# Poles, Jews, and the Politics of Nationality

# Poles, Jews, and the Politics of Nationality

The Bund and the
Polish Socialist Party
in Late Tsarist Russia,
1892–1914

JOSHUA D. ZIMMERMAN

The University of Wisconsin Press

The University of Wisconsin Press
1930 Monroe Street
Madison, Wisconsin 53711

www.wisc.edu/wisconsinpress/

3 Henrietta Street
London WC2E 8LU, England

Printed in the United States of America


Library of Congress Cataloging-in-Publication Data

Zimmerman, Joshua D.
    Poles, Jews, and the politics of nationality : the Bund and the Polish
Socialist Party in late Tsarist Russia, 1892–1914 / Joshua D. Zimmerman.
        p. cm.
Includes bibliographical references and index.
    ISBN 0-299-19460-4 (hardcover : alk. paper)
    1. Poland—Politics and government—1796–1918. 2. Jews—Poland—
Politics and government. 3. Socialism—Poland—History. 4. Poland—
Ethnic relations. 5. Ogólny Żydowski Związek Robotniczy "Bund" w
Polsce. 6. Polska Partia Socjalistyczna. I. Title.
DK4381 .Z56    2004
320.53'12'0943809041—dc21    2003008903

*For my parents, who raised me in a warm and loving home imbued with intellectual liveliness, humor, great music, and a profound respect for the academic pursuit*

# Contents

# Maps, Tables, Figures, and Illustrations

# Acknowledgments

IT IS A PLEASURE to acknowledge the contributions of those who aided me in conceiving, executing, and completing this book. First and foremost, I would like to thank Antony Polonsky, my dissertation committee chair and advisor at Brandeis University, who supported and encouraged me at every stage of the research and writing process. I would also like to thank my other dissertation committee members, Gregory Freeze at Brandeis University and Roman Szporluk at Harvard University.

During research trips in the United States, Poland, and Israel, I benefited enormously from contact with scholars, archivists, and librarians. In Warsaw, the historian and economist Jerzy Tomaszewski discussed at length archival holdings and library collections in Poland. I was also privileged to discuss my topic with Jan Kancewicz and Anna Żarnowska, the premier historians of the pre-WWI Polish Socialist Party. They read my research proposal with great care, helped direct my archival research, and invited me to seminars and conferences. Other Polish scholars who commented on my research include Feliks Tych, Szymon Rudnicki, Alina Cała, Alicja Pacholczykowa, Paweł Samuś, and Michał Śliwa.

I also benefited greatly from research conducted at the Yivo Institute for Jewish Research in New York City. Leo Greenbaum, head of the Bund Archives of the Jewish Labor Movement, provided invaluable assistance in locating materials, as did Marek Web, Fruma Mohrer, and the late Dina Abramovitch. I would also like to thank my former Yiddish instructor, Mordkhe Schaechter, of Columbia University, who took the time to answer several questions regarding variations in Yiddish orthography and dialects in nineteenth-century Russia.

While a postdoctoral fellow in Jerusalem, several scholars read my dissertation, in part or in whole, and provided valuable suggestions for revision. In particular, I owe a debt of gratitude to Jonathan Frankel, who read my manuscript and gave detailed comments. Avraham Greenbaum, a scholar at the Hebrew University's research center on the Jewish labor movement, gave freely of his time, carefully read my dissertation, and gave valuable suggestions as well. During my time in Israel, the American scholar Theodore Weeks, of Southern Illinois University, also read my dissertation and provided carefully prepared comments from which I have benefited.

I would like to give particular thanks as well to Jack Jacobs, of John Jay College of Criminal Justice in New York City. A specialist on the subject of nineteenth-century European socialists and the Jewish question, as well as on the Bund, Jacobs read the manuscript and provided several important comments during my period of revision. Robert M. Seltzer, of Hunter College in New York, graciously read my book proposal and gave thoughtful and insightful comments as well.

I would also like to extend my gratitude to two professors at UCLA, where I received an M.A. in the department of history. In particular, I would like to thank Ivan Berend, professor of history, who introduced me to the field of East European Studies and economic history. I also would like to thank David Myers, professor of Jewish intellectual history, in whose extraordinary course "Varieties of Jewish Nationalism" I first conceived the idea of this book. I have also benefited from conversations with, among others, Ezra Mendelsohn, John Klier, Peter Kenez, Shaul Stampfer, Robert E. Blobaum, and Norman Naimark, who took the time to answer queries on various aspects of East European history.

Research for this article was supported in part by a grant from the International Research and Exchanges Board (IREX), with funds provided by the National Endowment for the Humanities and the United States Department of State under the Title VIII program. It was also aided by a grant from the Kościuszko Foundation in New York and a generous dissertation fellowship from the Joint Committee on Eastern Europe of the American Council of Learned Societies and the Social Science Research Council. In addition, I am grateful to the Hebrew University of Jerusalem's Institute for Contemporary Jewry for providing me with a postdoctoral fellowship during the 1997–98 academic year, as well as to Haifa University's Bund Institute, which provided a summer fellowship. Three follow-up research trips to Israel and Poland during the summers of 1999 through 2001 were made possible by Yeshiva University's generous faculty research grants. A research grant from the Yivo Institute for Jewish Research in 2001 provided me with the means to conduct the final stage of research for this book.

Yeshiva University has been an ideal setting for teaching, writing, and research. In particular, I owe a debt of gratitude to my distinguished colleagues at YU, among them Arthur Hyman, Jeffrey Gurock, Ellen Shrecker, and Haym Soloveitchik, who have encouraged my research pursuits, given generously of their time, and provided stimulating intellectual companionship.

Finally, a special thanks to my wife, Ruth, an educator and student of history who read parts of the manuscript, provided wise counsel on various aspects of the book, and lovingly cared for our adorable son, Ezra, during my time tucked away in libraries completing the final stages of writing. Her dedication to teaching and family, to the art of cucina italiana, and her strong personal integrity are sources of comfort and inspiration.

# Note on Transliterations, Dates, and Terms

A FEW REMARKS on text mechanics are in order. All translations are mine unless otherwise noted. Transliteration of Yiddish follows the Yivo Institute for Jewish Research system as presented in Uriel Weinreich's *Modern English-Yiddish, Yiddish-English Dictionary*. Transliteration of Hebrew follows the style used in *Encyclopaedia Judaica* with the exception of diacritical marks, which have been omitted, while the Library of Congress style has been used for transliteration from the Russian. The spelling of place names follows *Merriam-Webster's Geographical Dictionary*, third edition. Instances when the contemporary name varies from the current form (for example, Lemberg, rather than present-day L'viv) are noted in the text.

The setting for this study is the area of legal Jewish residence in late tsarist Russia: the Pale of Settlement (*Cherta postoiannoi evreiskoi osedlosti*, "Boundary of Permanent Jewish Settlement"), comprised of fifteen provinces, and the Kingdom of Poland, created in 1815, comprised of ten provinces. While it is common to refer to these two regions as "the Pale," the Kingdom of Poland was in fact formally outside the Pale of Settlement and was administered by a different set of laws and institutions. Thus, the terms "the Pale" or "the Pale of Settlement" will be used throughout this book to refer to those borderland provinces between Russia proper and the Kingdom of Poland that roughly correspond to the present-day states of Lithuania, Belarus, Ukraine, and Moldova. Because the Kingdom of Poland itself went under different names (in Polish, *Królestwo Polskie, Kongresówka*, or simply *Polska*; in Russian, *Tsarstvo Pol'skoe* or *Privislinskii krai* after 1863), it will be used interchangeably with "Congress Poland," "the Polish kingdom," or "the Polish provinces."

With regard to dates, the Russian Empire prior to 1917 followed the Julian (Old Style) calendar, rather than the Gregorian (New Style) calendar used in the West. The Julian calendar was twelve days behind the Gregorian in the nineteenth century and thirteen days behind in the twentieth century. The Kingdom of Poland, reflecting its historic ties to the West, utilized the Gregorian calendar, except for official correspondence and publications, which followed a system of double dating. All dates in this book are New Style unless specifically noted, in which case they are double dated.

*The Pale of Settlement, 1900*

*Congress Poland (The Kingdom of Poland), 1900*

# Poles, Jews, and the Politics of Nationality

# Introduction

THE HISTORY OF the Jewish Labor Bund in tsarist Russia has received considerable scholarly attention since the Second World War. Both party histories and academic studies have focused on the evolution of the Bund's national program set against its struggle with Lenin and the Russian Social Democrats. Little research, however, has been conducted on the Bund's relations with the Polish Socialist Party (Polska Partia Socjalistyczna, PPS), with which the Bund fought a bitter struggle over the right to organizational and programmatic independence in its formative years. The decidedly Russian orientation of the pre-WWI Bundist leadership has obscured the fact that Jewish workers in tsarist Russia lived to the west of the Russian ethnic frontier and consequently had little or no contact with either Russian workers or Russian culture. In the industrial pockets of the Warsaw and Łódź provinces, the Jewish worker operated in a decidedly Polish cultural milieu, while Vilna (present-day Vilnius), the Bund's birthplace, was a prominent center of Polish national life throughout the nineteenth century and a city in which Poles made up a third of the population. Outside Vilna, Poles and Russians constituted small minorities amidst a largely Belarussian- and Ukrainian-speaking peasantry in the Pale of Settlement, the area to which the Jews of tsarist Russia were confined. Bundists active at the beginning of the century placed great importance on their dispute with the PPS and on the influence of Polish socialism on the development of a national program within the Jewish socialist camp. By 1903 the prominent Bundist Marc Liber characterized its dispute with the PPS as "the first page of our history."[1]

The PPS, which was established in 1892 by descendants of the Polish nobility and Polonized Jews from Warsaw, combined the ideology of socialism with the Polish insurrectionary tradition and saw its leading mission as the formation of a united ethnic front against imperial Russia. Its founding program demanded the breakup of Russia and the formation of a breakaway federal republic of the Polish, Lithuanian, and Ukrainian nations. While recognizing Lithuanians and Ukrainians as successor nations to the old eighteenth-century Polish Commonwealth, the same honor was not extended to the Jews, who constituted the single largest minority in the Kingdom of Poland, the ten western-most provinces of the Russian Empire acquired in 1815, as well as the second largest ethnic group in Lithuania.[2] Rather, the Polish leadership (both Catholic and Jewish) saw the Jews as potential recruits to the Polish nation who would be Polonized through linguistic, cultural, and civic assimilation.

But as the PPS was establishing centers throughout Russian Poland in the early 1890s and promoting the idea that the "Polish proletariat" consisted of Christian and Jewish workers, the national ferment then taking root throughout the Russian Empire began to spread to the Jews as well. In Lithuania, a buffer zone between ethnic Poland and ethnic Russia, a Jewish socialist center arose that began to compete openly with Polish socialists for the allegiance of the Jewish working class. By 1897 the Russian-Jewish socialist group would form its own empire-wide organization—the Jewish Labor Bund—and subsequently declare that the Jews were a nation distinct from Poles and Russians and attempt to spread this idea into Congress Poland. Ideologically straddling the PPS and the Bund stood the Jewish Section of the PPS (1893–1907), a group of Yiddish-speaking artisans in Congress Poland who embraced the program of social emancipation under a breakaway Polish republic, but who also championed a Yiddish cultural revival. Maintaining a unique identity as Yiddish-speaking Poles, the Jewish Section rejected the Bund's all-Russian orientation and neutrality on the Polish national question while opposing the assimilatory tendencies of such party leaders as Feliks Perl. Until the late 1970s, when Henryk Piasecki's pioneering monograph on the PPS's Jewish Section appeared, very little was known about the short-lived organization.[3]

Over the next seven years, between 1897 and 1905, and to a lesser extent in the period 1907–14, the Bund's relations with the PPS had a major impact on the development of a distinctive national program within Jewish socialism. This book thus argues that the Bund's path from advocate of civil rights to proponent of Jewish national autonomy was, to a large degree, the result of its search for an answer to the PPS. Besides the PPS's insistence that the Bund respond to the national question, the architect of the Bund's national program, John Mill, repeatedly emphasized the significance of the PPS as the model of a strong, disciplined socialist party committed to a national program. I also argue that the two parties under examination drafted their programs and developed their ideological platforms with each other in mind and that this mutual influence has not been adequately taken into account in the respective literature.[4] Thus, this study seeks to answer two questions: What precisely were the lines of influence between the PPS and the Bund in their formative years? What role did the struggle between the two parties play in the crystallization of the Bund's national program and in Polish socialist attitudes toward Jews?

The lack of interest in the Bund's relations with the Poles in the pre-WWI period is the result of the particular nature of Jewish historiography in the Cold War period. The first studies on the Bund and its national program were conducted in the two decades after WWII. These works, produced by immigrant historians and Bundist émigrés in the United States and Israel, viewed the development of the Bund's national program in isolation from the larger non-Jewish environment. The turn to a national program was seen as a response of the Bundist leadership to pressures from the Jewish working masses to adopt a more Jewish program, reflecting a general increase in national consciousness among East European Jewry.[5] In the 1960s and 1970s a new generation of Western-born scholars produced sophisticated studies that paid more attention to the influences of the larger environment on the Bund's national program. Trained in Russian studies and influenced by the Russian-orientation of the early Bundist leadership, these historians focused on the Bund's struggle with both Russian Social Democrats and labor Zionists and gave cursory treatment to the ideological influence of Polish socialism or the Polish socialist movement as a competing force for the allegiance of Jewish workers.[6]

An exception was the work of the late Polish-born Moshe Mishkinsky (1917–98), himself intimately acquainted with the Polish primary and secondary literature, who introduced one of the first revisions to the old school of Bundist historiography. Mishkinsky was among the first scholars to challenge the prevailing view, enshrined in the Bund's own postwar party history, that the development of a national program was the result of pressure from below, from the Jewish masses. By tracing the idea of an independent Jewish workers' movement back to the earliest documents of the movement, Mishkinsky persuasively argued that the national character of the socialist movement among Jews in Vilna had been present from the beginning.[7] Mishkinsky's discovery was linked to a second emphasis relating to the influence of Polish socialism on the early development of a distinctively Jewish socialist movement. Mishkinsky maintained that the polemic between the PPS and Jewish socialists in Vilna in the early 1890s over the national question led to the crystallization of a Jewish orientation within the socialist movement among Jews in Vilna.[8] Mishkinsky also emphasized the role of regional factors in the formation of the Jewish labor movement, pointing to the heterogeneous national character of Lithuania combined with Jewish predominance in urban life as causal factors in the development of a separate Jewish socialist movement.[9]

In the beginning of the 1980s Jonathan Frankel's magisterial work on Jewish socialism alluded to the "great, even crucial, importance" of Polish socialism on the origins of the Bund.[10] Jack Jacobs similarly suggested that more work was needed on the Bund's relations with Polish socialists, while Ezra Mendelsohn recently alluded to the importance of situating the emergence of the Jewish socialist movement in tsarist Russia within the context of other minority socialist parties in the Pale.[11]

This study thus aims to present a critical episode in the history of the Bund in general and in the study of Polish-Jewish relations in particular. The first chapter provides the historical setting and background for the topic and raises the central questions I hope to answer. In particular, I chronicle the rise of the Polish Socialist Party (PPS) under Józef Piłsudski in 1892–93 and its position on the national question in general and the Jewish question in particular during the first half of the 1890s. Drawing on Piłsudski's personal correspondence, housed in the Archive of New Records in Warsaw, as well as on the PPS press, chapter 1 thus examines the attitude of the PPS to the Jewish question before the founding of the Bund. Chapters 2 and 3 analyze the emergence of the Jewish socialist movement in Vilna in the first half of the 1890s and its spread to Congress Poland on the eve of the founding of the Bund. Two chapters follow on the founding and ideological consolidation of the Bund in the period 1897–1901. Chapters 6 and 7 discuss the political response of the PPS to the formation of the Bund by examining the rise of the PPS Yiddish press and the creation of the Jewish Section as a means of competing with the Bund. Finally, chapters 8–10 examine the impact of the 1905 Russian Revolution and its aftermath on the development of the Bund and on the attitude of Polish socialists to the Jewish question on the eve of WWI.

# ■ 1.
# Industrialization and the Rise of the Polish Socialist Party in Tsarist Russia, 1892–97

*The historical role of socialism in Poland is the defense of the West against reactionary Russia.*
JÓZEF PIŁSUDSKI (1895)

*I do not generally care very much for the national . . . by itself. But in the case of Poland I think that the only hope of pushing reactionary Russia back from central Europe lies in the reconstitution of a strong Poland, and I see no hope of any movement in that direction except from the Socialists.*
HENRY HYNDMAN (1896)

WHEN A JEWISH SOCIALIST CENTER arose in Vilna at the beginning of the 1890s, the Russian radical movement had long been in disarray. Only scattered groups of Russian Marxists and radical populists operated inside Russia, east of the Pale, as well as in émigré centers abroad.[1] Alongside the dense Jewish populations in the towns and cities of Russia's western provinces, the Polish Socialist Party (PPS) emerged as the dominant revolutionary party. With major centers in Vilna, Warsaw, and Łódź, the PPS organized strikes, disseminated propaganda through an illegal printing press, and appealed to the Jewish socialist intelligentsia in Lithuania for common action. Jewish socialists in Vilna, who were in contact with Jewish groups in Congress Poland, observed the Polish movement closely. Iulii Martov, active in Vilna at the time, recounted that the Vilna center drew on the Polish model, "which was well known to us" and which had a "direct influence" on Jewish socialists.[2] And in its first attempt at a history of the movement, the Bund explicitly acknowledged its debt to Polish socialists.[3] In the following pages,

we begin with a discussion of the broader transformations undergone by Polish and Jewish society in late nineteenth-century imperial Russia, followed by an examination of the rise of the PPS in the
1890s and its position on the national question in general and on the
Jewish question in particular.

## Poles and Jews under Russian Rule, 1864–1914

The rise of the PPS and the Bund in the 1890s followed
dramatic social, economic, and political changes in Russian Poland.
In Polish society the failure of the 1863 uprising led to a new conservative leadership that favored peaceful social and economic
advances while stressing the importance of scientific knowledge
and education. Instead of killing off the nation's finest sons in hope-
less armed rebellions, the new leadership argued, nation building
had to proceed in strictly social and economic spheres. The so-called
Triple Loyalists and liberal Warsaw Positivists—those who pledged
allegiance to the three partitioning powers and an "organic work"
program of peaceful social and economic development—thus came
to dominate Polish political life in the late 1860s and 1870s. On social
questions Polish liberals called for the integration of peripheral
social elements (peasants, Jews, and women) into Polish society
through the introduction of universal secular lay education and
equal civil rights.[4] Jews, they argued, could be nationalized by linguistic, cultural, and civic assimilation. As Roman Szporluk has
recently remarked, the attitude of Polish liberals during this time
reflected an attempt to compensate for the loss of Polish territory to
the east by integrating into the nation those social groups that had
been excluded previously.[5]

Jewish political life in the Pale and Congress Poland followed a
similar pattern. Political leadership revolved around proponents of
the Russian Haskalah (Enlightenment), who had gained ground
under the reign of Tsar Alexander II. During the 1860s and 1870s,
Russian and Polish Maskilim (proponents of the Jewish Enlightenment) advocated social integration through the secularization of
Jewish education and linguistic assimilation. The process of acculturation, Jewish leaders maintained, would bring an end to Jewish
separateness, a decline in anti-Jewish prejudice, and eventual political emancipation. Part and parcel of the Maskilim's integrationist

program was an almost universal disdain for the Yiddish language, which they argued was the single greatest barrier to acculturation.

The assassination of Tsar Alexander II in March 1881 and the period of reaction that followed led to a decisive rejection among young Poles and Jews of the politics of conciliation. In both societies a new "uncompliant" generation came of age during Tsar Alexander III's reign (1881–94), a period that saw the growth of anti-Jewish laws as well as an intensification of anti-Polish measures in Congress Poland. Born between 1865 and 1873 and educated in secular Russian schools, this new generation of young Jews and Poles rejected the complacency and conciliatory politics of their parents and instead formed conspiratorial national and socialist movements. It was precisely this core of young Poles and Jews, in their twenties and early thirties, who established new underground political parties in the 1890s.

The birth of new conspiratorial parties in the 1890s was partly a response to the rise of new social forces in the Pale of Settlement and the Kingdom of Poland. The Industrial Revolution, a development that fundamentally transformed European society in the nineteenth century, reached the Kingdom of Poland in the second half of the nineteenth century. Several factors brought about this industrial surge. First, the Russian government's decision in 1851 to lift tariff barriers between the kingdom and the empire opened up potentially lucrative Russian markets. The demand for industrial goods, partly spawned by the Crimean War in 1854, led to the mechanization of Polish textile production in the 1850s. The development of railway networks linking Polish industry with many distant parts of the Russian Empire between 1862 and 1871 and the abolition of serfdom in 1864 opened up new possibilities for economic growth. The combination of peasant emancipation and semiprotectionist trade policies in Saint Petersburg that favored the advanced Polish industry led to sustained industrial growth. Between 1870 and 1890, iron and steel production rose more than tenfold.[6] Congress Poland became the third leading industrial region in the Russian Empire, next to Moscow and Saint Petersburg, producing 40 percent of the empire's coal, 25 percent of its steel, 19.5 percent of its textiles, and 42 percent of its linen. Thus, although Congress Poland accounted for 7.3 percent of the general population, it produced one-fourth of the empire's industrial output.[7]

Economic development in the Kingdom of Poland was peripheral and disjointed, characterized by growth in the advanced modern sectors but by stagnation in agriculture. One result of peripheral modernization was rapid demographic growth, as the population grew from 5.3 million (1865) to 10 million (1900), set against a relatively slower pace of urbanization. While industrial centers such as Łódź, Sosnowiec, Żyrardów, and Warsaw experienced sharp population increases, the kingdom's total urban population increased from 26 percent (1872) to 31.5 percent (1897).[8] This process was most pronounced in the booming textile center of Łódź, where the population increased more than ninefold between 1872 and 1913 (from 50,000 to 459,000).

Industrialization in Congress Poland was concentrated in two of ten provinces. The province of Piotrków (Łódź, Częstochowa, the Dąbrowa coal basin, and Sosnowiec) contributed half the total industrial output and employed 52 percent of the work force; the province of Warsaw contributed 34 percent of output and employed 29 percent of the work force. One result of regional growth was that, by 1910, Warsaw (pop. 777,000) and Łódź were the only cities in the kingdom with a population exceeding 100,000. With the exception of Białystok, the northwestern provinces (Vilna, Grodno [present-day Hrodna], Minsk, Vitebsk, Kovno [present-day Kaunas], and Mogilev [present-day Mahilyow]) had scarce natural resources and were the least developed industrially. Vilna, with a population of 168,000 in 1910, was the only city in the northwest with a population over 100,000.

Urban growth came primarily from migration, not from an internal demographic rise. The rapid growth of industrial centers came from the influx of landless peasants and, to a lesser degree, from the disenfranchised nobility, leading to the growth of the urban intelligentsia and working class. In spite of agrarian reform following 1863, rural areas were unable to absorb the rising population. In 1864 there were 590,000 landless peasants. That number had increased to 827,000 in 1891 and to 1.2 million by 1901, or about a fifth of the rural population.[9] Thus it is not surprising that the landless peasantry provided the main source of the new work force.

The dual impact of industrialization and the abolition of serfdom unleashed new social forces. As table 1.3 indicates, the industrial work force in Congress Poland increased more than fourfold during

TABLE 1.1
## Population Growth in the Kingdom of Poland

| Year | Total Population | Jews | Jews as Percent of Population |
|------|------------------|------|-------------------------------|
| 1816 | 2,732,324 | 212,944 | 7.8 |
| 1827 | 4,032,335 | 377,754 | 9.1 |
| 1834 | 4,059,517 | 410,062 | 10.1 |
| 1856 | 4,696,929 | 571,678 | 12.2 |
| 1865 | 5,336,112 | 719,112 | 13.0 |
| 1885 | 7,687,893 | 1,087,204 | 14.1 |
| 1897 | 9,402,253 | 1,270,575 | 13.7 |
| 1907 | 11,505,112 | 1,576,000 | 13.7 |
| 1913 | 13,055,313 | 1,941,640 | 14.8 |

SOURCE: *Rocznik Statystyczny Królestwa Polskiego: Rok 1914* (Warsaw: Skład główny u Gebethnera i Wolffa, 1915), 15; *Rocznik Statystyczny Królestwa Polskiego: Rok 1915* (Warsaw: Skład główny w Księgarni Gebethnera i Wolffa, 1916), 26, 45–47; B. Wasiutyński, *Ludność żydowska w Polsce w wiekach XIX i XX* (Warsaw: Wydawn. Kasy im. Mianowskiego, 1930), 8; A. Eisenbach, "Ludność żydowska w Królestwie Polskim w końcu XIX wieku.," *BŻIH*, no. 29 (Jan.–Mar. 1959): 76.

TABLE 1.2
## Towns of 10,000 or More Inhabitants in the Kingdom of Poland

| Year | Number of Towns Exceeding 10,000 | Combined Population |
|------|-----------------------------------|---------------------|
| 1857 | 7 | 246,000 |
| 1872 | 15 | 524,000 |
| 1897 | 35 | 1,756,000 |

SOURCE: S. Koszutski, *Rozwój ekonomiczny Królestwa Polskiego w ostatniem tzydziestoleciu, 1870–1900* (Warsaw: Nakład Księgarni Naukowej, 1905), 201.

1877–1910, from 90,767 to 400,922 in 1910. In contrast the general population in the kingdom rose by about 70 percent during the same period.

The Jewish population of the Russian Empire numbered 5.19 million in 1897, or 4.13 percent of the total population. More than nine out of every ten Jews (93.9 percent) resided inside the Pale of Settlement and the Kingdom of Poland, comprised of twenty-five provinces on the Russian Empire's western rim.[10] Unlike their core-

TABLE 1.3
## Development of Industry in the Kingdom of Poland

| Year | Number of Factories | Percent Increase | Number of Workers | Percent Increase | Value of Production (in 1000s of Rubles) | Percent Increase |
|------|------|------|------|------|------|------|
| 1877 | 8,349 | 100 | 90,767 | 100 | 103,404 | 100 |
| 1883 | 9,516 | 113 | 144,786 | 159 | 208,483 | 201 |
| 1895 | 12,987 | 155 | 205,827 | 226 | 278,600 | 269 |
| 1903 | 13,209 | 170 | 252,126 | 277 | 429,424 | 406 |
| 1905 | 10,479 | 125 | 276,747 | 304 | 413,858 | 400 |
| 1910 | 10,953 | 131 | 400,922 | 447 | — | — |

SOURCE: Witold Kula, *Historia gospodarcza Polski w dobie popowstaniowej 1864–1918* (Warsaw, 1947), 42; Erasmus Piltz, *Poland: Her People, History, Industries* (London, 1909), 159.

ligionists in central and western Europe who had achieved legal emancipation by 1871 and who championed acculturation, the Jewish communities in the Pale and in the Polish kingdom remained socially isolated and politically unemancipated, while preserving distinct religious, linguistic, and cultural traits. Perhaps the strongest indicator of the persistence of Jewish separateness in tsarist Russia was the slow pace of linguistic acculturation. According to the first comprehensive census of the Russian Empire in 1897, 96.9 percent (5.06 million Jews) claimed Yiddish as their mother tongue.[11] At the same time a small but significant group claimed languages other than Yiddish, including Russian (63,383), Polish (47,060), and German (22,784). Reflecting the historical pattern of Jewish acculturation into the nearest high cultures (in this case, Polish and Russian), the Baltic and Slavic minorities in the western provinces made no impact, with 2,424 Jews citing Ukrainian as their mother tongue, 1,334 citing Belarussian, and 142 claiming Lithuanian.[12] It is important to note that only one-third of Jews claiming Russian as their mother tongue lived inside the Pale. Tables 1.4 and 1.5 also reveal that acculturation in Congress Poland (3.5 percent) was about seven times higher than that in the western provinces (0.6 percent).

The largely unacculturated Jewish masses in the Pale were close to 88 percent urban. The most compact communities lived in

TABLE 1.4
## Jewish Population in the Kingdom of Poland by Language, 1897

| Language | Number | Percent of Jewish Population |
|----------|--------|------------------------------|
| Yiddish | 1,254,902 | 94.9 |
| Polish | 46,390 | 3.5 |
| Russian | 5,000 | 0.3 |
| German | 2,000 | 0.15 |

SOURCE: Edward Czyński, *Etnograficzno-statystyczny zarys liczebności i rozsiedlenia ludności polskiej* (Warsaw, 1909), 57–58.

TABLE 1.5
## Jewish Population in the Pale of Settlement by Language (excluding the southern provinces), 1897

| Language | Number | Percent of Jewish Population |
|----------|--------|------------------------------|
| Yiddish | 2,608,946 | 99.4 |
| Russian | 11,582 | 0.4 |
| Ukrainian | 2,424 | — |
| Belarussian | 1,334 | — |
| German | 745 | — |
| Latvian | 502 | — |
| Polish | 268 | — |
| Lithuanian | 142 | — |
| Estonian | 26 | — |

SOURCE: Edward Czyński, *Etnograficzno-statystyczny zarys liczebności i rozsiedlenia ludności polskiej* (Warsaw, 1909), 68; Bauer, Kappeler, and Roth, *Die Nationalitäten des Russischen Reiches in der Volkszählung von 1897* (Stuttgart, 1991), 2:77, table 6.

Lithuania-Belarus ("the northwest territories"), numbering 1.42 million, or 14 percent of the general population, and over half the general urban population.[13]

In Congress Poland Jews numbered 1.32 million, or 14.1 percent of the population, and formed about 44 percent of the urban population.[14] Thus, while Jews formed more than half the population in only three cities in Congress Poland (Łomża, Chełm, and Zamość), they formed a majority in nineteen cities in the northwest provinces.[15]

TABLE 1.6
## Jewish Population in Ten Major Cities in the Kingdom of Poland, 1897

| City | Total Population | Jewish Population | Percent of total population |
|---|---|---|---|
| Warsaw | 638,208 | 219,141 | 34 |
| Łódź | 315,209 | 98,677 | 31 |
| Lublin | 50,152 | 24,280 | 48 |
| Częstochowa | 45,130 | 11,980 | 26 |
| Siedlce | 23,714 | 11,440 | 48 |
| Radom | 28,749 | 11,277 | 39 |
| Będzin | 21,190 | 10,839 | 51 |
| Piotrków | 30,824 | 9,543 | 31 |
| Kielce | 23,189 | 6,399 | 27 |
| Tomaszów | 21,041 | 9,386 | 44 |

SOURCE: Ignacy Schiper, *Dzieje handlu żydowskiego na ziemiach polskich* (Warsaw: Nakładem Centrali Związku Kupców w Warszawie, 1937), 493; *Pervaia vseobshcha-ia perepis' naseleniia Rosiiskoi Imperii 1897 g* (Saint Petersburg, 1905), 2:23–25.

TABLE 1.7
## Jewish Population in Twelve Major Cities of the Northwest Provinces (Lithuania–Belarus), 1897

| City | Total Population | Jews | Jews as a percent of total population |
|---|---|---|---|
| Vilna | 154,532 | 63,996 | 41 |
| Minsk | 90,912 | 47,562 | 52 |
| Kovno | 70,920 | 25,448 | 36 |
| Dvinsk | 69,675 | 32,400 | 44 |
| Białystok | 66,032 | 41,905 | 63 |
| Vitebsk | 65,871 | 34,440 | 52 |
| Grodno | 46,919 | 22,684 | 48 |
| Brest-Litovsk | 46,568 | 30,260 | 65 |
| Mogilev | 43,119 | 21,547 | 50 |
| Gomel | 36,775 | 20,385 | 55 |
| Bobruisk | 34,336 | 20,760 | 60 |
| Pinsk | 28,368 | 21,065 | 74 |

SOURCE: *Pervaia vseobshchaia perepis' naseleniia Rosiiskoi Imperii 1897 g.: Naseleniia mesta Rosiiskoi Imperii v 500 i bolie zhitelei* (Saint Petersburg, 1905), 10, 12, 44, 91, 104, 107, 108, 111, 113.

TABLE 1.8
**The Jewish Working Class in the Pale of Settlement and Kingdom of Poland, According to Data of the Jewish Colonization Association, 1898–99**

| Region | Industrial Workers | Artisans | Total |
|---|---|---|---|
| Polish Provinces | 12,380 | 119,371 | 131,371 |
| Northwest | 22,279 | 179,503 | 199,503 |
| Southwest | 9,596 | 140,849 | 150,445 |
| South | 2,058 | 61,263 | 63,321 |
| Total | 46,313 | 500,896 | 547,209 |

SOURCE: *Recueil de matériaux sur la situation économique des Israélites de Russie, d'apres l'enquète de la Jewish Colonization Association* (Paris, 1906), 1:118, 240.

The character of the Jewish working class differed from its Gentile counterparts in several ways. First, Jewish workers consisted primarily of artisans, unlike non-Jewish workers, who were employed predominantly in factories.[16] Of the approximately half-million Jewish wageworkers in Congress Poland and the Pale, 85 percent were artisans, laboring in small shops in traditional crafts such as tailoring and carpentry.[17] The low percentage of Jewish factory workers resulted primarily from the problem of the Shabbat rest day. Most factories, including some Jewish-owned ones, refrained from hiring Jewish workers. The Jewish Colonization Association's findings for 1898 reveal that of a total of 12,380 Jewish industrial workers in the Polish provinces, 11,944 were employed in Jewish-owned factories.[18] The Jewish worker in large modern factories was thus an exception in tsarist Russia.

## Origins of the Polish Socialist Party

By the early 1890s industrialization in the Kingdom of Poland brought about the rise of a sizable industrial working class. The rise of these new social forces corresponded with the decline of the Russian radical movement in the 1880s. These two developments led to a shift among Polish émigré socialists to a proindependence program. The early 1890s also saw the revival of socialist activity in the Kingdom of Poland, when three Polish socialist groups formed: the Second Proletariat, the Union of Polish Workers (Związek Robotników Polskich, ZRP), and the Workers' Unification. The most significant of these was the ZRP, the organization that rejected revolutionary terror in favor of economic struggle, including the organization of the large-scale strike movement. Unlike the Second Proletariat, an elite revolutionary group confined to Warsaw, the ZRP focused on agitation among workers and broadened its movement to all the major industrial pockets of the kingdom. As table 1.9 shows, strike activity significantly increased in the beginning of the 1890s among the two-hundred-thousand-strong industrial working class in the Polish kingdom, with the first major strikes in May 1891. The largely spontaneous strike movement reinvigorated the underground socialist parties, who could now claim to represent a constituency with revolutionary potential: the downtrodden, poor, and oppressed workers in the industrial pockets of Russian Poland.

A turning point came on May 6, 1892, when approximately sixty-five thousand workers went on strike in Łódź. A violent confrontation erupted between the workers, the police, and the army in what has been described in Polish historiography as the "Łódź Rebellion." When order was finally restored four days later, eighty people lay dead, 300 wounded, and 350 were placed under arrest.[19] This revival of strike activity in the early 1890s paved the way for the coming of a unified Polish socialist party.

TABLE 1.9

**The Growth of the Working-Class Movement in the Kingdom of Poland, 1889–92**

| Year | Number of Strikes | Number of Workers |
|------|------------------|-------------------|
| 1889 | 2 | 2,870 |
| 1890 | 7 | 10,400 |
| 1891 | 30 | 25,540 |
| 1892 | 12 | 70,000 |

SOURCE: Feliks Tych, *Związek Robotników Polskich, 1889–1892: Anatomia wczesnej organizacji robotniczej* (Warsaw, 1974), 421.

## Establishment of the Polish Socialist Party

In the early 1890s Polish socialists came to the conclusion that they could not serve as an appendage to the general revolutionary movement in Russia. An independent, unified Polish organization was thus essential. The opportunity to publicly present their plan came in August 1891 at the Brussels Congress of the Second International, when a Polish delegation declared its intention to form a single union of Polish socialists. In a resolution prepared for the congress, the Polish delegation declared that a unified organization of Polish socialists "is indispensable for the interests of both the development of socialism in Poland and international socialist politics." The resolution preserved the call for class struggle and international workers' solidarity, characterizing the goal of a Polish party as "a unified class struggle with one enemy: the *szlachta* [Polish nobility] and the Polish bourgeoisie." The Polish delegation also declared its solidarity with the Russian revolutionary movement: "Regarding our Russian comrades, Polish socialists are committed to the principle of international solidarity that it has always faithfully upheld."[20]

Following the Brussels congress, the delegation published an open letter explaining the need for a unified Polish group at future international congresses. Although the delegation's original aim was to create an all-Polish union of socialists from the three partitions, only a union from the Russian partition came into being.[21] To this end, the London center under the leadership of Stanisław Mendelson (1858–1913) made arrangements in early 1892 for the convening of a congress. Born to a well-to-do assimilated Jewish banking family from Warsaw, Mendelson had been a founder of the first Polish socialist circle at Warsaw University in 1878. To escape arrest, Mendelson settled in Geneva, where he founded and financed the first Polish socialist journals, *Równość* (Equality, 1879–81) and *Przedświt* (Dawn, 1881–93), and played a significant role in Polish socialism throughout the 1880s and early 1890s.[22]

The year-long plan to convene a congress of Polish socialists came to fruition in the fall of 1892 in Paris.[23] On 17 November, the first day of deliberations, eighteen Poles crowded into the apartment of Bolesław Jędrzejowski in the Paris suburb of Montrouge.[24] The participants represented four Polish socialist parties from

Congress Poland and abroad. These included eight members from the internationalist Second Proletariat, including Mendelson, four from the nationally oriented Workers' Unification, one from the Union of Polish Workers, and three from the Paris-based National Socialist Commune; two participants attended without any party affiliation.[25] Of the eighteen participants, only two came directly from Russian Poland.[26]

A biographical study of the Paris congress participants reveals significant social, economic, and geographic similarities. Of the fifteen participants for whom biographical material is available, twelve came from Congress Poland, while two (Witold Jodko-Narkiewicz and Bolesław Limanowski) came from the northeast *kresy*, or borderlands, and only one participant originated from Ukraine. The majority of participants were born in the 1860s and early 1870s, thus representing a second generation of Polish socialists. The younger participants began their activity in socialist groups *after* the Russian revolutionary groupings had waned. Consequently, their models of antitsarist activity were the three *Polish* radical groups that survived the crackdowns of the mid-1880s. Thus, their entry into revolutionary circles in the late 1880s did not occur under the influence of Russian radicalism, giving their activity a decidedly Polish orientation. At least six of the participants had fathers or uncles who had been persecuted in 1863 for their participation in the national uprising, while the most senior member, Limanowski, had been an insurgent in the 1863 rising.[27]

The Paris congress participants were also the first generation of Poles living under post-1863 Russification and were thus deeply affected by their status as a subject nation forcefully incorporated into an alien empire. It was this common experience of national defeat, Russification, and socioeconomic transformation that made possible the coming together of disparate Polish socialist groups under a single all-Polish program.

Significant organizational and programmatic decisions were made at the conference that produced two results. First, an outline program was drafted and agreed to by all members. Second, a Union of Polish Socialists Abroad (Związek Zagraniczny Socjalistów Polskich, ZZSP) was formed, which took over *Przedświt* as the union's official organ, and was entrusted with the responsibility of dispatching emissaries to Russian Poland to form a Polish socialist party.[28] With regard to programmatic developments, the congress did not consider questions of an ideological nature. Rather, the seven-day émigré gathering focused on development of a minimum program, the question of tactics, and the creation of a unified Polish socialist party in Russian Poland.[29] However, left and right divisions among the delegates surfaced over debates on two issues: the nature of the congress's national demands and the critical issue of relations with the Russian revolutionary movement.

The consensus in Polish historiography is that discussions on the national question played almost no role at the congress because everyone was in agreement.[30] However, a close reading of the protocols reveals significant divisions within the congress, particularly regarding relations with Russian revolutionaries. While a clear consensus existed regarding the aim of national independence, disagreements arose over the nature of that future Polish state and the means by which to achieve it. Feliks Perl first raised the national question when he asked whether the minimum *political* goal of the socialist movement was to be a constitution in Russia or a breakaway Polish republic. Edward Abramowski responded that as a goal the congress should include independence but added that the congress would in the future have to be prepared to compromise.

Unsatisfied with Abramowski's response, Perl maintained that "we must clearly place an independent Polish republic as our *nearest* goal." Abramowski agreed that independence should be a goal but argued that Polish socialists had to link that aim to the achievement of political freedom in Russia.[31] On the second day of deliberations, Mendelson submitted a draft of the program principles that he had drawn up the previous evening and which the delegates debated for the remaining days of the conference. As one participant recalled, "I went to the second day with the idea of defending the principle of the independence of Poland . . . when Mendelson rose . . . [and] to my great surprise, the struggle for Polish independence was given a central place in the program."[32] From that moment on, Limanowski concluded, "I felt in full harmony with the entire congress."[33]

The second major issue that divided Left and Right at the congress was the question of relations with the Russian revolutionary movement. The brief exchange between Perl and Abramowski on the first day revealed substantive differences on this question.

Abramowski argued that Polish socialists had to link their goals with the situation in Russia, possibly conceding or postponing the independence demand under conditions of a Russian revolutionary upheaval. But one delegate responded that the party platform had to unambiguously embrace the independence idea. "We must clearly underscore that we are a separate party that endeavors to eradicate the view that heaven will follow once the tsar is overthrown." Abramowski countered that "we cannot accomplish anything if we do not work together with the Russian movement." The congress chairman, Mendelson, then rose with a statement that reflected the dominant mood of the congress: "In the last few years, we, in the west and at home, have become disillusioned with the Russian movement . . . we should clearly put forth the demand for the breakup of the Russian state, framing it from the point of view of the interest of international socialist politics."[34] The latter quote revealed the extent of Engels's influence on Mendelson regarding the significance of the Polish question for European socialism. As late as 1891, *Przedświt* continued to link the success of the Polish movement to Russian revolutionaries. "Our victory over the tsar depends, if not in full, then at least to a great extent, on the strength of the revolutionary movement in Russia," *Przedświt* argued in one piece.[35] This favorable view of the Russian movement would gradually wane.

Despite differences over the means by which to achieve the goal of an independent Polish republic, a final program was drafted after six days of deliberations. Penned by Mendelson and approved by majority vote, the Outline Program of the Polish Socialist Party contained the following demands:[36]

**AIMS OF THE POLISH SOCIALIST PARTY**
The Polish Socialist Party, as the political organization of the Polish labor class, struggling for liberation from the yoke of capitalism, strives above all to overthrow the present political slavery and to obtain power for the proletariat. In this striving its aim is *an independent Democratic Republic*, based on the following principles:

POLITICAL
1. Direct and universal suffrage by secret ballot;
2. Complete equality of the nationalities entering into the composition of the republic on the basis of a voluntary federation;

3. Community and provincial autonomy with the right to elect administrative officers;
4. Equality of all citizens regardless of sex, race, nationality or religion;
5. Complete freedom of speech, press, and assembly;
6. Free court procedure, election of judges, and responsibility of officers before the court;
7. Free, obligatory, and universal education, with the state supplying student stipends.

ECONOMIC
1. An eight-hour work day;
2. Establishment of a minimum wage;
3. Equal pay for women for equal work;
4. Prohibition of child labor;
5. Complete freedom of workers' strikes;
6. Gradual nationalization of land, means of production, and communications.[37]

The attitude of the new party to the nationalities question can be discerned from the resolution on the Lithuanian and Ruthenian questions. Here the territorial ambitions were clarified in no uncertain terms. "The Polish Socialist Party, in agreement with point 2 of its program, regards it as necessary to expand its activity to cover the provinces formerly united with the Polish Commonwealth [*na provincje dawniej z Rzeczypospolitą Polską związane*]." Regarding Lithuania and Ukraine, the resolution called for a "unified political force" with the existing Lithuanian and Ukrainian socialist movements "with the aim of struggling against the yoke of oppression in our country." With regard to the new party's relations with Russian revolutionaries, the program favored cooperation with Russian revolutionaries, but only on the basis of complete independence and equality. It also demanded the right to serve as the sole representative of the workers living in Polish territories (*nasz kraj*).[38]

The outline program of the new Polish party contained many implications for the compact Jewish population in Polish lands. A formulation on relations with Jewish socialists followed under the section on Lithuania and Ruthenia. It contained a paragraph on the Russian-speaking Jewish Social Democratic group, which had recently formed in Vilna. "The congress has agreed," the resolution stated, "that our party should distribute a proclamation as soon as

possible to Russian Jewish circles in Lithuania and Ruthenia, exposing their Russifying activities to be contradictory to both the political interests of liberation and the interests of freedom in Russia."[39]
The resolution on the Jewish socialists had been proposed by
Mendelson at the congress, accepted without discussion, and printed unchanged in the program.[40] It revealed that the Lithuanian and
Ruthenian questions were regarded above all as territorial, not
national, which is why the statement on Jews was subsumed under
the latter heading. It also showed the degree to which Jewish assimilationists within the party led the struggle against the Jewish center in Vilna, as well as the importance the congress attached to the
activities of Jewish socialists in its self-declared sphere of interest.

Two points of the program concerned relations with Jews and
provided a point of departure for future resolutions on the Jewish
question. As the single nonterritorial group in the Pale and Congress Poland, the Jews were excluded from the resolution on the
equality of nationalities because the future Polish state was to be
formed on a national-territorial basis. The resolution on civil rights
for all citizens, however, included the Jews. Thus, at its founding
congress the PPS viewed the Jews in much the same way as the
French revolutionaries had in 1789: "The Jews should be denied
everything as a nation, but granted everything as individuals."[41] It
clearly underscored the integrationist assumption that the Jews on
Polish lands would come to identify politically as Poles and thus
have no separate interests. It was the western model of emancipation that the PPS leaders, including the Jews, advanced as their
solution to the Jewish question.

The establishment of the PPS was a watershed in modern Polish
history. Rooted in a belief in Poland's special mission to liberate
Europe from reactionary despotism, the outline program provided
the theoretical foundations for a unique synthesis of modern socialism and the Polish romantic-insurrectionary tradition. Although its
authors came from the first generation of Polish socialists, the majority of participants at the congress of 1892 were part of a new generation of revolutionaries who entered the movement after Russian revolutionary activity had gone into decline and were thus much less
predisposed toward linking the two movements. Left and right divisions within the Paris congress, however, were still connected to the
Russian question, something that became critical in 1905–6.

## The Establishment of the PPS in Tsarist Russia, 1893–94

In addition to the outline program, the Paris congress selected six participants to form the Union of Polish Socialists Abroad (ZZSP), which was entrusted with the responsibility of producing and transporting socialist literature into the country. The six members constituted the *Centralizacja*, or chief representative body, and included Bolesław Jędrzejowski, Edward Abramowski, Feliks Perl, and Stanisław Wojciechowski.[42] In January 1893 the ZZSP established itself in London, where it remained the official PPS body abroad.[43]

The émigré organization's immediate task was to send an emissary into Russian Poland to form the Polish Socialist Party, and to act swiftly to develop ties with socialists inside Russian Poland. All agreed that Mendelson was the best person to form the party inside Russian Poland. As an emissary of the ZZSP, the thirty-five-year-old Mendelson crossed into Russian Poland from East Prussia on January 16, 1893, at the border town of Wierzbołowie in the Suwalki province. Mendelson first traveled to Vilna, where he met the young Józef Piłsudski.[44] Mendelson then journeyed to Warsaw, where he made contact with activists from the Union of Polish Workers, Second Proletariat, and Workers' Unification. Under Mendelson's influence proponents of the outline program from among the three groups combined to form the Polish Socialist Party in February–March 1893.[45]

Sometime in February Mendelson journeyed back to Vilna to make contact with Piłsudski's group of Polish socialists. Shortly afterward the group of Polish socialists in Vilna accepted the outline program and renamed itself the "Lithuanian Section" of the PPS. There are almost no accounts of the discussions between Mendelson and Piłsudski. It is clear from Piłsudski's subsequent writings, though, that Mendelson had an influence on Piłsudski's ideological direction. As Garlicki writes, Piłsudski's meeting with Mendelson opened the possibility of action in the newly born PPS, a forum in which he could work to lift the yoke of foreign rule.[46] Within eighteen months the young Piłsudski would rise up the ranks of the party and become its unquestioned leader.

The figure of Józef Piłsudski (1867–1935) was typical of the new young socialists. He was born to an old Polish-Lithuanian noble family in Zułów, sixty kilometers north of Vilna. In his memoirs he described a childhood that would have been idyllic if it were not for one cause of bitterness that "ate away at my father's soul, drew tears from my mother's eyes and deeply impressed a child's mind. That was the memory of the national defeat of 1863."[47] He then described how his mother infused him with patriotic sentiment, calling on him to further the struggle. "From our earliest childhood, my mother acquainted us with the works of our national poets," he wrote. In addition, Piłsudski became enamored with the figure of Napoleon, who "overwhelmed me with emotion and inflamed my imagination. All my dreams were then concentrated around armed insurrection against the Muscovites, whom I hated with all my soul, every one of whom I considered a scoundrel and a thief." At the age of ten Piłsudski entered the Russian gymnasium in Vilna housed in the former Polish-language Vilna University, which had been closed in 1869. "The atmosphere of the gymnasium crushed me, the injustice and the politics of the schoolmasters enraged me," Piłsudski wrote, adding, "in these circumstances my hatred for the Tsarist administration and Muscovite oppression grew with every year. My cheeks burned, that I must suffer in silence while my pride was trampled upon, listening to lies and scornful words about Poland, Poles and their history. . . . The feeling of oppression . . . weighed on my heart like a millstone. I always count the years spent in the gymnasium amongst the most unpleasant of my life."[48]

Piłsudski graduated from the gymnasium in 1885, after which he studied medicine in Kharkov. During his first year of studies he became acquainted with Russian socialist literature. After members of the Proletariat were put on trial, bringing an end to the first Polish socialist party in 1886, Piłsudski became connected with Polish socialist circles.[49] In 1887 he returned to Vilna and was implicated in a plot to assassinate the tsar as a result of his brother's involvement. Piłsudski was consequently sentenced to five years exile in Siberia. When he returned to Vilna in June 1892, however, he found a society that had changed. In particular, a new patriotic socialist group had assumed leadership in emigration, and when Piłsudski met Mendelson in January 1893, he was ripe for entry into a conspiratorial organization that sought both to transform social relations and to struggle for a free and sovereign Poland. That new organization was the Polish Socialist Party.[50]

## The First Contacts with Jewish Socialists

One of the first issues Piłsudski addressed upon his entry into the PPS was to continue Mendelson's struggle against Russian Jewish socialists in Vilna. Mendelson had convinced Piłsudski that winning over the Russian Jewish socialist intelligentsia in Vilna to the PPS program was a key task. To this end, they made contact with Jewish socialist leaders Arkadi Kremer and Tsemakh Kopelzon, with whom they spent two evenings in heated discussions. They condemned the Jewish Social Democrats for leading educational circles in the Russian language and encouraged them to switch to Polish or Yiddish as the language of agitation among Jewish workers. They also invited the Vilna group to agitate under the banner of the PPS.[51] The discussions broke down, however, over the question of Polish independence, which Kremer and Kopelzon rejected as part of a Social Democratic platform.

While the details of the first contacts between the PPS and proto-Bundists are scant, the result was clear. In March 1893 the Union Abroad in London received a correspondence from Piłsudski, which they published the following month. Dated March 4, 1893, Piłsudski's first writing on the Jewish question, and third correspondence printed in *Przedświt*, revealed Mendelson's influence.[52] Piłsudski first informed the readers that Jews made up almost half the population of Vilna and were the majority of the urban population in the northwest territories. "If, since 1863, Russification has made progress in Lithuania [*w kraju*]," Piłsudski wrote, "it is precisely among the Jewish people." The Russified nature of the Jewish Social Democratic group made it difficult for the Jewish and Christian working classes in Lithuania to work together, he stated. "I do not take exception to the study of Russian culture and language in and of itself. This is about the denationalization and Russification of Lithuania, and with the current state of affairs," he declared, "no socialist for whom any manifestation of oppression is loathsome . . . has the right to hold a neutral position on this question, not to any extent." He concluded that a neutral stand on the national question among the Jewish socialists would paralyze the possibility of building a mass movement.[53]

Piłsudski continued to pressure the Jewish Social Democrats in the following issue of *Przedświt*, when he wrote the proclamation on

Russian Jewish socialists that was mandated by the Paris congress outline program. In addition to the proclamation, the May 1893 issue of *Przedświt* printed for the first time the outline program drafted at the Paris convention. The proclamation, titled "To Our Jewish Socialist Comrades in the Occupied Polish Territories," fluctuated between outright threats and invitations for Jewish socialists to join the ranks of the PPS. Whereas in the March correspondence, Jewish socialists' "neutrality" on the Polish question was condemned, that same neutrality was characterized as "hostile" one month later. The proclamation warned that an increasingly negative attitude toward Jews was forming among Polish people because of what he called "some Jews' hostile attitude toward the politics of [our] country." This new hostile mood, he continued, was being fomented by the young generation of Russian-speaking Jews, who, ignorant of the past, were "full of false ideas and principles" about Poland they had learned in Russian schools.[54]

These Russian-speaking Jews, he went on, were agents of Russification. "In our country . . . the brutal violence of tsarist despotism has found expression in the politics of 'unification,'" he wrote, "and Jewish socialists have begun working among the Jewish proletariat with the aim of imposing on them the Russian language as the path to culture." Piłsudski then moved to the crux of his argument, which revealed the extent to which he viewed the Jewish question within the context of Russo-Polish relations. "It has become increasingly clear," he wrote, "that the Russian government is using . . . the Russified Jews as a weapon against the political aspirations of the Poles."[55] The proclamation concluded with two demands. First, it called on Jewish socialists to take a "clear and unambiguous" position on the PPS program. Second, Jewish socialists had to struggle alongside Polish and Lithuanian workers, or they would be perceived as doing the work of the tsarist regime. After the proclamation and correspondences on the Jewish question in the first half of 1893, Piłsudski would begin to rise up the ranks of the party and write a series of increasingly sophisticated articles on the nationalities question.

Meanwhile, relations between the PPS in Warsaw and the ZZSP began to break down in May. A group of intellectuals from the former Second Proletariat began to raise objections to the political platform adopted in Paris.[56] Referred to in London at the time as the

"Old PPS," the breakaway group became convinced that the London émigré center was adopting a national program that had moved too far away from class and revolutionary aims. They also objected to the increasingly anti-Russian rhetoric employed in *Przedświt*.[57] At the same time proponents of the proindependence program, led by Leon Falski, formed a Central Circle (Centralne Koło) in Warsaw, which consisted of three workers and three intellectuals.[58]

The pace of events accelerated when ZZSP member Wojciechowski left London in June 1893 for Russian Poland in an attempt to broker an agreement with the breakaway Old PPS. Unable to convince the Old PPS to accept the Paris program, a frustrated Wojciechowski set out for Vilna at the end of June as a representative of the Central Circle in Warsaw. In Vilna, Wojciechowski met Piłsudski in person for the first time after receiving and printing his Vilna correspondences from the spring in London. At the beginning of July an illegal meeting was held in the Belmont Forest outside Vilna, near the home of Piłsudski's sister. It was attended by Piłsudski, Wojciechowski, Aleksander Sulkiewicz, and Ludwik Zajkowski, representing the Vilna, Warsaw, and Saint Petersburg party sections. Later referred to as the First Congress of the PPS, the meeting lasted the entire morning and afternoon. No mention was made of political demands, since they all supported the Paris program. Rather, the day was dominated by Piłsudski's insistence on revising the part of the program on Russian revolutionaries.[59]

Piłsudski's revised draft on Russian revolutionaries revealed the degree to which his deep disdain for Russia guided his politics. Leon Wasilewski, one of Piłsudski's closest confidants in the Union Abroad, commented later that Piłsudski's "profound disdain for Russia was one of the principle components of his political world view." And this was not just hatred for the tsarist government, Wasilewski wrote, but extended to Russian culture and to the Russian national character.[60] The connection between Piłsudski's articles on the Russian Jewish intelligentsia and his missionary struggle against Russian rule came to the surface in his article on Russian revolutionaries. "Indifference [on] the question of Russification," he wrote in July 1893 regarding Russian revolutionaries, "must be recognized by us as silent support for tsarist politics." He concluded with a set of principles on which relations with Russian revolutionaries had to be based. First, they had to explicitly accept the PPS program. Second, Russian revolutionaries agitating on Polish lands could only do so under the PPS banner.[61]

Piłsudski's rise to leadership in the PPS would take place over the following eighteen months. In October 1893 a Workers' Committee (Komitet Robotniczy) was chosen in Warsaw with Piłsudski selected as the representative from the Lithuanian section. At the second congress, which took place February 1894 in Warsaw, Piłsudski was among nine delegates. The congress selected a four-person Central Workers' Committee (CKR), which consisted of Piłsudski, Jan Strożecki, Julian Grabowski, and Paulin Klimowicz. The CKR was entrusted with the responsibility of smuggling into Russian Poland socialist literature and starting a party organ inside the country.[62] As a figure of increasing importance in the party, Piłsudski returned to his Vilna home in the spring of 1894. Shortly after arriving, he sent two letters to the Union Abroad in London regarding his party's organizational activities and the issue of propaganda literature. Although he had publicly condemned the Jewish Social Democrats in Vilna, in private he began to work with them at this time. While lamenting the Russian orientation of the Jewish socialists (*Żydkowie*), Piłsudski suggested the PPS could wield influence on the Jewish socialists in Vilna by pressuring them to switch to Yiddish as the language of agitation.

Piłsudski also recommended that the PPS assist the Jewish Social Democrats in the transportation of Yiddish socialist literature into the Empire. He suggested smuggling *Der arbeyter,* the Yiddish organ of the Polish Social Democratic Party of Galicia, into Vilna for the Jewish Social Democratic group.[63] He then forged a link between Jewish socialists in Galicia and the Jewish Social Democrats in Vilna. Beginning in 1893 Piłsudski helped to facilitate the transport of Yiddish socialist publications to Vilna from Galicia, New York, and London. Moreover, he entered into a friendship with Arkadi Kremer at this time.[64] Thus, largely on Piłsudski's initiative, the PPS smuggled 167 Yiddish brochures into the empire in 1893, according to a reliable source. And in 1894 it is estimated that the PPS smuggled 788 copies of Yiddish socialist brochures, including fifty copies of *Der arbeyter.*[65] The importance Piłsudski attached to his relations with the Vilna Jewish socialists was revealed in a May 1894 letter to the Union Abroad in London. He noted that some Jewish Social Democrats were beginning to develop sympathy for the PPS program. If they eventually joined the PPS, he wrote, "that would be the greatest triumph I could imagine."[66] In addition to linking Galician Jewish socialists with those in Vilna, which allowed for Yiddish socialist brochures to be funneled into Vilna from Lemberg (present-day L'viv), Piłsudski organized the smuggling of a special mimeograph machine with Hebrew typeface into Russian Poland, which he delivered to the Jewish Social Democrats in July 1894.[67]

Meanwhile, the CKR succeeded in smuggling a printing press into the empire, and in July 1894 the first issue of *Robotnik* appeared. But at the end of August, a wave of arrests hit the PPS. Of the four CKR members, only Piłsudski escaped arrest. The unfortunate arrests, however, would elevate Piłsudski to a top leadership role, as he then practically took sole charge of the party's activities. As editor of *Robotnik* and the only surviving member of the core leadership, Piłsudski would remain party leader in Russian Poland for the next seven years.

One of his first acts as party leader was to continue his polemic with the proto-Bundist center in Vilna. After private persuasion proved unsuccessful, Piłsudski decided to publicly pressure the Jewish Social Democrats to agitate in Yiddish. "Our Jewish comrades," Piłsudski wrote in September 1894, "continue to draw on Russian revolutionary writings from the 90s, 80s, and even the 70s. What's stranger, is that even publications in Yiddish are looked down upon by those who see in them a turn to a 'national' viewpoint . . . and this is so despite the fact that the available quantity of socialist literature in Yiddish now equals, or perhaps surpasses, what there is in Russian."[68]

Emboldened by his new status as party leader, Piłsudski used his influence to develop the general political program of the party. In April 1895 Piłsudski printed an article in *Robotnik* that for the first time fully revealed his position on the nationalities question. Reflecting the influence of Mendelson's writing from 1891 and early 1892, Piłsudski emphasized that the only guarantee of political freedoms was national sovereignty. The language he used, however, departed from Mendelson's works by calling unambiguously for "an independent democratic *Polish* republic" in the interests of freedom for the working class. Piłsudski then hinted at his territorial ambition, writing of the Poles, Lithuanians, Latvians, and Ukrainians in the western provinces of the empire who, "by sheer force are in chains and oppressed" and, having been part of prepartition Poland, "have an entirely different history, and different traditions." The inhabitants of these provinces, he wrote, all suffered from national and religious oppression under the tsar. Therefore, Piłsudski concluded, "all these conditions suggest that precisely from them will emerge the strength which will crush to dust the might of tsarism."[69]

Piłsudski then set out to formulate the principal task of his party. Drawing on the nineteenth-century patriotic-insurrectionist tradition and Marx's and Engels's long-time support for Polish independence, Piłsudski proclaimed that the mission of the Polish socialists was to defend the west against eastern despotism. "The historical role of socialism in Poland," he wrote in April 1895, "is the defense of the west against reactionary Russia." The Polish socialist movement, he continued, intended to garner all opposition forces in Russia against the tsarist regime.[70] Because of Piłsudski's writings on the nationalities question, the CKR made him responsible for relations with the nationalities of the western provinces at the third congress in June 1895. At the congress, Piłsudski passed through a significant resolution calling on the party to spread separatist aspirations among the nationalities of the western provinces.[71] With his new role as nationalities secretary, Piłsudski furthered his discussion of the national question in *Robotnik*.

A second figure that influenced the development of the party's ideological evolution was Witold Jodko-Narkiewicz. In a series of articles in 1894, Jodko-Narkiewicz advanced the idea of political independence while rejecting cooperation with Russian revolutionaries. Jodko's central argument was that the party's goals could only be realized in the context of an independent Poland.[72] To make this program attractive to all inhabitants in Russian Poland, Jodko maintained, the party had to link the party program to the specific interests of the non-Polish nationalities in the Baltic and Ukrainian provinces. "We will be on solid ground," Jodko wrote, "if, in our relations with Lithuanians, Ukrainians, and Latvians, the demand for an independent Polish republic is based on the slogan of complete equality for the nationalities as well as the right of each to independently determine its political future." Only in this way could the party convince the nationalties of the superiority of the PPS program over the demand for the transformation of Russia into a constitutional state. Besides, Jodko concluded, "we can rely on the

sympathy and eventually the active aid of all authentically democratic elements in Europe if our program will obliterate rather than
strengthen tsardom."[73]

### Rosa Luxemburg and the First Schism: Social Democracy of the Kingdom of Poland

Before Piłsudski rose to leadership and was able to push
through an increasingly anti-Russian separatist line, a group of
Polish socialists in Zurich linked with the Old PPS printed the first
issue of an oppositional newspaper, *Sprawa Robotnicza,* in July 1893.
The editorial board consisted of the brilliant Rosa Luxemburg, then
twenty-two years old, Lev Jogiches from Vilna, a member in the
1880s of the Second Proletariat, as well as Julian Marchlewski and
Adolf Warszawski, at one time members of the Union of Polish
Workers.[74] While the editors continued to function as an opposition
force within the PPS in July, *Sprawa Robotnicza* departed significantly from the Paris program on two points. First, it called for close
cooperation with the Russian workers, "our brothers in adversity,
comrades in struggle," without whom the tsarist regime could not
be crushed. Second, *Sprawa Robotnicza* refused to endorse the PPS's
independence program.[75]

The appearance of *Sprawa Robotnicza* in the summer of 1893 coincided with the Third Congress of the Socialist International, which
was to take place in Zurich the following month. In order to stake a
claim at being represented at the congress, Luxemburg wrote a
Polish minority report on behalf of *Sprawa Robotnicza* and submitted
it in advance to the congress.[76] The note comprised Luxemburg's
first writing on the question of Polish independence and contained
the seeds of her argument against Polish independence from which
she never departed. The socioeconomic history of Polish lands, she
wrote, "has led to their organic integration into the three partitioning powers and has created in each of the three parts separate aims
and political interests." She then took a stab at the PPS national program. "The realization of a program that states the overthrow of the
tsar as its nearest goal neither depends on a political transformation
in Europe, nor does it owe its existence to the wishes and ideals of
individuals or an antiquated class. To the contrary," she wrote, "it is
the product of the objective course of history."[77]

The spirit of compromise and cooperation between rival PPS factions broke down in August 1893 at the Zurich congress when the fiery Luxemburg voiced her opposition to Polish independence. When the distinguished delegation of PPS representatives from London and Galicia arrived, a group that included veteran socialists Maria Jankowska-Mendelson, Feliks Perl, and Ignacy Daszyński, they did not expect that someone from within the PPS would publicly challenge them. They immediately registered their opposition to Luxemburg's mandate to the congress chairman. Because their request was not granted, Daszyński took the matter before the congress. There, before the International, Luxemburg and Daszyński argued their cases. The Belgian socialist Emile Vandervelde described the scene in his memoirs: "Rosa, 23 years old at the time, was quite unknown outside one or two socialist groups in Germany and Poland, but her opponents had their hands full to hold their ground against her. . . . I can see her now: how she rose from among the delegates at the back and stood on a chair to make herself better heard. Small and looking very frail in a summer dress . . . she advocated her cause with such magnetism and such appealing words that she won the majority of the Congress at once and they raised their hands in favor of the acceptance of her mandate."[78] When it came to a formal vote, however, the congress revoked Luxemburg's mandate. The disputes between Luxemburg's group in Zurich and PPS leaders left a bitter residue.

Now that open war had been declared between the breakaway Zurich group and the PPS leadership, there was no longer a justification for the two groups to remain united. In late August Luxemburg's group broke officially with the PPS and announced the formation of a new party—Social Democracy of the Kingdom of Poland (Socjaldemokracja Królestwa Polskiego, SDKP).[79] The new organization spelled out a decidedly internationalist and pro-Russian position, marking the revival of the antinational Marxist current in Polish socialism.[80]

The emergence of the proindependence Polish Socialist Party in 1892 was linked to the decline of the Russian revolutionary movement. Feliks Perl stressed this point in his writings, noting the crisis of the Russian revolutionary movement as a major factor in the evolution of a proindependence program in Polish socialist circles.

"The influence of the Russian movement was so great, the tradition of *Narodnaia Volia* so strong," Perl wrote, "that for a long time we waited for the revival of the revolutionary struggle and its inescapable victory. But it finally came to light that waiting was undermining our movement and excessively hindering our revolutionary action. It was necessary to free ourselves from undue subordination to the Russian movement, the blind faith in its superiority, and in the certainty of its leading mission. The stagnation in Russia next to the magnificent development of our movement liberated Polish socialism from Russian influence and forced us to practice our own political credo."[81] In an earlier piece, Perl similarly wrote: "[T]he fall of the revolutionary movement in Russia awakened in us . . . a new level of thinking."[82]

The new separatist line in the Polish socialist movement constituted a fundamental ideological shift that had enormous influence on the evolution of its national program. Above all, the new program allowed Polish socialists to refocus their attention from Russia proper to the ethnic borderlands that divided them. Out of the new separatist view arose the seed of the federal idea, whereby the Polish party would seek to extend its influence throughout the western provinces in preparation for a future breakaway federal republic. That the Pale of Settlement—where the world's largest Jewish population resided—would become the PPS's main battleground would have serious consequences.

But a dramatic shift in political culture was not confined to Polish intellectual circles. The 1890s also witnessed the emergence of a separate Jewish socialist movement, to which we shall now turn.

# ■ 2.
# The First Sproutings of the Jewish Socialist Movement, 1890–95

*Since 1893, we have placed mass agitation at the center of our program, and now we must adapt our propaganda . . . to the masses. That is, to give it a more Jewish character.*
IULII MARTOV, MAY DAY RALLY IN VILNA (1895)

TO UNDERSTAND THE RISE AND GROWTH of the Jewish labor movement in imperial Russia, it is necessary to consider the unique setting of Lithuania, the movement's birthplace. In an important essay on Jewish assimilation in Polish lands, Ezra Mendelsohn makes a critical distinction between the process of Jewish "assimilation" in Congress Poland and Russia proper, on the one hand, and Jewish "acculturation" in Lithuania-Belarus, on the other.[1] In Congress Poland, which was overwhelmingly Polish demographically as well as in terms of high culture, the Jewish elite not only acculturated linguistically but also assimilated politically; they adopted the Polish language and regarded themselves as Polish in all respects except for religion. Jewish assimilation also took place in Russia proper, where a tiny percentage of "tolerated" Jews settled outside the Pale and where Russians were demographically and culturally dominant.[2] An altogether different pattern took place in Lithuania-Belarus, where Poles and Russians each made up about 6 percent of the population. Economic backwardness and a multinational character, where no single nationality dominated, combined to erect a barrier to full assimilation. As the late Moshe Mishkinsky similarly argued, the centrality of Lithuania in the Jewish labor movement was a function of slow industrialization, Jewish demographic concentration, and a heterogeneous national character, all of which "impeded the assimilatory tendencies in Jewish life" and endowed Lithuanian Jewry "with greater inner solidarity and stimulated its unique social self-determination."[3]

Russification nonetheless had a significant impact on the Lithuanian Jewish intelligentsia. The Jewish elite of Lithuania-

TABLE 2.1
**Ethnic Composition in the Pale of Settlement and the Kingdom of Poland by Language, 1897**

| Language | Number | Percent Total Population |
|---|---|---|
| Ukrainian | 16,071,756 | 38.0 |
| Polish | 7,672,359 | 18.1 |
| Belarussian | 5,624,250 | 13.3 |
| Yiddish | 4,815,212 | 11.4 |
| Russian | 3,398,772 | 8.0 |
| Lithuanian | 1,604,042 | 3.8 |
| Moldavian | 1,094,899 | 2.6 |
| German | 936,115 | 2.2 |
| Latvian | 299,250 | 0.7 |
| Other | 821,912 | 1.9 |
| Total | 42,338,567 | 100 |

*Source*: Yacov Lestschinsky, *Dos yidishe folk in tsiferen* (Berlin: Klal farlag, 1922), 53.

TABLE 2.2
**Population of the Kingdom of Poland by Language, 1897**

| Language | Number | Percent Total Population |
|---|---|---|
| Polish | 6,754,503 | 72.0 |
| Yiddish | 1,267,072 | 14.0 |
| German | 404,840 | 4.3 |
| Ukrainian | 333,255 | 3.5 |
| Lithuanian | 304,548 | 3.2 |
| Russian | 272,022 | 2.9 |
| Belarussian | 26,567 | 0.3 |
| Other | 39,446 | 0.4 |
| Total | 9,402,253 | 100 |

*Source*: *Pervaia vseobshchaia perepis' naseleniia Rosiiskoi Imperii 1897 g.*, vol. 7 (Saint Petersburg: Tsentralnii statisticheskii komitet, 1905).

TABLE 2.3
**Population of the Northwest Provinces of the Pale of
Settlement (Lithuania-Belarus) by Language, 1897**

| Language | Number | Percent Total Population |
|---|---|---|
| Belarussian | 5,446,085 | 54.1 |
| Yiddish | 1,414,151 | 14.0 |
| Lithuanian | 1,309,071 | 13.0 |
| Russian | 565,632 | 5.6 |
| Polish | 563,451 | 5.5 |
| Ukrainian | 379,168 | 3.9 |
| Latvian | 299,250 | 3.0 |
| German | 26,567 | 0.2 |
| Other | 59,436 | 0.6 |
| Total | 10,062,811 | 100 |

Source: *Pervaia vseobshchaia perepis' naseleniia Rosiiskoi Imperii 1897 g.*, vol. 7 (Saint Petersburg: Tsentralnii statisticheskii komitet, 1905).

Belarus looked to Moscow and Saint Petersburg for cultural inspiration, not to Warsaw. The Russian Jewish socialists in Vilna reflected this well, as they thoroughly identified with the Russian revolutionary tradition. Despite Russifying tendencies, the secular elite retained a strong sense of Jewish autonomous culture and identity. "This elite," Mendelsohn writes incisively, "spoke Russian but did not become Russian; it acculturated but did not assimilate. Indeed, the russified Lithuanian Jews became the pioneers of modern Jewish nationalism . . . and it was they who introduced this new ideology into Central Poland."[4] Raised in a buffer zone between ethnic Poland and ethnic Russia, the Lithuanian Jewish intelligentsia considered itself neither Russian nor Polish and thus never left the living Jewish milieu. A contemporary observer characterized Jewish socialists in Vilna as *intelligenty* who "sensed the pulse of the masses, of the 'average' Jewish worker, and sought a way to him, in his language."[5] These factors, among others, led to the emergence of a unique combination of orthodox Marxism and Diaspora nationalism. Later known as "Bundism," the new synthesis first took root in Vilna, the heart of Jewish Lithuania.

## The First Pioneers: A Biographical Profile

While the first open challenge to PPS hegemony in Russian Poland came in the form of a party schism that led to the formation of Rosa Luxemburg's rival party based in Zurich (SDKP), a serious problem was also posed by the formation of a Russian Jewish socialist center in Vilna. The Vilna center, calling itself the Vilna Group or the Jewish Social Democratic Group in Russia, considered itself the advanced guard of the Russian Social Democratic movement. It was formed in 1890–91 of an elite group of Russian Jewish intellectuals who had begun to organize Jewish workers in Vilna into illegal educational circles. Their goal was to create a core of "conscious Social Democrats" among Jewish workers for entry into the general Russian Social Democratic movement. The Vilna Group was also the first socialist group in the Pale to form on a non-territorial basis, claiming to represent *Jewish* workers scattered throughout the empire. This was a direct challenge to the PPS, the only existing socialist party operating in the empire at the time, which used the adjective *Polish* in a strictly *territorial* sense, claiming to represent all workers within the borders of prepartition Poland.

The Vilna Group was first organized in 1890 by Tsemakh Kopelzon (1869–1933) and Lev Jogiches (1867–1919), who later defected to the Polish Social Democratic movement (SDKPiL). At the beginning of 1891 a core of new members enriched the Vilna organization. These included Arkadi Kremer (1865–1935), who quickly became the leader; Pati Srednitskaia-Kremer (1867–1943); Shmuel Gozhanski (1867–1943), a graduate of the Vilna Teachers Institute; John Mill (1870–1952), a graduate of the *Realschule*, a modern German secondary school system adopted in several countries as well as of the polytechnic; Isai Aizenshtat (1867–1937), and Liuba Levinson (1866–1903). By 1893 the Vilna Group expanded to include the students Vladimir Kossovsky (1867–1941), Avrom Mutnik (1868–1930), Noyakh Portnoy (1872–1941), Pavel Rozental (1872–1924), Anna Heller (1872–1941), and *Realschule* student Pavel Berman (1873–1922). With the exception of Jogiches, who became an active member of Rosa Luxemburg's Social Democracy of the Kingdom of Poland, the latter group of *intelligenty* formed the nucleus of the future Jewish Labor Bund.[6]

An examination of the social background of the Jewish Social Democratic pioneers reveals striking similarities. First, the Vilna

Group leaders were born between 1865 and 1873 and came from enlightened families who had already embraced the Haskalah. Second, the Jewish socialist pioneers all came from the territories of the northwest provinces. Of the thirteen leaders, ten were from the Vilna region, two from Grodno, and one from Latvia. Similar to the PPS pioneers, who did not directly experience the 1863 insurrection, the Vilna Group leaders all came from the Lithuania-Belarus and thus did not experience firsthand the pogrom wave of 1881, which had taken place in the Ukraine. Third, the Vilna Group pioneers were products of a secular education in Russian schools and only had a rough knowledge of traditional Jewish subjects. Although most of them had been blocked because of their Jewish origin in their efforts to enter the professions, they were mainly concerned with the vast social and economic problems in Russia and drawn to radical Russian circles.[7] Born to Maskilic (enlightened) families, they were raised not in the traditional hadorim and yeshivot (Jewish primary and secondary schools), to which the vast majority of Jewish families sent their boys, but in the government-run Crown Jewish Elementary School, the Russian gymnasium, and the *Realschule*.[8]

Before discussing the Vilna movement itself, we shall sketch the backgrounds of Arkadi Kremer and John Mill, two major figures in the early history of the Bund.

Known as the "father of the Bund," Kremer was born in 1865 in the town of Svencionys in the Vilna province. Svencionys was a typical town in Lithuania-Belarus. Of 6,025 inhabitants, Jews constituted 52 percent of the population, with Poles and a few Lithuanians constituting the remaining population.[9] Kremer's father was a teacher of Jewish religious studies and a Maskil (proponent of the Jewish Enlightenment) who believed in the importance of secular studies and social integration.[10] Kremer, however, did not receive a traditional Jewish education. In 1877, at the age of twelve, he moved to his impoverished uncle's home in Vilna, where he enrolled in a *Realschule* and developed a love for mathematics and physics. It was in the Vilna *Realschule* that Kremer came under the influence of revolutionary currents when he befriended Jacob Notkin, a Russian populist (*narodnik*). In August 1885 Kremer, along with Notkin, journeyed to Saint Petersburg to take examinations for the technical institute. After spending two years in Saint Petersburg, Kremer settled in Riga to study at the Riga Polytechnic Institute.

Kremer's revolutionary career began in Riga under the influence of Polish revolutionaries. His studies in Riga came to an abrupt halt when he was accused of disseminating illegal literature and involvement with Polish revolutionary circles. Arrested in 1889, Kremer served six months in the notorious Pawiak Prison in Warsaw. After his release he returned to Vilna in the beginning of 1890. Soon after, he joined the Jewish Social Democratic Group, which had formed sometime in late 1890.[11] At the time Kremer was a faithful socialist revolutionary with no national leanings. One contemporary recalled that, in the early 1890s Kremer was "too de-Judaized" to discuss the Jewish national idea, which "ricocheted off him like balls off a stone wall."[12] Rather, his interest was in the general revolutionary movement in the Russian Empire; Jewish cadres, he believed, could be used in the larger Russian industrial centers. After Kremer's arrival in Vilna in 1891, he gradually replaced Kopelzon, who recalled that Kremer was a "well-educated young man, wise, witty, good-hearted but often very strict, very able, and untiring. His popularity grew rapidly and practically all without exception accepted him as the leader of the organization."[13] Mill similarly wrote that "the flesh and soul, and the head and heart of the Jewish labor movement in the pioneering days was none other than Arkadi Kremer."[14]

While Kremer's background is representative of the majority of pioneers, the early biography of John Mill, born Yoysef Shloyme, illustrates a figure who led the struggle for a national platform in the Jewish socialist camp. Mill was the one pioneer who had been raised in both a Russian *and* a Polish atmosphere. From an early age Mill established close relations with Polish people and took a special interest in the Polish national problem.[15] As veteran Bundist Frants Kursky commented, Mill was the first—and for some years the only—Bundist to bring a "Polish element" into Jewish socialist circles in Lithuania, that is to say, a sympathy and understanding for Polish issues, for their national aspirations and longings. In contrast, Kursky wrote, "the other pioneers of the Bund were classic Litvaks with a Russian education and very little familiarity with Polish life." Furthermore, they had no particular interest in the national question.[16]

Yoysef Shloyme Mill was born in the Lithuanian town of Panevėžys in 1870 in the Kovno province. Panevėžys had a large percentage of Jews, something characteristic of towns in the north-west provinces. Of a total population of 12,968 in Panevėžys, 6,627 were Jews (51 percent), 4,172 were Catholics (32 percent), most of them Polish, and the remaining were Orthodox.[17] At the age of four, Mill's Maskilic father began to teach him to read and write Russian and Yiddish. Soon after, however, Mill's father sent him to a government-run Jewish primary school, where Mill furthered his study of Russian but ceased study of Yiddish, which he lost by the time he reached his teens (his passive knowledge of Yiddish would none-theless help him when he later had to relearn it). In 1882 the government opened a *Realschule* in Panevėžys, where Mill became a student.[18]

Mill's experience in the Russian school system reveals the degree to which Russian schools became instruments of acculturation. "In school," he wrote, "I learned nothing [about Judaism]—neither Hebrew, Jewish prayer, nor even the basics of the Jewish religion." His subsequent knowledge of Torah and Jewish culture in general, he continued, "came not from heder, but thanks to the chance conversations with my grandfather, and from the weekly class on religion in *Realschule*." Mill's schooling, and the fact that he learned very little about Jewish matters at home, was typical for the first generation of children to grow up in an acculturated family environment. This is reflected in the fact that Mill's parents raised their children in the Christian section of Panevėžys, and the majority of his childhood playmates were non-Jews.[19]

While the government-run primary and secondary schools were successful at acculturating the second generation of Jewish integrationists to Russian culture, they were unable to shield them from revolutionary currents. Mill's revolutionary career first took root in the Panevėžys *Realschule* when, in his fourth year, he joined a secret reading group of radical students. Consisting of a few Polish and Jewish students, as well as one Russian, the group began with Russian literature. According to Mill, he was the only Jew in the group to develop friendships with Polish students during his time in the *Realschule*: "a thick wall of mistrust and traditional antipathy" still existed between the Poles, Jews, Russians, and Lithuanians in the Panevėžys *Realschule*.[20]

In the following year, 1887, Tsemakh Kopelzon, who had been helping Lev Jogiches organize workers in Vilna, came to Panevėžys to enter the fifth year at the *Realschule*. Through Kopelzon the group learned about the Russian revolutionary movement, as well as about the growth of the socialist movement in western Europe. Kopelzon exerted a great influence on the group, particularly among the Jews. Not only did he introduce them to ideas about the workers' movement, political struggle, and socialism, but he brought forbidden literature from Vilna, including socialist brochures and the organ of *Narodnaia Volia,* which, according to Mill, the group devoured.[21] After summer and winter breaks Kopelzon would bring back news from Vilna, to which the students listened with great interest.

The *Realschule* in Panevėžys graduated its students after six years. Thus, with a diploma in hand and a letter of recommendation from his school rector, Mill went to Vilna in 1889 to enter the seventh class at the advanced *Realschule*.[22] Soon after, the nineteen-year-old Mill met some students of the gymnasium and *Realschule* in Vilna and joined the socialist circle they had formed.[23] The group of Vilna students was very similar to Mill's radical circle in Panevėžys, as it was dominated by young Polish radicals. A few of them, Mill recounted, were Polish patriots whose fathers had been persecuted for involvement in the 1863 insurrection. One of the students, Okuniewicz, took a liking to Mill and recommended him to tutor his younger siblings at their Vilna home. Mill was required to converse and tutor at the Okuniewicz home in Polish, which he spoke with broken grammar and a Russian accent. For taking part in the 1863 rising, Okuniewicz's father had spent several years in Siberian exile, where he suffered permanent damage to his leg. Around the dinner table, Mill wrote, the father spoke of the uprising and his life in forced exile. The whole home, Mill recalls, "was imbued with hatred for Russians . . . whom they accused of ruining their lives."[24]

From the Panevėžys and Vilna student circles, Mill developed a particular understanding for the Polish cause. In the Polish socialist movement, "I found not only a basis for my search for truth . . . but an understanding for the special Polish approach to political problems and goals of that time."[25] Mill nonetheless described his work in radical Polish student circles as a temporary diversion. A new direction in Mill's thinking was linked with the figure of Kopelzon. After learning of Mill's work with the Polish student circle, Kopelzon introduced him to members of the radical intelligentsia as well as to workers. It was at the end of 1889 and the beginning of 1890 that the Jewish radical intelligentsia led by Kopelzon and Jogiches, after some years of agitation, formed a small group devoted to work among Jewish workers.

## Vilna: The Assimilationist Period, 1891–93

Despite some interest in national issues and in Polish political life on the part of Mill, the Vilna Group remained unequivocally integrationist in the period 1890–93. They were drawn to Russian culture and had no specific interest in founding a Jewish movement. As Jonathan Frankel describes in his superb study of Jewish socialism, the Vilna circles had been structured as a "pedagogical hierarchy—workers selected from the rank and file progressed upwards through a series of study circles. Starting with lessons in the fundamentals of the Russian language, natural history, and political economy, they advanced to lessons on Darwinism and Marxism."[26] The immediate objective in this period was to turn the workers into conscious Social Democrats. No particular interest in Jewish workers or in Jewish problems was expressed at these meetings. Kopelzon stated clearly the environment of the Vilna Group: "We were assimilationists who did not even dream of a separate Jewish mass movement. We saw our task as preparing cadres for the Russian revolutionary movement and acclimatizing them to Russian culture."[27] Kremer similarly recalled that those who first founded revolutionary circles in Vilna "only wanted to produce a few more developed workers, bring them to socialist consciousness, prepare them as agitators for Russia, for the industrial centers, and for the Russian working class. In those days, socialists still did not see the possibility of a conscious class movement among workers from small workshops, and even less so among Jewish workers widely scattered among the artisan shops."[28] Another historian of the workers' movement in tsarist Russia characterized the Vilna Group's assimilationist predisposition well: the Vilna leaders "sought to draw the Jewish workers into the Russian movement and to efface any peculiarly Jewish consciousness. In effect, propaganda activity in Vilna . . . served to 'russify' the worker elite and alienate it from the Jewish milieu."[29]

Shmuel Gozhansky was representative of the integrationist tendencies in the early period of the Vilna Group. Born to an upper middle-class family in Grodno, Gozhansky pursued a career in the government-run Jewish schools. After graduating from the Vilna Teacher's Institute in 1888, Gozhansky taught at a Crown Jewish school in Vilna.[30] While all classes, even those in Jewish religion, were conducted in Russian, one student, Hersz Abramowicz (1881–1960), recalled how strictly and uncompromisingly Gozhansky enforced the Russian only rule, refusing to allow even questions of clarification in Yiddish. "One day," Abramowicz wrote in his memoirs, "two friends and I walked out of the school conversing loudly in Yiddish, our mother tongue, unaware that Gozhanski was walking behind us. Apparently, I was the last one he heard speaking, for Gozhanski walked straight toward me, stopped our group and said (in Russian) in his staccato tone, 'Go back to school and report to Il'ia Isakovich [Lazarev, the school administrator] that you and your friends were speaking Yiddish outdoors.'" Abramowicz commented on the irony that not only were Jewish pupils at the government-run school forbidden to speak Yiddish "in the most pro-Yiddish city in the world," but "so, too, is the fact that the enforcing agent was none other than Gozhanski, who was later one of the founders of the Bund."[31]

By 1892 the Vilna Group had organized several circles of both intellectuals and workers. In the period 1891–92, according to Kopelzon, about sixty to seventy intellectuals were organized into secret conspiratorial groups of ten to fifteen people each. In addition, Kopelzon estimated that Vilna Group leaders had organized about 150 Jewish workers into propaganda *kruzhki* (circles). The fact that these educational circles were conducted in the Russian language severely limited the circles to the tiny minority of so-called worker-intellectuals who were literate in Russian.[32] By the following year, about three hundred Jewish workers were organized into professional *kases,* workers' organizations originally designed to provide strike funds.[33]

The internationalist spirit of the *kruzhki* was evident at the 1892 May Day events in Vilna. At that rally, when about a hundred Jewish workers demonstrated, four worker-intellectuals spoke alongside Kremer and Mill, and the speeches of the four workers were published abroad.[34] Constituting the first documents of the Jewish labor movement in the Russian Empire, these speeches reflected an internationalist position, staunchly assimilationist and hostile to Jewish tradition as well as a Jewish separatist stand.[35] Despite differences, the four speakers emphasized the need for economic struggle while almost wholly ignoring the question of anti-tsarist political action. The internationalist view was well articulated by one of the speeches. "And we, Jews, 'subjects' of Russia," said one speaker, who most clearly articulated the internationalist view, "renounce our holidays and fantasies as useless for human society. We join the ranks of the socialists and adhere to their holidays . . . which will exist for all the generations to come, for its goal is to raze to ground the pillars of the old world and to establish on its ruins a world of peace. Our holidays, which our grandfathers have bestowed on us, will disappear along with the old order. We maintain that no single god . . . can lift the yoke from the oppressed masses who are being pushed to the ground. Only knowledge and our own energy can lead us from the darkness."[36] Israeli historian Moshe Mishkinsky has written that the Vilna *kruzhki* members were taught a conception of the structure of society that declared that anything outside of the "bourgeoisie" and "proletariat" was destined by the "historical process" to disappear. "According to these ideas," Mishkinsky writes, "the reality of the existence of the Jewish people seemed to melt away, the inner ties within Jewry were severed, and they would not be restored—particularly since religion was losing its significance as a factor lending uniqueness to the Jews as a whole."[37]

Not all the workers, however, supported the internationalist tendency of the Vilna Group leaders. In fact, the first open challenge to the internationalist current then prevalent in Vilna came from the bootmaker Reuven Gershovski. Gershovski's speech, in turn, brought to the surface tensions within the labor movement among Jews over the question of whether or not the Jewish working class had special tasks of its own, or if the Jewish component of their movement would eventually become irrelevant. The working class in Russia was at the beginning of a historical stage in the evolution of the workers' movement. "One has only to look at the example of western Europe," he said, "where the workers, as now in Russia, began to unify by creating circles, at the beginning small, and afterward, with the growth of industry and from the propaganda among the workers, much larger." But unlike the interpretation of the previous speaker, Gershovski contended that the Jews must first organize themselves before entering the ranks of the international working class. "We cannot sit with folded arms and wait for help from above. We can gain freedom and salvation," he maintained, "only from ourselves." He concluded with an unpopular affirmation of Jewish identity. "And we, Jews, should not be discouraged or ashamed that we belong to the 'dishonorable' Jewish race. The history of our people gives us that right."[38] As Mishkinsky has insightfully noted in his introduction to the Hebrew translation, Gershovski's speech marked a departure from the strictly internationalist spirit of the circles and pointed toward a Jewish labor movement.

### From Propaganda to Agitation: The New Program, 1893–95

The entire approach of the Vilna Group was consciously abandoned in 1893, a change resulting from the influence of the Union of Polish Workers, which called for the large-scale organization of workers; the general growth of the strike movement in Russian Poland, including the massive 1892 May Day strike in Łódź; and pressures from the newly formed PPS to abandon agitation in Russian for Yiddish.[39] The turning point can be traced back to an ideological and tactical breakthrough in 1893, which saw the printing of Kremer's famous brochure *On Agitation* and of Gozhanski's critical piece *A Letter to Agitators*.[40]

In *On Agitation* Kremer argued for a tactical shift in the Social Democratic movement in which political agitation should broaden its base by a greater appeal to the working masses; it should cease being theoretical and instead launch a program integrating political and economic goals.[41] In line with the tactics of appealing to the masses, *On Agitation* implied that agitation would now have to be conducted in the language of the working masses. Kremer realized that his group could not attract a broad mass following unless Yiddish was adopted. After a debate with those opposed to the use of Yiddish, Kremer's program was accepted in 1894. The importance of the new emphasis on Yiddish, although at the time considered a mere tactical decision, would later be characterized as a central event in the Bund's history. "The switch to Yiddish," one Bundist later commented, "in fact signified [the birth of] an autonomous Jewish workers' movement. A special Jewish organization for the Jewish worker would now have to be created . . . with a revolutionary literature . . . and culture in Yiddish."[42]

By 1893 it had become clear that conspiratorial educational circles were inadequate to prepare the Jewish worker for the Social Democratic movement in Russia. Rather, the Vilna Group had to begin addressing the concrete practical needs and demands of Jewish workers. Frankel argues that the adoption of the new program signified the leadership's decision to recognize the labor movement in Vilna as an autonomous political entity. As now envisioned, the movement "was to become that of the Jewish working class with Yiddish as its language, the local workshop as its focal point, and 'trade unionism' . . . as its major form of activity."[43] Kremer, however, intended his work for the general Social Democratic movement in Russia, or, as Tobias observes, "as a kind of Social Democratic strategy paper."[44] It was written in Russian and addressed to the "Russian" Social Democratic movement with no explicit reference to Jewish workers. Allan Wildman has remarked that the remarkable feature of *On Agitation* was that its theoretical argument and practical guidelines, although designed to meet the crisis arising from the specific conditions of the small workshop, were placed within the general framework of Marxist theory and were thus universally applicable.[45]

While Kremer laid out the theoretical basis for a transition to mass agitation, Gozhanski applied the new program to the specific case of Jewish workers in *A Letter to Agitators*.[46] While earlier works on the Bund have emphasized the importance of *On Agitation*, two historians have revised that view and placed greater weight on Gozhanski's pamphlet.[47] Gozhanski was the first Vilna Group leader to hint at the need for a *Jewish* labor movement that would take into account the special tasks and needs of the Jewish working class. Moreover, *A Letter to Agitators* is the first document of the Jewish labor movement in Russia that refers to the Jews as a "nationality."[48] For this reason, Mishkinsky has rightly characterized *A Letter to Agitators* as "the source of Bundism."[49]

Gozhanski began his pamphlet with a discussion of parliamentary systems in Europe. The tsarist regime, he argued, would eventually give way to a more democratic regime. But it would be naive to assume that a constitutional government in Russia would necessarily grant equal rights to the Jews. "The Russian constitution," Gozhanski wrote, "will encounter a land divided between classes (the bourgeoisie and the proletariat), estates (the nobility and the peasantry), and nationalities (Russians, Poles, Jews, Finns, Tartars, etc.). The rights granted . . . will depend on the political power and interests . . . each group will have at the moment Russia attains political freedom. A constitution—a parliamentary regime—does not guarantee equal rights for all citizens," he warned. To prove his point, Gozhanski surveyed the various parliamentary regimes in Europe. While in Germany the classes had equal rights, they did not in Austria. In France, he continued, the nobility and peasantry had equal rights, while this was not the case in Austria. There were countries in which all nationalities had equal rights (France, England, Italy), whereas this was not the case in Germany and Hungary, where Poles and Romanians were persecuted. And in the case of Romania, one nationality was denied the right of citizenship—the Jews. As Gozhanski wrote, "[T]he Jews have fewer rights in constitutional Romania then in autocratic Russia."[50] The vastly different systems in Europe resulted from the crude fact that constitutions were drafted to protect political interests "from the power a group has built through political struggle." In contrast to the development of political interests, which Gozhanski called "internal" factors that had led to inequality in societies under constitutional governments, economic interests, or "external" factors, also played a role. The different systems could be explained, therefore, by each country's unique combination of political and economic conditions.

How, then, could Jews ensure that they, too, would attain equal rights in a future democratic Russia? The progressive Jewish *intelligenty* and worker-intellectuals had to raise the political consciousness of the Jewish working masses so that it would become an active force. That political struggle, Gozhanski continued, was to be carried on by the urban population. "Those rights that the Jewish proletariat receives without a conscious political struggle will be worthless," Gozhanski wrote, continuing that, "if the Jewish proletariat does not attain a proper level [of political consciousness], the majority will see to it that the constitution will present it nothing more than a piece of paper. Those rights will then not be granted and the Jewish proletariat will not be in a position to properly defend itself." The political level of the Jewish worker thus had to be raised to a proper level of maturity so that he or she would be prepared to engage in a political struggle. "We, Jewish Social Democrats," Gozhanski concluded, "must develop a consciousness among the Jewish proletariat strong enough so that it will be prepared to attain its rights and defend them once they have been won."[51]

The final part of Gozhanski's pamphlet revealed the extent to which the Vilna Group intended to link its organization with the Jewish masses. "Agitation," Gozhanski declared, "is the foundation of the Social Democratic program," whose new slogan is "all for, and by, the working masses!" *A Letter to Agitators* also assigned a specific role to the Jewish socialist intelligentsia: to create agitators out of the workers through education. To become a "conscious Social Democrat," an agitator had to have a certain level of knowledge, Gozhanski maintained, including that of political economy, politics, history, geography, and natural history. The agitator "should clearly comprehend the theory of evolution, the relation between economic and political change, and every aspect of the present class struggle."[52]

The change to mass agitation also required a major tactical shift—the question of language—which Gozhanski took up in the conclusion. In order to facilitate the change to mass agitation and to raise the level of consciousness among the Jewish workers, the Vilna Group would now have to use the language of the common folk, Yiddish. This would require, he noted, a large-scale campaign to translate and print socialist literature in Yiddish. The switch to Yiddish was considered a short-term tactical decision that did not contradict the Vilna Group's assimilationist position. Once agitation in Yiddish created conscious Social Democrats among Jewish workers, the process of full integration would naturally follow, and with it, the disappearance of Yiddish. Not only did Gozhanski attach no special significance to Yiddish, other than its value as a tool for the dissemination of socialism, but many Jewish socialists at the time were of the position that the preservation of Yiddish was wholly undesirable. This is supported by the fact that Gozhanski's *Letter*, while acknowledging the need for using Yiddish, mandated the use of Russian whenever possible and expressed the hope that Jewish workers would eventually master Russian. "We propose that the question of who should be taught in Russian and which scientific branches should be taught in Yiddish, as well as when, in general, Yiddish should be used as the language of instruction, will be decided jointly by the intelligentsia and agitators." However, for those aspiring to be "leader-agitators," knowledge of the Russian language was required, and once the agitators learned Russian well, the educational circles of the intelligentsia and agitators were to be conducted exclusively in Russian.[53]

Gozhanski's pamphlet expressed several radical new ideas that laid the foundation for a new direction in the Jewish labor movement. Among these was, first, the notion that Jewish workers had distinct and particular interests for which they had to wage a separate struggle. Second, Gozhanski maintained that the Jews had to actively fight for and defend their rights to equality before the law, as Jewish interests might be compromised in the struggle between different groups for the attainment of power in Russia. Third, he argued that the dissemination of socialist ideas among Yiddish-speaking workers could be accomplished through an appeal to particular Jewish economic, cultural, and political interests and concerns. As Peled has maintained, these ideas would become the ideological foundation of the future Bund.[54]

Taken together, *On Agitation* and *A Letter to Agitators* laid the basis for a new program in the socialist movement among the Jews of Vilna. Although printed together and intended as a single work, they nonetheless reflected left and right divisions within the Jewish socialist camp. In contrast to Kremer's *On Agitation*, the Jewish national overtones of Gozhanski's work discomfited some members.[55] At that time Kremer would not have identified himself as a "Jewish Social Democrat" as Gozhanski formulated, but as a Social Democrat preparing one section of the working class, distinguished, in his mind, only by a separate language, to enter the general movement in Russia. After 1893 the Vilna Group increasingly focused on the particular conditions of Jewish workers, as well as on Jewish problems in general.

The separatist current first hinted at by Gershovski in 1892 and Gozhanski in 1893 was first acknowledged and discussed at a conference held in Vilna in August 1894. The meeting lasted two days and was attended by all the major Vilna Group leaders.[56] According to Mill, it was at the 1894 meeting that the Vilna Group first clarified its position on the "Jewish question." "This was the first time that we declared our stand on the Jewish question so clearly, without any ambiguity whatsoever," he wrote. On that occasion, the speakers argued "that the Jewish worker suffers in Russia not merely as a worker but as a Jew; that in agitation all forms of national oppression should be stressed more and more; that, together with the general political and economic struggle, the struggle for civil equality must be one of our immediate tasks; and that this struggle can best be carried out by the organized Jewish worker himself."[57] The conference revealed the degree to which the socialist movement in Vilna had begun to adopt a distinctly Jewish character and was beginning to address the particular needs of the Jewish working class.

The second turning point in the Vilna movement's shift to a Jewish orientation is connected with the May Day events in 1895. The new recruit Iulii Martov delivered a speech to Jewish workers in Vilna unambiguously advocating the formation of an *independent* Jewish socialist movement that would demand *national* rights.[58] The movement in Vilna had reached a wholly new stage in its evolution from propaganda circles to mass agitation, Martov proclaimed. Before 1893 the Vilna leadership only looked at Jewish workers "with scorn," Martov maintained, represented by the fact that agitation was conducted in Russian. "Wishing to join the Russian movement," Martov said, "we forgot to establish links with the Jewish masses who do not understand Russian. Yes, our early movement expressed a mistrust of the masses, which we adopted from our bourgeoisie. . . . Consequently, we neglected to acknowledge that a Jewish movement was emerging."[59]

Martov characterized the switch to mass agitation in 1893 as a critical moment. Since 1893 "we have placed mass agitation at the center of our program, and now we must adapt our propaganda . . . to the masses; that is, to give it a more *Jewish* character." Drawing from Gozhanski's precepts, Martov stressed that the Jewish worker could not depend on the Russian or Polish movements for political freedom. Martov then took Gozhanski's arguments one step further by explicitly calling for the creation of an independent Jewish socialist party. "We need to categorically recognize," he continued, "that our goal . . . allows for the creation of a special Jewish workers' organization that will become the leader and educator of the Jewish proletariat in the struggle for economic, civil, and political freedom."[60]

Martov stressed, however, that the turn to a separate Jewish organization was a short-term *tactical* decision. The long-term goal was still to create "conscious Social Democrats" out of the Jewish working class. According to Martov, national and cultural difference were destined by "the historical process" to disappear eventually. "Yes, socialism is international," Martov proclaimed, "and the historical process that created the class struggle in modern societies will inevitably lead to the abolition of national boundaries and the merging of all peoples into one family. But . . . as long as modern societies with pressing needs exist, each nationality has to win for itself, if not political independence, then at least full equal rights." Martov thus concluded, "the development of national and class consciousness must go hand in hand." He acknowledged that the national part of the program could obscure class consciousness among Jewish workers. But he argued that "we have no fear of recognizing once and for all the distinct character (call it what you want—a national character) of our movement."[61] Iulii Martov was the first to formulate with full clarity the need for an independent Jewish workers' organization.[62]

## Reactions to the "New Program" Abroad

As major changes were taking place in Vilna, John Mill settled in Zurich to study at the university and make contacts with émigré socialist circles. At the time Polish socialist émigrés in Zurich grouped around two major figures: Feliks Perl of the PPS and Rosa Luxemburg of the newly formed Marxist party, Social Democracy of the Kingdom of Poland (SDKP), originally a PPS splinter group. The main ideological divide between the two parties—and the cause of the first schism within the PPS—was Luxemburg's rejection of Polish independence as a part of the party platform. During his two-year stay in Zurich between the summers of 1893 and 1895, Mill met Luxemburg and her close associate Lev Jogiches on several occasions. He recalled his first meeting with Luxemburg in the summer of 1893, soon after the SDKP had been formed. She asked him many questions about the activities of the Vilna Group and the working-class movement among Jews in Russia. She was more interested, however, in the Vilna center's position on the ideological dispute then taking place between her organization and the PPS.

From the very beginning of his stay in Zurich, Mill found himself caught in the crossfire between the internationalism of the SDKP and the national orientation of the PPS. Indeed, it was in Zurich that Mill's views on the Polish question began to take shape. In contrast to the PPS, which had openly castigated the Vilna Group as Russifiers of the Jewish working class, Luxemburg lent her full support to the Vilna Group's Social Democratic orientation, which made the SDKP more favorable in Mill's eyes.

Mill also came into contact with PPS leader Feliks Perl in Zurich. Mill's initial dislike of Perl would never soften. Until Mill's arrival in Zurich, he and the Vilna Group had never heard of Perl. "[Feliks Perl] made a disagreeable impression," Mill recalls, adding, "An assimilated Polish Jew, he used to avoid Russian and Jewish students like the plague. Stiff and high-strung, he behaved more Polish than the Poles. . . . The zealousness brought out by his Polish patriotism, his devotion to the new line in Polish socialism, and his hatred toward everyone who did not adhere to the PPS program often took a bizarre form."[63]

The situation in Zurich in the years 1893–94 was unique. The three central figures representing the SDKP, the PPS, and the Vilna Group were Jews from Lithuania and Congress Poland, representing three currents within the Jewish radical intelligentsia: a doctrinaire Marxist, a Polish patriot, and a Jewish socialist. After making key contacts in Zurich, Mill returned to Vilna in the summer of 1894 to bring back socialist literature and report back to the Vilna Group.

In September 1894, after the important Vilna Group meeting in Vilna mentioned earlier, Mill recalled that something in him had changed, that he was then more certain than ever of the correctness of the Vilna Group's new program.[64] The most enthusiastic support for the new program was mainly among latecomers: Martov, who arrived in Vilna in 1893, and Vladimir Kossovsky and Avrom Mutnik, who came in 1894. Of the veterans, only John Mill gave his wholehearted support. Pioneers such as Aizenshtat and Kopelzon were clearly uncomfortable with the national focus Gozhanski and Martov were seeking.

From Zurich and London both the SDKP and the PPS did not refrain from expressing their stark opposition to the new separatist line then forming in Vilna. In the face of an onslaught of attacks from the SDKP, Mill was fully prepared to defend the new program in Zurich. Upon Mill's return from Vilna in 1894, Luxemburg and Jogiches accused the Vilna Group "of being 100 percent separatist, as a kind of PPS-ism in the Jewish street, as a step that would logically lead us nearer to the ideology of the petty bourgeoisie." In a view that reveals the degree to which the integrationist solution to the Jewish question had been incorporated into radical circles in the 1890s, Luxemburg and Jogiches argued that the new policy in Vilna would retard the process of acculturation. The movement in Vilna, Luxemburg insisted, "needed neither the Yiddish language nor a separate Jewish workers' organization, but the language of the surrounding population and a blending with the Christian proletariat." Any other line, it was argued, would lead the socialist movement down a nationalistic road.[65] What was at stake in the dispute between the SDKP and Mill, however, went far beyond specific concerns with the socialist movement in Vilna. Luxemburg was intent on winning over Mill and the Vilna Group to her anti-PPS program, and the separatist turn in Vilna indirectly gave credence to the national orientation of the PPS.

Emboldened by the Vilna conference from which he had just returned, Mill openly challenged Luxemburg's positions, including her dogmatic opposition to Polish sovereignty. In the fall of 1894, Mill wrote, Luxemburg and Jogiches "had expressed outrage" when he informed them of his position in Vilna vis-à-vis their program. Mill and other Vilna Group members did not agree with the view that Poland was "organically linked" to Russia, as Luxemburg had argued. Mill then reminded Luxemburg and Jogiches that Plekhanov, Kautsky, and Engels "had publicly and unambiguously expressed their support for a free and independent Poland."[66] Yet, while Mill sympathized with Polish national aspirations, he did not favor the PPS program in particular. The PPS program had argued that Polish independence was necessary *before* a political revolution in Russia, something to which the Jewish Social Democrats could not lend their support. It was precisely this sticking point that placed the Bund between the Polish Marxists and patriotic socialists in the pre-WWI period.

At the beginning of the 1890s, an elite Russian Jewish socialist center arose in Vilna ideologically and culturally linked to the Russian revolutionary tradition. Its birthplace was Lithuania, a buffer zone between ethnic Poland and ethnic Russia ideal for the spread of Jewish autonomous movements. While in 1891–92 its activity was confined to elite propaganda circles, the period 1893–95 saw the movement's dramatic shift "from propaganda to agitation," which involved the critical decision to agitate in the language of the Jewish masses. The switch to Yiddish thus solidified a "Jewish orientation" in the movement and would dramatically increase the movement's following. But the decision to establish a separate Jewish socialist party two years later was intricately connected with the spread of the Vilna movement to Warsaw, the Polish heartland, in the years 1895–97.

*Arkadi Kremer (1865–1935), c. 1895 (Yivo Institute for Jewish Research)*

*John Mill (1870–1952), Switzerland, c. 1905 (Yivo Institute for Jewish Research)*

*Pati Srednitskaia-Kremer (1867–1943), Mogilev, Russia, 1901 (Yivo Institute for Jewish Research)*

*Shmuel Gozhanski (1867–1943), Geneva, 1907 (Yivo Institute for Jewish Research)*

*Noyakh Portnoy (1872–1941), Minsk, 1904 (Yivo Institute for Jewish Research)*

*Vladimir Kossovsky (1867–1941), Geneva, 1906 (Yivo Institute for Jewish Research)*

*Vladimir Medem, Geneva, 1906 (Yivo Institute for Jewish Research)*

*Marc Liber (1880–1937), Vilna, c. 1905 (Yivo Institute for Jewish Research)*

*Liuba Levinson (1866–1903), Vilna, c. 1895 (Yivo Institute for Jewish Research)*

*Pavel Rozental (1872–1924), c. 1905 (Yivo Institute for Jewish Research)*

*From left to right: Henryk Erlich (1882–1941) and Bronislav Groser (1883–1912),
with their wives, Sophia Dubnow-Erlich and Sara Groser, Saint Petersburg,
1907 or 1908 (Yivo Institute for Jewish Research)*

*Max Weinreich (1894–1969), a founder of the Yivo Institute for Jewish Research in Vilna and seminal scholar of the Yiddish language, at the age of nineteen with fellow Bundists (standing, second from left), Tsarist Russia, 1913 (Yivo Institute for Jewish Research)*

# ■ 3.

# Into the Polish Heartland:
# The Spread of the Jewish
# Movement to Warsaw, 1895–97

> *Until recently we had relations [with Jewish workers] in*
> *Warsaw, but now, even there, the Vilna Jews are making their*
> *influence felt.*
> JÓZEF PIŁSUDSKI (LETTER OF FEBRUARY 1897)

> *The very choice of Warsaw as [John Mill's] field of action in 1895*
> *was indicative of his single-minded determination to prove that*
> *the Jewish proletariat throughout the empire had to be seen as a*
> *single political entity.*
> JONATHAN FRANKEL, *PROPHECY AND POLITICS*

IN THE PREVIOUS CHAPTER we traced the emergence of a Jewish socialist movement in the first half of the 1890s. The period 1895–97 marked a new chapter in the movement, when the Jewish Social Democrats spread to other parts of the Pale and Congress Poland. Not only did it expand to the southern provinces, but the Vilna leadership sent trained agitators to the Polish heartland as well. Expanding the movement to Congress Poland, however, proved substantially more difficult than to areas of the Pale. While the Jewish Social Democrats were pioneers of the general socialist movement in the western provinces, the same could not be said of Congress Poland, where the Polish socialist movement had been active organizing Jewish and non-Jewish workers.

In the following pages, I examine the rise of a pro-Polish socialist movement among Warsaw Jewry in the years 1891–95 and the subsequent encounter between Polish Jews and Lithuanian Jewish "colonizers" on the eve of the founding of the Bund. Indeed, in the years

1895–97, Warsaw became the main battleground between the PPS and Jewish Social Democrats for the allegiance of the Jewish working class.

### The PPS and the Jewish Working Class in Warsaw

Before the Vilna Group expanded to Congress Poland, Polish socialists had already begun to organize Jewish workers in Warsaw. From its inception, the PPS had support from both the Polonized Jewish intelligentsia and traditional Yiddish-speaking artisans. Prominent members of the party leadership, such as Stanisław Mendelson, Feliks Perl, and Kazimierz Róg, came from middle-class assimilated homes in Warsaw and had been raised in the Polish patriotic-insurrectionary tradition. Feliks Perl's father, for example, had been arrested in 1863 for involvement in the Polish uprising.[1] The party's assimilated Jewish members often had unusual talents as writers and publicists and, similar to their counterparts in Vilna, were separated from the bulk of Jewry by virtue of the fact that they did not speak Yiddish. In contrast, members of the first circle of Polish Jewish workers, who joined the PPS in 1893, were Yiddish-speaking artisans who had only recently taken interest in Polish language and culture. While the Polonized high-ranking members had been long-time activists in the Polish socialist movement going back to the 1870s, the Jewish Section consisted of newly won converts to the PPS program. These Yiddish-speaking members were natives of Congress Poland, born in the early 1870s, and had received traditional Jewish educations.[2]

The beginnings of the party's Jewish Section can be traced back to the Polish Jewish socialists Maksymilian Heilpern (1858–1924) and Israel Faterson (1875–1938). Heilpern had been a long-time activist in Polish revolutionary circles. He was arrested in 1878 for membership in the first illegal socialist circles among Warsaw University students. Sentenced to penal servitude in Siberia, he was first placed in the notorious Pawiak Prison in Warsaw between 1878 and 1880 and then spent four years in Siberia. On his return to Warsaw in 1884, Heilpern became active in both the Proletariat and later the Second Proletariat groups.[3] In 1891 he assumed directorship of a school for young Jewish artisans in the Warsaw district of Nalewki.[4] Heilpern was a staunch assimilationist who formulated a program of intensive instruction in Polish language and literature at his school.[5]

At the time a few members of the radical Jewish intelligentsia were beginning to lead circles of Jewish workers in Warsaw. Faterson, a student at Heilpern's artisan school, formed the most influential underground socialist circle, which later provided the first Jewish cadres to the PPS. Faterson's circle resembled in many ways the socialist circles then forming in Vilna, although in the entirely different context of Congress Poland and the Polish Jewish intelligentsia. In contrast to the Vilna Group, which sought to raise the Jewish worker's consciousness through the study of Russian, Faterson, an ideological assimilationist, chose Polish as the path to high culture, and his circle was led in the Polish language.[6]

Israel Faterson was born in October 1875 to a lower middle-class Jewish family in Warsaw. While we have no information regarding his primary school education, we do know he attended Kronenberg's Trade School in Warsaw in the late 1880s. Kronenberg's Trade School had functioned as the only Polish national institution of higher education after 1863 and had produced leaders of Polish radical groups in the late 1880s.[7] Faterson's first circle, formed in 1891, consisted of ten worker-intellectuals who were literate in Polish because of their training at Heilpern's school.[8] They would later provide the party with a critical mass of *polu-intelligenty* (worker-intellectuals) able to serve as a bridge between the Yiddish-speaking worker and the local party leadership. By introducing Jewish workers to Polish language and culture, Faterson sought to form a bridge between the Jewish and the Christian working class.

Like the Vilna Group in the period 1891–93, Faterson's first *koło*, or circle, had sought to prepare the Jewish worker in Congress Poland for entry into the Polish socialist movement. And to this end, the language question was key, for at the beginning of the 1890s "the Yiddish language separated the Jewish and the Polish worker like the Chinese wall," a contemporary Warsaw Jew, Mojżesz Kaufman, recalled. That same wall also isolated the Jewish intelligentsia from its constituency, for the Polonized Jews not only were illiterate in Yiddish but also often regarded it with disdain. "Polish socialists (as well as the first Polish Jewish socialist group)," Kaufman wrote, "believed the only way to link the Jewish worker to the world of socialism was through study of the Polish language," for Polish "opened the ghetto walls to the path of enlightened European culture." In hindsight, though, Kaufman acknowledged that the Polonization platform of the Polish socialist movement "was simply an impossible goal for the vast majority of the Jewish working masses."[9]

In the two years prior to the establishment of the PPS, Faterson's circle operated independently. After the formation of the PPS in 1893, its Warsaw leaders approached the banker Kazimierz Róg (1873–1933), an assimilated Jew who had been active in Polish revolutionary circles. At the time Róg was active in the Warsaw branch of the PPS and would later serve on the party's Warsaw Worker's Committee.[10] Sometime in the second half of 1893, Róg, who did not know Yiddish but was connected to the Jewish community, entered into talks with Faterson.[11] As a Jew, Róg was able to build trust with members of Faterson's circle who agreed to join the PPS and act as an unofficial Jewish Section.[12]

By 1893 Faterson's circle had expanded to include nine new members.[13] This unofficial Jewish Section of the PPS, now with eighteen *polu-intelligenty*, committed itself to winning over the Jewish masses to the idea of socialism and Polish independence. But Faterson's preeminence in PPS Jewish circles came to an end in June 1893, when he fell victim to a police crackdown and was arrested with thirty-six others. Róg consequently became the de facto head of the new Jewish Section.[14] Before his arrest, however, Faterson made his mark in the history of the Jewish socialist movement by authoring the first known May Day proclamation in Yiddish. The circular was distributed in Warsaw on 1 May 1893 in a bilingual Yiddish-Polish form.[15]

## The Spread of the Vilna Movement to Warsaw, 1895–97

The establishment of a Russian Jewish socialist center in Congress Poland was considered by many Poles and Polish Jews as a provocation. Russian Jewish socialists in Vilna, Białystok, and Minsk were the pioneers of the general socialist movement in Lithuania-Belarus, where non-Jewish workers had not yet become politically active. But in Congress Poland, the situation was quite different. There the Jewish population lived in an area of rapid industrial growth and Polish demographic concentration in the cities. The organization of Jewish workers thus grew out of the existing Polish socialist movement, one that formed the advanced sector of the working-class movement in the Russian Empire at the time.[16] The new arrivals from Vilna, Russian-speaking radicals with no particular interest in Polish affairs, encountered resistance from both Poles and Polish Jews who objected to their aim of unifying all Jewish workers into a single all-Russian organization.

The first attempts to establish links between the Vilna Group and Jewish workers in Congress Poland can be traced back to a conference in Vilna held in August 1894. The conference participants came to the conclusion that closer cooperation with Jewish workers in other cities was the next logical step in the development of the Jewish worker's movement. Plans were then made to dispatch emissaries to large urban centers. Soon after, a number of Vilna pioneers, both workers and intellectuals, set out to found new Social Democratic organizations throughout the Pale in a process that became known as "colonization."[17] Between 1894 and 1896, the Jewish Social Democrats in Vilna established centers in Minsk, Odessa, and Białystok.[18]

In addition to establishing "colonies" in Białystok, Minsk, and Odessa, the Vilna Group selected three delegates to organize Jewish workers in Warsaw under an empire-wide Social Democratic banner. Those chosen were the seamstress Tsivia Hurvitsh, John Mill, and Leon Goldman.[19] The Jewish Social Democratic center was established gradually in the years 1894–96. In the fall of 1894 Tsivia Hurvitsh became the first "colonizer." The process of forming a Jewish center in Warsaw was made easier by the fact that Hurvitsh was welcomed by an existing group of Lithuanian Jewish students at Warsaw University who had immigrated from Vilna in the years 1890–91. They included Israel Peskin, Yasha Vitkind, Albert Zalkind, and Yona Antokolsky.[20] With the aid of these Lithuanian students at Warsaw University, Hurvitsh organized a small circle of Jewish workers by the end of 1894.[21]

Before his arrival in Warsaw, Mill had spent two months in Zurich during the summer of 1894, learning about Polish history in general and about the history of Polish socialism in particular. He turned to SDKP member Julian Marchlewski, who for the next two months briefed him on the situation in Warsaw. Thus, when Mill

departed to Warsaw in August 1895, he entered Poland more educated, more familiar with west European life, more informed about
the international socialist movement abroad, and better acquainted
with the socialist movement in Warsaw.[22] At the time, two groups of
Jewish workers had formed in Warsaw—a Lithuanian one led by
Tsivia Hurvitsh and a circle of PPS Jews. By all accounts, the PPS
group was more influential and had even begun to produce and distribute the first printed Yiddish circular in the Russian Empire during May Day 1895.[23]

### The Clash: Russian Jewish Socialists
### and the PPS in Competition, 1895–97

The period 1895–97 constituted a turning point for the
socialist movement among Jewish workers in Warsaw, as it saw the
crystallization of two major currents: the Jewish Social Democratic
movement, which received fresh impetus with Mill's arrival, and
the influence of the PPS. The PPS's influence among Jewish workers
was challenged in the late summer of 1895 with the arrival of "colonizers" from Vilna. The most important emissary, John Mill, immediately set about expanding Tsivia Hurvitsh's group and the existing colony of Russian Jewish students. In addition, shortly afterward Mill arranged for Leon Goldman (the only member of the circle besides Mill who spoke Polish), Maria Zhaludsky, Albert Zalkin,
and Meryl Ginsburg to come to Warsaw.[24] During the fall of 1895
and January 1896, the Union of Jewish Workers in Warsaw came
into being under Mill's leadership.[25]

In the face of a new rival Litvak worker's organization in
Warsaw, the local leader of PPS Jews, Róg, expressed concern about
the possibility of eroding support among Jewish works. In particular, PPS Jews noted the Litvak organization's advantage: the possession and distribution of socialist literature in Yiddish. Whereas
the Vilna Group had already switched from Russian to Yiddish as
the language of agitation in 1893, the PPS continued to agitate
among Jewish workers in Polish. A contemporary active in PPS
Jewish circles recalled the discussions then taking place about the
problem of attracting Jewish workers: "For a long while propaganda was limited to only a few groups because agitation was conducted in Polish. But when there were mass actions, the Jews had to

TABLE 3.1
**Underground Yiddish Literature Produced by the Jewish Social Democrats (Bund), 1893–97**

| Year | Brochures / Periodicals | May Day Proclamations |
| --- | --- | --- |
| 1893 | — | — |
| 1894 | — | — |
| 1895 | 9,000 | — |
| 1896 | 7,400 | 3,000 |
| 1897 | 13,400 | 6,700 |
| Total | 20,800 | 9,700 |

*Source*: A. Cherikover, "Di onheybn fun der umlegaler litaratur in yidish," *Historishe shriftn* (Vilna) 3 (1939): 592; *Historya żydowskiego ruchu robotniczego na Litwie, w Polsce i Rosyi*, rev. ed. (London: Bund, 1902), 25, 28, 30; *Materialy k istorii evreiskago rabochego dvizheniia* (Saint Petersburg: Tribuna, 1906), 59, 62–63.

be addressed in Yiddish. . . . The need for publications in Yiddish thus began to be felt."[26] Róg responded by addressing a letter to the party's Warsaw branch. But the party leadership's response was hardly encouraging. The absence of propaganda in Yiddish, Róg was reportedly told, was not regarded as a pressing need, and therefore limited party resources could not be utilized for such a purpose.

The Polish party's negative response led Róg to begin talks with the Litvak leaders in Warsaw. When news about the gesture reached Vilna, Kremer promptly sent Róg an invitation for talks. Both Kremer and Mill were present during the meeting, which took place in Vilna, when Róg proposed giving the Social Democrats more access to Polish Jewish workers in exchange for socialist propaganda material in Yiddish. The main stumbling block, however, revolved around attitudes to the Polish question. Kremer made it clear that no aspect of the PPS program, including the demand for Polish independence, would be incorporated into the Vilna-based movement.

Róg returned to Warsaw without an agreement and appealed a second time to the PPS leadership. In an official letter to the party's central committee in Warsaw, dated December 1895, PPS Jews warned of the dangers of Russian Jewish agitation in Warsaw and concluded with a set of demands. The letter opened by expressing its disappointment with the previous party congress held June 1895.

"Neither a resolution at the last congress nor any special articles in *Przedświt* or *Robotnik* have addressed the party's relations with Polish Jewish workers." The issue of how the PPS was to agitate among Jews was not raised, nor was the importance of this issue in any way discussed, the letter protested.[27]

The letter then enumerated several points. First, it stressed the need for party literature in Yiddish. "The PPS has not provided any writings for Jews," the letter stated, "neither newspapers, brochures, or Yiddish publications from abroad, whether from Europe (Galicia, London) or from America." The letter then reported that the Vilna Group's new center in Warsaw was drawing Jewish workers away from the PPS. "So long as that party, whose program calls for 'the equality of Jews in Russia' and is otherwise identical with the program of the Social Democrats, does not meet with competition from the PPS," the authors wrote, "it will harmfully influence the further development of political consciousness among the Jewish masses. . . . Considering the above, we, Jewish members of the PPS, protest against [the Union of Jewish Workers] and confirm our solidarity with the program and aspirations of the PPS."[28] In order to successfully compete with the Social Democrats, the letter concluded, a special section of the PPS devoted to Jewish issues had to be created.

While the letter highlighted a kind of crisis confronting the organization of Jewish workers under the PPS banner in Warsaw, it

TABLE 3.2

**Underground Yiddish Literature Produced by the PPS, 1893–97**

| Year | Brochures / Periodicals | May Day Proclamations |
|---|---|---|
| 1893 | 167 | — |
| 1894 | 788 | — |
| 1895 | 1,253 | 500 |
| 1896 | 1,674 | 300 |
| 1897 | 1,034 | 800 |
| Total | 4,916 | 1,600 |

*Source*: A. Malinowski, *Materiały do historyi PPS* (Warsaw, 1907), 1:46, 91, 173, 243–47, 313–16; [Stanisław Wojciechowski], *Polska Partya Socyalistyczna w ostatnich pięciu latach* (London: PPS, 1900), 30; P. Shvarts, "Di ershte yidishe oysgabes fun der PPS," *Historishe shriftn* (Vilna) 3 (1939): 527–39.

was not entirely true that the PPS had not been providing, and even producing, Yiddish language material. As table 3.2 shows, the PPS smuggled increasing quantities of American Yiddish materials into the empire during this period. But with the aim of forging an alliance with the Vilna Group, the majority of this Yiddish socialist literature smuggled into Russian Poland by the PPS during this early period was earmarked for Jews in Lithuania.[29] Not only had the party's foreign committee in London been smuggling Yiddish socialist periodicals into the empire since 1893, the PPS had also printed one of the earliest Yiddish circulars in 1895 (and the first printed one in a nonhectograph form).[30] Printed in London and smuggled into Russian Poland in April 1895 with a print run of five hundred, the May Day leaflet stressed the common goals of Jewish and Christian workers and the need for unified action. "Brothers! Comrades! The same yoke oppresses both the Christian and the Jewish worker. Our interests are one in the same! . . . We must boldly demand our rights together!" Interestingly, the proclamation, while calling for the attainment of "political rights," did not include the specific demand for Polish independence.[31]

## The Failure of Cooperation

By 1896, according to contemporary participants, three distinct socialist groups were active among Jewish workers in Warsaw. These included John Mill's Union of Jewish Workers in Warsaw, Kazimierz Róg's unofficial Jewish Section of the PPS, and a group of workers under the leadership of Yitzkhok Pesakhzon, who stood ideologically between the two groups.[32] While Mill's memoirs offer few details of his organization's activities in 1896, Pesakhzon's writings offer a more detailed picture of Warsaw in the summer and fall of 1896.

Pesakhzon, a native of Lithuania-Belarus who settled in Warsaw with his family as a young teenager, became active in Jewish socialist circles in Warsaw at the beginning of the 1890s. In the spring of 1895 Pesakhzon fell ill and left Warsaw, to return one year later in April 1896.[33] Upon his return, he began to organize Jewish workers from glass, lace, and clothing factories into *kruzhki* of eight to ten persons each. At the time, he claimed, he did not belong to any party. While "psychologically far from Polish life," he felt Mill's group had no understanding for the specific conditions of Polish Jewish workers.[34] Pesakhzon recalled that the biggest obstacle to the growth of a Jewish worker's movement in Warsaw at that time was "an appalling lack" of socialist literature in Yiddish. He acknowledged that most of the Yiddish material then circulating was provided by the PPS, including American Yiddish brochures and a few of their own publications.[35]

Pesakhzon's recollection of a dearth of socialist literature in Warsaw is reflected in the internal correspondences between PPS Jews and the party leadership. In August 1896 the PPS central committee received a second letter signed, again, by "Jewish members of the PPS." The letter focused on the PPS's neglect of the Jewish group. "The party has not given us any aid: not with materials, not with a sufficient amount of essential Yiddish literature, not with our people. Nor have you provided advice, suggestions, or moral support by raising issues especially relevant for Jews in party newspapers," the letter stated.[36]

In order to compete with Mill for the allegiance of Jewish workers, these PPS Jews put forth three suggestions. These included providing steady supplies of Yiddish literature, forming an official Jewish Section with representation in the central committee, and raising the Jewish question in the party press. "Not a single one of our demands [from the last letter] has been taken into consideration. And what do we see?" According to the letter, Mill's campaign to draw Jewish workers away from the PPS was becoming increasingly aggressive. The new Union of Jewish Workers "is heaping slander at us Jews and at the whole PPS. What's more, they have a tendency to falsify the PPS program, persuading Jews that the PPS does nothing for them . . . that the behavior of the PPS demonstrates total indifference to Jewish workers and that only their party is concerned with Jewish issues."[37]

The letter stressed that without official status as a group, no effective action could be taken to counter Mill. The conclusion of the letter appealed to the party to address the needs of Jewish members. "We must make it clear that . . . our existence is ephemeral and that . . . we will dissolve into thin air" without party aid. They ended with the following demands: (1) the creation of a Jewish Section (as an official opponent to the Union of Jewish Workers); (2) at least the import of existing American Yiddish publications; (3) the publication of all PPS proclamations in Yiddish; (4) the publication of Yiddish proclamations drawn up specifically for the Jewish worker; (5) the inclusion in *Robotnik* of a column reserved for the Jewish Section; and (6) the discussion of the Jewish question in party organs. The letter concluded with a request that the party provide "a precise description of our rights and obligations regarding our relations to the party."[38]

The only preserved response of the PPS came from none other than Piłsudski. In a letter to the Union of Polish Socialists Abroad in London, Piłsudski complained there was not enough interest within the party to devote resources to a party organ in Yiddish. What the PPS could do is continue smuggling American and Galician Yiddish materials into the empire, and possibly make *Der arbeyter,* the Yiddish organ of the Polish socialists in Galicia, a joint organ with the PPS.[39] More revealing was a subsequent letter in which Piłsudski lamented the lack of interest in Jewish affairs on the part of the PPS. "The majority of our members (and I belong to the minority)," Piłsudski wrote from Vilna in December 1896, "are of the opinion that we do not need Yiddish literature in Congress Poland. But I know we cannot win over those who know only Yiddish [with propaganda in Polish]."[40]

The lack of Yiddish propaganda materials in Congress Poland and the PPS's failure to address the concerns of its Jewish group forced Róg to reconsider his alliances. With no concrete action from the PPS leadership, and the general lack of Yiddish literature threatening to stunt the growth of the socialist movement among Jewish workers, Róg and Mill entered into negotiations for a second time during the fall of 1896.[41] In December of that year, Róg, Mill, and Pesakhzon discussed conditions for unifying into a single organization. Negotiations focused on the question of Polish independence and the name of the new organization. Róg retained the right to defend the idea of Polish independence among his group but agreed that the Polish question would not be considered in general meetings or mass agitation. On the question of the name, Mill proposed "The Jewish Social Democratic Bund in Warsaw." Róg opposed the use of "Social Democratic" in the title and offered instead "The Jewish Socialist Bund in Poland." The two groups came to a compromise and in January 1897 agreed to unite under the name "The Jewish Workers' Bund in Poland."[42]

The Jewish Workers' Bund in Poland, which combined both Social Democratic and PPS elements, barely outlived the winter of 1896–97. The fragile agreement on which it was based—that the PPS group could agitate independently for the PPS program, but that the Jewish Workers' Bund itself would not discuss the matter at meetings—was bound to break apart soon. Regarding the question of Yiddish literature in Warsaw distributed by the PPS, Pesakhzon wrote that it consisted in early 1897 of six to seven Yiddish brochures from abroad.[43]

The defection of Róg's group came as a blow to the PPS leadership, which now feared it had wholly lost contacts with Jewish socialists in Warsaw. "Until recently we had relations [with Jewish workers] in Warsaw," Piłsudski lamented from Vilna, "but now even there the Vilna Jews are making their influence felt, for [PPS Jews] have fused with them and have formed the Union of Jewish Workers in Poland."[44]

Ideological and tactical differences between the Polish and the Lithuanian element of the Jewish Workers' Bund came to the fore with the coming of May Day 1897. At a gathering of some two hundred Jewish workers, Róg registered his protest over the first May Day proclamation produced and distributed by the Jewish Workers' Bund.[45] Instead of including a point that the Jewish worker should struggle alongside the Christian worker "in Poland," the proclamation had called on the Jewish worker to unite "with the proletariat of all nations."[46] Soon after, Róg was told to either sever once and for all any links with the PPS and its political program or withdraw from the Jewish Workers' Bund. Mill advanced the argument before Róg that Jewish workers should "struggle for general political freedom and equal civil rights, and not for the independence of Poland." But the arguments of Lithuanian Jews were unpersuasive; Róg and his group left the meeting in protest.[47] After Róg's group withdrew from the Jewish Workers' Bund in Poland, the Jewish workers sympathetic to Mill and Pesakhzon renamed their organization. As of May, the Jewish Social Democrats in Warsaw operated under the name "The Jewish Social Democratic Workers' Bund in Warsaw."[48]

Thus, shortly after May Day 1897 Róg's group rejoined the PPS. The creation of an official Jewish Section, however, was not permitted. The members thus rejoined the PPS as individuals. The news of the breakup of the Jewish Workers' Bund was received with great joy by the PPS. "The alliance of Warsaw Jews has fully come to naught!" Piłsudski joyously wrote from Vilna in July. "Now I hope we can undertake serious Jewish work." A local Polish Jew, Piłsudski noted, was of the opinion that the antipathy between Polish and Lithuanian Jews was too great for any alliance. In an optimistic note, Piłsudski concluded that the PPS was "significantly closer" to being able to win over the Jews.[49]

Piłsudski's letters to London were the most reliable source of information for the Union Abroad. And on the eve of the founding of the Bund, the breakup of the Mill-Róg alliance between Vilna and Warsaw Jews seemed to confirm the view of many PPS leaders that with time the Jewish workers would embrace the PPS. Before Piłsudski was informed of Róg's return to the PPS, however, the fear of a Vilna-Warsaw alliance of Jewish socialists can be discerned from his letters. There are rumors, Piłsudski wrote on 30 May, that the Polish Jewish and Lithuanian Jewish groups intended to form a unified organization, "and that they intend to enter into a Russian party. Can you imagine the scandal—Warsaw Jews in a Russian Party!"[50]

In the face of Mill's growing influence, Piłsudski steadily increased his request for American Yiddish publications in 1896 and 1897. Due to the often slow response of the party's contacts in New York, however, there were delays in smuggling American Yiddish publications into Russian Poland in the spring and summer of 1897. In response to Piłsudski's request to increase shipments of *Tsukunft* and other American Yiddish publications, the Union of Polish Socialists Abroad in London sent a series of letters to New York in the summer of 1897.[51] "We wrote you on 9 June but until now have no reply," wrote Bolesław Jędrzejowski, the secretary of the PPS's London branch. "We therefore repeat our request regarding Jewish socialist publications, which we need most urgently for sending to Russian Poland. [At this very moment] our comrades in Poland request that you send larger quantities." Jędrzejowski's requests included six copies of each issue of *Tsukunft* and enumerated the titles of four Yiddish brochures. "In the next year we hope to be able to write particulars about the growing [sic] of our movement among the Jewish proletariat in Russian Poland. We conclude for today by asking you to answer *promptly* and to execute our request if only possible."[52]

In the same year as *On Agitation* and *A Letter to Agitators* set into motion the movement toward a "Jewish orientation" in the Vilna Social Democratic camp (1893), emissaries from the Union of Polish Socialists Abroad in London organized the Polish Socialist Party in Vilna and Warsaw. From the outset, the new Polish Socialist Party, raising the banner of the romantic insurrectionary tradition, sought to unify revolutionary groups in Lithuania and Congress Poland and placed the struggle for an independent federal republic of the Polish, Lithuanian, and Ukrainian nations at the top of its program. Contrary to the consensus in Jewish historiography, which claims that the PPS had no particular interest in matters particular to the Jewish worker, the party's leader, Józef Piłsudski, placed great emphasis on winning over the Russified intelligentsia and Jewish workers. Instead of the development of a Polish orientation in the Vilna movement, however, PPS pressure had the unintended consequence of crystallizing a Jewish path, as Mishkinsky has astutely observed.[53]

It is thus no surprise that the PPS viewed the spread of the Vilna movement to Congress Poland as a grave threat. The Litvak leaders of the Warsaw division imported two ideas into Congress Poland inimical to the PPS: the link with the general Russian revolutionary movement; and the idea of a separate Jewish workers organization. Unlike historians of the Jewish labor movement who argue that PPS hostility to the Vilna movement stemmed from its Polonized Jewish elite, this study of the PPS's Jewish Section suggests that many Polish Jewish workers and *polu-intelligenty* were fervent adherents of the PPS program and bitter opponents of a separate Jewish workers movement, suggesting that the integrationist ideology of the Polish Jewish intelligentsia had trickled down to a section of the Jewish working class.

# ■ 4.
# Organizational Breakthrough: The Formation of the Jewish Labor Bund, 1897–98

> *According to the thinking of the Polish Socialist Party, we were 'Russifiers,' Jewish nationalists, and haters of the political and national aspirations of the Polish people. For those active in Warsaw, it was clear that a 'counteroffensive' against the PPS could be waged only when an organized Jewish working class from all cities in the Pale would be unified in one party.*
> JOHN MILL (1922)

THE MAN WHO BECAME KNOWN as the "father of the Bund," Arkadi Kremer, first entertained the idea of a founding congress of Jewish socialists in the summer of 1897. At that time the Russian socialist organization the Group of Free Labor, which included Plekhanov, Pavel Axelrod, and Vera Zasulich, had invited Kremer to accompany them to an international labor conference in Zurich. On their way to Switzerland, Kremer and Plekhanov discussed the future of the Social Democratic movement in Russia. Plekhanov informed Kremer that the formation of a Russian Social Democratic party was imminent and raised the question of how Jewish workers would be represented in the future party. "The father of Russian Marxism," Kremer recalls, "posed to me a tough question: 'How will we represent you [at future congresses], for you are not unified? Formally there is now nobody to represent.'" Plekhanov's question made a strong impression.[1] Why, Kremer asked himself, had the Jewish socialists failed to unite? On his return to Vilna, Kremer discussed the idea of unification with fellow Vilna Group members.

The prospect of entering a future Russian Social Democratic party as representatives of a unified Jewish organization was a great impetus for Kremer. "The fear that our organization would attend the founding of a Russian Social Democratic party disunified, with different plans and without a general program, had forced Arkadi to think things through," Mill recalled, "and to evaluate the extraordinary importance of calling forth our own congress beforehand."[2]

While Kremer placed great importance on the approval of leading Russian socialists, John Mill's struggle with the Polish Socialist Party in Warsaw proved more significant. For the Jewish socialist movement in Warsaw, the first half of 1897 was a period of great optimism. That optimism was challenged, however, when in May 1897 the alliance between Lithuanian Jewish and Polish Jewish socialists broke down. The defection of PPS Jews threw Mill on the defensive. The PPS had begun to produce and distribute its own literature in Yiddish among Polish Jewish workers in 1896 and stepped up its attacks on Mill's group. In July the group of PPS Jews returned to the PPS and vowed to undertake "serious Jewish work." It was precisely this PPS offensive that made the need for a united Jewish party keenly felt.

At the same time that the conflict between Mill and the PPS was intensifying, Kremer visited Warsaw to discuss the possibility of founding a Jewish Social Democratic party in Vilna.[3] Mill's recollection of that meeting reveals the centrality of the conflict with the Poles. He told Kremer on that day that the growing conflict with the PPS required the imminent formation of a separate Jewish party. "To compete with the PPS," Mill said, "we needed the power and authority of a centralized and disciplined Jewish socialist *party* with a clear set of goals in order to challenge them on the basis of far-reaching influence over the masses. . . . It was essential for us to have a party that would take an unambiguous position on grievous political and national problems and on the question of the independence of Poland."[4]

Following Kremer's meeting with Mill, a date was set for the founding congress, and invitations were sent out to the various centers. Shortly after, Mill departed for Vilna in early September 1897 with Leon Goldman and Maria Zhaludsky. Waiting at the Vilna train station to greet them was none other than Kremer. Unexpectedly, Kremer had a stunned look on his face: his wife had been arrested, and the streets of Vilna were filled with spies and informants. It was, Kremer decided, too dangerous to convene the congress. Mill insisted, however, on going ahead, claiming that the situation in Congress Poland "is such that the conference is a question of life or death for the Warsaw organization."[5] Kremer hesitatingly conceded.

## The Founding Congress of the Bund

In the early evening hours of October 7, 1897, thirteen young Jewish men and women crowded into the attic of a Jewish artisan's home on the outskirts of Vilna.[6] The delegates included Kremer, Mutnik, and Kossovsky from Vilna, as well as the workers Dovid Katz, Israel Kaplinsky, and Hirsh Soroka; Pavel Berman from Minsk; Mill, Zhaludsky, and Leon Goldman from Warsaw; Rosa Greenblat and Hillel Katz-Blum from Białystok; and Yudel Abramov from Vitebsk.[7] The group of thirteen delegates attested to the centrality of the Vilna Group, as ten were trained in Vilna and had been sent out to establish centers throughout the Pale. In addition, the more or less equal balance of workers and intellectuals (eight of the thirteen delegates were workers) showed the congress had recognized their mutual dependence. The conference lasted for three days and was conducted in the Russian language.[8] For the sake of secrecy, no official records were kept, although Kossovsky took hand-written notes used later to prepare a congress report for the party press.[9]

Kremer officially opened the congress with a discussion of the goals of the new organization, relations with Russian and Polish socialists, the press, and propaganda literature. The unification of Jewish Social Democratic forces was necessary, Kremer maintained, because of the anticipated formation of an empire-wide Russian Social Democratic Party. The goal of the new Jewish organization, Kremer proclaimed, was the following: "A union of all Jewish socialist organizations will have as its goal not only the putting forth of general political demands in Russia. It will also have the special task of defending the particular interests of Jewish workers, conducting a struggle for their civil rights, and, above all, waging a campaign against anti-Jewish legislation."[10]

Kremer followed with a discussion on relations with Russian and Polish socialists. The Jewish Bund will join the future Russian party "as a solid, autonomous organization with the right to decide on matters particular to the Jewish proletariat as well as to print its own literature for the Jewish working class." With regard to the Poles, Kremer dwelled on "the embittered struggle" that the PPS had been conducting against Jewish workers' organizations in general and the Warsaw section in particular. The PPS campaign, Kremer continued, "was accusing the Jewish Social Democrat movement of 'Russification' and the propagation of hatred toward Polish socialists and their national aspirations."[11] The congress thus resolved that the two most important tasks of the Jewish socialist movement were the production and distribution of socialist literature in Yiddish and the struggle for the attainment of civil rights for the Jewish people. Other party aims did not differ from those of non-Jewish socialist groups.[12] Following a debate over the new organization's name in which Mill insisted on including "Poland" in the title, the "General Jewish Workers' Bund in Russia and Poland" came into being.[13] The late Mishkinsky has suggested that in demanding the inclusion of Poland in the title, Mill intended to send a clear message to the Poles that the new organization represented Jewish workers in the whole empire.[14]

In addition to the formulation of a party platform, important practical results came out of the three-day conference. First, *Di arbeyter shtimme*, the Vilna-based organ of the Jewish Social Democratic group in Russia that had first appeared in August 1897, received official status as the central organ of the Bund. Second, Kossovsky, Mutnik, and Kremer were selected to form the Bund's central committee, which assumed control over the printing press in Vilna. Immediately following the congress, the three-member central committee relocated because of suspicions of police surveillance. They chose Minsk as their new center. Thereafter, they arranged for the transport of printing facilities to a secret location and set about preparing their underground newspaper.[15]

## "Scandalous!": Polish Socialists Respond to the Formation of the Bund

The formation of a separate organization claiming sole representation of Jewish workers "in Russia and Poland" came as a shock to proindependence Polish socialists who had pinned their national aspirations on unifying all national groups in Russian Poland into a single party.[16] The events of October 1897 were thus, as Piłsudski commented in a letter, "scandalous!"[17] Most abhorrent to Poles was the process by which Russified Litvaks had established a center in the Polish heartland and organized Polish Jewish workers under a banner that affirmed the unity of Russia, including the Polish lands.

Just one month after the founding of the Bund, in November 1897, thirteen senior PPS members gathered in Warsaw to convene the fourth party congress.[18] High on the agenda was a resolution on the new Jewish labor party. "We resolve," the resolution stated, "that the Jewish proletariat can have common goals only with the proletariat of the nation among whom it lives." It continued, proclaiming that it regarded the "organizational and program separateness" of the newly formed Bund as "harmful" to the Polish movement. The resolution concluded with harsh words, accusing the Bund of "renouncing solidarity with the Polish and Lithuanian working class in the struggle for liberation from tsarist occupation."[19] After a short discussion, Piłsudski's resolution on the Bund passed with a single abstention.[20]

To address the issue of the PPS's declining influence among Jewish workers, the congress acknowledged the lack of Yiddish-language material sympathetic to the PPS and committed itself to creating a Yiddish-language organ to be printed abroad.[21] The protocols record the delegates' resolve that the new Yiddish organ and brochures were "to explain to the Jewish workers the significance of waging a common struggle with the Polish proletariat."[22] The congress also drafted statements on relations with the Russians, presenting a set of conditions on which cooperation with a future Russian socialist party would be based. Piłsudski persuaded the congress to accept three principles of Russo-Polish cooperation: that the demand for Polish independence be incorporated into the program of the Russian party; that the Russian party secure PPS approval before entering into relations with revolutionary organizations "in Poland or Lithuania"; and that the Russian party recognize the right of non-Russian groups to form separate organizations.[23]

The PPS was similarly antagonistic to the recently formed Lithuanian Social Democratic Party (LSDP). Founded in 1896 in Vilna by Alfonsas Moravskis (1868–1941) and Andrius Domasevicius (1865–1935), the LSDP was led by descendants of Polonized Lithuanian noble families whose native tongue was Polish. The

LSDP's Polish cultural orientation was clearly indicated by the party's publications. Of the four short-lived organs published by the LSDP in the period 1896–99, three were in Polish and one was in Lithuanian.[24] Initially the party supported the idea of a federal union with Poland, Latvia, Belarus, and Ukraine. At its second party congress in January–February 1897, however, the LSDP came out against the PPS program when it decided to include Russia in a future union.[25] From the beginning, however, Lithuanian socialists favored the right of Jews to form an independent workers' party. In a resolution from 1896, the LSDP declared, "The Lithuanian Social Democratic Party [resolves] that the socialist party organization of the Jewish proletariat is fully entitled to put forth its own political and national goals."[26]

From the PPS resolution on Lithuanian socialists one can derive the PPS's first formulation on the definition of nationality as an ethnolinguistic group inhabiting a particular territory. "The congress recognizes the organizational separateness of revolutionary Lithuanian groups (that is, those that exclusively employ the Lithuanian language in their agitation)," the resolution stated, "as long as they do not spread hatred toward the Polish nation in their agitation, which would be so beneficial to the tsar."[27] Thus, the congress used "Lithuanian" exclusively to denote persons whose mother tongue was Lithuanian. According to this view, members of the Polonized intelligentsia of Lithuania who defined themselves as Lithuanian by nationality were, according to the PPS, Poles.[28]

The PPS definition of "Lithuanian revolutionary groups" as those that agitate exclusively in the Lithuanian language thus excluded the one Lithuanian socialist party operating at the time—the Lithuanian Social Democrats. Historians of Polish socialism, however, often omit this crucial distinction. In his standard history of the PPS, for example, Tomicki misleadingly writes that "the [fourth] congress recognized the separateness of Lithuanian revolutionary groups," without any mention that they in fact did not recognize the LSDP.[29] Marian Żychowski, a prominent historian of nineteenth-century Polish socialist thought, similarly writes that the fourth congress resolution "was theoretically a vote for the autonomy of nationality groups [in] Lithuania." He acknowledges, however, that "in practice, their goal was to absorb [the groups] under the PPS, or at least to impose a leadership role."[30]

The congress resolution concluded with a condemnation of the two organizations "whose aspirations do not accord with the interests of the working class." Those two groups were the Lithuanian Social Democrats and the Bund. Drafted by Piłsudski, the resolution maintained that Polish-speaking socialist groups in Lithuania had no justification for agitating except under the PPS banner. "The vast majority of the proletariat in Lithuania do not know the Lithuanian language," the resolution stated, "and are linked with the Polish proletariat in both speech and historical traditions. We resolve that neither political nor economic conditions require a separate party organization for the [the Polish-speaking] proletariat . . . under the name of Lithuanian Social Democracy."[31] The congress thus resolved that it did not recognize the rationale for the formation of the LSDP and called on the Lithuanian party to agitate under the PPS banner. In the PPS press the LSDP was referred to as a part of the "Polish socialist movement," which should "work for the separation of the largest possible territory from Russia and the creation of a federal republic. . . . There is no other alternative."[32]

The resolutions of the PPS fourth congress were made public in the beginning of 1898, when both *Przedświt* and *Robotnik* printed the congress report.[33] *Robotnik* also ran a separate piece by Piłsudski, titled, "On the Jewish Question," which derided "Jewish separatism" in general and called on Jewish socialists to sever their political links to Russia while allying with the Polish and Lithuanian workers. The socialist movement was now eroding the foundations of old prejudices and hatreds, Piłsudski wrote, and a phenomenon had arisen in which the sons of Polish nobles and Jews were struggling together for the future of Poland. Anti-Semitism, he emphasized, would not be tolerated in the Polish socialist movement. "Any trace of anti-Semitism among our comrades will be persistently fought against, and under no conditions will we allow anti-Semitism to manifest itself in the life of our movement."[34]

Despite opposition to anti-Semitism, Piłsudski derided Jews in Lithuania for their Russian cultural orientation: "Jews in Lithuania, in spite of the interests of the whole country, do not present any resistance to Russification, and even, to a certain extent, support it." Piłsudski concluded by casting PPS-Bund relations within the broader context of Russo-Polish antagonism. "It must be stressed," he wrote, "that the separateness of the Jews serves, above all, the interests of our most significant enemy—the Muscovite tsar." The chief threat to the tsar, he continued, was the solidarity of the different peoples. Piłsudski concluded with a call to Jewish workers to form a union with Polish socialists: "We are exploited as a proletariat, we are oppressed by barbarism and persecuted as Poles and Jews. Our only salvation [is] common struggle under a single banner."[35]

Together with Piłsudski's article and the party congress resolutions, one Bundist characterized the February 1898 issue of *Robotnik* as a "declaration of war" on the Bund.[36] Soon after the February issue of *Robotnik* appeared, delegates gathered in Minsk to commence the founding congress of the Russian Social Democratic Workers' Party (RSDRP) on 1 March 1898.[37] Three of nine delegates at the congress—Kremer, A. Mutnik, and S. Katz—were Bundists, while Kremer was selected to sit on the new party's central committee. The congress granted the Bund limited autonomy, which was a great achievement for Kremer, who had accomplished his aim of integrating the Bund into a general all-Russian party with its autonomy preserved. However, the Bund's participation in the RSDRP's first congress was followed by the worst crisis in its early history. The first congress had scarcely concluded when a wave of arrests crushed the newly born party. And from that time on, the tsarist secret police had agents and informants trailing the Bund all over Minsk.

To the PPS the unification of the Bund and with the new empire-wide Russian Social Democratic Party was nothing less than scandalous. In the wake of these events the PPS printed several articles condemning the Bund, dwelling at length on the claim that the Bund was a Russifying agent on the Jewish street. When "a socialist organization, [whose aim is to] represent the entire Jewish proletariat in the Russian partition, expresses a Pan-Russian slogan on its banner, then we shall brand such tactics as harmful and struggle against it with all our might," the PPS declared in April 1898.[38] Another article on the Bund, this time by the head of the PPS's Jewish Section, continued to raise the accusation of Russification. Alleging indifference to Polish national sensitivities, Róg derided the Bund for referring to Congress Poland as "Russia" in a leaflet distributed to Polish Jewish workers.[39]

The tone of the anti-Bundist polemic did not escape criticism within PPS circles. In August 1898 the PPS's central committee received a letter protesting the party's hostile attitude to the Bund. Penned by Władysław Goldberg (1877–1919), a PPS member since 1893 who was exiled to Irkutsk at the time, the letter castigated the PPS for its uncompromising platform.[40] "I agree completely with the PPS program," Goldberg wrote, "but the PPS's attitude toward Jews is shameful and cannot be honored. . . . The PPS demands autonomy for all nationalities. So why, then, do you deny this right to the Jews, slinging mud at them for organizing a separate party? . . . If the Jews regard themselves as a nationality, that does not give the PPS the right to proclaim them as enemies of the Poles."[41]

### The Bund's "Counteroffensive"

Attacks in the PPS press during the spring and summer of 1898 deeply disturbed the Bund. Central committee members Kremer and Kossovsky emphasized the humiliation they felt in the face of PPS allegations. Printing an official response was thus an important task during the first year of the Bund's existence. Emboldened by their status as members of the strong empire-wide Russian party, the Bund's core leadership, now with the printing facilities they lacked in the period 1893–97, was determined to strike back.

It will be recalled that after the Bund's first congress in October 1897, Kremer and Mutnik, along with the printing press, moved to Minsk. Shortly afterward, the printing press was transferred to Bobruisk.[42] The third central committee member, Vladimir Kossovsky, had remained in Vilna and did not settle in Minsk until the beginning of March 1898. Upon Kossovsky's arrival, Mutnik departed to Łódź, where he helped form a Bund division. Thus, after March the core leadership in Minsk, with control over the party press and printing facilities, consisted of Kremer and Kossovsky.[43]

Following the founding congress of the RSDRP, the Bund's central committee began preparing a statement of aims. "It was necessary to clarify the special demands of the Jewish proletariat, drawing a sharp principled distinction between the Bund and bourgeois nationalism on the Jewish street," Kossovsky wrote. In addition, the statement of aims "was to establish a clear relation to the difficult question of 'civil' and 'national' equality." In the second part, he continued, it was necessary to answer the PPS. "It was necessary to wage a campaign against the PPS," Kossovsky wrote, "and to wrest from under its influence the Jewish worker, whom [the PPS] had organized in its 'Jewish Section.'"[44]

Kremer similarly recalled the urgency with which the central committee considered its relations with the PPS. Just as in the period immediately before the formation of the Bund, when John Mill emphasized the need to wage a "counteroffensive" against the PPS, Kremer and Kossovsky were now feeling the sting of PPS attacks. They also came to the conclusion that the PPS was increasing its influence among Jewish workers with Yiddish-language propaganda. "It was impossible for us to cease our work," Kremer recalled. "We had to get out *Der arbeyter shtimme* and answer the PPS's sharp attacks against the Bund."[45] As Kremer wrote, "In successive resolutions from their [fourth] congress, [the PPS] sharply assaulted the Bund. These resolutions challenged the right of the Jewish worker to his own organization and held that [the Bund's] very existence was detrimental. We had not anticipated such a conflict and had to provide a proper response." Kremer maintained that a lengthy response to the PPS was necessary not only for the PPS but "for our friends alone," referring to the Russian Social Democrats and some Bundists, who, "by their poorly understood internationalism," were questioning the right of the Bund's existence.[46]

But before the Bund began distributing *Di arbeyter shtimme,* intensive police activity led to what the Bund has called its first "catastrophe." On 27 July 1898 the secret police, headed by Sergei Zubatov, undertook major raids and arrests in the western provinces and Congress Poland: not only was the Bund's entire three-member central committee apprehended, but its main weapon—that most important Bobruisk press—was confiscated.[47] The July arrests marked the end of the era of the Bund's first central committee. In all, it is estimated that some seventy Bund followers were arrested.[48]

In the captured materials of the Bobruisk press was the crucial issue of *Di arbeyter shtimme,* issue 9–10. In this issue, which would never leave the confines of the secret police headquarters, the central committee had drafted and prepared a lengthy programmatic statement, "Our Aims," which included its report of the founding of the RSDRP and the meaning of the PPS attacks. The captured material also included copies of Kossovsky's brochure on the PPS.[49] Before the arrests the Bund had finished printing and already distributed their long-awaited response to the PPS. Written with Kossovsky's biting pen, it consisted of two pieces that appeared together: the statement of aims, "Our Aims," and Kossovsky's thirty-seven-page brochure, *The War of the Polish Socialist Party against the Jewish Workers' Bund.* Significantly, the title page bore the emblem of the Russian Social Democratic Workers' Party with the Bund's title at the bottom, making it an official RSDRP publication.[50]

"Our Aims" presented the program of the Russian party to the Jewish worker and sought to clarify the Bund's role within it as well as present the argument explaining why, with the new Russian party, a separate Jewish organization was necessary. The second part was a discussion of the PPS. The most important phenomenon in Russian life during the 1890s, the authors wrote, was the founding of the Russian Social Democratic Workers' Party, which had unified various Social Democratic groups into one political organization. For the authors, the formation of the Bund and its entry into the RSDRP fulfilled a decade-long dream. The new party had given a unified form to different workers' organizations that had begun to work together in their struggle against the bourgeoisie and the tsar. In terms of party organization and center-periphery relations, members from each city and town would elect a representative body—a committee—which would have the freedom to govern its own affairs.[51]

"Our Aims" followed with a discussion on the Bund's relations with the RSDRP. According to the new party's manifesto, the Bund would have full autonomy in Jewish affairs. "[The Bund] has entered the Party as an autonomous organization that is independent solely in questions pertaining to the Jewish proletariat," stated the RSDRP manifesto. In addition to its autonomous status, Bundists also pushed through a statement acknowledging the Jews' unique condition in the Russian Empire: "The situation of the Jews in Russia—the politics of the tsarist government directed against them, as well as other particularities [*bezonderheyt*] (such as a different language)—has created special interests among the Jewish proletariat that need to be defended. Defending Jewish interests can only be undertaken by a separate Jewish organization . . . and the party will not interfere in the Bund's affairs. However, the Jewish Bund, as a party member, must defer to the central committee in affairs that concern the whole proletariat in Russia." The manifesto stressed, however, that the Bund did not have separate privileges. Rather, the party's resolution on the Bund was the result of "wise and practical" considerations. "The party treats [*ferhalt zikh*] the 'Jewish Bund' as it treats each workers' organization that defends the special interests of its own nation."[52] The manifesto's implicit recognition of the Jews as a nationality would be subsequently challenged, and ultimately rejected, by the Russian party. But for the time being, the Russians deferred to the Bund on Jewish matters.

In order to defend the Bund against its Polish and Russian critics, "Our Aims" advanced arguments to justify the need of a separate Jewish organization. The argument, which closely resembled Kremer's address at the Bund's founding congress, began with a survey of tsarist policies toward the Jews. The creation of the Pale of Settlement, whereby Jews were restricted to urban areas in a specified area, was the result, it was argued, of tsarist politics that sought to pit one nationality against another, as well as to divide Christians and Jews in the Pale. This policy also retarded the process of Jewish integration, thus preserving Jewish isolation. In addition to the exterior factor of official anti-Semitism, language also separated Jew from Christian. The combination of government anti-Semitism and the linguistic divide required a separate Jewish workers' organization. First, only a Jewish party could produce socialist literature in Yiddish. And second, only a Jewish party was able to defend Jewish rights against official government anti-Semitism. When the tsarist regime toppled, only the Bund would be able to maintain the level of energetic struggle needed "to attain equal civil rights for its nation." The latter argument revealed the degree to which the intellectual roots of the Bund's program could be traced back to Gozhanski's and Martov's positions laid out in the period 1893–95. It also demonstrated the degree to which Kremer had acquiesced to the party's national wing. "We shall state once again," Kremer and Kossovsky wrote, "that only a special Jewish workers' organization can provide enough strength and means to successfully lead the struggle of the Jewish proletariat. Only [the Bund] alone is able—at the right time . . . and with enough energy, to put forth their demands. Only the Bund can . . . acquaint the Russian worker with the political and economic movement of the Jewish proletariat through articles in the [Russian party's] organ and thereby aid in developing solidarity among the proletariat of Russia."[53]

"Our Aims" also responded to its Polish critics. Emboldened with its newfound legitimacy, the authors attempted to expose the PPS's alleged intolerance. They reiterated the central message of the piece: that a separate Jewish workers' organization was necessary for the interests of Jewish workers, just as for the Christian. Only such an organization was able to tend to the special needs of the Jewish worker. Their Russian friends were sufficiently astute, they wrote, to understand this and to allow the Bund a measure of independence. The RSDRP recognized "the right of all nations to have an independent workers' organization. For this is the best guarantee that the party will gravitate to all the living strength of the proletariat of Russia."[54] The central committee's statement of aims nonetheless achieved its goal of laying out the Bund's program, demanding its right to exist, and answering its critics. Its discussion of the PPS, however, was cursory. Although it answered accusations in the PPS press, it nonetheless ignored the so-called Polish question.

In contrast to "Our Aims," which sought to sell the Bund platform to Polish and Russian skeptics, as well as to the rank-and-file Jewish worker, whom the PPS was trying to recruit, Kossovsky's brochure lashed out against the PPS in a biting and slashing style. The thirty-seven-page brochure constituted the Bund's first sustained response to a half-decade of PPS accusations and claims. Provocatively titled *The War of the Polish Socialist Party against the Jewish Workers' Bund*, Kossovsky's brochure presented the party's position on such important matters as the national question and argued that the PPS's attitude to the nationalities question was conveniently formulated to further the PPS's political agenda. Taken as a whole, Kossovsky's brochure challenged three PPS claims: that the Bund had cut itself off from the Christian working class by creating a separate organization; that the Bund had formulated aims "separate" from the Christian workers in the Pale and Congress Poland; and that the Bund furthered the tsarist politics of Russification.

Between 1893 and 1896, Kossovsky acknowledged, the PPS was the only socialist party operating inside the empire. But that "golden age" of the PPS had passed and new movements had arisen among the Lithuanians and the Jews. Here he began his use of biting sarcasm. With the formation of the Lithuanian Social Democratic Party and the Jewish Labor Bund, Kossovsky wrote, "the 'Polish' party has taken note and raised a cry to heaven. She drums and sounds the trumpet: the fatherland is in danger! . . . [For] on a piece of land that belongs to her by virtue of historical rights, on her very own 'terrain,' a few organizations have arisen that have the audacity to challenge her authority. Some nerve!"[55]

According to the PPS's fourth congress resolution, the existence of separate Jewish and Lithuanian Social Democratic parties was contrary to the interests of the Polish and Lithuanian working classes, for economic and political conditions had required the need for a single party under one banner. Such a claim, Kossovsky maintained, represented the "arrogance" of PPS leaders in their belief that only they knew the correct socialist path. According to the resolution, "the PPS has a monopoly on [what are] the correct aims of the working class movement, and it alone possesses the correct understanding of socialism." By what logic, he asked, did the PPS claim it would struggle against the LSDP and the Bund, but support "revolutionary groups" in Lithuania? Kossovsky maintained that a native Polish speaker living in Lithuania could very well be of Lithuanian nationality. According to the resolution that claimed Polish-speakers were bound to Poland by "language and historical traditions," there were two types of people in Lithuania: Polish speakers who shared a common historical tradition and non-Polish speakers who had a different language and culture. Such a dichotomy, Kossovsky argued, defined two Lithuanias: "[T]he Lithuania that speaks Lithuanian belongs to 'Lithuanian revolutionary groups', while the Lithuania that speaks Polish belongs to the PPS."[56]

Kossovsky then moved to the crux of his argument. Following from the position on Lithuania, Lithuanian-speaking socialists, by virtue of the fact that they spoke a different language and did not share a common cultural tradition with the Poles, had the right to form a separate independent organization. With such a view on Lithuania, only "logical trickery" could claim that the Yiddish-speaking working class did not have the same right as Lithuanian-speaking workers: "The PPS maintains that a different language is enough to make necessary a separate organization," Kossovsky wrote. He continued: "Why, then, do you pronounce the Jewish workers' organization harmful and entitled to all kinds of vilification? For the Jews also speak a separate language, and it is in this language that [the Bund] agitates. Why do you deny [the Jews] what you grant the Lithuanian speakers?"[57]

The most politically charged issue that Kossovsky addressed was the accusation of Russification. Kossovsky acknowledged that, yes, the Vilna Group during the early 1890s had sought to teach the workers Russian in order to acquaint them with Russian radical literature. But to call the teaching of Russian revolutionary writers to Jewish workers "Russification," Kossovsky wrote, was thoroughly indefensible. "We always thought," Kossovsky wrote, "that by 'Russification' one meant the politics of the tsarist government, which suppressed the literature and language . . . of the oppressed peoples in Russia. [It meant] the prohibition of the Polish language . . . that in schools instruction must be carried out exclusively in the Russian language . . . and a prohibition on printing Yiddish newspapers." Given the common understanding of Russification, Kossovsky marveled that "the PPS is the first to arrive at the view that disseminating the ideas of Dobroliubov, the closest confidant of the father of socialism in Russia—Chernyshevskii—could be termed 'the Russification of Lithuania'! How shameful!"[58]

In the last part of Kossovsky's brochure, he addressed the April 1898 article "The Question of the Jewish Proletariat," which had constituted the PPS's most biting attack on the Bund.[59] Here the PPS press had argued that the Jews, because of their social isolation, had not taken part in Polish uprisings and that their inactivity had aided the tsar. Kossovsky disputed this claim, arguing that (and the historical facts bear this out) Jews took part in the 1830, 1848, and 1863 uprisings. The PPS, Kossovsky maintained, had stooped so low as to falsify history in the service of their political agenda.[60]

Having presented all the PPS attacks on the Jewish socialist movement, Kossovsky concluded with his most damning response: that the PPS leaders were not free from anti-Semitism themselves. Why else had they opposed so staunchly the formation of an independent Jewish party and had preached to their readers that the Jews were opponents of Polish freedom, he asked. In response to the PPS's stated opposition to anti-Semitism, Kossovsky responded, "How can it be expected that such gentlemen who are not free from religious and racial anti-Semitism themselves . . . [will] eradicate it from the Polish worker . . . ?" Consequently, he concluded, the Bund refused to believe the PPS leaders' claims to oppose anti-Semitism, "for they are not free from the racial anti-Semitism that they have inherited from the haughty Polish aristocracy." According to Kossovsky, socialism was not liberating the PPS leaders from anti-Semitism, as *Robotnik* had argued in February 1898. Rather, and this was Kossovsky's most controversial statement, the cry of the PPS against the Bund's energetic activities and success "is the same hatred for Jews that was suckled with their mother's milk."[61]

Kossovsky's strongly worded brochure was a shock for that time. "It made an enormous impression even on the PPS itself," Kremer recalled, stressing that Kossovsky's brochure was not an explanation or apology, but an open counterattack on the PPS, a sharp critique of its tactics and positions. "With biting irony, we spoke of [the PPS's] socialism, and with resentment of their nationalism." Kossovsky's brochure raised eyebrows even within the Bundist leadership. Tsivia Hurvitsh, for example, was fully opposed to distributing the brochure, which she argued was too harsh. Hurvitsh was not alone in protesting what she considered Kossovsky's overly hostile and accusing tone.

In the years prior to the formation of the Bund the debate between the PPS and the "Jewish Social Democratic Group in Russia" had centered on programmatic questions. A revived Russo-Polish struggle over the eastern borderlands, the PPS insisted, required a clear response from minority socialist groups in the Pale on the national question. The formation of the independent Jewish Labor Bund, however, shifted the center of that debate. In the first year of its existence, the Bund was forced to defend the right of Jews to form a separate workers' party. The bitter struggle for organizational independence in the empire, it will be argued, led some Bundists abroad to search for a comprehensive answer to the PPS, and they arrived at the provocative theory of *Jewish nationality*, to which we now turn.

*Student member of the Bund, Świsłocz (Grodno Province), 1908 (Yivo Institute for Jewish Research)*

*Group of Bundists, Siedlce (Congress Poland), 1903 (Yivo Institute for Jewish Research)*

*Studio portrait of Chaim Shnayer (standing, right), later a leading actor in the Vilna Troupe, with a group of Bundists, Vilna, c. 1910 (Yivo Institute for Jewish Research)*

*Groups of Bundists, Lyady (Mogilev province), 1902 (Yivo Institute for Jewish Research)*

*A Bundist circle, Minsk, 1903 (Yivo Institute for Jewish Research)*

*Circle of Bundist women, Suwałki (Congress Poland), 1904 (Yivo Institute for Jewish Research)*

*Group of Bundists, Włocławek (Congress Poland), 1912 (Yivo Institute for Jewish Research)*

# ■ 5.
# Ideological Transformation:
# The Turn to a National Program,
# 1899–1901

> *We vigorously maintain that the Jewish nation, like all others, should possess equal political, economic, and national rights. We shall even fight for it.*
> FOREIGN COMMITTEE OF THE BUND (1899)

> *When in 1893 we urged the Jewish organization in Lithuania to conduct agitation in Yiddish, we never expected that these same comrades . . . would later return to oppose us with such obstinacy. To a significant degree, we understand this as being the result of the Russian school system from which the Jewish intelligentsia has adopted a perfidious view about Poland and its history.*
> FOREIGN COMMITTEE OF THE PPS (1900)

WHILE THE NEWLY FORMED BUND defended its right to organizational independence within the larger Social Democratic movement in Russia and suffered a dramatic setback with the arrest of its central committee in 1898, a few surviving members escaped abroad and set about preparing a theoretical challenge to the PPS. That the man who came to head the Geneva center—John Mill— was the party's most nationally minded member would have a significant impact on the ideological evolution of the Bund. It will be argued that the seed of the Bund's future program of national cultural autonomy can be traced back to a polemic with Polish socialists over the national question.

## The Bund's Foreign Committee

Following the liquidation of the Bund's central committee, a few *polu-intelligenty* organized an interim second party congress in Kovno in October 1898. Representing the Vilna, Kovno, Warsaw, Białystok, Minsk, and Łódź regions, the second congress consisted of twelve members, including Dovid Katz and Maria Zhaludsky, the only participants who had been present at the founding congress. Their tasks included reestablishing a press and selecting a new central committee, which Katz, Tsivia Hurvitsh, and Sender Zeldov now headed.[1] Perhaps the greatest feat of the new central committee was its ability to restart *Di arbeyter shtimme*, the Bund's central organ inside the empire. With the previous issue now in the hands of the police, the Bundist organ had not appeared since February. But in December 1898, to the chagrin of the secret police, *Di arbeyter shtimme* reappeared with a report on the second congress and a reprint of materials from the confiscated issue, including the programmatic piece, "Our Aims."[2]

While the Bund reestablished itself inside the empire, the wave of arrests in July 1898 had the effect of strengthening the organization's leadership abroad. The only member of the core leadership to survive the police crackdown was John Mill, who, by a stroke of luck, had departed to western Europe just before the arrests. With the devastating events at home, the burden of continuing the organization and literary prowess of the Bund now shifted to Geneva. Mill thus set about establishing links during the late summer and fall of 1898 and was able to make contact with Kopelzon, who had been in exile in western Europe since 1897. In December 1898 Mill established an official foreign committee in Geneva and made *Der yidisher arbeyter* an official organ of the Bund with himself as editor-in-chief.[3]

With new authority as foreign committee head, Mill used the pages of *Der yidisher arbeyter* as a forum for discussions on the national question, now establishing himself as the unabashed leader of the Bund's national wing. The first issue of *Der yidisher arbeyter* under Mill appeared in March 1899 with a host of articles on the national question in what one historian of the Bund characterized "as a virtual national Manifesto."[4] The entire project of publishing a Bundist organ devoted to the national and Jewish questions in the Russian Empire derived from the debates that had taken place in Warsaw before Mill's departure.[5]

In a review of *Der arbeyter*, the PPS 's first Yiddish organ, which had appeared in December 1898, Mill castigated PPS Jews for their

*Cover of* Der yidisher arbeyter, *organ of the Bund's Foreign Committee in Geneva, 1901 (Yivo Institute for Jewish Research)*

belief that the restoration of Poland would bring about the emancipation of the Jews. From both a socialist and a Jewish point of view, he maintained, Polish independence had to be subordinated to more pressing issues relevant to all workers in Russia. Yes, independence would alleviate the oppression of Poles, but a democratic Polish republic would not necessarily protect Jews against legal discrimination. Mill took care, however, to emphasize that the Bund was not in principle opposed to Polish independence and even declared that "no true socialist" could be against the right of Poles to national sovereignty. The problem was one of stages. The Bund supported an empire-wide constitutional solution that would *precede* all attempts to resolve territorial disputes. In sum, the overthrow of absolutism had to be every socialist's primary goal. Echoing the Bund's polemic against the Zionists, Mill also maintained that the struggle for Polish independence under current conditions was a utopian fantasy. By what means, Mill asked, did the PPS expect to separate from the powerful Russia state? Insurrection? War? Clearly, a Polish armed uprising was doomed to utter failure. Also, why should Jews support Polish independence, Mill queried, given that they had no assurance a Polish state would bring them full emancipation.[6]

For Jews, then, a different solution had to be sought. Mill invoked the model proposed by the Marxist leader Karl Kautsky, who had argued for the preservation of the Austro-Hungarian Empire through a system of national self-determination.[7] Applying Kautsky's purported analysis to the Russian Empire, Mill argued that only a nonterritorial answer to the national question could be employed in multinational states. "Not only Poles live in [Russian Poland]," Mill wrote, "but also Jews, Germans, Lithuanians, and Belarussians. If Poland was separated from Russia, power would be in the hands of the Poles, and it would be highly unlikely if Jews, Germans, and others would obtain national rights." He concluded with the Bund's soundest argument yet against the PPS program. In a statement that would form the kernel of the future program of national-cultural autonomy, Mill concluded that the solution to national oppression in Russia "is not the separation or federation of countries, but only the autonomy of *nations*: each nation shall have equal rights in all matters. . . . There can be no other national program for socialists."[8]

Mill later recalled that the PPS-Bund polemic over the national question had forced him to reconsider the Bund's party platform. In the concept of Jewish nationality, the Bund found a powerful rhetorical weapon with which to fight the PPS. "Why does the PPS and its organ, *Przedświt*, struggle against the Bund?" asked *Der yidisher arbeyter* in the summer of 1899. "What can the Jewish proletariat expect from 'the separation of Poland'?" Mill asked, "Can it expect that persecution against it *as Jews* will cease? Will it really receive *national equality*? This is the entire question. Nobody can prove to us that we will really gain national rights. We will be the minority in free Poland and the future Polish regime can persecute us just as much as the present Russian regime."[9]

Mill's rejection of the territorial solution can be traced back to the first month of 1898. At the time a consensus arose within the Bund's Warsaw division that the demand for equal civil rights was insufficient, and intensive discussions began on the national question. The "national problem" required a comprehensive solution, it was decided. The bitter struggle that the PPS had waged on the Bund was beginning to dominate the party's Warsaw branch and led Warsaw Bundists to reconsider the party platform. While rejecting the PPS program, the Warsaw section nonetheless concluded that the Bundist platform was inadequately suited to Polish conditions. The PPS had raised significant questions. "We searched for a solution," Mill recalled. "The national question became a perpetual theme at almost all our meetings, Bundist gatherings, and debates. We were opposed to the historic-territorial aspirations of the PPS, but we could not see the right direction in equal civil rights [Bund] and the self-determination of nations [program of the RSDRP]."[10]

The solution Mill was searching for came to him shortly thereafter. In the beginning of 1898, Mill came upon an article by Karl Kautsky that would transform his thinking on the national question. That article proposed a solution to the national problem in the Austro-Hungarian Empire and argued that the working class had to have an adequate answer to the national question before it could correctly lead a class struggle. Workers should not be hostile to national movements. Rather, it was in the interests of the working classes to promote the cultivation of, and demand rights for, their respective national cultures. There was thus one solution to the national problem in Austria-Hungary: a federation of nationalities on the basis of language borders. "There remains only one possibility," Kautsky wrote, "that is *the autonomy of nations*. Austria must become divided by languages, and the language borders must become autonomous regions of Austria." Under Kautsky's formula, a state of various provinces and crown lands would be replaced by a state of nations. Kautsky emphasized the importance of addressing the national question for the international working class. "*The autonomy of nations* is today a necessary foundation for every class struggle."[11] Thus, Kautsky formulated an integrative solution to the nationalities problem—one that could satisfy national longings while preserving the territorial integrity of multinational states.

To Mill, Kautsky's proposed solution to the national question in Austria-Hungary came as a revelation. It answered his objections to both the Bund's international wing and the PPS. First, it gave legitimacy to the idea that socialists need not avoid the national question. One of the most respected and renowned European socialists was now endorsing the idea put forth by Martov in 1895: that class and national consciousness had to go hand in hand. Kautsky's idea also challenged the PPS's historic-territorial platform. "We used all of [Kautsky's] arguments in our struggle against the territorial solution to the national question," Mill recalled. "We supposed that we had finally found that which we had so passionately searched for."[12] As Jack Jacobs has rightly stressed, the Bund used Kautsky's theory specifically in the context of its search for an answer to the PPS.[13]

If Mill's article was radical in its arguments for national autonomy for the Jews, it was nonetheless superseded by a more startling piece in *Der yidisher arbeyter*. Under the pseudonym "Ben Ehud" (Son of Unity), Chaim Zhitlovsky, in his article, "Zionism or Socialism?" argued that the Yiddish-speaking worker must reject Zionism as a movement strictly of the Jewish bourgeoisie. The Jewish people (*folk*) had their own *national* culture and its core was the Yiddish language, which Zhitlovsky called upon the Jewish *folk* to cultivate into a modern European language. The "sacred" Yiddish tongue, Zhitlovsky wrote, had to develop into a richer language in both vocabulary and expression, and everything the young generation produced in science and art was to be produced in Yiddish. This, in turn, would contribute to the growth of secular Yiddish culture. This would mean that Jews should have their own middle schools and universities with Yiddish as the language of instruction.[14]

Responding to political Zionists, Zhitlovsky argued that the Jewish people had to liberate itself from the "bourgeois misconception" of territorial aspiration. Whereas in the Old World, it was believed that a *folk* naturally strove for territorial independence, culture and education defined the New World. Only through the preservation of culture (Yiddish), he argued, could Diaspora Jewry be preserved.[15]

The decision of the Bund to print Zhitlovsky's article was rather astonishing. At the time the Bund's official platform called for equal civil rights for the Jews in Russia. As Frankel has commented, Zhitlovsky's call for the Jews to develop a modern nation, "worldwide in scope, socialist and secular in content, Yiddish-speaking in form" was wholly unprecedented in revolutionary circles in the 1890s.[16] In fact, Mill included a disclaimer in which he explained that Zhitlovsky's ideas were the opinion of the author alone. The text that followed revealed the limits of Mill's own national tendencies. He informed the reader that *Der yidisher arbeyter* fully supported the principle that all nations—including the Jews—were entitled to equal political, economic, and national rights. "But whether the Jewish folk language, the 'jargon', will develop into a cultural language; whether . . . a special Jewish literature and science in Yiddish . . . [and] Jewish gymnasiums, universities and other schools [will develop]; whether it is necessary to link the Jewish workers in different countries . . . all these are questions which it is as yet hard to answer definitely."[17]

In addition to Mill's article, which is the first Bundist document to use Kautsky in its polemic with the PPS, Mill printed an article about the Lithuanian Social Democrats. In the brief article, it was argued that the LSDP rose because of the inadequacies of the PPS. The Lithuanian socialists organized into a separate party because "neither the program nor the tactics of the Polish Socialist Party was adequate for the young Lithuanian workers' movement." Avoiding the question of nationality, *Der yidisher arbeyter* noted that the LSDP agitated mainly in Polish because Polish was widely used in Lithuanian cities by the "Christian" workers.[18] A protest letter of the Lithuanian party condemning the PPS followed the article. "The Polish Socialist Party wants the right [to organize independently] only for itself," the LSDP stated. "It struggles for the independence of its own workers' movement. And yet, it does not recognize that same right for the Lithuanian worker. It strives . . . to destroy the independence of the Lithuanian workers' movement."[19] The Lithuanian socialist response to the PPS thus closely resembled the Bund's position.

Under Mill's leadership the new foreign committee put out two more issues of *Der yidisher arbeyter* in 1899. In the August and December issues, Mill filled the pages with more theoretical articles on the national question and continued to use the Bundist organ as a forum for PPS opponents. First, it was the LSDP. But now, Mill allowed the PPS's archrival, Rosa Luxemburg, to argue her controversial and dogmatic case against Polish independence.[20] The fact that Mill allowed *Der yidisher arbeyter* to be used as a forum for both the LSDP and the SDKP to rail against the PPS would further strain PPS-Bund relations. Although Mill included an editorial note disclaiming responsibility for Luxemburg's views, the fact that her forceful arguments against Polish independence were now disseminated in Yiddish to the Jewish worker in Russia greatly angered the PPS leaders.

The third issue of *Der yidisher arbeyter* under Mill appeared in the wake of the historic Austro-Marxist congress. Taking place in September 1899, the All-Austrian Social Democratic party met in the Moravian city of Brünn (present-day Brno). Because of the increase in tensions between the various nationalities in the Austro-Hungarian Empire, the Austro-Marxists discussed the national question at length. During the course of the debate, Etbin Kristan, a South Slav delegate from Trieste, argued a case that would later be seized upon by the Bund: Kristan argued that a resolution on the national question should endorse the rights of extraterritorial nationalities.[21] A free society had to emancipate itself, the South Slav delegate proclaimed, from the assumption that a nation was defined by territory. "The principle of a free society finds its parallel," Kristan declared, "in the separation of the idea of nation from that of territory. We have to make it clear that equality of rights is possible only if the nation is defined not as the population living in one territory, but as the sum total of all individuals claiming a particular nationality."[22]

The congress nevertheless rejected the South Slav delegate's proposal. Instead, the Austro-Marxists adopted the principles set out in Karl Kautsky's writings and declared the following:

1. Austria shall be transformed into a democratic federation of nationalities.
2. The historic provinces (crown lands) shall be replaced by nationally delimited, self-governing areas in each of which legislation and administration shall be entrusted to national chambers, elected on a basis of universal, direct, and equal suffrage.
3. All the self-governing regions of one and the same nation shall jointly form a single national union which shall manage its national affairs on the basis of complete autonomy.
4. The rights of national minorities shall be protected by a special law to be adopted by the parliament of the empire.
5. We do not recognize any national privilege and therefore we reject the demand for an official language [*Staatssprache*]. A parliament of the empire shall decide as to whether and in which degree a common language is necessary.[23]

The Brünn resolution defined national autonomy in terms of territorial units, rejecting the principle of extraterritorial autonomy. As Kogan writes in his study of Austrian Social Democracy, the Brünn program advocated a national autonomy along territorial lines.[24]

Three months following the Brünn congress, Mill informed readers of *Der yidisher arbeyter* that a long-awaited answer to the difficult "national question" had arrived. That solution was the transformation of a multinational empire into a federation of nationalities, each of which would be granted autonomy. The solution of federation or autonomy "rests on the principle . . . that each nation should have its own workers' organization; [that] each language, literature, and national culture be given equal rights," Mill wrote, adding that "no Social Democrat can in any form be against the national strivings of each *folk*." Mill continued his polemic with the PPS, arguing that the new Austro-Marxist platform had made territorial solutions to the national question obsolete. Galicia was a perfect example, Mill claimed. Despite the existence of some three million Ruthenians and other minorities, the Poles claimed the whole territory by virtue of historical rights. He thus concluded that "Social Democrats, who stand for equality and truth, and who want to defend the right of all working peoples, cannot lead such a struggle."[25]

Mill emphasized two important principles that were raised at the Brünn congress. The first, which had clearly been influenced by Kautsky, was that all nations had equal rights and that the development of their national cultures, languages, and literatures was in the interests of the working class. Despite the fact that the Austro-Marxist congress had advocated national autonomy along strictly territorial lines, Mill stated that the congress had made "a great distinction between land and the nation [*folk*], and does not hold that only a people with territory should be regarded as a nation and can demand national rights." Borrowing from Zhitlovsky's ideas, Mill wrote that a new concept of the nation was now becoming accepted—that *"the nation is its culture."* The Jewish workers of Poland and Russia also had a "national question," which had to be addressed. "We must also find an answer to our national question. What our answer will be, we do not know. But an answer will come sooner or later."[26]

## The First Debate on Jewish Nationality: The Third Congress of the Bund, 1899

The crystallization of the Jewish national idea in Geneva coincided with the Bund's third party congress, which took place in Kovno in December 1899. At the time the gap between the national wing of the Bund in Geneva and the party's central committee inside the empire was widening. The new central committee—organized in the wake of the 1898 arrests of Kremer and Kossovsky—was decidedly internationalist in orientation. Since the appearance of *Der yidisher arbeyter* under Mill's control, the party leadership inside Russia expressed concern about the "nationalism" of the Geneva Bundists.[27] Opposition to the new line in Geneva also found expression in the Bund's Warsaw branch. Rakhmiel Weinstein, who joined the Warsaw Bund in 1898, received *Der yidisher arbeyter* in March 1899. Instead of distributing the first issue of the Bund's foreign committee as is, he appended a note to each issue stating that the Warsaw Committee of the Bund disclaimed all responsibility for the "nationalist views" expressed. Specific mention was made of Zhitlovsky's and Mill's articles as particularly objectionable. Significantly, the Warsaw committee's protest note was first made public by the PPS, which delighted in printing Weinstein's "protest" in their organ.[28]

When fifteen delegates, representing twelve cities, arrived in Kovno for the third congress, the debates focused largely on the proposal of one participant.[29] During a full day's discussion, Mill argued before his fellow delegates that in addition to civil rights, the Jewish worker should demand equal *national* rights. To bolster his argument, Mill used the example of Prussian Poles. There, in the region of Posen, Poles had equal civil rights and, like Germans, the right of peaceful assembly. But they were required to use German at public meetings. This clearly demonstrated, Mill maintained, that the attainment of individual civil rights did not guarantee the protection of one national group against discrimination. As long as Yiddish was not elevated to an equal status with Russian, civil freedoms would be useless to the Jews of Russia.[30]

Despite Mill's strong appeal for the introduction of Jewish national rights into the party platform, the delegates Dovid Katz, Pavel Rozental, and Rakhmiel Weinstein remained steadfastly opposed.[31] They responded that the Prussian Polish example only demonstrated that the German constitution was insufficiently democratic. One only had to look to England and America, they said, for examples of democratic systems whereby separate national demands were not needed.[32] The delegates also raised broader concerns with Mill's proposal. They feared that such a demand would alienate the Bund from non-Jewish workers and fracture the empire-wide movement. They accused Mill and his Geneva division of having become more nationalist than socialist. One delegate maintained that *Der yidisher arbeyter*, by printing several articles on the national and Jewish questions, had contradicted "all the dear and sacred traditions" of scientific socialism.[33]

The uniformly negative reaction to Mill's ideas in Kovno reveals how new was the Jewish national idea. Mill recalled that the majority of delegates were not in a position to discuss the national question intelligently. Another delegate present at the Kovno congress confirmed Mill's recollections. Hillel Katz-Blum, a native of Dvinsk (present-day Daugavpils) who had been present at the Bund's first congress and represented Białystok at the 1899 congress, recalled that the issue of Jewish "national" rights was new for most of the delegates, some even going so far as to consider them "heretical" ideas.[34] Another delegate at the congress—Tsivia Hurvish—similarly noted that the first time she ever seriously considered the idea that the Jews constituted a nation was at the third party congress.[35] Mill described the atmosphere at the congress: "The debates were heated and excited. Some of the delegates did not want to know or hear anything about our changes on the Jewish question. Cosmopolitans from head to toe, they refused even to touch upon national questions. For them, anything that smelled of nationalism, that had any relation to national problems, was treyf."[36] In the end the delegates in Kovno chose to preserve the party platform. The Bund's third party congress resolved the following: "The 'Bund,' among its political demands, calls only for equal civil—not national-rights." The resolution did state, however, that further discussions on the national question should continue in the pages of *Der yidisher arbeyter*.[37]

The question of the Bund's relations with the PPS was also debated at the congress. While the delegates decided against issuing an official declaration for or against the PPS political platform, they did pass a resolution on the PPS's tactics. The resolution acknowledged the significance of the political question of Polish national aspirations and decided to open a free discussion in *Der yidisher arbeyter* on the independence of Poland. The resolution on the PPS concluded with the following statement: "Given that the existence of the Bund is necessary for the development of class consciousness among the Jewish proletariat, and that the PPS works to undermine the Bund's independence and existence, the congress resolves to fight against the tactics of the Polish Socialist Party by all appropriate means."[38]

While the Bund's original platform survived its first challenge in 1899, significant new developments strengthened the national wing of the Bund, both at home and abroad. The year 1900, for example, saw significant developments in the Bund's foreign committee. Kremer, Kossovsky, and Mutnik had been released from prison in the spring and settled abroad in Switzerland.[39] Upon joining the foreign committee, the members of the first central committee embraced the new national line in Geneva. The fact that the most highly esteemed Bundist pioneers were now active in the party's foreign committee was of great significance for the evolution of the

Bund's national program, for it gave the foreign committee's position more authority in the eyes of Bundists inside the empire.[40]

The Bund inside the empire also underwent a significant change. In 1900, after four years of forced exile, veteran Bundist Noyakh Portnoy escaped from Siberia and made his way illegally to Vilna. Portnoy had been a graduate of the Vilna Teacher's Institute and an important member of the proto-Bundists in Vilna before his arrest in 1895. Soon after rejoining the party in the spring of 1900, Portnoy was coopted into the central committee by Dovid Katz, thus putting the central committee back into the hand of a pioneer intellectual.[41] The new central committee, now based in Białystok, consisted of Portnoy, Dovid Katz, and Pavel Rozental.[42] As a Bundist pioneer and *intelligent*, Portnoy quickly rose to leadership in the central committee, filling the vacuum caused by Kremer's arrest.[43] From Portnoy's crucial role in the fourth congress, it is clear that he, too, unlike Katz and Rozental, was sympathetic to the position put forth in Geneva.[44]

### The Bund's Foreign Committee and the Polish Question, 1899–1901

Among the internal factors that led to the historic fourth congress, at which the principle of Jewish nationality was endorsed, was the return of Kremer, Kossovsky, and Mutnik from prison and Siberian exile in 1900 and their subsequent activity with the foreign committee. Noyakh Portnoy's return from prison in the same year and his rise to leadership inside the empire was similarly consequential. One could also mention the impact of *Der yidisher arbeyter* and its consistent focus on the Jewish national idea as a contributing factor in the growing attention given to the national question in Jewish socialist circles. Since the third party congress, every issue of the Geneva Bundist organ contained articles under the headings "Discussions on the National Question" and "Discussion on the Question of the Independence of Poland."[45]

With regard to external factors, however, Mill maintained that the PPS had an enormous influence on the Bund's national program and, to a lesser extent, on the growth of labor Zionism. In addition to the polemic that transpired between party elites, the PPS was important as the sole model of a strong, disciplined socialist party with a national program. Mill wrote of "the great influence" that the "national strivings" of the PPS had on the ideological development of the Bund, as well as the PPS's wide network of local organizations in the Pale and Congress Poland.[46] And as the PPS established itself more and more in the small towns of Congress Poland and in Lithuania, the conflict between the two was no longer confined to the Bund's Warsaw branch.

In almost every issue prior to the fourth congress, Mill continued his polemic with the PPS in the column, "From the Press."[47] In these columns Mill maintained that the two main PPS arguments against the Bund—that it separated Jewish and non-Jewish workers, and that the Bund was Russifying the Jewish movement—were baseless and slanderous. The first charge was "meaningless," for as part of the Russian Social Democratic Workers' Party, the Bund was strongly unified with the Christian worker. Of course, Mill's counterarguments did not always directly respond to PPS claims: by "Christian worker" the PPS referred to ethnic Poles and Lithuanians and their movements towards independence.

Differing conceptions of nations and nationalities were at the heart of the PPS-Bund dispute, Mill maintained. The PPS failed to recognize the gradual and irreversible penetration of the Jewish national idea among the Yiddish-speaking working class. "Why does the PPS and its organ, *Przedświt*, struggle against the Bund? Why is that which is good for the Polish proletariat bad and harmful for the Jewish worker?" Mill asked. The answer, according to Mill, was clear: "[To the PPS] there is no Jewish nation, and there is no Jewish proletariat: there are only Polish, Lithuanian, and Russian workers of the Hebrew faith, and thus no separate Jewish interests. Such a view would be very, very naive."[48]

### Consolidation of the National Wing: The Fourth Congress of the Bund

The penetration of the national idea in the Jewish socialist camp led to the historic party congress in April 1901, when twenty-four delegates met in Białystok to convene the Bund's fourth congress.[49] In the fifteen months since the previous party congress, the pioneer-intellectuals who had emerged in 1900 from prison and Siberian exile had taken over leadership both at home and abroad.

Emboldened by the new developments, the foreign committee delegates arrived at the congress with an ally in the central committee—Noyakh Portnoy. At the twelve-hour session on the national question, Katz and Rozental voiced opposition to the foreign committee's national program proposal. With Portnoy's intervention, however, Katz and Rozental agreed to a compromise solution.[50]

Combining Kautsky's position on the national question with the theory of extraterritorial nationality, the congress passed the following resolution: "The congress resolves that a Social Democratic program must not allow the oppression of one class over another, or of one nation or language over another. The congress recognizes that a state such as Russia, which is made up of many different nations, will in the future be transformed into a federation of nationalities, and that each will have full autonomy independent of the territory in which it resides. The congress maintains the term 'nationality' should also apply to the Jewish people [*Der tsuzamenfor halt, az dem bagrif natsyionalitet darf men onvendn oykh oyfn yidishn folk*]."[51] Katz pushed through the following statement, revealing the hesitancy with which the congress as a whole endorsed the principle of Jewish national rights: "The congress, however, regards it as premature in present circumstances to put forward the demand of national autonomy for Jews. The congress maintains that, for the time being, we should only struggle for the repeal of all anti-Jewish laws; to protest against the oppression of the Jewish nationality; and to guard against inflaming national feelings that can only obscure the class consciousness of the proletariat and lead to chauvinism."[52] Both contemporary reports and memoirs suggest the compromise resolution at the fourth congress was the result of difficult negotiations between Portnoy and Rozental.[53] Since both men—representing the national and the international wing of the party—were able to garner the support of delegates, the official resolution recognized the principle of Jewish national autonomy while excluding it from the official movement. But the endorsement of Jewish national autonomy was a watershed in the history both of the Bund and of European Jewry in general.

Historians of the Bund have had to grapple with the difficult task of explaining just how the views of a tiny minority at the 1899 congress were able to win over the majority of delegates in April 1901. Frankel has argued that two main factors brought about the dramatic shift.[54] First, ideological pressure from abroad influenced the Bundist leadership inside the empire by publicizing the works of Karl Kautsky and the resolutions of the Brünn congress, both of which argued that the working class had an interest in formulating a response to the national question. Thus, the smuggling of the eighth issue of *Der yidisher arbeyter* (Dec. 1899) into the empire with Yiddish translations of Kautsky, the Austro-Marxists, and Mill certainly raised the level of knowledge among Bundists on the subject and provided them with a new vocabulary with which to discuss the national question.

The two most important primary sources on the fourth congress confirm Frankel's contention of the significance of ideological currents from abroad. These are the published congress report, written by Portnoy and Rozental, and the memoirs of Pavel Rozental.[55] Both remark that the 1899 Brünn program of the Austrian Social Democrats was the basis on which the national question was discussed.[56] The congress protocol attempted to explain the dramatic shift in the period 1899–1901, emphasizing the increasing influence of the Jewish national idea on the Bundist leadership in the fifteen-month period between the third and fourth party congresses.[57]

The second main factor in the ideological shift, according to Frankel, was the mechanics of decision making. Here contemporary sources attest to Noyakh Portnoy's central role. According to Rozental and the congress report, three views surfaced on the national question: a left position led by Rozental and four others, a centrist position led by Portnoy with two supporters, and a right position held by a single delegate, Marc Liber. Liber had argued that as a long-term goal, the congress should inscribe the demand for Jewish national autonomy on its banner. "We must prepare the Jewish proletariat for national autonomy by developing their national consciousness," Liber proclaimed. "Until now, we have been too cosmopolitan—we should become more national [*nacyonalny*]. There's no need to fear that word: *national* does not mean *nationalistic*."[58] Liber nonetheless did not find a single supporter among the congress delegates. The result, Rozental wrote, was a compromise resolution worked out by himself and Portnoy, which included two parts—a programmatic statement theoretically endorsing Jewish national rights and a practical statement, making the national question unofficial. "True, equal national rights were not put forth as an actual demand," Rozental later reflected. "But at the same time the resolution was an attempt to give a programmatic answer to the national question, not in the sense of national-territorial autonomy, but rather in that of personal and cultural [autonomy]."[59]

Basing their interpretation on two primary sources—the congress report and Rozental's memoirs—historians have assumed that no debate on the PPS program took place at the congress. According to this consensus, the territorial solution, as formulated by the PPS, did not have a single adherent at the congress.[60] One delegate, however, contradicts such a view. Leyb Blekhman (1874–1962), who represented Vitebsk at the congress, vividly recalled that a small group argued for the breakup of Russia into national states based on ethnolinguistic frontiers as the only realistic long-term solution to the national question. At the Bund's fourth congress, Blekhman wrote, "a small group maintained that to solve the national question, Russia had to break apart into separate states according to nationalities, such as Poland, Lithuania, Ukraine, and White Russia."[61] But the congress rejected the motion with the claim that a territorial solution would only create new oppressed national minorities. Blekhman's recollections suggest that the ideas of the PPS and the Lithuanian socialists, who at that time were becoming more nationalistic, had made their way into Bundist circles, and that the lower level leadership did not necessarily share the position of party elites.

What is clear is that the debates and resolutions were adopted with the PPS consciously in mind, not to mention the Zionists (to which I shall return later). The official congress report stated triumphantly that no delegates had advocated the PPS program, and used the PPS program as a point of departure to argue *in principle* against territorial solutions. If the restoration of Poland was to be based on historic rights, the congress report asked, would it choose boundaries from the sixteenth, seventeenth, or eighteenth century? "It can be charged . . . that we recognize the present borders as an unalterable fact. In essence, [the Russian Empire] was created by the help of fire and sword, swindle and the gallows," the report stated, "but were the so-called historic provinces of Poland . . . formed any differently?" The congress continued: "We, Social Democrats, are generally not concerned with the state, and it is not our intention to alter its borders and carve out new ones. We are for total freedom and equality. With regard to national equality, its only guarantee is to be sought in national autonomy, not in territorial independence."[62]

In addition to the crucial resolution on the national question, the fourth congress decided to add "Lithuania" to the Bund's name.[63] The new addition was significant in that it faithfully reflected the leadership's evolving conception of Lithuania as a territory distinct from Russia. If by using the term "Poland and Russia" they wished to differentiate between historic provinces, one delegate asked, then certainly "Lithuania" should be included, given that it was the main area of Bundist activity. In spite of the growing Ukrainian national movement, however, the congress reported no advocate of appending "and Ukraine" onto its title, suggesting that the Ukrainian question was of little concern.[64] The addition of "Lithuania" to the title was both the result of the emerging Lithuanian nationalist movement as well as a desire to renounce claims to Lithuanian soil by the PPS, which at that time was increasing its activities in Lithuania. It may also have been the result of repeated PPS reminders that the Bund was agitating not "in Russia," but "in Poland and Lithuania."

The addition of "Lithuania" to the Bund's name represented a changing regional perception. Henceforth, "Russia" receded in order; Lithuanian Jewish socialists went from being "The Jewish Social Democratic Group *in Russia*" (1893) to "The General Jewish Bund *in Russia and Poland*" (1897) to "The General Jewish Bund *in Lithuania, Poland, and Russia*" (1901). Mishkinsky has noted that placing the words Lithuania and Poland in the title reflected "a factual shrinkage" of Russia to the southern Pale (the Ukraine).[65]

## The PPS and the Bund's Fourth Congress

In its official response to the Bund's fourth congress, the assimilated Jew and PPS intellectual Feliks Perl set out to refute the Bund's new position on the national question. In the pages of *Robotnik,* the central organ of the PPS, Perl derided the Bund for attempting to import into the Russian Empire a theoretical model for solving the national question in Austria-Hungary.[66] But what was behind the Bund's opposition to a breakaway Polish republic? Why did the Bund fear Polish cultural domination in a future Polish state, while it harbored no corresponding concern for a future Russian democratic republic? The faulty logic of the Bund's position, Perl wrote, derived from the idea that "Russia, a despotic state . . . , a conglomerate carved from [a host of] provinces, will transform itself into a . . . union of free nations. But Poland—no! Poland will oppress Jews, Germans, and Russians! Here the influence of Russian government 'science' appears, which always paints Poland in the darkest colors in relation to the glory of Russia."[67]

More importantly, Perl maintained, the Bund's vision of a democratic federal republic was undemocratic in character, for under the Bund's plan, the nationalities of the western provinces and Congress Poland would be coerced into a federation ruled from Moscow. To the PPS leadership, this position on the state reflected the Bund's political immaturity. "Unlike the Bund, we will not force anyone into a federation," Perl emphasized. "We fully recognize the right of other nations to [either] an independent state or a *voluntary* union with Poland. The Bund's federation is impossible, but even if it were not, it would be a *forced* union." In an effort to formulate a theoretical justification for its refusal to support Polish independence, Perl continued, the Bund had resorted to intellectual "acrobatics" and "prevarications." How did the Bund arrive at such a position? Perl's answer is revealing: "It derives from the Bund's original sin—its *all-Russian* position. In the country in which it is active—in Poland-Lithuania—the Bund has separated itself from the local population, neither shares its aspirations nor understands its interests, and does not sympathize with the exceptional predicament in which these subjugated people find themselves." By linking a movement in Poland-Lithuania (*w kraju*) to Russia, "the Bund plays a false and harmful political role."[68]

The Jewish Labor Bund underwent a major transformation in the first four years of its existence. At the founding congress, the Bund declared itself the defender of equal civil rights for the Jews and favored unification with the Russian socialist movement. From its inception, the Bund had to withstand harsh critics from the PPS, the largest and most influential socialist party in the Russian Empire at the time. PPS pressures forced the Bund to formulate an official position on the national question. Because of a host of internal and external factors—PPS pressures, Karl Kautsky's theoretical formulations, and the national wing's domination of the foreign committee—the Bund decided to endorse the principle of Jewish national autonomy in April 1901.

This chapter has argued that the Bund's path from defender of civil rights to proponent of Jewish national autonomy was, to a large degree, the result of its search for an answer to the PPS. Besides the PPS's insistence that the Bund respond to the national question, the architect of the Bund's national program, John Mill, repeatedly emphasized the significance of the PPS as the model of a strong, disciplined socialist party committed to a national program. Also, the Bund's adoption of the Austro-Marxist solution to the national question must be understood within the context of its struggle with the PPS. At the height of PPS attacks on the Bund in 1897–98, nationally leaning Bundists were unable to respond. It was thus the urgent need to answer the PPS that made Kautsky's conception of national autonomy so significant. Kautsky's injunction that workers from each nationality should preserve and develop their national cultures gave the Bund's national wing an argument with which to answer both the PPS on the Right *and* the internationalist on the Left. At a 1903 Bundist gathering Boris Frumkin remarked in a debate on the national question that the fourth congress resolution had been passed in reckless haste "under the influence of the PPS and Zionists."[69] Jacobs has thus rightly revised the old school and argued that "the initial impetus for this development [of a national program] was . . . the necessity of answering the PPS, and the kernel of the Bund's platform was derived from Kautsky's article on Austria-Hungary."[70]

# ■ 6.
# Polish Socialism Responds:
# The First Years of the PPS
# Yiddish Press, 1898–1902

> *We, Jewish workers in Poland, share the same . . . interests and*
> *needs as our Christian brothers in the same country. Their future*
> *is also our future, their aspirations, ours: an independent Polish*
> *Republic is therefore our political program.*
> DER ARBEYTER (1898)

> *Down with programs that disturb the brotherly harmony*
> *between the Polish . . . and the Jewish worker. May the walls*
> *crumble to the ground that today separate these two great sec-*
> *tions of the proletariat inhabiting our land.*
> W. JODKO-NARKIEWICZ, *DI YIDN IN POYLN* (1901)

IN THE YEARS 1897–1901 both the crystallization of a
national program in the Jewish socialist camp and the Bund's growing influence brought about a concrete response in PPS circles.
While continuing its old tactic of publicly deriding the Bund's "Pan-
Russian" orientation as contrary to Polish aspirations and beneficial
to the tsarist regime, the PPS recognized that expanding the Polish
movement among Jewish workers required the formation of a party
press in Yiddish. The production and dissemination of a PPS
Yiddish press and its impact on the socialist movement among
Jewish workers is thus the focus of this chapter. In the period under
examination, the PPS produced several Yiddish-language leaflets
annually, two Yiddish organs, and an uninterrupted series of
Yiddish-language agitation brochures. Despite this considerable
output of party material in Yiddish, constituting the largest production of Yiddish literature of any non-Jewish political party, historians of the Jewish labor movement in eastern Europe have heretofore

never evaluated the PPS Yiddish press. And because historians of the Polish labor movement were not able to use Jewish sources, the PPS's party press in Yiddish has fallen through the cracks of historical research.[1]

### "Jewish Socialist Post from America to Poland": The First Attempts, 1896–97

The story of the PPS's Yiddish press goes back to the mid-1890s, when the Warsaw party leadership failed to procure Yiddish propaganda material for its Jewish Section leaders. In the wake of protest letters from PPS Jews warning of the need to offset the infusion of Yiddish literature from Vilna, the London-based Union of Polish Socialists Abroad (ZZSP) looked across the Atlantic, where a considerable number of Polish Jewish socialists had recently settled in New York. The idea, first entertained by the party's London secretary, Bolesław Jędrzejowski, was to enlist Polish Jewish socialists in New York to write party publications in Yiddish. With the additional goal of making contacts with Polish socialists in America, the ZZSP sent one of its members, Bolesław Miklaszewski, to America in 1896.

Miklaszewski made contacts with Jewish socialist émigrés soon after his arrival in New York in February 1896. In his unpublished memoirs Miklaszewski described how he met several prominent figures of the Jewish socialist community in New York, among them Abe Cahan, with whom Miklaszewski was very impressed.[2] His most consequential contact among the Jewish socialist émigré community, however, was with the Polish Jewish socialist Benjamin Feigenbaum (1860–1932), a native of Warsaw who had immigrated to New York in 1891.[3] In a letter to the ZZSP in London, Miklaszewski reported that "on Feigenbaum's initiative, the best and most active Jewish comrades from Warsaw have established themselves here, and have taken it upon themselves to gather funds for the creation of Yiddish literature to aid our cause." These Polish Jewish socialists from Warsaw, Miklaszewski continued, were solid backers of the PPS program and wanted to establish an American Jewish division of the party. "Let me remind you that [Feigenbaum's] group includes some of the most talented Yiddish writers."[4] Miklaszewski took a personal liking to Feigenbaum during his stay in the United States; he wrote, "it was easiest for me to come to an understanding with Feigenbaum, a native of Warsaw, with whom I entered into close relations."[5]

Piłsudski, who was in London at the time, expressed interest in Miklaszewski's contacts. Concerned with the political orientation of these Jewish socialists, however, Piłsudski cautioned Miklaszewski, commenting, "it must always be remembered that in regard to the Jewish question, Russia's influence on Jews . . . will always be in our way." To establish any formal relationship, Miklaszewski would have to determine that they did not have a "gravitational tendency to Russia," as did the Lithuanian Jews. "In any case," Piłsudski continued, "we must try, and even more so, because our work among Jews is terribly deficient. We lack the literature and the people."[6]

Assured that Feigenbaum's circle was composed of Jews from Congress Poland sympathetic to the PPS program, Piłsudski and the ZZSP formally announced in 1896 the formation of a new organization devoted to the production and dissemination of party literature in Yiddish. Under the direction of Feigenbaum, the organization was named "Jewish Socialist Post from America to Poland."[7]

One of the first tasks of the Jewish Socialist Post, which had about fifteen members, was to write an original socialist brochure for distribution in Congress Poland.[8] In the spring of 1896 Feigenbaum corresponded with Piłsudski regarding the brochure's contents. "In a rather impolite tone," Piłsudski wrote, "the Jews [*Żydy*] from America replied to my letter that only they will judge what is appropriate to publish for their comrades in Russian Poland."[9] Piłsudski nonetheless continued to correspond with Feigenbaum, urging him to use simple and clear prose. Taking advice from Jewish party members inside the empire, Piłsudski wrote to Feigenbaum, "many Yiddish publications [from abroad] are really written in German, only with Hebrew letters." In addition, they recommended that Feigenbaum avoid the use of abstract terms such as "despotism" and "absolutism," which tended to be the norm in such publications. Such a brochure would expand the PPS's influence among Jewish workers. Piłsudski then passed to Feigenbaum a letter he had received from Russian Poland. "'We are very pleased'," the letter read, "'that Jews [in New York] have come to an understanding with [the PPS]. We hope this will result in building a [pro-PPS] movement among Jewish workers [in Warsaw]. What we lack is not people, but a Yiddish-speaking intelligentsia and popular [Yiddish] publications sympathetic to our movement.'"[10]

In an effort to influence the content of Feigenbaum's brochure, Piłsudski sent Miklaszewski a set of guidelines and principles to be incorporated into the party's Yiddish publications. "Remind them," Piłsudski wrote, "of the necessity of having a set of unified *political* goals for the entire proletariat in Russian Poland [*w kraju*], among which is the necessity of spreading the idea of the independence of Poland among the Jewish proletariat." If the Jewish Socialist Post produced brochures that discussed only general principles of socialism, "then they would be no different from those publications put out by the Lithuanian Jews, and we would not be producing anything new." It was not that economic aims should be marginalized, he continued, but only that the publication project would be ineffective "without full solidarity with [our political program]."[11]

Feigenbaum completed the manuscript in July 1896, initially titled, *The Socialist Movement in Russia and the Local Jewish Population: A Propaganda Brochure Published for Distribution among the Jewish Workers in Russia in General, and in Russian Poland in Particular.*[12] For distribution in Russian Poland, however, Feigenbaum altered the title page to elude the Russian censors. Probably in response to Piłsudski's suggestions to use simple language, Feigenbaum came up with a folksy, neutral title. Thus, the ZZSP in London received initial copies of the brochure under the title *Paradise on Earth: A Wonderful True Story about How the Road to Paradise Was Found, and How We Can All Get There.*[13] Although written in the form of a story told through the character of a simple Jew, in compliance with the suggestions from Warsaw, it nonetheless fell short of explicitly presenting the PPS aim of national independence.

Feigenbaum's brochure attempted, in plain, colloquial Yiddish, to explain the basic concept of class struggle. In a not-too-subtle way, Feigenbaum's character promoted the idea that the Jewish worker had more in common with the Christian worker than with the Jewish bourgeoisie, and that the common interests of the working class of different groups required common action. "Only the workers in Russia and Poland alone," the main character said, "can achieve freedom, fairness, truth, equality, and brotherhood." What is more, socialism, the new Garden of Eden, had created "a new religion," and its most sacred holiday was the May Day celebration.

The brochure attempted to allay Jews' traditional distrust of the goyim. "To you, poor Jewish artisans, workers from Poland and Russia, your brother, the local Christian worker, is extending his brotherly hand and asks you to understand that he is rebelling not against you . . . but against the rich capitalist thieves, whether Polish, Russian, German, or Jewish. They want this for themselves and for you as well, Jewish workers, and they only ask: look to them as comrades in arms!" The Christian worker, the narrator concluded, did not consider race or religion, but only common economic interests. "O brothers! Come, let us be one with them! Let us help them bring forth salvation from hardship and suffering!"[14]

The first mention of the PPS came at the very conclusion of the thirty-one-page brochure, where it stated that everywhere socialist parties were arising, and in Poland that party was the PPS, an organization "of noble men." It urged the Jewish worker to join the party, which the tsarist government was trying to crush and banish. Although no explicit mention was made of Polish independence, it alluded to the PPS program when it argued that political freedom had to be achieved in order to liberate the Jewish worker, and that this freedom would come only when all "nations" dwelled in their own state, with the Jews becoming Poles and Russians of the Hebrew faith.

### The Second Initiative, 1897–1900:
### Maurycy Montlak and the Aid Alliance of New York

The Jewish Socialist Post from America to Poland failed to survive beyond a year, disbanding shortly after *Paradise on Earth* appeared in print.[15] Its only major publicist, Feigenbaum, was becoming increasingly involved in the New York Jewish socialist press. But unlike Feigenbaum, who had never been directly affiliated with the Polish socialist movement, the Post's organizer in 1897, the *polu-intelligent* Maurycy Montlak, had been active in the PPS for four years before he immigrated to America.[16] Thus, when the Post disbanded in 1897, Montlak informed London that the organization's members who "are in full agreement on the need for PPS literature in Yiddish" were intending to establish a new organization.[17]

Montlak succeeded in gathering a group of Polish Jewish émigrés sympathetic to the PPS in the fall of 1897. The new Aid Alliance, as it was called, was founded to provide PPS literature in Yiddish. "In the place of the 'Post,'" Montlak announced from New York, "we have founded a new 'Aid Alliance' [Związek Pomocy], which has stirred some interest in the PPS [here]."[18] The formation of a pro-PPS Jewish group in New York proved a difficult task, however. Because of the dearth of PPS Jews in New York in 1898, Montlak chose not to use the PPS in its name, calling the organization the "Aid Alliance of the Jewish Workers' Movement in the Russian Empire" (Hilf ferband fun der yidishe arbeyter bavegung in rusishen reykh).[19] In the first document to mention the Aid Alliance, Montlak referred to local opposition from Bundist sympathizers. "In particular," Montlak wrote in April 1898, "[Bundists] are attacking us with the claim that we are developing literature for Poland, and not for all of Russia."[20]

By July 1898 the Aid Alliance had forty-two members, including Benjamin Feigenbaum, and had drafted a set of principles.[21] The program, "Our Tasks," reflected Montlak's desire to broaden the organization to an empire-wide orientation. The Aid Alliance intended to aid "in the economic struggle of the Jewish workers under the Russian government." That aid would come in the form of agitation literature. The principle task was to produce socialist literature in Yiddish ("Jewish jargon") "for general agitation as well as for propaganda" in the Russian Empire. No reference was made to the PPS.[22]

The non-Polish character of the Aid Alliance changed in 1899 and 1900. Developments in New York were influenced by those in Congress Poland when Jewish members of the PPS fell victim to police crackdowns. First, Kazimierz Róg, the head of the party's Jewish Section in Warsaw, was arrested in late April 1898.[23] A second crackdown followed in the summer and fall of 1899 and led to the arrest of socialist circles in Warsaw and Białystok.[24] Of those arrested, some fifty belonged to the PPS, including many PPS Jews.[25] By 1900 all members of the original PPS Jewish circles from the early 1890s were arrested, not to mention Maks Horwitz in December 1899.

As a result, the geographical focus of PPS Jewish circles shifted from Russian Poland to New York and London in 1900. With the release of Jewish Section leaders in 1899 and 1900, two waves of emigration took place. The first wave of emigration included Saul

Degenfisz and Leyb Burgin, who arrived in New York in September 1899.[26] A second wave brought a significant core of Jewish PPS leaders to London in 1899 and 1900, including such figures as David Perlmutter, Kadish Altglas, I. Kornblit, and Mendel Rubinstein, all of whom were freed from the Warsaw Citadel in September 1900.[27] With the wave of emigrants, the London PPS division formed a Jewish Section. In November 1900 thirty-two PPS Jews signed a "Mandate of Jewish Socialists in London," which pledged full support for the PPS program.[28] According to Leon Wasilewski, a PPS leader in London at the time, the PPS Jews newly arrived in London were "fanatically bound" to the party's independence program.[29] Even though the PPS Jews in London were native Yiddish speakers, Wasilewski described them interestingly as "assimilated, if not always by language, then at least politically."[30]

With the arrival of Degenfisz and Burgin in New York in the fall of 1899, Montlak reconstituted the Aid Alliance into an official PPS branch. The Aid Alliance of the Jewish Workers' Movement in the Russian Empire now became the Aid Alliance of the Polish Socialist Party (Związek Pomocy PPS) in July 1900.[31] The new statute required each member to recognize the PPS program and act under its banner. "We, Polish émigrés living in New York, and organized in the Alliance," the statute stated, "stand by the goal of morally and materially aiding the PPS in the Russian partition, to propagate its program and literature among Jews and Christians, to inform workers in America about important events in our country [*w Kraju ojczystym*] . . . and to send socialist literature printed in America that will be of service for agitation and propaganda in Russian Poland [*w Kraju*]."[32] The PPS Aid Alliance would play a significant role in providing Jewish writers and propagandists for the PPS Yiddish press.

### *Der arbeyter:* The London Period, 1898–1901

Not long after the Jewish Socialist Post from America to Poland formed in New York, the PPS's first Yiddish organ appeared in December 1898. Printed in London, the new organ—*Der arbeyter*—had a circulation of fifteen hundred copies for distribution in Congress Poland and was edited by Maks Horwitz (1877–1937), a member of the PPS since 1896 and the only Jewish intellectual party member at the time able to edit a Yiddish-language organ.[33] According to Leon Gottlieb (1878–1947), who worked as Yiddish editor and translator for the PPS beginning in 1901, he himself smuggled out of the empire the material for *Der arbeyter,* which included the lead editorial, city chronicles, and factory reports.[34] The appearance of *Der arbeyter* marked a critical step in the PPS's struggle for the allegiance of the Jewish working class in Russian Poland. As tables 6.1 and 6.2 show, while the PPS produced the largest socialist press in the Pale and Congress Poland, it nonetheless lagged far behind the Bund with regard to Yiddish publications.

The first issue led off with an inaugural note, in Yiddish and Polish, by the central committee. The open letter called for the elimination of barriers between Jewish and Christian workers, "children from one land," while emphasizing the need for a common struggle for the liberation of the working class.[35] Following the open letter, *Der arbeyter*'s eighteen-page inaugural issue consisted of a lengthy programmatic piece, correspondences from factories in Warsaw, Białystok, and Grodno, and a piece on the Zionist movement. Conspicuously absent was any mention of the Bund. Mendel Rubinstein, a member of the first circle of PPS Jews in the early 1890s, composed the lead editorial, "The Tsarist Regime and the Worker."[36] Rubinstein would later play a major role in the party's Yiddish-language publications as editor of *Di proletarishe velt* (1902–3) and *Der arbeyter* (1903–5).

In "The Tsarist Regime and the Worker," Rubinstein maintained that absolutism was incompatible with the demands and needs of the working classes and that Jewish workers should sympathize with the Polish cause. While the attainment of civil rights had to be every worker's aim, the oppression of one nation against another also had to end. Poland, he wrote, had been robbed and looted for a century "by a government that strives to destroy the Polish nation and make Poland one with the Russian Empire." The imposition of Russian as the language of administration and education on Polish lands, he contended, was retarding the process of Jewish integration into Polish society. The government was thus deliberately Russifying Jews as part of their war against the Polish nation and culture. Thus, he concluded, civil and national liberation could only be attained by the breakup of the empire into its "natural parts," and the Jewish worker was obligated to combat the politics of

TABLE 6.1

**The Bund and the PPS: Party Organs in Yiddish, 1896–1901**

| Bund | Appearance of First Issue | Issues by 1901 | Polish Socialist | Appearance of First Issue Party | Issues by 1901 |
|---|---|---|---|---|---|
| *Der yidisher arbeyter* (Geneva) | 1896 | 13 | *Der arbeyter* (London) | 1898 | 4 |
| *Di arbeyter shtimme* (Vilna) | 1897 | 25 | | | |
| *Der veker* (Vilna, Warsaw) | 1898 | 10 | | | |
| *Der varshaver arbeyter* (Warsaw) | 1899 | 9 | | | |
| *Der bialostoker arbeyter* (Bialystok) | 1899 | 6 | | | |
| *Der minsker arbeyter* (Minsk) | 1900 | 4 | | | |
| *Der klasenkamf* (Warsaw?) | 1900 | 5 | | | |
| *Der kamf* (Gomel) | 1900 | 3 | | | |
| Total | | 75 | | | 4 |

*Source*: "Żargonowe wydawnictwa 'Bunda," *Di arbeyter shtimme (Głos Robotniczy)*, no. 25 (Dec. 1901): 22; Ch. Kazdan, "Der bundishe umlegale prese un literatur," in Hertz, Aronson, and Dubnow-Erlich, *Di geshikhte fun bund,* 1:257–68; Kormanowa, *Materiały do bibliografii druków socjalistycznych na ziemach polskich w latach 1866–1918* (Warsaw, 1949).

Russification through endorsing the PPS program. "We, Jewish workers in Poland," Rubinstein wrote, "undoubtedly share the same worker interests and needs as our Christian brothers in the same land. Their future is also our future, their aspirations, ours: an independent Polish Republic is therefore our political program, for it is the only form of government that will give us the needed political rights for our class struggle."[37]

Rubinstein concluded with a set of five principles, which, taken together, constituted the ideological and tactical underpinnings of the PPS Jewish program. The Jewish worker, he wrote, had to realize the following principles: (1) the tsarist system was incompatible

TABLE 6.2
### The Socialist Press in Russian Poland, 1892–1901

| Party | Appearance of First Issue | Number of Party Organs by 1901 | Total Number of Issues Appearing through 1901 |
|---|---|---|---|
| PPS | 1892 | 10 | 187 |
| Bund | 1896 | 8 | 75 |
| SDKPiL | 1893 | 5 | 33 |
| PPS Proletariat | 1901 | 1 | 4 |

*Source*: "Żargonowe wydawnictwa 'Bunda," *Di arbeyter shtimme (Głos Robotniczy)*, no. 25 (Dec. 1901): 22; Z. Kormanowa, *Materiały do bibliografii druków socjalistycznych na ziemach polskich w latach 1866–1918* (Warsaw, 1949).

with workers' demands; (2) autocracy had to be abolished: (3) a constitutional solution was "impossible" in Russia because of the uneven development of different areas; (4) the task of the "conscious proletariat" was to struggle for the breakup of Russia: and finally, (5) the Jewish and the Polish working class had to struggle hand in hand "for one independent democratic republic in Poland."[38] "The Tsarist Regime and the Worker" constituted the first attempt to link the PPS program with Jewish interests. Rather than lash out at the Jewish socialist intelligentsia of the Bund, *Der arbeyter* tried to sell the PPS program to the Jewish worker.

Circumstances beyond the party's control thwarted attempts to regularly produce *Der arbeyter*. In 1899 Horwitz was arrested in Warsaw, which eliminated the only PPS intellectual who was capable of editing a Yiddish organ at the time. In an extraordinary sign of the importance the party attached to its Yiddish press, Leon Wasilewski, a descendant of the Polish *szlachta*, learned the Jewish vernacular in order to continue production of *Der arbeyter*.

Wasilewski produced the second issue of *Der arbeyter* with the help of Teresa Reznikowska-Perlowa and Leon Gottlieb. Reznikowska-Perlowa (1871–1939) came from a lower middle-class Lithuanian Jewish family in Slonim and had become active in socialist circles in Warsaw. Following her arrest in 1890 for participation in a May Day rally in Warsaw (where she first met Feliks Perl), she went abroad to Zurich and then to Paris, where she became active in the ZZSP as well as among Russian socialists. In 1900 Reznikowska settled in Paris and worked as a typesetter for

פּראָלעטאַריער אַלער לענדער פֿעראײניגט אײך!

# אַרבּײטער

אָרגאַן פֿון דער פּוילישער סאָציאַליסטישער פּאַרטײ.

## די באַדײטונג פֿון דער פּוילישער סאָציאַליסטישער פּאַרטײ צו דער יודישער פֿראַגע.

*Cover of* Der arbeyter, *Yiddish organ of the Polish Socialist Party, 1905 (Sejm Library, Warsaw)* the PPS organs *Przedświt* and *Światło* (The beacon). During this time Feliks Perl moved to London as well. Shortly after, they were married.[39] Perlowa's arrival in London came just at the time a Yiddish speaker was sorely needed. Wasilewski thus recruited Perlowa to assist him in preparing materials for their Yiddish organ.

Leon Gottlieb played a more substantial role in producing the second issue of *Der arbeyter*. Gottlieb, who wrote and corresponded under the pseudonym Jacob Hartman, was born in Grodzisk, west of Warsaw, to a traditional Jewish family. His grandfather was the town's rabbi. Gottlieb received a traditional education in the Grodzisk heder and then studied in different yeshivot in Łódź, Skierniewice, and Radom. But at age seventeen, Gottlieb came under the influence of secular currents and moved to Warsaw, where he entered the artisan school for young Jews in the Nalewki district.[40] It will be recalled from chapter 3 that the artisan school in Nalewki had produced Jewish recruits for the PPS in 1893. It was in the artisan school that Gottlieb learned Polish and became a socialist.[41] He joined the PPS in 1897 and was arrested the following year for participation in a May Day rally in Warsaw. After spending six weeks in the Pawiak Prison in Warsaw, Gottlieb worked for the PPS in Łódź, where he agitated among Jewish workers and became a proponent of Polonization. In 1900 he went abroad and arrived in London in September.[42] The fact that Gottlieb settled in London in the beginning of the fall was of great consequence for the party's Yiddish press. Gottlieb was bilingual with some experience in Yiddish writing and printing. As the typesetter, Gottlieb helped produce a Yiddish newspaper superior to that of his predecessor, Horwitz.[43]

While Gottlieb and Perlowa improved the language and style of *Der arbeyter*, the content remained the same. The feature article, written by Feliks Perl and translated from the Polish by Gottlieb, discussed the Russian government's Jewish policies.[44] "The Politics of the Russian Government regarding the Jews" was less about the Jews than about the nationalities question in the Russian Empire. Perl began by proclaiming that the greatest obstacle to the liberation of the working class was autocratic Russia, a regime that promoted interethnic strife between the nationalities in order to prevent unifying alliances. "The murderous Russian government is the greatest and most destructive anti-Semite," stated *Der arbeyter*, "so much so that Haman, may he rest in peace, was altogether a saint in comparison."[45] The tsarist regime, *Der arbeyter* continued, used its power to inculcate hatred for Jews in other people, inciting the Poles, Lithuanians, and Russians. Moreover, the Russian government desired the Jews "to always be sunk in the swamp of superstition and darkness" and did not intend to grant them civil rights.

But the government's anti-Jewish politics should not be viewed in isolation. Rather, the Jewish question had to be seen within the broader context of the regime's nationalities policies in general and the Russo-Polish conflict in particular. One of the greatest fears of the government, he wrote, was that the Jewish and Christian workers would combine into one party—the Polish Socialist Party. "The despotic government wants the Jews to remain alien from everything . . . Polish—to all that concerns Polish land—[to remain] a people apart [without] common aims with the Poles."[46] The conscious effort of the government to undermine Polish-Jewish solidarity was reflected in the government's Russification program, *Der arbeyter* argued. Without Jewish acquaintance with the Polish language and culture, alliances would be difficult to establish.

The Russian government restricted not only Jewish access to higher education but the movement of Jews outside the boundaries of the Pale as well. Government policy thus demonstrated, *Der arbeyter* maintained, that the tsarist regime sought to retard Jewish integration and had no intention of making Jews citizens. By way of comparison, the last king of sovereign Poland, Stanisław August-Poniatowski, with support from Polish society, instituted reforms to modernize the Jewish population, "to civilize them," and to transform them into full citizens of the country. But under Russian rule the tsars propped up a fence of laws around the Jewish population that resulted in the persistence of Jewish alienation from Polish society. While avoiding mention of the Bund, *Der arbeyter* castigated Zionists for a political program that sought to "separate the Jews, severing them from the country's inhabitants." Thus, the only way to achieve liberation from tsarist despotic rule was to create an antitsarist front with the Poles. "In line with the Polish Socialist Party," the author maintained, "we, Polish Jews, must fight for liberty, independence, and good fortune for the country in which we were born and in which we suffer from the capitalist yoke and the tsarist regime together with our brotherly Christian workers. . . . Only in an independent Polish Republic will we obtain living conditions under which we will not be oppressed and will have such political arrangements in which the working classes living in Poland [will be able to realize] . . . the socialist ideal. In this lies the only help, the only future for us, Polish Jews!"[47]

The final pages of issue 2 of *Der arbeyter* contained a chronicle of PPS activities in Warsaw. The content of the chronicle is much less important than what the language reveals about the party's conception of Jewish workers. The writer proclaimed that the party had to spread working-class consciousness among the masses. "When all the Polish working people, *without regard to faith*, will understand their interests and enter into the ranks of the Polish Socialist Party," the author wrote, "we will [create] a tumult that will cleanse from the earth tsarist rule over Poland."[48] The notion that the Polish working class consisted of peoples of different religions clearly suggested the Jewish worker was perceived as a part of the *Polish* working class and, by extension, of the Polish nation.

While the appearance of *Der arbeyter* was a mark of significant progress, the ZZSP received several critical responses from Jewish readers. In January 1901 Henoch Kowalski, a member of the PPS division in Karlsruhe, outlined his critique of *Der arbeyter* in a letter to London. Kowalski expressed his disappointment at the absence of a polemic with the Bund and complained that too much space was occupied with tedious factory reports, and that the Yiddish organ lacked articles of a theoretical nature. It was odd, Kowalski commented, that the PPS printed articles on the Bund in *Przedświt* and *Robotnik*, which the Jewish worker did not read, and yet the Bund was absent in the pages of its Yiddish-language organ, written for Jews.[49]

The ZZSP secretary, Jędrzejowski, justified the editorial policy. Above all, *Der arbeyter* addressed the day-to-day concerns of the masses: exploitation in the factories and life in workshops. For such readership, he contended, articles of a theoretical and propaganda nature were unnecessary.[50] Kowalski also suggested that in addition to *Der arbeyter,* the London branch print the PPS cultural-intellectual organ, *Światło,* in Yiddish.[51] Jędrzejowski's response revealed a perception of the Yiddish-speaking worker as insular and backward and the assumption that the Polish Jewish worker interested in worldly matters would have already assimilated to

Polish culture. "We will not print *Światło* in Yiddish," Jędrzejowski replied, "because, for the most part, those Jewish workers who would make use of it can already read Polish."[52]

Jędrzejowski also defended the decision to refrain from direct references to the Bund. Just as the London leadership did not regard articles of a theoretical nature essential for *Der arbeyter*, Jędrzejowski replied, it had agreed that explicit mention of the Bund would be counterproductive. The Jewish masses had until then not been aware of the PPS-Bund conflict, he argued, nor was it necessary for them to know. "It is enough [to propagate that] the Jewish worker should struggle arm in arm with Christians," Jędrzejowski argued, "and to inculcate in them love for the Polish Socialist Party." The fact that *Przedświt* and *Robotnik* ran polemical articles on the Bund was a different matter, he insisted, because potential recruits for the Bund did not read the party's main organs. "*Przedświt* is not read by people whom the Bund could recruit, nor do we hope to recruit a single member of the Bund through articles in *Przedświt*. Rather," he wrote, "[our articles] are only intended to inform our . . . comrades of the Bund's stupidity and dirty trickery."[53]

Jędrzejowski nonetheless acknowledged the party's shortcomings regarding Yiddish literature and so-called Jewish work. Because the language barrier would continue to separate the Polish and the Jewish worker, winning over the Jews to the PPS program would have to be accomplished before the eventual Polonization of the Jewish masses. "With time," he wrote, "we will come to see a commonality of ideals, and later, perhaps, in language as well." For now, "the sense of belonging to one organizational whole" was the main link between the Jewish and the Polish worker.[54]

Meanwhile, the Polish Socialist Party Aid Alliance in New York met to critique *Der arbeyter*. Montlak reported the results of the meeting in a letter to London. He began by voicing concern over the party's lack of "zhargonists" in London to oversee a Yiddish press. This was reflected, Montlak maintained, in *Der arbeyter*'s "poor quality" of style. Such an evaluation was the consensus "of *all of the oldest* PPS members who have firsthand knowledge of the Jewish movement in Russian Poland . . . and are now members of the 'Aid Alliance of the PPS,' New York branch."[55]

The Aid Alliance held that the first two issues had failed to link the reader to the wider PPS movement by confining the contents to the movement among Jewish workers. What was needed, Montlak implied, was a middle ground between *Robotnik* and a wholly Jewish-centered organ. First, each issue should contain articles of a social-scientific and theoretical nature, particularly given the fact that the PPS had no Yiddish-language brochures for distribution. Second, the correspondences from factories should consist of reports from Jews *and* Christians but should not occupy the bulk of the issue. Exclusively Jewish factory reports gave the impression that the movement only consisted of Jewish workers. The reports were to provide an example to the politically inactive worker of the need to enter into a struggle with his fellow Christian workers. Moreover, the chronicles should include a section on events in the Prussian and Austrian partitions, as well as on international socialism abroad. Montlak also suggested that *Der arbeyter* print excerpts from Yiddish fiction writers. Lastly, Montlak was unequivocal in his opinion that *Der arbeyter* had to respond to the Bund's position vis-à-vis the PPS platform.[56] Jędrzejowski replied straightforwardly that "neither I nor any others have changed our view of the contents [of *Der arbeyter*]."[57]

In the months following Montlak's letter, the situation in London improved with the arrival of Dr. Feliks Sachs (1869–1935) in 1901. A native Yiddish-speaker who had taken a particular interest in disseminating the PPS program among Jewish workers, Sachs was born and raised in Warsaw to a lower middle-class Jewish family. After graduating from the Fifth Gymnasium in 1888, Sachs entered the School of Law at Warsaw University and the following year switched to medicine. Sachs became involved in a radical student group during his studies and by the beginning of the 1890s became a self-defined socialist. In 1895 he completed his studies, became a doctor of medicine, and began work in a Warsaw hospital. He joined the PPS in 1898 and became a member of the party's Warsaw Workers' Committee. In 1899 Sachs settled in Vilna, where he joined the editorial staff of *Robotnik* alongside Piłsudski. Shortly after, *Robotnik*, along with the editorial board, moved to Łódź, where in February 1900 the entire editorial staff and illegal printing press was discovered. After being placed under arrest, Sachs was released in May and returned to Warsaw, where he was coopted into the party's central committee.[58]

In February 1901 Sachs left Russia for London, where he became active in the party's Yiddish press. Sachs was the first PPS member in London who spoke and wrote Yiddish well and had previous editorial experience. With his particular interest in attracting Jews to the party, Sachs energetically joined the editorial staff of *Der arbeyter*. As Wasilewski recounted, with Sachs's arrival in London, the problem of Yiddish publications began to proceed on a normal path.[59] In a separate letter to Montlak, Wasilewski optimistically reported that the London center no longer lacked "zhargonists" (Gottlieb and Perlowa) and Yiddish-speaking intellectuals (Sachs).[60]

With Sachs in London, the PPS was able to produce two issues of *Der arbeyter* in 1901. The contents of issue 3 of *Der arbeyter*, printed in April 1901, revealed a few key changes. The eight-page issue contained a lead article on May Day and a piece on the history of May Day in Congress Poland. In line with suggestions from the Aid Alliance, chronicles of labor activities in the Austrian and Prussian partitions, as well as a theoretical piece, "European Socialists on the Polish Question," followed the two lead articles. The lead article spoke of the need for "international solidarity" among the working classes, referring to that between the working classes of different countries. It called upon workers to "unify into one family, in one brotherly union" that would fight the common enemy: the Russian government and capitalism. While workers were demonstrating in western Europe, Polish Jews should remember how great was the suffering "of the workers in Poland," who were "oppressed by a savage Russian tyrant."[61] The article concluded with the slogan "Long Live a Workers' Poland!"

With the abundance of Jewish PPS members now in London, Wasilewski was able to print a fourth issue of *Der arbeyter*, this time with the direct involvement of Feliks Sachs. Appearing in August 1901, this issue followed the same pattern as the previous one, although with more factory and workshop reports. The lead article contained the same message as the first three issues, urging solidarity between Jewish and Christian workers for the aim of separating "Poland" from Russia and forming a democratic republic.

In the lead article, "What the Jewish Worker in Poland Ought to Do," the author began by explaining the unique predicament of Polish socialists. In other countries, socialists fought in conditions of national freedom, that is, against their own governments. But in Polish lands, socialists fought also against foreign rule. "One thus finds in the program of Polish socialists a demand that is not found in other socialist parties: that for the independence of Poland. . . . That is to say, an independent democratic republic in which working people would govern." To achieve this goal, "the Polish Socialist Party endeavors to enlighten the working masses in Poland." Alluding to the Polish romantic-insurrectionary tradition, the author declared that "[w]hen the working masses become conscious and all the conditions exist for a victorious revolution, we will at last . . . oust the tsarist government from our country."[62]

An analysis of terms and definitions in *Der arbeyter* is revealing. *Der arbeyter* consciously used the terms "Jewish" and "Christian" to denote members of ethnic—not national—groups. To minimize the link between Catholic and Polish, "Poland" as both noun and adjective was used in a territorial and ideological sense, while the Jewish and the Catholic workers were strictly referred to as two religious parts of one whole—*one* working class "in Poland" (of course, the boundaries of this "Poland" were left undefined). Thus the frequent call in leaflets and May Day proclamations for "international solidarity" of the "working masses of every country" was an attempt to inculcate the Jewish worker with the idea that Jewish and "Christian" workers "in Poland" were part of a single working class.

An analysis of the first four issues of *Der arbeyter* reveals that PPS Jewish leaders had a very different conception of nationality than did the Bund. The PPS view, propagated as late as August 1901, ran directly counter to the Bund's bold assertion, made earlier that year, that the Jews were a nationality separate and distinct from the peoples among whom they lived. Jewish activists in the PPS, however, argued that the Bund's organizational separateness ran counter to the socialist agenda on Polish lands. Mojżesz Kaufman (1878–1936), who joined the PPS in 1899, reflected on the organization's Jewish activities in the late 1890s. He recalled that in the process of organizing a Jewish section, its leading activists fought against two foes within the Jewish community : religious "fanaticism," and the idea of "national separateness," as represented by the Bund and Zionism.[63] "I convinced myself," Kaufman wrote, "that a socialist movement has no place for a separate nationalist party. The working class in each country, without national differences, must create one unbroken whole."[64]

The fourth issue of *Der arbeyter* addressed precisely the issue of the Bund's organizational separateness, although without mentioning it by name. "If the Jewish worker in Poland fights separately," *Der arbeyter* warned, "he will not be able to achieve any significant results." The Jewish worker was a part of the general factory work force in Warsaw, Łódź, and Białystok, and without organizational and program unity, the factory owner would exploit divisions and undermine workers' demands. The writer concluded with the most succinct argument yet put forth against the Bund: "The historic fate of our country has tightly bound the Jewish proletariat with the Polish worker. Calamities that befall the Polish worker befall us, and the Jewish worker will benefit from the triumph of the Polish proletariat. The tighter the unity between the Jewish and the Christian worker, the faster and nearer victory will come. The Jewish worker who struggles under the banner of the Polish Socialist Party understands this." *Der arbeyter* concluded: "But he who declares that the Jewish worker should not unify with his Christian brother—who says that the Jewish worker has separate interests—does great harm to the proletariat. Whoever utters the notion that the Jewish worker should separate himself from Christians and fight alone is the worst enemy of socialism, [and serves only] the bourgeoisie and the tsarist government."[65]

*Der arbeyter* also provided valuable information about the party's influence on Jewish workers in the period 1898–1901. Although we do not have membership figures for this period, the factory/workshop reports and the distribution of PPS Yiddish circulars suggest that the unofficial Jewish Section was strongest in Warsaw and Białystok, while the local Jewish divisions in Łódź and Grodno were in their beginning stages.[66] Jews were first organized into PPS circles in Grodno in the fall of 1898, when some twenty Jewish workers met to discuss the formation of the Bund and came out strongly opposed to a Jewish organization outside the PPS. By 1899 the Grodno division included fifty to sixty Jewish members, and by 1901 the Grodno organization of the PPS was almost exclusively composed of Jews.[67] One of the main tasks of the PPS division was to offer Polish-language courses for Jewish workers, although few attended.[68]

## The Yiddish Brochure

In 1900 the Bund began to mock the PPS for its lack of Yiddish literature. "In a period of five years," John Mill wrote, "the PPS has not published a single Yiddish brochure," demonstrating the PPS's "indifference" to Jewish workers.[69] But in the same year, the London and the New York branch of the PPS began a series of correspondences regarding possible translations of relevant socialist works into Yiddish. By December the two branches agreed on eight titles as well as plans for reprinting original Yiddish works.[70] The planning paid off, as four Yiddish propaganda brochures appeared in 1901.[71] At the same time the PPS's Aid Alliance in New York experienced an increase in membership and was "becoming more popular among the Jewish masses" according to its new secretary, H. Bassel.[72] During the next four years, the PPS would print a total of twenty-four Yiddish brochures, mostly translations from the Polish, but some original Yiddish works.

Feigenbaum's brochure had originally appeared in 1891 and was one of many popular works he published during his London peri-

TABLE 6.3

**The Bund and the PPS:
Propaganda Brochures in Yiddish, 1896–1905**

| Bund | Translated from Russian/Polish/German | Original Yiddish Publication | Polish Socialist Party | Translated from Polish | Original Yiddish publication |
|---|---|---|---|---|---|
| 1897–1900 | 15 | 7 | 1896 | | 1 |
| | | | 1901 | 3 | 1 |
| 1901–4 | 36 | 15 | 1902 | 5 | |
| | | | 1903 | 5 | 1 |
| | | | 1904 | 4 | 2 |
| | | | 1905 | 1 | 1 |
| | 51 | 22 | | 18 | 6 |
| Total Yiddish Brochures | 73 | | | 24 | |

*Source*: Holdings of PPS Yiddish brochures in the Sejm Library (Warsaw), Yivo Library, and the Bund Archive (New York); *Głos Bundu* (Geneva), no. 1 (May 1904), 15–16; Ch. Kazdan, "Der bundishe umlegale prese un literatur," in Hertz, Aronson, and Dubnow-Erlich, *Di geshikhte fun bund*, 1:257–68.

od (1888–91).[73] The PPS's foreign committee first proposed printing a second edition of Feigenbaum's brochure in January 1901. In a letter posted to New York, Jędrzejowski asked the party's Aid Alliance to request permission from Feigenbaum to publish a second edition. It also wanted to commission Feigenbaum to translate Edward Abramowski's 1892 brochure, *Sprawa Robotnicza*.[74]

In March 1901 the foreign committee was informed that Feigenbaum had agreed to both requests. Jędrzejowski then posted a letter to Feigenbaum expressing the foreign committee's gratitude. "We understand from comrade Bruzel that you do not object to our reprint of your pamphlet, *Vi kumt a yid tsu sotyialismus?*, and we are very much obliged to you," Jędrzejowski wrote in English. "Although the large majority of our committee does not read Yiddish, still all of us are able to understand it when spoken or read out loud. Your pamphlet was read to us, and we are sure it will be very useful in our movement."[75] In a separate letter we learn that Leon Gottlieb read Feigenbaum's brochure out loud in the presence of the PPS's foreign committee, which afterward unanimously voted in favor of its publication.[76] Jędrzejowski also organized a meeting between Gottlieb and Feigenbaum. "We profit by this opportunity to introduce to you comrade Hartman, who shall be glad to speak with you about our projects concerning Yiddish socialist literature."[77] Shortly after, on 4 May, Gottlieb arrived in New York.[78]

The PPS edition of *Vi kumt a yid tsu sotsyialismus?* appeared in May 1901 with a print run of three thousand copies for transport to Russian Poland.[79] Under the title appeared a passage from the bible in Hebrew, perfectly applicable as a socialist slogan: "You shall eat your fill of bread and dwell securely in your land (Lev. 26:5)." This passage gave an indication of what was to come: a popular socialist agitation brochure adapted to the Jewish worker, sprinkled with quotations from traditional Jewish texts.

*Vi kumt a yid tsu sotsyialismus?* maintained that a deep connection existed between Judaism and socialism. "Yes, brothers, socialism is redemption for us, the Jews. Socialism will rescue all the unfortunate people, Jews as well, and give them equal rights." Socialism's victory, he continued, would spell the only effective defeat of the forces of anti-Semitism. "I alone have heard many good [men] declare that they were Jew haters before they became socialists." Socialism, he maintained, was emancipating non-Jews from prejudice, as it enlightened its followers to the fact that "it was not the Jew who was the bloodsucker, but the capitalist, whether a Jew or a Gentile, and that the Jewish poor are his brothers [as well]." Rejecting Zionism as utopian, Feigenbaum reformulated the idea of *goles* (exile) as a state of persecution, not dispersion from Palestine. The triumph of socialism would therefore liberate the Jew from his greatest curse—exile: "Socialist belief will save the Jew from *goles*." He urged Jews to rid themselves of the "sorrowful illusion" of associating *goles* with the exile from Palestine.[80]

Starting with Feigenbaum's thirty-one-page work, all PPS Yiddish brochures included a Yiddish translation of the "Program of the Polish Socialist Party." The Yiddish version of the program differed in subtle, but significant, ways from the original. In a paragraph introducing the party program, the Yiddish version stated that "the Polish Socialist Party, as a political organization of the working class *in Poland* that fights for liberation from the capitalist yoke, strives for the overthrow of today's political slavery and the rule of the proletariat. The party's aim is an independent Polish People's Republic based on the following principles" (emphasis mine). In contrast, the original Polish text stated the following: "[T]he Polish Socialist Party, as the political organization of the *Polish* working class, struggling for liberation from the yoke of capitalism, strives above all to overthrow the present political slavery and to obtain power for the proletariat. In this striving, its aim is: An independent Democratic Republic."[81]

The party carefully adapted the program to the Jewish and the Polish reader, respectively. To Jewish readers, the program was different in two ways. First, instead of demanding "an independent democratic republic," as in the original Polish text, the Yiddish translation called for "an independent Polish People's Republic."[82] This was consistent with the way national demands were framed in the party's Yiddish-language leaflets, which were intended to deflect accusations of chauvinism by couching demands in socialist terminology. Second, while the original Polish addressed its program to the "Polish working class," the Yiddish text, in an attempt to reformulate the concept of "Polish" from ethnic to territorial, used the inclusive phrase "the working class in Poland."

The year 1901 also saw the appearance of *Di yidn in poyln*, a translation of Witold Jodko-Narkiewicz's article bearing the same title.[83]

By comparing the two versions, we discover that the Yiddish translation was adapted to the Jewish readership. First, the Yiddish brochure included a publisher's forward, which informed the reader that the purpose of distributing Jodko-Narkiewicz's brochure was "to acquaint the Jewish worker with important historical facts from the life of Jews in Poland, facts that shed light on the history of Jewish-Christian relations, and on the causes of Jewish separateness." Such a brochure would provide insight into contemporary times, when "the union of the Jewish and Christian working peoples has become daily a burning issue on which the whole future of the Jewish working people depends."[84]

Jodko-Narkiewicz had been an important figure in the Polish socialist movement. A participant of the Paris congress of 1892, he was editor-in-chief of *Przedświt,* the organ of the PPS abroad, between 1893 and 1898 and became a leading figure in the party's London branch.[85] Born and raised in a well-to-do Polish noble family from Lithuania, he graduated from the gymnasium in Warsaw and in 1885 entered the School of Medicine at Warsaw University.[86] Known by his contemporaries as well read and highly educated, Jodko-Narkiewicz knew all the major European languages and was politically astute and a talented publicist.[87]

Jodko-Narkiewicz began his brochure with a survey of Polish-Jewish relations in Old Poland. Despite their one-thousand-year-long presence on Polish soil, Jodko-Narkiewicz wrote, the vast majority of Jews were entirely foreign to the Poles in terms of religion, language, and customs. The persistence of Jewish separateness had far-reaching implications for contemporary Polish politics. It was thus no surprise that all political parties were concerned with the "age-old question" of Jewish separateness. Jodko-Narkiewicz suggested two main causes of Jewish isolation: the clergy and the Jewish rabbinate. The former, he wrote, preached hatred of the Jews through the persistent charge of deicide. The spread of anti-Semitic sermons in the church, he noted, clearly played a role in separating Christians from Jews. The rabbinate, however, was even more culpable; Jewish religious authorities did everything to separate Jews and were still attempting to lock the ghetto walls from the inside, as they had been doing for centuries. The rabbinate even preferred a state of anti-Semitic persecution to a democratic system, for fear that equality would lead to assimilation, he argued.[88]

It was the tradition of tolerance in medieval Poland that allowed for such a high proportion of European Jews to settle there, a tradition that had extended to Germans, Lithuanians, Czechs, Tartars, and Armenians as well. Through autonomous institutions, the Jews were able to remain separated from the Christian population. With the spread of the Enlightenment to Poland in the last third of the eighteenth century, however, and particularly under Stanisław August-Poniatowski (1764–95), a reform movement called for the modernization of Polish state and society, including a plan for Jewish integration. Although there were disagreements among reformers, Jodko-Narkiewicz continued, Jewish Maskilim and Catholics alike agreed that limiting the authority of the Kahal (or abolishing it altogether) and establishing state schools for Jews (in which mastery of Polish would be compulsory) was essential. The reform projects came to an abrupt halt, however, with the partitions of Poland.

One success of that period, Jodko-Narkiewicz argued, was the appearance of Jews who fought and died for the Polish cause. The most notable Jewish hero of the Kościuszko rising, Jodko-Narkiewicz noted, was Berek Joselewicz, a Polish Jew who had formed a Jewish militia to support Kościuszko's rising. Although Kościuszko failed, Joselewicz, Jodko-Narkiewicz observed, also fought with Napoleon for the Duchy of Warsaw, for which he paid with his life in 1809.

But the vast majority of Jews were still isolated and poor, despite the beginnings of Jewish integration. "Common sense says," Jodko-Narkiewicz maintained, "that Jews can escape from their wretched situation only by working with Christians." And it was the socialists who could provide the most happiness to the greatest amount of people. Given that Zionism was an undesirable and unrealistic movement, the Jewish worker had no other alternative than to embrace a socialist movement uniting the Jewish and the Christian working class; both were exploited and both lived in wretched conditions. To alleviate the miserable conditions of the Jewish worker, it was necessary to create a united front with common aims. "That is why," Jodko-Narkiewicz wrote, "Jewish workers also have to recognize the aims of Polish workers as their own and accept the program of the Polish Socialist Party." It was in the Jews' collective interest, then, to fight for the separation of Poland: "Jewish workers

should accept the goal of an independent Polish democratic republic . . . not only because Poles have raised this demand, but because
it answers to the best interests of the Jewish working masses. We do
not need to write at length on the fact that we can bring about true
freedom only after winning our independence. Only then can the
Jewish proletariat secure the conditions of full development."[89]

The first Yiddish brochure to appear in 1902 was a translation of
Edward Abramowski's 1892 brochure, *Sprawa Robotnicza* (The labor
question).[90] Abramowski had been present at the Paris Congress of
Polish Socialists in 1892. *Sprawa Robotnicza* presented the future PPS
program, emphasizing that "political freedom" and "national independence" were two integral parts of the Polish socialist program.
Thus, a Polish socialist party could not support a general empire-
wide constitution: such a system would require the use of Russian
in administration, schools, and the courts. "It is therefore evident,"
Abramowski maintained, "that if we are to bring about such freedom and political rights . . . then *we must create a constitution for
Poland*, or, to put in another way, *we must overthrow the tsarist government together with Russian workers and expel it once and for all from
our country—to form an independent Poland*."[91]

In the Yiddish version the PPS made several changes. Whereas
the original text was addressed to Poles, the Yiddish translation
purged the text of all references to "Polish workers," the "Polish
language," and the "Polish nation." For example, a paragraph in the
original that began "We, *Polish workers*, have neither freedom nor
political rights" was changed in the Yiddish version to "We, *workers
in Poland*, have neither."[92] Like other PPS Yiddish materials,
Abramowski's Yiddish brochure distinguished between the Jewish
and the Christian "working peoples" (*dos yidishe un khristlekhe
arbeyterfolk*) and "the working class in Poland" (*di arbeyterklas in
poyln*). In this case "Polish" was used in a historic-territorial sense.

In addition, the focus on the oppression of Poles in the original
was rewritten for a Jewish readership. Instead, the Yiddish text
either expanded the examples in the original to include other ethnic
groups or included wholly new paragraphs. The most overt change
was in the section on the PPS demand for territorial sovereignty. In
the original text Abramowski included a long paragraph on the partitions. Then he followed it with a statement on national oppression:
"Today, the child of a Russian worker may learn at school in his

own language. When the [Russian] worker goes to court, to other administrative departments, or speaks with a factory inspector, he may conduct his affairs in Russian. But we have none of this. The Polish language is forbidden, and everywhere Russian must be spoken. The bureaucrats, gendarmes, and inspectors persecute, harass, and cheat us not only because we are workers, but specifically because we are Poles, a conquered nation, who must constantly be held under whip and sword." That was why a Russian constitution was insufficient for the Polish worker. "Even if we belonged to a [constitutional] Russia," the Polish version stated, "the oppression of our language and nationality would not be removed. And thus from political rights and freedom [alone], we would not obtain adequate benefits."[93]

In contrast, the Yiddish version omitted the two passages quoted in the preceding paragraph. In their place, the editors inserted the following passage: "For the Jewish worker, and for all Jews in particular . . . Poland [must] become an independent state. Jews will enjoy greater freedom in a free Poland than in Russia, for the Polish people are more civilized, and the Polish working class is more conscious and more advanced. The Jewish working class would therefore be more secure in a free Poland. . . . Jews would moreover have more clout in Poland because they are a sixth of the whole population, whereas in the whole of Russia Jews make up one-fiftieth of the inhabitants."[94]

The appearance of Yiddish brochures marked an important step in the PPS's so-called Jewish work. It reflected a gradual move away from the party's assimilationist stand on the Jewish question. Now the PPS acknowledged that attracting Jewish workers required a carefully constructed propaganda linking the "Polish question" to specifically Jewish concerns. In particular, the PPS's Yiddish press would now use the Polish cause to refer more generally to principles of democratic freedoms, arguing that democratic institutions could only be established under a Polish democratic republic. The idea of the Polish insurgents of 1830, "For Your Freedom and Ours," reappeared in the party's Yiddish press. These developments led to more sustained consideration of Jewish needs *as a group* over the next few years.

## The Yiddish Leaflet

The PPS was one of the first socialist parties to disseminate Yiddish-language circulars. Between 1893 and 1898 PPS leaflets in Yiddish were produced abroad and smuggled into the empire. But in 1898 local PPS committees began printing their own Yiddish leaflets. It was Piłsudski who instructed the ZZSP to purchase Hebrew printing characters in February 1898.[95] Shortly after, the printing device arrived in Congress Poland, and by April 1898 the Białystok and Warsaw committees printed their first Yiddish-language May Day proclamations.[96] By the end of 1899 the CKR, as well as the Warsaw and Białystok branches, would use the new printing capabilities to produce seven more Yiddish leaflets totaling some seven thousand copies.

The contents of PPS Yiddish leaflets, from 1898 and 1899, reveal that central and local committees were hesitant to flaunt a national independence platform to Jewish workers. Instead, the leaflets focused on concrete bread-and-butter issues, such as wages and hours. An exception was the CKR's May Day leaflet for 1899, which called on Jewish workers to raise the banner of "a free and independent workers' republic in Poland."[97] When the national platform was expressed to Jewish workers, the authors avoided the ethnic connotation of *Polish* in favor of the *territorial* sense of a "workers' republic *in Poland*." It is important to note, however, that leaflets distributed to Polish workers similarly tended to stress local concrete demands over abstract political goals. In fact, before 1904 leaflets rarely included national demands but stressed international workers' solidarity instead. Only in 1904, in the wake of the Russo-Japanese War, did PPS circulars begin to stress national demands.[98]

In the period 1900–1902 PPS Jews distributed only a few leaflets, owing to the emigration of its core leaders following arrests. PPS Jews nonetheless managed to produce two circulars during this time.[99] Both put forth slogans consistent with the party leadership. The May Day leaflet, for example, reminded the Jewish worker that "Jewish-Christian solidarity" was necessary to defeat the dual enemies of "capitalism" and "the tsarist regime." May Day was a workers' holiday "when workers from the whole world jointly protest against bondage and injustice, [and promote] the brotherhood of

Jewish and Christian workers." The leaflet concluded with the slogans "Long Live the First of May!" "Long Live Solidarity among Workers of All Peoples and Religions!" and "Long Live the Polish Socialist Party!"[100]

PPS circulars distributed to Polish workers similarly advanced the theme of Jewish-Christian solidarity. A March 1901 circular, distributed by the PPS division in Białystok, urged the Polish worker to regard workers of different religions as comrades in arms. On the question of the workers' struggle, the Polish leaflet stated, "there should not be any distinction between faith and nationality! For us socialists, Polish, German, Russian, Jewish, and Tartar workers are brothers with whom we share common interests, and with whom we are jointly fighting against our exploiters, whether Poles, Germans, Muscovites, or Jews."[101]

Jewish PPS members sometimes paid a heavy price for distributing party leaflets. With the Jewish Section's leadership abroad, the distribution of party leaflets was sparse in the spring of 1902. The hectograph Yiddish-language May Day proclamation of the PPS's Warsaw division, dated April 1, 1902, had called for the overthrow of the tsar.[102] But the leaflet fell into the hands of the Russian secret police. For its possession, Israel-Shmuel Weisman, age sixteen, and Moishe Zhelikhover, seventeen, were arrested on 8 April; Moishe Kafenbaum, sixteen, and Eizer Leybman, twenty-one, on 12 April, and Eduard Tsirts on 15 April. The five remained in prison for over a year and were sentenced to three years of penal servitude in Siberia in June 1903.[103]

During the period under examination, the PPS attempted to infuse a "Polish orientation" into the workers' movement among Jews through the introduction of a Yiddish press. Among the goals advanced in *Der arbeyter* were: (1) to instill Jewish workers with sympathy for the Polish cause, including resistance to the suppression of Polish culture and language and the harmful effects of Russification; (2) to link the Jewish question with the Polish struggle for freedom; and (3) to argue against a constitutional solution to the national question in Russia.

*Der arbeyter* was produced under the direct editorial control of the foreign committee, and thus any tendency within the Jewish Section leadership to stray from the party line was suppressed. Both

Wasilewski and Jędrzejowski clearly attested to this fact, writing that, without exception, they screened every article before it went to the typesetter. The innovation of *Der arbeyter* in its London period was to link the PPS program to *Jewish* interests for the first time. Regarding the Jews and the nationalities question, *Der arbeyter* advanced the idea that Jews were members of the Polish nation separated by faith and language. The "Polish proletariat" thus consisted of "Jewish" and "Christian" workers.

At the same time the growth of a PPS Yiddish press marked the beginning of a departure from the party's assimilationist leanings of the 1890s. The commitment of valuable party resources to the production and dissemination of propaganda material in Yiddish derived from a recognition of the special needs of Jewish workers. The formation of the Bund created a sense of urgency, as Jewish party members repeatedly complained of the lack of Yiddish material in the face of the Bund's energetic and prolific publishing activities. The party leadership thus concluded that Polonization was no longer an immediate aim. Rather, winning over Jews to the Polish state idea, or "political assimilation," would now become the party's principle focus. Jędrzejowski articulated the new position in January 1901 when he wrote that the party had to first create a "commonality of ideals" with the Jewish working masses. Only after, he concluded, would linguistic assimilation occur, if at all.[104]

*Józef Piłsudski (1867–1935), London, 1896 (National Museum in Warsaw)*

*Stanisław Mendelson (1857–1913), Paris, c. 1892* (Niepodległość, *Warsaw, 1929)*

*Maria Jankowska-Mendelson (1850–1909), c. 1890* (Niepodległość,
*Warsaw, 1929)*

*Feliks Perl (1871–1927), c. 1895 (Archive of New Records, Warsaw)*

*Witold Jodko-Narkiewicz (1864–1924), c. 1904 (Niepodległość, Warsaw, 1929)*

*Bolesław A. Jędrzejowski (1864–1914), c. 1900* (Niepodległość, *Warsaw, 1929*)

*Stanisław Wojciechowski, c. 1898, later, president of the Polish Republic from 1922–1926 (Archive of New Records, Warsaw)*

*Leon Wasilewski (1870–1936), 1900 (Archive of New Records, Warsaw)*

*Kazimierz Kelles-Krauz (1872–1905), Paris, c. 1902 (Archive of New Records, Warsaw)*

*Kamila Horwitz-Kancewiczowa (1879–1952), c. 1906, a leader of the PPS's Warsaw division and activist in the party's Jewish Section (Archive of New Records, Warsaw)*

# ■ 7.

# Toward a Recognition of Jewish Nationality: The PPS and Its Jewish Section, 1902–4

*The Bund cannot comprehend how a Jew can call himself a Polish socialist.*
JEWISH MEMBER OF THE PPS (1903)

*The proletariat in Poland and Lithuania cannot fight for political freedom without a simultaneous struggle against the occupiers. They cannot strive for . . . democracy without also fighting for independence.*
PPS RESOLUTION (AUGUST 1902)

THE YEAR 1902 WAS A MAJOR TURNING POINT for the PPS's work among Jewish workers. With the formation and consolidation of the Bund in 1897–1901 and a corresponding decline in PPS influence among Jewish workers, the PPS felt the need to respond. That organizational response came at the party's sixth congress in June 1902 when the delegates voted to create an official Jewish Committee to oversee the Yiddish press and to represent the Jewish Section in the central committee. Henceforth, the Jewish Section of the PPS (ŻO) became a semiautonomous body within the party, held its own conferences of *intelligenty* and worker representatives, and passed resolutions. The conference minutes offer a window into the Jewish Section's ideological and tactical disputes as well as its attitude to the party platform and the Bund.

The sixth congress also marked the rise to leadership of Feliks Sachs. As head of the PPS's Jewish Committee, editor of *Der arbeyter*, and a member of the party's central committee, Sachs became a major voice in forming the party's policies both toward its Jewish Section and in its relations with the Bund. Sachs also became the spokesperson for the party's emerging left-wing opposition during this time, challenging the PPS leadership on issues of tactics and ideology. The party had to revise its official position on the Lithuanian and Jewish questions, Sachs argued, and recognize both as *equal* partners rather than as "sections" of the party. This entailed two critical changes. First, the party had to recognize the Jews as a distinct nationality as well as their right to form an independent worker's party. Second, the PPS had to abandon its conception of Lithuania as a Polish province and clearly inscribe Lithuanian independence on its banner.

The ascendancy of Sachs to leadership reflected deeper changes in the party leadership. For two major party leaders—Piłsudski and Kelles-Krauz—had already begun to soften their position on the Bund and demonstrated openness to the idea of Jewish nationality in the late winter and early spring of 1902. Indeed, we can observe a rhetorical shift in the public and private writings of Piłsudski whereby he surrendered the idea of a multicultural nation, in which he entertained the dream of building a state of hyphenated Poles on the American model, to that of a federation of nationalities. This conceptual shift would have important consequences for the evolution of Polish-Jewish relations. With the tacit recognition of Jewish nationality, Piłsudski would abandon the idea of *asymilacja narodowa* (national assimilation) and instead embrace the aim of *asymilacja państwowa* (state assimilation). The idea of *asymilacja państwowa*, which would mark Piłsudski's attitude to national minorities in interwar Poland, demanded Jewish loyalty to the Polish state idea while officially recognizing the right of Jews to cultivate a distinctive national culture and identity.

### Piłsudski's Transformation on the Jewish Question

During the 1890s Piłsudski led a campaign to expose the Bund as a Pan-Russian organization that—regardless of intention—contributed to the Russification of Polish lands. But in February 1900 Piłsudski's campaign against the Bund came to an abrupt halt when he was arrested in Łódź. For the next fourteen months Piłsudski was imprisoned in Łódź, Warsaw, and Saint Petersburg. He finally escaped in May 1901. After spending a few months in Galicia, he made his way to London, where he arrived in November 1901 and was greeted by Bolesław Jędrzejowski and Leon Wasilewski.

At the time, Bund leader Arkadi Kremer was also in London. Despite the bitter polemics that had passed between the two in the 1890s, Kremer invited Piłsudski to his home shortly after he arrived. According to Wasilewski, Piłsudski and Kremer were on "very friendly" terms in London. In fact, Piłsudski accepted Kremer's invitation to speak at a Bund gathering. Piłsudski spoke publicly on only one other occasion during his time in London.[1] It was probably through Kremer that Piłsudski learned of the Bund's fourth congress, at which it committed itself in principle to the idea of Jewish national autonomy. While there are no accounts of the discussions that took place between the two most significant figures in the Bund and the PPS, it is clear from Piłsudski's letters that they discussed the possibility of cooperation.

At the time, Piłsudski responded to several letters on the Bund's new national program and its implication. On January 9, 1902 he received a letter from Władysław Gumplowicz, a member of the party's Zurich branch, requesting suggestions on an official response to the Bund's new program. Piłsudski's response reveals the extent to which he viewed the Bund in the context of a Russo-Polish struggle over control of the western, and particularly the northwestern, provinces. The PPS thought the Russian Social Democrats would use the Bund as a pretext for territorial claims in Lithuania and even Congress Poland. This "open war" had left deep resentment and mistrust between the two groups. Addressing the suggestion that the PPS recognize the Bund's independence in exchange for the Bund's recognition of the PPS program, Piłsudski objected to the term "independence": a PPS-Bund partnership had to be based on "party and program unity" and "full autonomy" for the Bund.[2] In another letter Piłsudski acknowledged that the PPS's old tactics of condemnations and threats had achieved little success and were no longer effective.[3]

Meanwhile, the PPS foreign committee in London received a letter from Kelles-Krauz regarding the possibility of a rapprochement with the Bund through the Galician Jewish PPSD member Max Zetterbaum. Although Zetterbaum was an assimilationist, he proposed that for tactical reasons the PPS "should recognize the Bund's organizational autonomy and the right of Jews to 'regard themselves' as a nationality (even though, in reality, they are not)." Kelles-Krauz recommended offering the Bund "autonomy in Jewish affairs within PPS territory." In exchange the Bund would pledge allegiance to the PPS's independence platform.[4] Piłsudski replied that he had had discussions with the Bund in London on a whole range of issues. Influencing the Jewish party, he concluded, would have to be done in stages, first by personal contacts. Talks with Kremer led Piłsudski to the conclusion that the PPS program, drafted in 1892, now needed a specific clause guaranteeing Jewish rights. He then proposed the wording for a resolution at the upcoming party congress: "a point should be introduced into the program especially about the Jews—that in a future Poland they would have the right to remain Jews if they so wish, and that we would defend their rights *as a nationality*."[5] To win over Jewish socialists, Piłsudski continued, the Bund had to be convinced that in a future Polish state "the Jews would not be denied independence in their own internal affairs, for those are 'the rights of national minorities' . . . which Poland will . . . grant to the Jews." He also came to the conclusion that the party's old assimilationist line was bankrupt, and consequently the party's founding program would have to be revised. "Our program," Piłsudski wrote, "lacks a guarantee for the rights of Jews *as a group*." The program contained guarantees for Lithuanians and Ruthenians, he continued, "but on the Jews, nothing explicit is put forth, with the exception of the general phrase on equality for all nationalities and faiths."[6] This marked Piłsudski's first concession to the Bund on the question of Jewish national autonomy.

### The Jewish Question at the PPS's Sixth Congress, June 1902

Anxious to rebuild the organization in Russian Poland, Piłsudski left London for Kraków in April 1902 and proceeded to Congress Poland that same month.[7] In June 1902 Piłsudski summoned eight delegates to Lublin to convene the party's sixth congress. The delegates included such figures as Feliks Perl (*Robotnik* editor), Jodko-Narkiewicz (foreign committee), and Feliks Sachs, representing the Lithuania and Jewish party divisions.[8]

The PPS's sixth congress was the first party gathering since the Bund's historic 1901 declaration recognizing Jews as a nationality. It is thus no surprise that the PPS's congress report included a lengthy section on the Bund, one that occupied more than half of the entire report.[9] Appearing in August 1902, the report repeated the PPS's opposition to the Russian orientation of the Bund. The Bund's "gravitational pull to Russia" and "indifference and even hostility" to the struggle for national independence on Polish and Lithuanian lands, the congress resolved, testified to a "weak sense of solidarity" with local non-Russian nationalities. A democratic republic of Poland and Lithuania, free from foreign rule, constituted the only political form that could guarantee legal equality and civil rights to all without regard to nationality and faith. It thus followed that an independent Polish republic was also in the best interests of Jews as well: "The demand for independence and a democratic republic is in the interest of the Jewish proletariat not only as workers, *but as Jews*. A democratic republic would secure equality for Jewish citizens and give them the possibility to freely develop and exert a formidable influence in public affairs."[10]

The attitude of the PPS to the Jewish question was linked to the general national question in Lithuania. Historical and cultural ties linked Congress Poland and Lithuania, the congress resolved. Lithuanian socialists therefore should join the PPS as an "autonomous section." With regard to the Jews, the congress downplayed the significance of the debate over Jewish nationality. Whether or not the Jews were a nation "in the full sense of the word" merited further debate. Resolving the theoretical question of Jewish nationality, however, had "no practical significance: even if we recognize the Jews as a separate nation, we would still have the right to demand from them loyalty to the general interests of the country." At the same time anti-Semitism was a reactionary ideology that had to be unambiguously fought against. "With all its energy, the Polish Socialist Party will struggle against anti-Semitism as a harmful and reactionary political current." Anti-Semitism, "awakens religious hatred," and "strengthening the influence of the clergy," it spreads "backwardness and fanaticism."[11]

To compete for the allegiance of Jewish workers, the PPS resolved that concrete measures had to be taken. In order to regularly produce and disseminate party literature in Yiddish, the congress created a special committee for agitation among the Jewish working class.[12] The new Jewish Committee (Komitet Żydowski, KŻ), under the direction of Feliks Sachs, received official status and representation in the party's central committee. Soon after, Piotr Szumow (1872–1936), an activist in the party's Grodno branch, and Józef Kwiatek (1874–1910), a prominent party member from Warsaw, joined the KŻ.[13]

Following the PPS congress, Sachs relocated to Vilna in order to strengthen the party's organization in Lithuania. From Vilna, Sachs reported back to the foreign committee in several letters, focusing on three issues: the Yiddish press, the nationalities question in Lithuania, and PPS-Bund relations. Contact with the Jewish community in Vilna led Sachs away from the abstract and theoretical atmosphere of the London foreign committee, and the patriotic tendencies of the party's Warsaw branch, toward a more pragmatic outlook. It was during his stay in Vilna that Sachs began to change his views on the Jewish question, concluding that the PPS position was in need of reformulation.

In late June Sachs informed London that the sixth issue of *Der arbeyter* would soon appear as the first issue printed in the empire. Printing *Der arbeyter* in Russian Poland, he added, was an important step in combating the influence of the Bund. He emphasized, however, that *Der arbeyter* alone was insufficient. In order to build a Jewish movement sympathetic to the PPS, "publishing brochures of a programmatic and theoretical nature is, along with *Der arbeyter*, essential." Without it, he stressed, the PPS would be unable to compete with the Bund.[14]

The first issue of *Der arbeyter* produced in Vilna appeared in July 1902. Without the watchful eye of the foreign committee, Sachs strayed from the orthodox party line. When produced in London, *Der arbeyter* was "too far from the day-to-day struggle, from the real needs of the Jewish proletariat." Now *Der arbeyter* would be close to the Jewish worker and better reflect his interests. "We are convinced," stated *Der arbeyter*, "that our organ . . . will better fulfill its task: to disseminate socialist ideas among the Jewish working masses, to aid them in their struggle, and to show them the right path . . . to a better future."[15]

The most striking change in editorial policy under Sachs was that Jews were now characterized as a "nationality." Also *Der arbeyter* appeared to define "Poland" in its ethnographic frontiers. Whereas *Robotnik* and *Przedświt* envisioned a single federal republic of Poland and Lithuania, *Der arbeyter* consciously referred to two distinct entities.[16] "Once the working masses in Poland and Lithuania are freed from the capitalist yoke," we read in *Der arbeyter*, "they will take political power in their own hands, that is, when Poland and Lithuania will become independent peoples' *republics*. The liberation of these *two countries* is thus our most important task." At present, he continued, it was impossible to predict whether these "two republics" would be united into one state or if they would be separate. It was more important "that all workers in Poland and Lithuania, without regard to nationality, understand that they have the same interest; that they are all equally interested in the liberation of these two countries, and that the struggle for freedom should be jointly led, for the separation of Poland and Lithuania means the liberation of Poles, Jews, Lithuanians, and Belarussians, and inasmuch as the interests of these *nationalities* are common, so we must lead a joint struggle."[17]

Sachs's argument, couched in a mixture of Marxist and romantic nationalist phraseology, led to the same conclusion as his fellow right-wing party leaders. If all the nationalities had the same interests, as Sachs argued, then the PPS could act as a kind of RSDRP of Congress Poland and the northwest provinces. Workers from four nationalities living in the two countries, Sachs wrote, "must unify under the banner of one common party. They all should have one common program and strive for one common goal." He continued that each "organization" and each "nationality" that formulated a separate party program weakened the united front and "brings shame not only on all the others, but upon themselves as well."[18] *Der arbeyter* thus concluded that the PPS's goal was to form a single party with a joint program for all the nationalities of Congress Poland and Lithuania.

Sachs remained in Vilna throughout the summer of 1902. The correspondence between Vilna and London attests to Sachs's emerging conviction that the party's position on Lithuania had to soften. The PPS should give up its habit of treating Lithuania as a province of Greater Poland, Sachs maintained. "People here regard Lithuania on the same footing as Poland and recognize the complete equality of all *nationalities*—Poles, Lithuanians, Belarussians, *and Jews*," Sachs wrote. He continued "each nationality now speaks in the name of its, and *only* its, interests." In no uncertain terms, Sachs recommended that the term "nationality" had to be applied to the

Jews: "We now treat Jews as a nationality equal to all others," Sachs informed London. In recognizing Jewish nationality, Sachs continued, "we are following 'the spirit of the times': if you were here, you would understand and even feel this 'spirit.'"[19]

By late August Sachs began to moderate his position on the need for total organizational unity between the socialist parties in Lithuania and the Polish provinces. The Poles had yearned for their own state for a century. But the situation for Lithuanian Jews, Sachs now wrote, was different. After a century of Russian rule Lithuanian Jews had cultivated sympathy for Russian culture and had begun to identify with the Russian working class. Sachs wondered aloud whether the PPS could reverse a century-long process. "The notion that the interest of the Jewish working class could only be the same as the interests of the nationalities among whom it lives," Sachs wrote, seemed to him the expression of the "exaggerated Polishness" of a handful of Warsaw Jews.[20]

Sachs also challenged the party's second reason for demanding Jewish loyalty to the PPS program: that of historical tradition. The fourth and sixth party congresses had advanced the romantic-insurrectionary idea of reconstituting the Polish-Lithuanian Commonwealth. But according to Sachs, the Polish romantic-insurrectionary idea had little significance in Lithuania. "I don't think the history of [Polish] insurrections can in some way exert influence," Sachs wrote. "Certainly not in Lithuania where Jews are not at all concerned with this 'past.' It speaks neither to their heart nor to their intellect. Besides, the Polish question is something foreign and very distant for Lithuanian Jews." Because of their distance from Polish matters, Sachs reported that Lithuanian Jews "possess a Lithuanian patriotism and a fear of [Polish] hegemony just like the Lithuanians." They were of the opinion, Sachs continued, that the PPS was doing too little to combat anti-Semitism among Polish workers. Sachs agreed: "We must recognize that there is much truth to these [concerns]."[21]

Sachs thus contended that the PPS had to adapt its program to new conditions. Above all, the PPS had to grant the different movements an independent (*samodzielny*) existence fully equal to the Polish movement. And this meant giving up once and for all the notion that Lithuania was a Polish province. "The more closely I come to know the conditions [here]," Sachs wrote, "the more poorly I regard the [sixth] congress resolutions on Lithuania," adding that treating Lithuania like a province was simply in bad taste. "We will have to unambiguously stress that [we regard] Lithuania as a sister, *not* a daughter, of Poland."[22] Revising the position on Lithuania thus required a change in the party's name, for if the PPS claimed to represent all the nationalities of Congress Poland and historic Lithuania, then the name had to reflect that aim. The name "*Polish* Socialist Party," Sachs suggested, implied hegemony for Poles. Instead, the party should change its name to "The Socialist Party . . . *of Poland and Lithuania.*"

### The Polemic between *Der arbeyter* and *Di arbeyter shtimme*, 1902–3

The revival of PPS activity on the Jewish street did not go unnoticed in Bundist circles. In August the Bund responded to the PPS's sixth congress in the pages of its central organ in Vilna. Titled "An Old Song with an Old Tune," the article in *Di arbeyter shtimme* addressed the PPS accusation of Bundist "indifference and even hostility" to Polish national aspirations.[23] "We call upon the PPS to attest to *one* incident when . . . we, Jewish socialists, acted with 'indifference' and 'hostility' against the [demand for] Polish independence," stated *Di arbeyter shtimme.* "Show us *one* word in our literature that indicates a 'hostile' view against [Polish] independence."[24] Sachs noted the Bund's editorial in a letter to London. "Lately, [the Bund] has been openly provoking us" with an "insulting" article. "Our Jews here are extremely resentful and eager to respond."[25] Reflecting the wishes of local party members, Sachs responded to the Bund directly, something the PPS had heretofore consciously avoided in its Yiddish press. "By actively supporting [Polish and Lithuanian] independence in today's circumstances," Sachs argued in *Der arbeyter,* "we mean propagating the idea . . . at every opportunity. Has the Bund ever done this? It would not deny that the answer is *no.* We understand further, that [support] for the independence of Poland and Lithuania means aspiring to it, *not* neutrality. Does the Bund have such a demand in its program? *No.* Not only does the Bund *not* support it, but it oftentimes despises this goal. We therefore have the full right to say that [the Bund] is indifferent and hostile to the independence of Poland and Lithuania."[26]

The brief exchange in August and November 1902 was only a hint of what was to come. After Sachs's editorial appeared, *Di arbeyter shtimme* featured a sixteen-column polemic against the PPS. This, in time, would receive a full response from Feliks Sachs, and both pieces would be printed separately as official party brochures in 1903 and 1904.[27]

In arguments founded on the Bund's traditional international-ism and increasingly strong national views, the Bund castigated the PPS for failing to recognize the right of Jewish workers to organiza-tional and programmatic independence. Instead of recognizing the Bund's positive role in organizing Jewish workers, as all other rev-olutionary groups in Russia had done, the PPS greeted the forma-tion of the Bund with accusations that it was Russifying Polish lands. In the ensuing five years, *Di arbeyter shtimme* stated, the PPS had forgotten much and learned little. It failed to realize that it was not, nor would it ever be, in a position to represent the interests of the Jewish working class. The PPS had forgotten that in spite of the "aspersions and insinuations" with which it had greeted the Bund since its founding, the Bund's influence among Jewish workers had dramatically increased. In no uncertain terms, *Di arbeyter shtimme* claimed *"only* the Bund leads the struggle for the liberation of the Jewish proletariat."[28]

The Bund exploited divisions within the Polish socialist move-ment to bolster its own claims, for the PPS was not the only Polish socialist party in Russian Poland. What about the SDKPiL, which favored a Russian constitution and autonomy for Congress Poland, but did not demand independence? And the PPS Proletariat, which believed the demand for Polish independence had to be suspended until after the achievement of liberal constitutional government in Russia? Or the Lithuanian Social Democrats, who favored a federal union with Poland and Russia? These three parties favored cooper-ation with the Russian Social Democrats and believed national demands could be addressed only *after* a general social and political revolution was achieved in the Russian Empire. Most importantly, the three rival socialist parties all recognized the right of the Bund to organizational independence. "Each of these [parties]," *Di arbeyter shtimme* stated, "claims that it *alone* correctly expresses the wishes and aspirations of the Polish and the Lithuanian proletariat; that only its banner [expresses] the *general* [will] of the whole proletariat. We therefore ask the PPS: if we have no right to put forth our own demands, if we are prohibited from fighting under our own banner, if we must only take part in 'the general struggle under a common banner,' then with *which* of the Polish and Lithuanian parties should we fuse? Under *which* 'common' banner shall we fight?"[29]

The answer, *Di arbeyter shtimme* continued, was clear. As a party of the *Jewish* working class, the Bund could not fuse with any of the Polish or Lithuanian parties, as the PPS had demanded in June 1902: "The Jewish working class is not only 'a part' of the Polish-Lithuanian proletariat. As with the proletariat of *each* nation, so [the Bund] is also an *independent party* of the universal proletariat, a party that possesses its own historical form, and which must advance the general socialist ideal in its own distinct way. In its class struggle the Jewish proletariat has certain obstacles not shared by the proletariat of other nations: only the Jewish proletariat can struggle [against them], and in this sense it possesses its own historical aims and tasks. To realize them, the Jewish proletariat must build a separate revolutionary organization, an independent revolutionary force."[30]

The central committee's polemic with the PPS demonstrated the degree to which the national idea had won over the Bund since 1897. Whereas in the spring of 1901 the central committee only hesitatingly adopted a resolution recognizing the Jews as a "nationality," in the following year the Bundist leadership seized upon the nationality card as a rhetorical tool in its polemic with the PPS. *Di arbeyter shtimme* thus declared that the PPS's mistake was to believe that it could lead the struggle of the Jewish workers, "the proletariat of a foreign nation to which [the PPS] does not belong."[31]

The PPS-Bund polemic reached a new stage with the Bund's increasing national orientation. Beyond tactical and organizational objections to PPS demands on the Jewish proletariat, *Di arbeyter shtimme* claimed that the working class of each nation "has its own psychology, which its own history has produced; its own traditions and customs, its own national goals." The particular qualities of each nationality played a role in determining a minimum program. Each party that desired to work among Jewish workers or any other national group, *Di arbeyter shtimme* claimed, would have to instinctively adapt to those particular conditions in their agitation.

Agitating among the working class of a particular nation "is possible only for the party that belongs to that proletariat, whose struggle it will lead. That party itself must have grown out of that proletariat, must be permeated with its ideals and understand its psychology." The Bund consequently derided, and even mocked, the PPS's growing body of party literature in Yiddish: "With great stir and clamor, [the PPS] has . . . announced before the whole world that it has begun to direct its activity to the Jewish proletariat. Then why is it that its work among the Jewish proletariat has never yielded any substantive results? Why has it never succeeded in striking roots in the Jewish working masses? Why, to date, has it given nothing to the Jewish worker, other than a few brochures written in garbled Yiddish [*tsugeynershe shprakh*]?"[32] The answer, *Di arbeyter shtimme* maintained, was clear. The PPS did not understand the special circumstances and needs of the Jewish working class: "Working among the Jewish proletariat in Poland, the PPS has not aspired to accommodate the special interests and ideals of the Jewish proletariat. That is because to the PPS, these interests do not exist and are not recognized, as [evidenced] in the resolution of its sixth party congress. Rather, [the PPS] has organized Jewish workers to aid its own cause. It has thus endeavored to solve the Jewish question *not from the standpoint of the Jewish proletariat*, but only from its own, Polish interests. It has never understood, and never will comprehend, the psychology of the Jewish proletariat. For this reason, it is not in a position to bring an independent spiritual physiognomy to the Jewish workers' movement, something essential for the growth and development of the Jewish working class."[33]

In its polemic with the PPS, the Bund suggested that in ethnically mixed areas of eastern and southeastern Europe, socialist parties could not represent a given territory, as the PPS claimed, but only organize workers of one nationality in a particular territory. To claim exclusive control over workers in a given territory on the basis of so-called historic rights, the Bund suggested, was nothing less than chauvinism: "We do not reproach the PPS for not knowing, and not wanting to know, the life and needs of the Jewish proletariat. In the best case, the PPS can only be a *national* Polish party. That is, a party that can respond to the needs of the *Polish* proletariat, and among it lead socialist propaganda. . . . But the PPS sees itself not as a *Polish* socialist party, but as the party *of Poland*. That is, it desires to represent not only the interests of the Polish proletariat, but of *all* workers living in Poland without regard to nationality."[34]

*Di arbetyer shtimme* also replied directly to the question of Polish national aspirations. It supported Polish independence as a long-term aim but *not* as part of a minimum program: political freedom had to come *before* national liberation. As *Di arbeyter shtimme* declared: "The freedom of Poland is possible only when absolutism in Russia is overthrown. Only then, when Russia is a free country, when the proletariat of all nations are in a position to express their own ideals and aspirations, will the realization of the *national* goals of the proletariat of all nations in the Russian state be truly possible."[35]

The severity of *Di arbeyter shtimme's* attacks put PPS Jews on the defensive. "The Bund has taken alarm at our advances in Lithuania," Sachs wrote from Vilna in January 1903, "and has come out against us in a sixteen-column article!" He continued that *Di arbeyter shtimme* based its attacks not so much on the PPS program as on the party's opposition to the Bund's organizational independence.[36] Sachs would return to *Di arbeyter shtimme*'s attack with a full response one year later.

Meanwhile, at a PPS party conference in November 1902, the central committee instructed both *Przedświt* and *Der arbeyter* to respond to the Bund.[37] The delegates passed a resolution condemning the Bund for allegedly weakening political solidarity among the working classes of Poland and Lithuania. The latter statement passed with five votes in favor (including Piłsudski's) and two abstentions, while only Sachs opposed.

PPS-Bund relations were also discussed at a December conference at which Józef Kwiatek and Maks Horwitz were present. Here, for the first time, the division between the party's Polonized Jewish elite and Jewish Section members came to the surface. Opposing any change in the party's official position, Horwitz attributed the Bund's position vis-à-vis the PPS to "Russified people whose dislike of the PPS is a reflection of a genuine antipathy to Poles." But Kwiatek, a leader of the party's Jewish Section, took a different position, arguing that anti-Bundist statements only diminished the party's standing in Jewish eyes. Moreover, one had to recognize that the party's political program simply did not resonate among non-Poles. "The independence program of the PPS," Kwiatek maintained, "is only accepted by those Jews *who regard themselves politically as Poles.*" But to the Yiddish-speaking masses, the Bund had easier access because of language. The party had to recognize, Kwiatek maintained, that the Bund was playing a very positive role by revolutionizing the Jewish working masses, thus preparing the ground for PPS influence. It was essential that the PPS and the Bund reach an agreement.[38]

The PPS's response to the Bund was entrusted to Witold Jodko-Narkiewicz, a leader of the party's Foreign Committee in London. Written in a detached manner, Jodko-Narkiewicz's response focused on core programmatic differences, followed by a step-by-step challenge to each Bundist argument. Jodko-Narkiewicz began by reaffirming the party's fundamental belief in a territorial solution to the national question. The break up of Russia was necessary not just for Poles but for all the non-Russian nationalities of the western provinces and Congress Poland. To date, Jodko-Narkiewicz declared, the Bund held that Jewish interests lay in preserving Russia's territorial integrity. "Such a view constitutes the greatest obstacle to a rapprochement between . . . the conscious proletariat under the Bund's influence and the socialists found in our ranks, both Christians and Jews."[39] Jodko-Narkiewicz reminded the Bund that not only the PPS demanded territories from Russia, but also the Lithuanian Social Democrats, the Ukrainian Socialist Party, and the Revolutionary Ukrainian Party. Thus, with few exceptions the Bund's program was contrary to the majority of inhabitants among whom it lived.

Jodko-Narkiewicz then took issue with the Bund's contention that the PPS could never legitimately represent the Jewish working class. "From the beginning of our movement we have had Jewish comrades, we will always have them and, we hope, in greater and greater number," Jodko-Narkiewicz reminded the Bund. The Bund had "arrogantly" supposed that all Jewish socialist intellectuals and workers supported their program. What about those Jews active in the PPS's Jewish Section? Were they incapable of understanding the psychology of the Jewish people because they did not agree with the Bund, the self-proclaimed "sole representatives" of the Jewish working class? Jodko-Narkiewicz continued: "Why can a Jewish Bundist understand the 'psychology' of the Jews, but a PPS Jew is not in a position to do the same? Why do Bundist resolutions answer to the needs of the masses, when the resolutions of . . . working-class Jews belonging to the PPS and comprising an autonomous body within the party are automatically judged as futile?"[40]

## The First Conference of the PPS's Jewish Section, April 1903

The Jewish Section's first conference took place in Grodno, just east of Congress Poland, on April 15 and 16, 1903. Four *intelligenty* were present, as well as seven workers representing Warsaw, Białystok, Grodno, Gródek (present-day Gorodok), and Vilna. Reports were also heard on Jewish agitation in Żyrardów, Płock, Łomża, Siedlce, and Brześć Litewski (present-day Brest). Among the participants in the two-day proceedings were Sachs, P. Szumow, and Maks Horwitz ("Henryk Walecki"), who had recently escaped from Siberian exile. Other delegates included David Perlmutter and I. Kornblit, founders of the first PPS Jewish circles.[41] Subjects of discussion included agitation, the question of producing party material in Russian, relations with the Bund, and the party's Yiddish press.

Dominating the conference was the question of the Bund. First, the Jewish Section debated at length the question of possible joint demonstrations. "Seeing that our fundamental position differs from that of the Bund," one resolution read, "the conference regards it as impossible to conduct any type of common political action."[42] The conference delegates nonetheless favored joint demonstrations of an exclusively economic character. In a discussion of the Yiddish press, the conference considered various ways of increasing the popularity of *Der arbeyter* and *Di proletarishe velt*, the party's Yiddish organ in London, which had first appeared in 1902. The Jewish Section's organ, the conference stated, should contain articles on the party program, articles on all aspects of Jewish life, including Zionism, and columns on the Polish and Russian revolutionary movements. For *Di proletarishe velt*, the congress resolved that each issue should be prepared in cooperation with the New York Aid Alliance and expressed hopes that Benjamin Feigenbaum, the Warsaw-born Yiddish editor and polemicist in New York, would agree to review each issue for style and language.

The Jewish Section presented its conference resolutions to the party in June 1903, when the central committee met in Vilna for a three-day conference. The conference included the entire eight-member central committee, including Piłsudski ("Mieczysław"), Sachs ("Jan"), Perl ("Juliusz"), Adam Bujno ("Jerzy"), Bolesław Czarkowski ("Leon"), and Jan Rutkiewicz ("Wicek").[43] Under point four on the agenda, "Relations with the Bund," three positions surfaced: Sachs proposed unconditionally recognizing the Bund's organizational independence; Piłsudski proposed conditional recognition; and Czarkowski opposed any change.

Piłsudski opened the debate by noting the growing schism between himself and Sachs. Sachs's stand on the Bund was contrary to the party's long-standing position on relations with other socialist organizations "on PPS territory." Sachs defended his view, declaring that the PPS could no longer harbor the illusion that it could absorb the Bund into the party. Given the Bund's greater influence among Jewish workers, there was only one option: compelling the Bund to recognize the PPS program, and in exchange the party would recognize the Bund as an independent party and enter into a federal relation with it. "We can . . . demand recognition of our program from the Bund," Sachs declared, "but we cannot order them to relinquish their organizational independence, for such a demand is . . . impossible to achieve."[44]

Opposed to Sachs's conciliatory position, Czarkowski countered that the "the vast majority [of Bundists] are Russians who know nothing of our country" and were ignorant of all things Polish. Consequently, the "profound schism" between the two parties was simply too wide to mend, and the party should maintain its present stand. Perl and Jan Rutkiewicz supported Czarkowski, arguing that preserving the party's position would eventually force the Bund to change its view. The party had already granted its Jewish Section organizational autonomy and formed a Jewish Committee to preside over Jewish affairs. "The Bund must either express its solidarity with us by entering [into the Jewish Section of the PPS] or struggle against us," Rutkiewicz maintained.[45] Piłsudski expressed general agreement that the party could not recognize the Bund's organizational independence, even if it agreed to accept the PPS program. If the Bund remained independent, its "ignorance" of Polish life would only persist, and thus nominal acceptance of the PPS program would be in name but not in spirit. Only Adam Bujno, representing the party's left wing, rose to support Sachs. The old tactic of unconditionally condemning other socialist parties had to be abandoned, for it merely undermined worker's solidarity. Bujno thus expressed hope that "healthy elements" within the movement would force the PPS to change its "ruinous and unsocialist" tactics. In light of the differing views, the central committee resolved that Sachs and Piłsudski should cowrite a response to the Bund.

The party leadership also debated the Jewish Section's resolution in favor of limited joint demonstrations with the Bund. Piłsudski declared he would support the resolution on the condition that it applied exclusively to Lithuania. The central committee thus instructed the Jewish Section to insert "in Lithuania, and only in Lithuania" alongside the resolution. Only Bujno raised an objection to Piłsudski's corrective, which he argued unnecessarily restricted the autonomy of the Jewish Section in Congress Poland.[46]

## The PPS's Official Response to the Bund, August 1903

In consultation with Piłsudski, Sachs prepared the long-awaited response to the Bund. The fifteen-page piece, printed in *Przedświt* and *Der arbeyter,* constituted the most precise line of argument to date clarifying the party's position.[47] Moreover, the fact that it was written by Sachs, the head of the party's Jewish Section and *Der arbeyter* editor, lent it a greater degree of credibility within the Jewish world.

Sachs argued that throughout the six-year polemic between the two organizations, the Bund had distorted the PPS's position. He reminded the Bund that the PPS had not been invited to the first congress of the RSDRP, which the Bund attended and entered into, and at which Polish independence was not recognized. The actions of the Russian Social Democrats as well as those of the Bund "clearly demonstrated that they were opponents of our demands for independence." Not only did the RSDRP's program omit any reference to Polish independence, Sachs continued, but it did not express any interest in the nationalities question in general. "That such a program cannot satisfy the workers of nationalities oppressed under the tsar" was obvious, Sachs wrote. Thus, Sachs concluded, the RSDRP itself rejected an alliance with the PPS by not meeting its conditions, and the Bund, as a member of that party, mistakenly followed suit. "Supporting the Russian Social Democrats on such a central point for us demonstrates . . . indifference, and even a hostile position, to our struggle for independence. And all the activity and tactics of the Bund testify to the fact that our charges our correct."[48]

Sachs continued: "Bundist organs, . . . which exhibit such sympathy for the Russian people's aspirations for freedom, both past and present, do not say a single word about the extreme oppression of Poland and Lithuania, which suffer much greater than that of Russia proper, or about the fight for freedom that has gone on for so many years in these two countries, not to mention the thousands who lost their lives in that struggle." Moreover, the Jewish worker agitating under the Bund's banner, "does not even sense that beside him lives the Lithuanian nation, whose literature has been *entirely* banned . . . and that in these same cities live the Poles, who are not free to publish and print in their own language. . . . It has not even occurred to Bundists to express their sympathies to Lithuanians and Poles or to protest against the oppression of their languages and literatures. . . . Bundists are almost wholly unconcerned with such matters, for they aren't aware of [the oppression of Polish and Lithuanian culture] because their leaders have said nothing about it."[49] Regardless of its position on independence, Sachs argued, the Bund had an obligation to inform Jewish workers about the oppression of Poles and Lithuanians. He gave the example of Finland, on which the Bund reported several times. Why, he asked, would the Bund be more sympathetic to the oppression of Finns than to that of the people among whom it lived? Why was the Polish question alien to the Jewish worker, who was informed about faraway provinces of Russia?

Sachs then took issue with the Bund's claim that the PPS was contributing to the spread of anti-Semitism through its public attacks on the Bund. According to this "strange logic," Sachs contended, the PPS was not permitted to advance even the slightest criticism of the Bund, for, according to the Bund's logic, criticizing its program would spread anti-Semitism among Christians. "*Di arbeyter shtimme* forgets that the Bund and the Jewish people are not one and the same; that, in coming out against the Bund, we are in no way standing out against the Jewish people."[50]

Sachs also reflected on the deeper, long-term causes of the antagonism between Polish and Jewish socialists and pointed to two basic causes. The first concerned the historical relations between Polish nobles and their Jewish subjects. "In general," Sachs wrote, "the majority of Lithuanian Jews don't like the Poles." The experience of centuries past when Polish lords wronged and humiliated Jews with impunity understandably persisted in the memory of Lithuanian Jews. It was nonetheless wrong, Sachs argued, to project that hatred for the *szlachta* onto the entire Polish nation, for the Polish people had suffered more from the *szlachta* than had the Jews. Second, Sachs maintained that those Jews who graduated from Russian gymnasiums and universities adopted a "hatred and disdain" for Poles, because everything Polish was presented in the worst light, everything Russian in the best way possible. Finally, Sachs countered the Bund's accusation of anti-Semitism within PPS ranks by pointing to alleged anti-Polish sentiments among Bundist intellectuals. "Instead of working for close relations between Jews and Poles, [the Bund] fans the flames and increases hatred toward the Poles."[51]

## The Jewish Section's Second Conference, October 1903

On October 9 and 10, 1903 delegates gathered in Grodno to participate in the Jewish Section's second conference. The members included three *intelligenty* (Kwiatek, M. Horwitz, and Sachs), workers from Warsaw, Białystok, and Vilna, and two workers from Grodno. The first point on the agenda, "Revision of the First Conference Resolutions," focused on the party's position on the Bund. Kwiatek reiterated his support for the resolution favoring joint demonstrations with the Bund in certain cases. Principled opposition to joint demonstrations would alienate Jewish workers, Kwiatek argued. In certain cases, such as funerals, pogroms, and armed defense, the Jewish Section had to act jointly with the Bund. Kwiatek nonetheless failed to sway the majority.[52] Backed by a majority, Horwitz argued that in the intervening months since the first conference, the Jewish Section's overtures to the Bund had been met with indifference; that in Lithuania, where the Bund was strongest, they felt no need to work with the PPS's Jewish Section.

Horwitz thus proposed a resolution opposing joint actions *unless* the Bund changed its tactics regarding the PPS program.

Jewish worker representatives were even less inclined toward compromise with the Bund than were the Jewish Section's intelligentsia. These representatives included the worker from Vilna, who had formerly favored compromise at the first conference but had changed his position. A worker from Grodno took the position that the party could no longer harbor any illusions that the Bund, which was becoming more nationalistic and chauvinistic, would change its tactics. "The only path for us rests in strengthening our own organization," the Grodno worker maintained. In the end, Horwitz's proposal was accepted (five votes for, three opposed).[53]

Sachs took it upon himself to reconcile the first conference resolutions with the central committee's objections voiced earlier in the year. He succeeded in overturning the previous decision on the unofficial participation of Jewish Section members in Bundist demonstrations, although some delegates were dissatisfied. Kwiatek in particular favored openly defying the party leadership. Interestingly, it was the worker representatives from the northwest provinces—recent converts to the Polish cause—who opposed any concession to the Bund. It thus appeared that PPS Jews from Grodno, Białystok, and Vilna often strongly identified with the Polish national struggle. Monachim Wajner, who was a leader of the Grodno division in 1900–1903 and of the Białystok division in 1904, later commented that those few Jewish workers in the Lithuanian-Belarussian provinces who joined the PPS did so chiefly out of identification with the "historic injustice" done to the Polish nation.[54]

## PPS-Bund Relations, 1903–4

In 1903 relations between the Bund and the PPS began to improve as the polemic over the right of Jews to an independent socialist organization shifted away from the PPS to the RSDRP. The conflict between Lenin's Iskra faction and the Bund came to a head at the second congress of the RSDRP in July 1903, when the Bund withdrew from the Russian party after its demand for autonomous status was denied. Piłsudski and Kelles-Krauz sought to exploit the Bund's conflict with the Russian Social Democrats. To the PPS, the

Bund's disillusionment with the RSDRP reaffirmed what they had been arguing all along: that true freedom could only be achieved by severing the western provinces from Russian rule. Consequently, the PPS urged the Bund in the second half of 1903 to join with the Lithuanian and Polish socialist parties. Kelles-Krauz appealed to the Bund in August 1903, arguing that unlike the Russian revolutionaries, the PPS was ready to grant the Bund full autonomy. Consistent with the PPS sixth congress resolution, Kelles-Krauz wrote, "those Jews who so desire would have full rights to create Jewish schools and other cultural institutions in the whole territory of a free Poland." He concluded that "having thus the assurance of full national rights and corporate autonomy in independent Poland, the Bund should at last depart from its absurd 'reflections' on such a political question as the independence of Poland, and embrace the aspirations of the proletariat of the country in which the vast majority of Jews live."[55]

Meanwhile, Piłsudski went about gathering PPS members in Vilna to aid in the production of *Walka*, the new PPS organ in Lithuania, and reflected further on the Bund and the Jewish question. "The existence of the Bund," he wrote, "is closely connected with an important issue—the Jewish question—which . . . complicates all our political evaluations and all social relations, particularly when we take into account that the Bund's main area of influence lies both in Lithuania, where our relations until now have been weak, and in Belarus, where we have no influence whatsoever."[56] In the third issue of *Walka,* which appeared in November 1903, Piłsudski published his last articles on the Bund. For the first time, Piłsudski began to praise the Bund's success in spreading antitsarist sentiments among Jewish workers. "Although we cannot agree with the Bund on some of their positions," Piłsudski wrote, "we have to recognize that their activities have developed into a strong revolutionary movement in Lithuanian cities and have created civic mindedness among those in Lithuania who heretofore had been wholly separated from political life."[57]

Piłsudski also reflected on the transformed situation in Russian Poland since the 1890s. Above all, he wrote, several political parties had evolved in the previous years. In particular, the National Democrats and the Bund had begun to organize workers and distribute illegal literature on a mass scale comparable to the PPS. The party had to recognize, Piłsudski wrote, that "the Bund puts out better and livelier writings than we; the literature in Russian, Yiddish, and Polish is plentiful; they [organize] demonstrations and disturbances everywhere in the empire and even [their use of] terror is sufficiently effective." The second most important development, he maintained, had been the spread of national consciousness in the eastern borderlands. In addition to the growth of the Polish Right and the Jewish socialist Left, he remarked, the Ruthenians and Lithuanians were now "becoming visible," not to mention the Caucasians and Finns. Consequently, "we must [act] in a spirit of compromise, not of control, and not of conquest."[58] The year 1903 also saw the publication of Piłsudski's essay on the underground socialist press, in which he also praised the Bund. In a discussion of the PPS's role in smuggling large quantities of illegal literature into the empire, he wrote, "So far, only the Jewish Section 'Bund' has followed the example of the PPS and succeeded in setting up a secret mechanism for producing books in the country."[59]

Piłsudski also wrote two feature articles on historic Lithuania and the Jews, both of which he linked to a wider context. With regard to Lithuania, Piłsudski stated clearly that an alliance of all socialist forces in the territory of historic Lithuanian was central to the realization of political freedom. The mistake of the Bund, he argued, was that its faith in a constitutional solution was misguided, for it only addressed the question of individual freedoms. Any comprehensive solution had to take into account the national aspirations of the Poles and Lithuanians. "This is not about fusing socialist organizations in Lithuania under the control of the PPS," he declared. "It is about the creation of a powerful union of all socialist parties in the territories of historic Lithuania. Without this, victory cannot be achieved." To allay their fears of territorial conquest, he concluded by stating that it would be premature to discuss whether the result would be three separate states or one federal republic.[60] Piłsudski followed the article on Lithuania with an emotional plea to the Bund. In the last article he would ever write on his party's relations with the Bund, Piłsudski castigated the Bund for continuing to refuse to enter into an alliance with the Lithuanian and Polish socialist parties. "The Bund, which is the main representative of the worker's movement among Jews in Lithuania," he wrote, "heretofore does not want to take into consideration the aspirations and needs of the Polish and Lithuanian people, nor does it regard it necessary even to acquaint the Jewish working masses with the life, history, pains, and hopes of its [Polish and Lithuanian comrades]." They forget that "without the Christian proletariat, the Jewish worker is powerless in the face of the tsarist state."[61]

But Piłsudski's longtime hope for a PPS-Bund union failed to materialize. Despite the bitter conflict with Lenin and the Bund's withdrawal from the Russian party, the Bund never wavered from its all-Russian orientation. Even while *Di arbeyter shtimme* tried to deflect accusations of Bundist "hostility" to the national aspirations of Poles and Lithuanians, the Russified Bundist leadership preserved the view that the breakup of Russia into national states would undermine the unity of the Jewish working class. "With all their arguments with the Russians," one historian of the Bund has stated, "the Bundists stood together with them in giving the class war priority over their own national goals. They thus saw the PPS as divisive and nationalist."[62]

In addition to Piłsudski's changing position, the year 1904 saw the appearance of theoretical works on the Jewish question by two prominent PPS activists, Kelles-Krauz and Józef Kwiatek. Kelles-Krauz (1872–1905), born in Congress Poland to a Polish gentry family, received his formal education in Paris, where he studied at the Sorbonne and afterward, at the Haute École des Sciences Politiques.[63] As a PPS activist, Kelles-Krauz became increasingly interested in the national question in general and in the Jewish question in particular. In a 1902 essay Kelles-Krauz insisted that the rise of the Zionist movement signified the emergence of a modern Jewish nationality. "I call the Jews a modern nationality," Kelles-Krauz wrote in 1902, "because the Jewish nationality is being formed under the influence of these same factors that have strengthened or revived [the] French, German, Italian, Slovene [nationalities]."[64] But it was in the pages of the prestigious Kraków monthly *Krytyka* that Kelles-Krauz developed his most original analysis of the Jewish national question. In "On the Question of Jewish Nationality," Kelles-Krauz observed that emigration was certainly not the solution to the Jewish problem, because the majority of Jews will remain in eastern Europe, while Jewish assimilation would not take place in the near future. The rise of political parties demanding that Jews be regarded as a nation confirmed, Kelles-Krauz argued, that Jewish national identity was not a temporary phenomenon. Kelles-Krauz thus concluded that Jews had to have the right to freely develop the Yiddish language and culture. "In my opinion, the answer [to the Jewish question] is very simple: we should broaden the idea of equal civil rights for Jews to encompass the right to posses their own nationality. We should recognize this nationality to the extent that Jews adopt it." Kelles-Krauz concluded that it was inconsistent to support the right of Jews to full civic equality while simultaneously limiting the right to develop a distinct Jewish nationality.[65]

A less renegade view on the Jewish question was expressed by Kwiatek. Kwiatek came from a Polish-speaking Jewish household in Congress Poland and received a secular primary and secondary education. He entered the faculty of law at Warsaw University, where he became active in the PPS. As a member of the party's Jewish Committee beginning in 1902, Kwiatek took a special interest in Jewish affairs. In his study *The Jewish Question*, Kwiatek, like Kelles-Krauz, linked the origins and causes of Jewish separateness in Polish lands to nineteenth-century developments. In a survey of the Jewish problem in the first half of the nineteenth century, Kwiatek commented that assimilation became the principle slogan of the Jewish intelligentsia. "Until recently," Kwiatek wrote, "[assimilation] was universally regarded as the only answer to the Jewish question." But on Polish lands the Jews had preserved a distinct national-cultural identity. And this was not simply a transitory phase toward assimilation. "Jewish separateness will endure for quite some time and is even conducive to the development of a separate Jewish culture." Unlike Kelles-Krauz, Kwiatek expressed little interest in the theoretical side of the problem of Jewish nationality. Rather, he was concerned with the practical question of how to respond to the phenomenon of Jewish separateness on Polish lands. Kwiatek maintained that as long as the Jews regarded themselves as a nation, the Poles had to extend recognition of this fact, for "it would be absurd in today's climate to deny the distinct character of the Jews." However, the right of Jews to cultural-national development did not mean that the Jewish working class had to struggle separately from the working class of the country in which it lived. "True socialists must march together in one political organization." Kwiatek thus came to the following conclusion: "Not with empty chatter about the superiority of assimilation over cultural distinc-

tiveness or vice versa, but with the idea of the necessary cooperation of the working classes . . . is socialism coming closer to resolving the Jewish question. . . . Every socialist should engrave this elementary truth on his memory. Let every socialist, if he be a Jew,
fight Zionism with word and deed, and if a Christian, combat anti-
Semitism with word and by his own example."[66] Thus, on the eve of
the 1905 Revolution, it appeared that the PPS was poised toward the
full recognition of Jewish nationality. It was not until the split of the
PPS into two parties in 1906 that some members would come out
publicly against the idea of Jewish nationality.

At the beginning of the period under examination, the PPS continued to boldly defend the principles inscribed in its founding party
platform. But with the Bund now applying the term "nationality" to
the Jews, several prominent party members (Piłsudski, Kelles-
Krauz, Sachs, Bujno, and Kwiatek) believed that conceding on this
point was politically expedient. The willingness of some party
members to recognize the principle of Jewish nationality represented a fundamental shift. The old assimilationist view had been
reflected in *Der arbeyter*'s London period (1898–1901), when the
Yiddish organ spoke of the "Polish proletariat" as one comprised of
different faiths. But beginning in 1902 *Der arbeyter* began to refer
regularly to Jews as a separate nationality while simultaneously
advocating Jewish support for Polish independence. But despite
Piłsudski's new position, the June 1902 congress resolutions reflected a view of Lithuania as Polish territory, for all Lithuanian and
Jewish revolutionary groups, the congress declared, should agitate
as "autonomous bodies" within the *Polish* Socialist Party.

In the course of eighteen months the party's left wing, led by
Sachs, formed an oppositional faction which sought to reform the
hallowed outline program from 1892. They argued that the PPS did
not have the right to demand that the Bund relinquish its organizational independence. Until the end of 1903 Piłsudski continued to
oppose the right of the Bund to such independence. We have
shown, however, that Piłsudski began to reevaluate his position in
1903 after giving up hopes of programmatic unity between the two
parties and began to openly praise the Bund's role in Lithuania for
the first time. This chapter has argued that Piłsudski's increasingly
conciliatory stand on the Bund was linked to a shift in his concep-

tion of the nation; by recognizing the right of Jews to national autonomy in a future Polish state, the conception of that state had to be altered. Henceforth autonomy in the future state would have to be based on both territory (Lithuania, Ukraine) *and* extraterritorial nationality (Jews, Germans).

# ■ 8.
# The 1905 Revolution in Russia and the Transformation of PPS-Bund Relations

*The mere granting of equal civil rights for Jews is too little. As with all other nationalities, they must be guaranteed the full freedom to develop their own culture and to use their own language . . . in schools, administration, and the courts.*
CENTRAL COMMITTEE OF THE PPS (DECEMBER 1905)

*And what a sight it was! In the middle of the meadow stood a huddle of men like a black mound or a shadow cast by the moon. The mound was silent, straining towards the center where the debaters were holding forth. First one, then the other of the Sedletzer Bundists faced off against the Warsaw PPS man, and the crowd stood on tiptoe, necks craned, wedged together in a thick silent mass that blackened the field around. The debate went on and on, argument against argument, ever more spirited and biting . . .*

*There will be no end to this, decided one of the Sedletzers, and suddenly called aloud: "Brothers, friends! Are you with the Bund?"*

*"Yes! Yes!" cried the crowd.*

*"Friends, brothers!" countered his rival, "are you with the PPS?"*

*"Yes! Yes!" came the answer, even louder than before.*
I. M. WEISSENBERG, *A SHTETL* (1906)

THE 1905 REVOLUTION was a watershed in the history of imperial Russia. With concessions to worker demands, the relaxation of censorship, and the transformation of Russia into a semi-constitutional monarchy, the empire's inhabitants were abruptly thrust into mass electoral politics. Within a matter of months newly legalized parties drafted political programs, issued legal newspapers in the vernacular, and organized electoral campaigns. In the pages that follow, I assess the impact of the social and political upheaval on the two parties under examination and argue that the 1905 revolution paved the way for closer relations, both in terms of practical work and ideological affinities. First, I show that in December 1905 the PPS became the first European socialist party to officially recognize the principle of extraterritorial autonomy for Jews, including the right to use one's native language in schools, administration, and courts of law. PPS support for Jewish *national* rights challenges a consensus in Jewish historiography; namely, the view that in the pre-WWI period, all Polish parties, including the socialists, were opposed to Jewish national rights.[1] Finally, I analyze the evolution of the Bund's position on the question of Polish independence.

### Prelude to Revolution:
### The 1904 Russo-Japanese War

By the first three years of the twentieth century, the PPS and the Bund represented the dominant socialist organizations in tsarist Russia. With an estimated membership of 5,600 in 1900 and leaping to some 30,000 in 1903, the Bund in fact became the largest workers' party in the empire.[2] Despite the PPS's influential role, by the end of 1903 the illegal Polish party exercised only a slight influence on the industrial and artisan work force it claimed to represent, with no more than a 1,000 to 1,500 organized members.[3] The onset of the Russo-Japanese War in February 1904, however, led to increased popularity for the socialist parties in imperial Russia's western borderlands. In the first two months of the war, opposition within Russia and the Kingdom of Poland was confined to a small percentage of industrial workers, students, and underground socialist groups. But as the war began to drain vital human and material resources and retard the growth of important sectors of the economy, domestic opposition grew. The decision to confine use of the Trans-Siberian Railway to the transport of military goods had an adverse economic effect. In the course of 1904 the production of silk goods declined by over 25 percent and of woolen goods by 15 percent, while the production of cotton goods, chemicals, and some other industrial products fell by smaller amounts. In addition, the call to arms of some 1.2 million reservists gutted the empire of some its most productive workers.[4]

The economic decline hit the Polish kingdom especially hard. In the second half of the nineteenth century, war-driven demands for raw material during the Crimean (1854) and the Russo-Turkish (1878) Wars had stimulated economic growth in Congress Poland. But whereas previous Russian war involvement dramatically increased demand for Polish industry, Russia's front with Japan was too remote from the kingdom to receive orders for heavy or light industry. The economy in the kingdom consequently declined in the spring of 1904 and reached crisis proportions in September. By the fall many industries in the Warsaw provinces were forced to fire between a fourth and a third of their workers, while wages fell by between a third and a half.[5] A report from the Piotrków provincial governor estimated that wages had dropped by more than a half and that Christian and Jewish charity groups were running soup kitchens to feed unemployed workers.[6] By the end of December approximately one hundred thousand people were out of work, and overall production in the kingdom had declined by more than a third.[7]

Meanwhile, socialist parties in the Polish provinces mobilized antiwar sentiment through demonstrations, agitation, and propaganda. Sympathy for revolutionary groups was thus especially pronounced in the kingdom. During this period the PPS played a disproportionate role in the antiwar movement, helping to transform the organization from a small conspiratorial group to the beginnings of a mass party. Through agitation leaflets and its clandestine organ *Robotnik*, the PPS led the campaign to discredit the war effort, propagating the idea that the kingdom was providing a disproportionate share of recruits.[8] Although it exaggerated the numbers, it helped create an environment whereby the antiwar movement became stronger in the kingdom compared with other parts of the empire. Indeed, from November 1904 to January 1905, when Russia sustained major defeats by Japan, the antiwar movement in the kingdom attained a mass character, as demonstrations were almost a daily occurrence. During the course of the Russo-Japanese War, some eighty demonstrations took place in the kingdom, forty-four of which were organized by the PPS.[9] Still, the demonstrations were relatively small, with the majority consisting of between one hundred and five hundred participants.[10] The Bund similarly began to take a leading role in Jewish life during this time. Its revolutionary vision was expressed in a December 1904 leaflet: "The order of the day is the liquidation of the Autocracy. Mighty blows, which nobody can parry, will drive the decrepit monster into the abyss. . . . The sun will shine joyfully on this great land where the heavy chains of political oppression will clank, where the dark shades of violence move, and the muffled groans of the victims—of millions who have been destroyed—can be heard. That will be the sun of freedom. The slave will give way to the citizen."[11] The PPS, the Bund, and the SDKPiL gained considerable popular support for their efforts to mobilize sentiment against the war. By the end of 1904 PPS membership had grown fourfold in Warsaw (368 to 1,500) and fivefold in Łódź (100 to 500), while it had developed strong local organizations in Kalisz, Lublin, Radom, and Zagłębie. In the fall of 1904 the Bund's membership grew to 900 in Łódź and 1,200 in Warsaw.[12] Similarly, the SDKPiL in Łódź grew from 25 members in the summer of 1904 to 120 by January 1905.[13]

## Bloody Sunday and the January–February General Strike in Russian Poland

By the beginning of 1905, when the Russian army's capitulation at Port Arthur to the Japanese raised domestic opposition to an acute form, a strike movement at the great Putilov works on January 3/16 grew to embrace over one hundred thousand persons. The massive strike gave rise to a plan for presenting a petition to the tsar. The petition demanded a legislative assembly elected with universal suffrage, an eight-hour workday, equal civil rights, and amnesty for political prisoners.[14] On the early morning of January 9/22, Father Gapon led some one hundred thousand persons in a peaceful march in Saint Petersburg to present the petition to the tsar. But as the demonstrators approached the Winter Palace, the army opened fire into the crowd, killing 130 people and wounding 299, according to official sources. "Bloody Sunday" in Saint Petersburg, as it came to be known, led to a widespread revolt among the middle and lower classes and sparked an empire-wide revolutionary upheaval. A vast, spontaneous strike movement ensued, making the Russian industrial workers a powerful revolutionary force. One day after the Saint Petersburg massacre, some 160,000 workers in Russia abstained from work in protest, of whom 45,000 were from the Moscow region alone. During the month of January an unprecedented 410,000 workers went on strike throughout the empire, throwing it into complete disarray. As one historian of late imperial Russia commented, "Bloody Sunday activated the working class to a degree unprecedented in Russian history."[15]

News of the Saint Petersburg massacre spread rapidly throughout the empire's industrial regions. The actual socialist parties, however, were slow to respond. The PPS program had been based on a lack of faith in the potential of the Russian revolutionary movement. It was thus no surprise that the PPS responded with hesitation and uncertainty to the spontaneous strike movement in Saint Petersburg and Moscow. This hesitation was not limited to the PPS. Even the SDKPiL and the Bund did not respond immediately, so surprised were they by the events in Saint Petersburg.[16] While the SDKPiL was the first to issue a leaflet in solidarity with the strike in Saint Petersburg, the local Warsaw section of the PPS followed suit, refusing to wait for directives from the executive committee, led by anti-Russian Old Guardists like Piłsudski.[17] In the Warsaw organization's excitement, old taboos broke down. On January 24 the PPS consulted the Bund on the possibility of joint action, and the PPS's Warsaw organization, led by Józef Kwiatek, organized a strike committee with divisions all over the city. The PPS, the Bund, and the SDKPiL then agreed to issue a strike call for January 28, which was preceded by the distribution of leaflets outlining economic demands. Thus, the PPS now actively courted the Bund and the SDKPiL, once bitter rivals. The workers themselves, however, began the strike one day earlier in Warsaw and Łódź.[18]

The local PPS committees in Warsaw and Łódź formulated a set of political demands in response to the Saint Petersburg–led strike movement. Józef Kwiatek, a leading PPS figure in Warsaw and a Jewish Committee member, drafted a manifesto in the form of a party leaflet, "Our Political Declaration." Distributed on January 30 in Warsaw and other parts of the kingdom, the Warsaw committee's political declaration included the demand for basic democratic freedoms, including freedom of speech, press, and assembly; equal civil rights regardless of faith or nationality; and the right of workers to strike and to form trade unions. It also called for "an independent national life" and demanded the use of Polish in all public institutions. Moreover, the leaflet put forth a new slogan in the PPS movement: that for a Polish constituent assembly in Warsaw chosen by universal suffrage and equal, secret, and direct elections.[19]

Kwiatek's political declaration departed from the PPS's founding program in two ways. First, it explicitly linked the goal of national liberation to a general revolution in Russia.[20] For the first time, the PPS based a political declaration on cooperation with a political transformation in the Russian Empire. In her authoritative study Anna Żarnowska remarked that Kwiatek's leaflet marked a new political line in the party and the "emancipation" of the PPS from the hegemony of the Old Guard.[21] Second, the WKR declaration included a separate point on the Jews, demanding "the guarantee of free cultural development for the Jewish people and other national minorities."[22] The significant WKR political declaration was subsequently reprinted by local workers committees in Łódź, Kielce, Częstochowa, Zagłębie, Lublin, Zawiercie, and Kalisz.[23]

The declaration of the PPS's Warsaw organization appeared on the first day of the socialist-led general strike. By January 30 47,000 striking workers made Warsaw one of the empire's major revolutionary centers.[24] Clashes with the army, which brought twenty-nine companies of infantry, five squadrons of cavalry, and four Cossack units into Warsaw, resulted in ninety-three deaths and several hundred casualties, according to official sources.[25] The largest strike area in the kingdom, however, was in the Piotrków province, where some hundred thousand workers left work. After massive walkouts on January 17/28 in Łódź, strikes embraced other industrial pockets in Piotrków, spreading to Częstochowa and the Dąbrowa basin on February 1. A state of alert, imposed on January 30 in the provinces of Warsaw and Piotrków, was extended to the provinces of Kalisz, Radom, and Siedlce on February 4 and to the whole kingdom by February 14.[26] The Polish kingdom thus played a major part in the general empire-wide strike movement, providing one-third of the 410,000 striking workers in January. In January–March 1905 over twenty times as many workers participated in strikes than in any one year between 1895 and 1905.[27]

The January–February general strike was a major turning point for the revolutionary parties in Russian Poland. For the Bund and the SDKPiL, whose social democratic programs called for a general

*Arthur Szyk, "The Italian Page" (1928) from* The Statue of Kalisz
*(1926–30). Jews and Poles with banners of the Polish Socialist Party erecting
a barricade in Łódź against Russian troops during the 1905 Revolution. The
lower banner reads, in Yiddish, "PPS: Jewish Section." (The Jewish Museum
of New York / Art Resource, N.Y.)*

empire-wide transformation, the revolutionary events in Russia only strengthened party unity. But for the PPS the spontaneous rise of an organized Russian working-class movement split the party into two factions: a left-wing Young (*Młodzi*) faction and the right-wing insurrectionist Old Guard (*Starzy*). During the dramatic January events local PPS divisions acted independently not only in matters of tactics but also in drafting a revised political program. At the time the Old Guard leadership was abroad: Piłsudski, Jodko-Narkiewicz, Jędrzejowski, and Wasilewski were in Kraków, while Wojciechowski was in London.[28] The two factions differed on two fundamental programmatic issues: the place of independence in the party program; and the party's relation to the revived Russian revolutionary movement. For the PPS organizations in Congress Poland, the January–February strike movement clearly tipped the balance in favor of the Young faction, which now linked the attainment of Polish freedom to the overthrow of autocracy, and argued that the Old Guard leadership had underestimated the revolutionary potential of the Russian working class.

### March–June 1905: The Rise of the PPS Young Faction

Following January–February 1905 both the Warsaw committee and the Regional Workers' Committee of Warsaw (Warszawski OKR) took the initiative to convene a party congress, but without the prior consent of the party's executive committee. At the time Piłsudski was in Kraków.[29] In March 1905 thirty delegates gathered in Warsaw for the seventh congress to reassess the party program in light of current revolutionary conditions. The Old Guardist executive committee chose not to attend and instead sent Aleksander Malinowski. The majority of delegates sympathized with the Young faction, although its leadership was weakened by the absence of Kwiatek and Sachs, both of whom were imprisoned at the time.[30] Maks Horwitz, however, played a prominent role at the congress.[31] The party congress voted on a new CKR, which included Piłsudski, even though he was not present.[32]

The congress's programmatic pronouncements revealed declining support among rank-and-file members for the separatist leanings of the Old Guard. It retained Polish independence as a party aim, but now in the form of the demand for a constituent assembly in Warsaw. That the demand for a constituent assembly was made dependent on the overthrow of the tsar was a radical departure from the outline program of 1892. The congress also revealed its lack of support for the Old Guard's position on the Bund. In a compromise statement, the congress called on the Bund to recognize the demand for a constitutional assembly in Warsaw, but also favored limited cooperation, resolving that "the congress regards it as desirable to make joint arrangements with the Bund for May Day demonstrations."[33] Finally, the congress entrusted the CKR with the task of creating a new military wing—the Conspiratorial Fighting Organization (Organizacja Spiskowo-Bojowa, OSB).[34]

Although the seventh congress divided power between the left and right wings of the party, the Old Guard still had considerable influence. They maintained a strong presence on the CKR as well as control of *Przedświt* in Kraków. In comparison to their former dominant position, however, the Old Guard had been isolated after the March congress, although not yet marginalized.

Following the seventh congress, the PPS's Jewish Section convened its third conference to take a position on the events in Russia and in the party. Taking place April 1905 in Warsaw, the conference had some thirty-one participants, representing Warsaw, Łódź, Pabianice, Kalisz, Siedlce, Białystok, Grodno, and Vilna, reflecting a distinct growth in the Jewish Section's membership.[35] In fact, the conference noted a "significant increase" of the Jewish Section's influence in the two intervening years since its last conference, although it acknowledged the Bund remained stronger. The conference report reveals that in the big cities like Warsaw, Vilna and Grodno, the Jewish Section had one hundred to two hundred dues-paying members, with a total of between five hundred and one thousand. It estimated that the Bund had about twice as many members. The major reasons for the Bund's greater influence, the congress resolved, were the lack of Yiddish party material and the lack of a Yiddish-speaking intelligentsia.[36]

Debates showed the Jewish Section's sympathy for the left-wing Young faction. Regarding the presentation of the party's political program, the conference expressed its solidarity with the struggle of Russian workers. The party press, the report advised, should emphasize the "internationalism" of the PPS program. One delegate from Białystok protested the use in *Przedświt* of the derogatory word *moskal* for Russians. Another complained that many leaflets had employed slogans such as "Long Live a Free Polish People" and "Long Live Polish Lands," which, it argued, alienated Jewish workers. The slogan of a "democratic republic," it was argued, clearly articulated the party's political ideals and thus should be the party's main political slogan. Delegates also presented a critique of party leaflets translated into Yiddish that had employed such terms as "the Polish people." Instead of the term "the Polish proletariat," PPS leaflets should employ "the proletariat of Poland."[37] The conference passed a motion urging the PPS to emphasize a class-based point of view, to publish brochures on anti-Semitism, and to clarify the party's new political program to Jewish workers at every opportunity.

The conference participants also debated a resolution on PPS-Bund relations. Significantly, the majority of delegates argued against the seventh congress resolution on the Bund, characterizing it as too conciliatory. The PPS should continue to fight against the Bund's "separatism," it was argued. The majority was uncomfortable with the idea of joint PPS-Bund demonstrations, given the programmatic gap between the two parties. The Jewish Committee representative, however, supported the position taken at the March congress, maintaining that in revolutionary times the party had to unite against the common enemy. The delegates agreed to a compromise resolution. The conference accepted the seventh congress resolution on the need for limited cooperation between the two organizations but vowed to continue its struggle against the Bund's "programmatic exclusivity."[38]

Meanwhile, the ideological and tactical positions of the Young and the Old Guard faction emerged more clearly after the March congress. In an effort to reach a programmatic compromise, Young faction leaders from Warsaw organized the first of a series of party councils in June 1905, which took place in Józefów outside of Warsaw. Jodko-Narkiewicz, Feliks Perl, and A. Malinowski represented the Old Guard, while Piłsudski represented the OSB. The more influential Young faction, led by Marian Bielecki and supported by Bujno, Szymon Posner, Horwitz, Kamila Horwitz-Kancewiczowa, and Feliks Sachs, numerically overwhelmed the Old Guard.[39]

The party debated several issues, including the relation of the

PPS to the Russian revolution. First, the Young faction complained that, under Jodko-Narkiewicz's editorship, *Przedświt* had continued to promote the Old Guard's position. In order to make the foreign committee organ reflect the party's new orientation, the council voted to replace Jodko-Narkiewicz.[40] On relations with Russian revolutionaries, Bielecki argued for a further modification of the 1892 Paris program, declaring that the party's most important task was the overthrow of the tsar through cooperation with other revolutionary groups. The party's political aims, Bielecki argued, could now be represented in the demand for a constituent assembly in Warsaw. Piłsudski and Jodko-Narkiewicz, however, countered that the goals of the Polish and the Russian movement had to be clearly separate; the PPS could only achieve its aim through increased terrorist actions leading to a national armed uprising.[41]

The arguments of the Young faction prevailed. "The triumph of revolution in the Polish kingdom and Lithuania," the final resolution stated, "is directly linked to the victory of revolution in all parts of the Russian Empire, and particularly in Russia proper. Revolution in the kingdom thus must be a constituent part of a transformation in the Russian Empire as a whole." With regard to the party's military wing, the council recognized the use of terror as a revolutionary tactic. OSB division leaders, however, were to be subordinate to and directed by the CKR.[42] In addition, the council voted on a new CKR, putting the central committee entirely into the hands of the Young. The new CKR included Feliks Sachs, Feliks Kon, Jan Rutkiewicz, Adam Bujno, and Maks Horwitz.[43] Finally, the party council resolved to establish a commission to revise the Paris program of 1892.

The PPS's seventh congress and June council marked a de facto rejection of the Paris program of 1892. The revisionist sentiments of the Young faction led to a bitter rivalry, with the Old Guard treating the June council as a virtual coup. The Old Guard was nonetheless able to regain a foothold in the party in October 1905. Just as the Young faction wrested control of the party, the tsarist police cracked down on PPS circles, arresting three CKR members in August.[44] Struck by the arrests of its major leaders, a provisional central committee organized a second party council, which took place October 1905 in Minsk.[45]

At the Minsk party council, the Old Guard persuaded the delegates to restructure the fighting organization. Henceforth, the Technical Fighting Organization (Organizacja Techniczno-Bojowa, OTB) replaced the OSB as a military training school. Furthermore, the Minsk council agreed to create a new Central Fighting Circle under the direction of Piłsudski, which at the time consisted of some 1,345 fighters (*bojowcy*).[46] With these concessions to the Old Guard, Piłsudski was able to gradually remove the Fighting Division (Wydział Bojowy) from the control of the CKR. The decision of the second council thus constituted, as Blobaum has observed, a power-sharing formula intended to uphold party unity.[47] This unity, however, would barely outlive the remaining months of 1905.

### The 1905 October Manifesto and the Rise of the Polish Nationalist Movement

Before the summer of 1905 only socialist parties competed with the PPS for the allegiance of the working class in Russian Poland. With the explosive rise of Polish working-class activity in 1905, however, Polish nationalists began for the first time to organize workers, competing directly with the PPS and the SDKPiL. In the late spring of 1905 Dmowski made efforts to form an Endecja labor division. The new antisocialist labor organization appeared shortly after, calling into being the National Workers' Union (Narodowy Związek Robotniczy, NZR). The NZR held its founding congress in June 1905 and issued a newspaper, *Pochodnia* (The torch). Its program called for Polish national solidarity and the defense of workers' interests, but came out against the principle of class struggle and international proletarian unity.[48] The NZR nonetheless committed itself to improving workers' conditions, to forming a labor union, to sponsoring cultural and mutual-aid activities, as well as to creating its own fighting organization. By July 1905 the NZR, even if supported by only a small group of workers, became engaged in antistrike and antisocialist agitation among workers, particularly in Łódź, where it declared war against the "anarchy" spread by socialist "criminals."[49]

With the inauguration of a strike wave in October and the dramatic October Manifesto, which announced the creation of a representative parliament, the Polish nationalists were able to make significant progress in drawing workers to their movement. The

October–November general strike began in the kingdom as an expression of solidarity for the All-Russian Union of Railroad Employees and Workers in Moscow, which organized a general strike on October 4/17. So successful was the strike that by October 10/23 service in Moscow, the hub of the empire's railroad system, came to a complete halt, and the strike quickly spread to Saint Petersburg.[50] The railroad-worker strike, which gradually spread to factory workers and artisans, spread to Congress Poland on October 11/24 with little forewarning and largely without party leadership, reaching a peak just as the October Manifesto was proclaimed on October 17/30. By the end of October the strike movement had encompassed the majority of workers in the Piotrków and Warsaw provinces. In Łódź, for example, the number of striking workers rose from 2,879 on October 24 to 64,000 by October 31.[51]

The announcement of the October Manifesto transformed the general strike in Russian Poland. Earlier the strike movement had been a vague expression of solidarity with the railway strike in Russia. The October Manifesto, however, brought about a pronounced phase of political protests among industrial workers when attempts were made to test the validity of the government proposals and ensure that its provisions were carried out. Led by the socialist parties, workers made demands for the release of political prisoners. They also demanded further political reforms, pointing to autonomy—but not independence—for the Polish kingdom. The October–November strike thus provided support for the political protest movement waged by socialist parties. Yet, it is significant that no worker-led strike employed the demand for Polish independence.[52]

As the strike movement in Russian Poland continued into the first week of November, the NZR began to challenge the socialist monopoly on working-class demonstrations. Following a PPS-led strike on November 1, a nationalist-led rally in Warsaw the next day drew seventy thousand people.[53] On November 4 an NZR rally attracted close to two hundred thousand participants. And on November 5, one hundred thousand persons participated in a nationalist march.[54] In the wake of the massive strike wave, the Russian government imposed martial law in the Polish kingdom on November 10, troop reinforcements were brought in, and the October–November general strike came to an end. .

The October Manifesto brought about two major shifts in the working-class movement in the Polish kingdom. First, it created a more favorable view of the tsarist government not only among the middle and upper classes but also among workers through concrete concessions, particularly the right to form unions. It also revived hopes for a settlement of the Polish question through some form of autonomy. Although martial law destroyed the October euphoria, the government-proposed reforms politicized the masses. The second main result of the October–November general strike was the penetration of the Polish nationalist movement into the ranks of the working class. This, in turn, was a victory for the Russian government. As Endecja became more conciliatory toward the tsarist regime and attracted more workers, the Polish socialist movement lost some support from the industrial working class. With government reforms and improved economic conditions for workers, the NZR's more moderate political program and antisocialist agitation began to make inroads. The NZR's openly anti-Semitic propaganda also contributed to its support among Polish workers, according to Richard Lewis.[55]

In sum, the October–November "Days of Freedom" splintered the working-class movement in Congress Poland into a unified nationalist Right and a fractured socialist Left. The politicization of the masses, the shift from revolution to reform, and the revival of the nationalist movement seriously challenged the socialists. The rapid expansion of nationalist sentiment and mass electoral politics led to the emergence of political anti-Semitism in the Polish kingdom.

## The "Completion" of the Bund's National Program, 1904–5

While the revolutionary events of 1905 widened divisions within the PPS, it had the opposite effect on the Bund. For the Bund, the 1905 revolution strengthened party unity in terms of both ideology and tactics. Even on the contentious national question, the old left and right divisions within the Bund became almost indistinguishable by the fall of 1905, a process that included an accommodation of former differences over the principle of national-cultural autonomy and the Polish question.

In the two years following the contentious fifth congress of June 1903, the combined events of the Russo-Japanese War and the revolutionary upheaval of 1905 made the national question more and more significant for underground political parties. Thus, even when the Bund debated the national question in 1901 and 1903, it was not a burning issue at the time. During the course of 1904, when Russia's successive defeats in the Far East were met with growing domestic opposition, the need to adopt a clear position on the national question grew more urgent. According to Vladimir Medem, one of the Bund's most important theorists on the national question at the time, the period 1903–5 witnessed much debate within the Bund on the national question. He recalled that by 1905 most skeptics within the party leadership switched allegiances to the national wing.[56]

In fact, it was in 1904 that the Bund's central committee put forth national-cultural autonomy as a *political* demand for the first time. In a widely distributed central committee proclamation with a print run of fifty-eight thousand, it was argued that the demand of equal civil rights was no longer sufficient for workers of subjugated nations. To freely develop, to proceed toward true freedom, it was now necessary to put forth demands shared by all oppressed nations: the freedom, guaranteed by law, of cultural development for all nations; and the equal right of one's native language in all government and social institutions. Jewish workers, the central committee proclaimed, "must have the opportunity to receive education in their own language. They must have the right to use their language in all governmental institutions, courts of law, in their relations with factory inspectors, at public gatherings, and so on." It stressed that the demand for cultural autonomy applied to the working classes of all oppressed nations. The leaflet concluded with the slogans, "Down with National Oppression!" "Long Live a Democratic Republic!" "Long Live Equal National Rights!" and "Long Live Socialism!"[57] As Medem commented, the December 1904 proclamation "represented more than a significant political step. It also indicated that the doubts and vacillation in our own ranks were gone." He continued: "Our Central Committee had always been exceedingly careful, always conscious of its heavy responsibility, and it never would have taken a decisive step without first ascertaining that the mass of party members was in accord with it. Here was clear testimony that the sentiment of the party had become solidified as early as the end of 1904."[58]

The decision to make national-cultural autonomy an official part of the Bund's program came in the fall of 1905, when the central committee summoned thirty delegates to Zurich to attend the party's sixth congress. Discussions on the national question predominated at the congress. The main concern was whether to preserve or revise the fourth congress's resolution of April 1901. Medem led off the debate with a speech in favor of the official inclusion of Jewish national-cultural autonomy in the Bund's program. The motion passed with twenty-five votes for and four opposed.[59] The official resolution called for the equality of all nationalities, which it defined in an extraterritorial manner, as well as written guarantees for the right of each nationality to free cultural development. "Seeing that Russia is inhabited by different peoples who are becoming more and more mixed together with the development of capitalism," the resolution stated, "the above-mentioned governmental-juridical arrangements can only be framed in an extraterritorial [manner]: in the form of national-cultural autonomy." The Bund's solution to the national question in general and the Jewish question in particular thus consisted of three points: full civil and political equality for Jews; legislation guaranteeing the right of Jews to use their native language in courts and in all public institutions; and national-cultural autonomy.[60]

Meanwhile, the Bund still had not taken an official position on the Polish question since its establishment. In fact, shortly before the sixth congress report appeared, the central committee printed an article in the Warsaw-based monthly, *Der bund,* outlining its position on the Polish question in the wake of the 1905 revolution. *Der bund* argued that under current conditions, the independence of Poland was unattainable. First, it was against the interests of both the bourgeoisie and the working class. Clearly, the middle classes were benefiting greatly from the growth of Polish industry under Russian rule. Similarly, the struggle for independence was contrary to the class interests of Polish workers. Even the PPS, the Bund maintained, was now seeing that social upheaval in Russia demanded the unification of all revolutionary groups in the struggle for the overthrow of autocracy. "The proletariat of Poland," it declared, "must therefore struggle together with the proletariat in all parts of Russia for the annihilation of tsarism and the formation of one democratic republic of Russia." Second, the independence of Poland was unattainable militarily. A Polish uprising would have no chance of defeating the combined forces of the partitioning powers. Only a war between the partitioning powers could bring about a restored Poland, and this, the Bund claimed, was "an impossible scenario." Because the restoration of Poland was an unrealizable goal under conditions existing in 1905, the Bund argued that Poles had to link their freedom to the advance of democracy in Russia. "A free Poland," *Der bund* stated, "is only possible in a free Russia."[61]

The article nonetheless acknowledged that a future democratic Russia would have to grant the Polish kingdom a degree of self-rule. Under the influence of the Bund's Warsaw division, whose original Lithuanian leadership had been replaced by 1905 with native Polish-Jewish intellectuals raised in Polonized households, *Der bund* came out in favor of "provincial self-government" for Congress Poland. But because "the Poland question" concerned all nationalities inhabiting Polish lands, the Bund went one step further. Territorial self-rule in Congress Poland had to be accompanied, it argued, by a legal guarantee for the right of non-Polish nationalities to freely develop their culture. "How can we be certain that schools will not be exclusively Polish in an autonomous Congress Poland?" *Der bund* asked. "How can we be guaranteed that [Jews, Germans, and Lithuanians] will have the free opportunity to develop their cultures?" The answer was national-cultural autonomy: "In addition to territorial self-government, the proletariat must demand national-cultural autonomy guaranteeing each nation in Russia the freedom to develop its own culture and the opportunity to receive education in its own language." The Bund reminded its readers that Poles too would benefit from national-cultural autonomy. Such a system would guarantee the right of Poles living outside Congress Poland to their own schools, that is, the right of free national-cultural development. The Bund's answer to the national question in general, and the "Poland question" in particular, was thus threefold: a democratic Russian state; territorial self-government for Congress Poland; and national-cultural autonomy for minority nationalities.[62]

The central committee's article in *Der bund* set the stage for the official resolution that was passed at the Bund's sixth congress in the fall of 1905. The congress delegates included members from the central and foreign committees and representatives from eighteen cities inside the empire and was attended by such leading figures as Vladimir Kossovsky, John Mill, Shmuel Gozhanski, Vladimir Medem, and Marc Liber.[63] Significantly, however, delegates from both the Warsaw branch, including Bronislav Groser, and the Polish Regional Committee, were not able to attend.[64] Thus, at the very congress at which the Polish question was seriously discussed, representatives of the Bund's Polish-Jewish intelligentsia, who had been the most sensitive to Polish concerns, were not present. Despite the absence of Polish Bundists, the congress proceeded with the debate and, without a single opposing vote, came out against the demand for Polish independence. With twenty-five voting in favor and one abstention, the congress passed the following resolution: "The Sixth Congress of the Bund holds that the demand for the independence of Poland cannot be part of a Social Democratic program, and finds that agitating for such a goal can only divert the proletariat . . . , obscure its class consciousness, and shatter the strength of the revolution."[65]

In addition, the congress fell short of explicitly endorsing the PPS demand for a constituent assembly in Warsaw. Instead, it adopted a general position in support of regional autonomy throughout the Russian Empire without a specific clause for Congress Poland. While some acknowledged the need for autonomy in Congress Poland, the majority believed, according to one firsthand account, that demanding a separate Sejm in Warsaw "would have been tantamount to a breaking of the revolutionary front and a splintering of forces."[66] The line between a separate constitution for Poland and outright independence, the delegates concluded, was very thin. The congress thus declared that "the interest of the proletariat from Poland demands the transformation of the Russian state into a democratic system with wide territorial self-government [*zelbstfarvaltung*] and national-cultural autonomy."[67] The Bund's resolution on the Polish question came as no surprise to the PPS. The organ of the PPS's Old Guard faction condemned both the Bund and the SDKPiL for their opposition to PPS demands while mocking the argument that national-cultural autonomy was the only solution to the national question in imperial Russia.[68]

To many Polish Bundists, however, the party's declaration on the

Polish question had not gone far enough. Although the Warsaw Bund was in agreement on the question of Polish independence, it nonetheless supported the specific demand for Polish autonomy. In the pages of the Warsaw Bund's Polish-language organ, *Nasze Hasła*, which first appeared in 1906 and was edited by Groser and Henryk Erlich, the Polish question received considerable attention. While Congress Poland could not exist on its own from an economic point of view, Groser argued, the Poles nevertheless had a right to "administrative autonomy" and a separate legislative Sejm that would deliberate on all questions pertaining to local affairs. But these arrangements, he emphasized, would have to be accompanied by legal guarantees of "full equality for all nations in Poland with regard to use of one's mother tongue in all civil service and state institutions."[69] The opportunity of the Warsaw Bund to put forth its position to the Lithuanian-dominated central committee came in the spring of 1906, when delegates met in Bern to convene the party's seventh conference.[70] Led by Groser, the Warsaw branch garnered support for a revised statement recognizing the demand for Polish autonomy. In a compromise between the Litvak and *poylisher* positions, the Bund issued the following resolution that would remain unchanged until the collapse of the Russian Empire in 1917: "[We] recognize that the position of the Bund's Warsaw committee, which interprets the . . . resolution on territorial self-government in terms of autonomy for Poland, does not violate the accepted congress resolution."[71]

## The PPS and the Jewish Question

The Bund's shift to a national program between 1901 and 1905 increasingly influenced PPS approaches to the Jewish question. We have seen that by 1902, Piłsudski, Kelles-Krauz, and Sachs believed that official recognition of Jewish nationality would help the party compete with the Bund. By 1905 Maks Horwitz ("Henryk Walecki") became the main PPS advocate of Jewish cultural autonomy. As an influential theorist and polemicist within the Young leadership, Horwitz maintained that a guarantee of Jewish rights had to be incorporated into the party's official platform.

Horwitz formulated the PPS's new position in the fall and winter of 1905 both while in prison and in his capacity as coeditor of *Kurjer*

*Codzienny* (Daily courier), the party's first legal daily. Horwitz had joined the party's central committee in June 1905 but was arrested in August. While imprisoned in the Warsaw Citadel he composed, among other things, a manifesto on the Jewish question. When freed on November 1 in the wake of an amnesty for political prisoners, Horwitz gave official expression to his views in the pages of *Kurjer Codzienny*.[72] Appearing under the title "On the Jewish Question," Horwitz's article presented the Young faction's position on the Jewish question for the first time.[73] Meanwhile, *Der arbeyter*, which had become a Warsaw-based weekly with a circulation of twenty thousand copies per issue, published Horwitz's article in Yiddish translation.[74]

With Horwitz's article, the PPS became the first non-Jewish socialist party to advocate full cultural autonomy for Jews. The PPS, Horwitz maintained, demanded the immediate repeal of all anti-Jewish decrees, laws that "must be completely and utterly torn out from the roots, never to reappear." Second, the PPS program now demanded the right for Jews to "full freedom of cultural development," on an equal footing with other nationalities. This form of Jewish autonomy would extend to all public institutions, schools, administration, and courts of law. "The mere granting of equal civil rights for Jews is too little," Horwitz wrote. "Equal to all other nationalities, [Jews] must be guaranteed the full freedom to develop their own culture, and to have the opportunity to use their own language . . . in all public institutions."[75]

Horwitz also took a stand on the language question. He rejected outright the tendency of assimilated Jews and Maskilim to deride Yiddish as a backward language of the ghetto. "Such a view is wholly false and unjust," Horwitz countered, for east European Jewry had the full right to cultivate its language. "Under the phrase, 'freedom of language,' we refer not to private affairs . . . [but] to all political and cultural institutions, such as schools, administration, and courts." Such a system would guarantee the freedom of cultural autonomy for all parts of the population: "Jews will be able to freely educate their children in Yiddish or Hebrew schools, supported by general municipal or state funds."[76]

The dual program of equal civil rights and full cultural autonomy for Jews, Horwitz maintained, would fully solve the political side of the Jewish question. The extension of cultural autonomy to the

Jews, Horwitz reminded his readers, was not a mere concession. In a bold rejection of the assimilationist program, Horwitz argued that the cultivation of Yiddish into a modern language was also in the interests of the Polish working class. "Just as the Jewish proletariat has a great interest in receiving education and culture . . . in the shortest and most effective manner, that is, in their own language," Horwitz wrote, "so too the Polish proletariat, linked by class solidarity with the Jewish worker, has . . . a direct interest in seeing that the Jewish proletariat becomes educated and enlightened. The interests of the Polish proletariat therefore lies . . . in seeing that a democratic administration and court will not favor the persecution of one language by another, but will serve the true, genuine needs of the people."[77]

Despite support for full Jewish autonomy, Horwitz opposed the Bund's program, for the Bund's nationalities platform failed to address the problem of Polish statelessness. "According to the Bund's understanding, the program [of national-cultural autonomy] will resolve all nationality problems in Russia. The Poles would have no need whatsoever to demand separation and political independence for that territory where they form a compact mass, but . . . would only need cultural autonomy." But any solution to the national question in the Pale and Congress Poland that did not address the Polish question was a "utopian fantasy, unrealistic and unattainable."[78]

One could not solve the century-long Polish liberation struggle, Horwitz continued, by Saint Petersburg "granting" the Poles cultural autonomy. Thus, any proposal for solving the Jewish question in imperial Russia had to simultaneously address the problem of Polish statelessness. "Our party, which from its inception has brought together the great masses of the Polish and the Jewish proletariat under one banner," Horwitz wrote, "represents the common economic and political interests of these two [peoples] and strives to create a legal system in which both Polish and Jewish workers are guaranteed full freedom of cultural development."[79]

The opportunity for the PPS's Jewish Section to discuss the party's new position on the Jewish question came in February 1906, when it held its fourth conference.[80] The conference report, reprinted in *Der arbeyter*, reveals that the Jewish Section had expanded significantly in 1905, as it included regional committee delegates from

Lublin, Płock, Kielce, Radom, and Zagłębie. The Jewish Section had divisions in all the major urban centers in the kingdom, not to mention Vilna, Białystok, and Grodno. Beyond Warsaw and Łódź, local branches had formed "in nearly every large city" in Congress Poland, including towns in the provinces of Radom, Siedlce, Kalisz, Kielce, Płock, and Piotrków. On the Jewish question, the Jewish Section officially endorsed Horwitz's position, resolving: "The fourth Jewish conference turns to . . . the PPS with a motion to append [two points] to the [party] program: (1) a separate demand of full political and civil equality for Jews; and (2) the assurance of free cultural development for all national minorities inhabiting the territory of Poland, according to the proposal [put forth] in *Kurjer Codzienny* in the article, 'On The Jewish Question.'"[81] Horwitz's position on the Jewish question came to be accepted in the party's left-wing leadership and would later be inscribed into the program of the PPS Left in 1908.

### The PPS Schism: The Rise of the PPS-Left and the PPS-Revolutionary Faction

An attempt to resolve the conflict between the PPS's Young and Old factions was made at the party's eighth congress, which met in Lemberg in February 1906. Expectedly, the Young faction retained a majority on the CKR. While no Old Guardists retained positions on the CKR, Piłsudski retained control of the Fighting Division. In addition, all fighting organizations, previously subordinate to the CKR, were now under the Fighting Division's control, putting the entire military wing in Piłsudski's hands.[82] But the question of the relations between Piłsudski's Fighting Division and the CKR was left unresolved.[83]

Throughout 1906 Piłsudski sought to remove his Fighting Division from CKR supervision.[84] His decision to undertake terrorist actions without consulting the CKR was roundly condemned. These military operations culminated in the so-called Bloody Wednesday action of August 15, 1906, when Piłsudski's fighters carried out attacks on Russian police, gendarmes, state officials, and soldiers throughout the kingdom, resulting in seventy-six dead, some of whom were innocent bystanders.[85] When the CKR instructed the Fighting Division to limit its activities to self-defense measures, Piłsudski defiantly authorized more attacks. The most prominent was an attack on a postal train near the Rogów station in the Piotrków province on November 7. Although the fighting squad managed to seize thirty thousand rubles from the postal train, they wounded eighteen Russian soldiers. In response, the CKR ordered a halt to all Fighting Division actions.[86] Piłsudski responded by organizing a conference of fighters in Zakopane at which the actions at Rogów were defended.

The growing divisions within the party culminated at the PPS's ninth congress, which took place November 1906 in Vienna. For two days, forty-six delegates debated the Fighting Division's unilateral actions. A resolution, written by Feliks Sachs, declared that the Fighting Division had formulated a political program and employed tactics "extremely divergent from the general politics of the party," a program that "aimed at the separation of the revolutionary movement in Poland from the general movement in the whole of the Russian Empire" and had "the character of a national uprising." The resolution concluded that all participants in the recent Zakopane conference of fighters, as well as their sympathizers, had placed themselves "outside the party's sphere."[87]

The acceptance of Sachs's resolution spelled the final end to party unity. The Old Guardists stormed out of the congress in protest. Later that month the Old Guardists met in Kraków and accepted Feliks Perl's recommendation to reconstitute themselves as the "PPS-Revolutionary Faction," or PPS Right.[88] In a programmatic statement, the PPS Right declared that the new party would fight for the suppression of capitalist exploitation and the victory of socialism. It added that "the only political system that answers to the political, social, and cultural-national interests of the working class is an independent democratic Polish republic [which] . . . constitutes the first point of our political program."[89]

In March 1907 the Revolutionary Faction held its first congress, at which it called for an independent Polish Republic. Probably on Feliks Perl's recommendation, the delegates refused to endorse the Jewish Section's motion of February 1906 to include a separate point on the rights of Jews to cultural autonomy. Instead, the program included a statement guaranteeing "the rights of national minorities in administration, schools, and courts," although this did not necessarily apply to Jews given the fact that Perl consistently promoted an assimilationist policy for East European Jews in general and for Polish Jews in particular.[90]

The program of the PPS Left differed substantially with regard to both the national question in general and the Jewish question in particular. At its first congress in January 1908, the PPS Left expectedly removed the demand for Polish independence from its minimum program, demanding instead "wide autonomy" for Poland based on a legislative Sejm. Advocates of Jewish national rights could be found both in the central leadership (Bielecki, Horwitz, Sachs) and among the representatives of the Jewish Section. The new party program specifically recognized the rights of Jews as an extraterritorial nationality, demanding "the guarantee of the rights of national minorities (Jews, Germans, etc.) not separated into autonomous territorial units."[91] Now that it no longer demanded independence, the PPS Left openly sought alliances with the Bund and the SDKPiL. Indeed, from 1907, the PPS Left began to work closely with the Bund, running with the Bund and the SDKPiL in the Third Duma elections.

On the eve of the schism, the PPS had a total of 55,000 members.[92] The PPS's Jewish Section made up almost 10 percent of the party, with 5,200 members.[93] The next largest socialist party was the SDKPiL, which had close to 35,000 members in late 1906.[94] The Bund, according to official figures, had 33,890 members in the Russian Empire, with its organization in Congress Poland confined to 5,320, less than one-fifth of its total party membership.[95] In addition to socialist organizations, the NZR claimed 23,000 members in 1906 while the Association of Christian Workers (Stowarzyszenie Robotników Chrześcijańskich [SRCh]) claimed 22,000.[96] Although official membership figures are surely exaggerated, they do provide a sense of the organization's relative strength. The combined membership of socialist parties thus increased to between 100,000 and 120,000 in late 1906.[97]

### Electoral Politics in the Polish Kingdom: The Duma Elections of 1906–7

The dramatic split of the PPS into two parties took place in the wake of Russia's election campaign to the First Duma. The Election Law of December 1905, although more liberal than earlier proposals, was still heavily weighted in favor of the gentry and middle class. In European Russia, peasants were to elect 42 percent of the electors; urban dwellers 24 percent, and workers 3 percent. The vote of one landowner was thus equal to that of three and one-half city dwellers, of fifteen peasants, and of forty-five workers.[98] Because the electoral law was weighted heavily against workers, most socialist parties boycotted the elections.

Radical left-wing Russian groups responded ambivalently to the Duma election. The Socialist Revolutionaries decided to boycott the elections at a party congress in January 1906 in Finland. The Russian Social Democrats, however, split in April 1906 at their fourth party congress in Stockholm. While the majority of the congress voted in favor of boycott, a group of Mensheviks emerged in favor of participation. In a surprising turn around, Lenin, who had previously stood for active boycott, conceded to the Menshevik faction and the congress resolved that such party members would be authorized to propose candidates to form a Social Democratic group in the Duma.[99] But the vast majority of Bolsheviks would not budge from their pro-boycott position. The result was that only Mensheviks would represent the Russian Social Democrats in the Duma. In addition, a group of agrarian socialists mainly of peasant origin ran as the Labor Group (*Trudoviki*). In a resounding electoral defeat for the government, opposition parties gained a majority of the votes. The greatest electoral success went to the liberal Constitutional Democrats, or Cadets, who gained 179 seats, while the right-wing parties gained 32. The Labor Group gained some 94 seats, making it the second largest party, and the Social Democrats 18.[100]

Whereas the liberals and socialists were victorious in Russia, the right-wing National Democratic Party won a landslide victory in the Polish kingdom. Because most socialist parties boycotted the Duma elections, only the nationalists, conservatives, and liberals ran for office. From mid-February through April 1906, when the campaigning took place, the two main contenders from the kingdom were the National Democrats, who claimed to represent ethnic Poles, and an alliance of the liberal Progressive Democratic Union (Związek Postępowo-Demokratyczny) and the Jewish Electoral Committee, both of which had considerable Jewish support.[101] The main conservative party was the aristocratic Party of

Realistic Politics (Stronnictwo Polityki Realnej), although it had no popular base.

The League for the Attainment of Full Rights for the Jewish People of Russia had formed the Jewish Electoral Committee to help bring about favorable election results. To this end, it sought alliances with liberal Polish and Russian parties partial to Jewish equal rights.[102] Thus, they supported the Russian Cadets and the Progressive Democrats in the Polish kingdom. The Progressive Democratic Union, which was formulated in January 1905, demanded autonomy for Congress Poland administered through a separate Sejm in Warsaw, the reintroduction of Polish in schools and administration, and equality before the law, a combination that drew support from Warsaw's educated Jewish elite.[103] But unlike the large following of the liberal party in Russia, the Progressive Democratic Union claimed only two hundred members, composed of influential middle-class intellectuals, lawyers, doctors, and Warsaw bankers. The party had a large Jewish component, estimated at one-third of its membership.[104] Among its leaders were famous positivists like Aleksander Świętochowski and Aleksander Lednicki, as well as influential "Poles of the Mosaic faith" like economist Stanisław Kempner, publisher and editor of *Gazeta Handlowa,* and Kazimierz Natanson, vice president of the Bank Handlowy in Warsaw.

The rise of these two contending parties set the stage for a bitter campaign during the weeks leading up to election day, which took place on April 26. The National Democrats furiously attacked the Progressive Democrats as a "Judaized" party. Jews, the Endecja held, could have no place in Polish political life. The Endecja routinely referred to its opponents as the "Judaized Progressive Democrats" despite the fact that its Jewish members were self-identified Poles. As Stephen Corrsin has shown, the main theme in the National Democrats' press prior to election day was the "defense of Warsaw against the Jews" and the "Jewish danger" lurking over Warsaw.[105] The nationalists distributed a flood of agitation leaflets in Warsaw before election day, warning in one circular that "[p]rogressive democracy has sold Warsaw to the Jews!"[106]

Another Endecja leaflet accused the Jews of national betrayal. In the middle ages when Jews were being persecuted and expelled from western Europe, Poland gave the Jews a safe haven, the circular stated. But at the precise moment when Poland lost its freedom and fell under despotic foreign rule, the Jews began working against Polish interests. "From now, we will treat you as enemies. On every front—in trade, industry, in the city and countryside—we will struggle against you," the leaflet stated. "You will come to your senses in time, for we will not permit someone other than a Pole . . . to represent Warsaw."[107] "When it has come time to defend Polishness and our rights," another leaflet declared, "Jews and the Judaized Progressive Democrats stand against [us]." These Jews aimed at imposing their will and "electing foreign deputies [to the Duma] who will sell Poland to foreign interests. . . . Enough! We will not permit Jews to dominate us!"[108] Two days before election day, a leaflet proclaimed that the Polish people would never permit Jews to represent their capital: "[W]e must show that we are the rulers of this country—that our vote predominates here."[109] The nationalists thus propagated the idea that their opponents had placed elections in Warsaw "entirely in Jewish hands."[110]

Despite the socialist boycott, the National Democrats used the Jewish card to discredit the socialists. Leaflets characterized the socialist movements as part of a Jewish conspiracy to control the kingdom. In March 1906, for example, the Endecja derided socialists for characterizing Polish landowners, priests, and factory owners as its class enemies while failing to inform its followers of the danger of "Jewish exploitation" to the Polish people. "A large part of our socialist parties consists of . . . learned Jews," the pamphlet declared. "These Jews lead the parties, and Polish workers are under their command."[111]

The PPS countered with leaflets exposing the Endecja's "disgraceful" use of anti-Semitism as a political weapon. One leaflet stated that Endecja was inciting hatred of Pole against Jew "for its own electoral aims," which was a "shameful tactic."[112] Just before election day, the Częstochowa branch of the PPS distributed a counteragitation leaflet condemning anti-Semitism.[113]

In the end the nationalists emerged victorious in the first Duma elections. Of sixty-seven thousand votes cast in Warsaw, Endecja won 54 percent, with the Progressive-Democratic-Jewish Electoral Commission earning a combined share of 40 percent. The National Democrats thus earned thirty-four of thirty-seven Duma seats from the kingdom.[114]

Within a few months, however, the First Duma was dissolved. Preparations for the Second Duma elections, which took place in February 1907, saw the consolidation of right-wing, liberal, and left-wing currents in Congress Poland. In December rightists formed the "National Concentration," consisting of the National Democrats, the Polish Progressive Party (a small breakaway group of the Progressive Democrats), and the Realists. Meanwhile, both the Bund and the SDKPiL formed a socialist bloc in Congress Poland and took part in the Duma elections for the first time. With more contestants for Duma seats, the Second Duma elections proved livelier than the first.

Although the National Concentration officially came out in favor of equal rights for Jews, it continued to warn of the "Jewish danger" threatening Warsaw and attempted to discredit the Progressive Democrats by pointing to its prominent Jewish members. On the eve of election day, the headline in a National Democratic newspaper proclaimed, "Tomorrow Warsaw must decide who is her master: We, the Poles, or the Jewish nationalists."[115] Once again the National Democrats and their Concentration were victorious. Of fifty-three thousand votes cast in Warsaw, 53 percent went to the nationalists, 45 percent to the Progressive Alliance-Jewish Electoral Committee, while all three electors from the three seats reserved for workers came from the Bund-SDKPiL bloc.[116] In Russia the decision of the Russian Social Democrats to enter the electoral process resulted in an increased showing for socialists, surprising the tsarist regime, which hoped for a conservative-right victory. The Second Duma thus lasted only three months before its dissolution and was followed by a Stolypin-led government coup against the semiparliamentary system. A new electoral law was designed to ensure a rightist victory and would bring about an end to the revolutionary days.[117] The first phase of imperial Russia's constitutional experiment left a dark shadow over Polish-Jewish relations.

In the period under examination, socialist parties in Russian Poland were transformed from small conspiratorial propaganda groups to mass parties. The emergence of electoral politics encouraged the various parties to clarify their positions on a host of issues. In the Polish kingdom, the national question was among the most pressing. Consequently, the PPS and the Bund were forced to draft platforms on the Jewish and the Polish question. The interest of the PPS's right wing in the Jewish question clearly diminished in 1905–6, as it focused its energies on developing the party's Fighting Division. The party's left-wing faction, however, devoted much energy to formulating a programmatic response to the Jewish question and endorsed the idea of Jewish national autonomy by late 1905 in the official party press. At its founding congress in January 1908, moreover, the PPS Left officially recognized the Jews as an extraterritorial nationality. Despite these significant developments, it has been argued that that the PPS Left's position fell short of supporting Jewish national autonomy. "The left wing of the Polish Socialist Party," wrote the Bundist J. S. Hertz, "did not accept the demand for national-cultural autonomy. However, it supported a number of Jewish demands that were in the spirit and character of that autonomy."[118] The Polish historian Jerzy Holzer similarly argued that "the PPS-Left tended towards the Bund and started to take a more sympathetic view of its basic position, though still retaining a critical attitude, especially of its separate activity."[119] An examination of the PPS press during the revolutionary period reveals that it clearly supported the principle of Jewish national autonomy while criticizing the Bund for viewing the Jewish question in isolation from the larger nationalities problem in imperial Russia's western regions.

The events of 1905 also saw the birth of political anti-Semitism in Polish party politics. This development challenged many cherished assumptions about working-class loyalties. In particular, the penetration of the right-wing nationalist movement into the ranks of the working class undermined the PPS's long-held view that anti-Semitism was an ideology of the middle and upper classes. Despite the party position, the PPS's Jewish Section had been urging the party to print a brochure on anti-Semitism since 1902. No such propaganda literature ever appeared, partly because the mainstream leadership refused to acknowledge the presence of anti-Jewish prejudice among workers. The rise of nationalist sentiment among workers also weakened the PPS's long-held position that Jews would be protected in a future Polish state. In response to these events, the PPS's left-wing leadership endorsed the principle of extraterritorial autonomy, thereby demonstrating its willingness to accommodate a Jewish national presence on Polish soil.

*Maksymilian Heilpern (1856–1924), founder of the first circle of PPS Jews, Warsaw, c. 1888* (Niepodległość, Warsaw, 1929)

*Maks Horwitz (1877–1938), founding editor of* Der arbeyter, *the first Yiddish organ of the PPS, c. 1898 (Archive of New Records, Warsaw)*

*Feliks Sachs (1869–1935), editor of* Der arbeyter, *1901–5, who represented the Jewish Section in the PPS's central committee (Niepodległość, Warsaw, 1929)*

*Józef Kwiatek (1874–1910), activist in the PPS's Jewish Section, c. 1905 (Archive of New Records, Warsaw)*

*Jewish section of the PPS's division in Paris, 1904 (Archive of New Records, Warsaw)*

*Sonia Dawidowska-Burginowa (1878–1965), an activist in the Jewish Section of the PPS since the early 1890s, a nurse by profession, and a typesetter for illegal party publications in Yiddish, including* Der arbeyter *and* Sotsialistishes flugblettel (Niepodległość, *Warsaw, 1929)*

*Mojżesz Kaufman (1878–1936), c. 1918, activist and chronicler of the PPS's Jewish Section (Jewish Historical Institute, Warsaw)*

# ■ 9.

# From Politics to the New Yiddish Culture: The Bund in the Period of Revolutionary Defeat, 1907–11

> *Jewish Social Democracy . . . must conduct the struggle against the assimilationists and Hebraists so that the Yiddish language will acquire in all areas of Jewish public life—especially in the schools and cultural institutions—the prominent position it merits as the national language of the Jewish people.*
> BUND RESOLUTION (1910)

THE 1905 RUSSIAN REVOLUTION saw the Bund's rise to great prominence in Jewish life. The Bund become history's first political party to demand national-cultural autonomy (October 1905), while its dramatic growth in membership made it one of the largest socialist parties in Russia. But a fresh wave of pogroms in 1905–6, the resulting exodus of some 330,000 Jews out of Russia by 1908, and the resumption of political repression led to a crisis in socialist parties in general and in the Bund in particular. Emigration dramatically depleted the ranks of the party, disillusionment with revolutionary politics set in, and the Bund went into a period of decline from which it did not recover until 1917. While at the height of the revolution in 1906, the Bund represented 274 local organizations in Russia and a membership of 33,890, only 10 local organizations were represented at the eighth party conference in 1910 with a total membership of no more than 2,000.[1]

Due to the postrevolutionary crisis, the historical literature on the Bund has largely overlooked the period 1907–14. Rather, it has focused on the pre-WWI Bund to 1905, the Polish Bund (1918–39), and the period of the Holocaust and its aftermath (1939–49).[2] The existing literature suggests, therefore, that no significant developments in the Bund's history took place between 1907 and the First World War.

It is true that the Bund officially endorsed the program of national-cultural autonomy at the height of the revolutionary storm of 1905, and that this constituted a milestone in the party's ideological evolution. But the *elaboration* of this complex national program, I will argue, was carried out in the period between the two Russian revolutions. Yoav Peled implicitly acknowledged this point when he remarked that the adoption of national-cultural autonomy in 1905 marked "the completion of the *first stage* in the ideological development of the Bund."[3]

The second stage of the Bund's ideological completion, I maintain, took place between 1907 and the First World War. It culminated both in the resolutions adopted at the eighth (1910) and the ninth (1912) party conference, as well as in the lengthy debates over the *shul-frage* (the school question), the *shprakh-frage* (the language question), the *kehila-frage* (the community question), on the party's attitude to the Jewish future, and on the question of a Shabbat rest day for Jewish workers. A. Litvak, a central committee member active in Russia at the time, stressed this very point when he characterized party debates in the years 1908–12 as "fertile." They "clarified our national program, and helped work out its particularities."[4] In the only narrative account of this period of the Bund's history, Sophia Dubnow-Erlich commented that in the feverish atmosphere of the 1905 revolution, it was not possible for either the Jewish working masses or the party leadership to absorb the new national ideas. "This became possible in the years after the [1905] revolution," she argued, when "organized Jewish labor became the most active element in the newly created Yiddish cultural and educational societies."[5]

## The Impact of the 1905 Revolution on Jewish Life

The Bund's new emphasis on *kultur-arbeyt* after 1905 was the result of several factors. Not only did the postrevolutionary reaction under Stolypin bring socialist agitation to a virtual standstill inside Russia, but the 1905 revolution brought about new political and cultural forces in Jewish life. These included the consolidation of the labor Zionist movement, the rapid growth of the Yiddish daily press, and an emerging consensus among Jewish political parties in favor of autonomous rights. The proliferation of Jewish political parties led to the gradual erosion of the Bund's dominance on the Jewish street. Nowhere was this more apparent than in the relative decline of Bundist domination in the Yiddish press. Whereas by 1900 the Bund produced thirteen of fifteen Yiddish periodicals in tsarist Russia, that share dropped to about one-fifth by 1914.[6]

The Bund increasingly came under scrutiny in the party presses of labor Zionists, Jewish liberals, the RSDRP, and the SDKPiL.[7] Among Jewish liberals the fact that the Bund consistently refused to enter into general Jewish coalitions led some to brand it as a radical group operating without regard for Jewish interests. At the height of the pogrom wave in December 1905, Simon Dubnow expressed profound disappointment at the Bund's refusal to join the League for the Attainment of Full Rights for the Jews of Russia. "As a party with an exclusively proletarian class program," Dubnow wrote in the pages of the Saint Petersburg Russian-Jewish journal *Voskhod*, "the Bund consciously and knowingly works, not for the good of the Jewish people as a whole, but only for the good of one part, and the smallest part at that. For the Bund the struggle between the interests of the bourgeoisie and the proletariat completely displaces the struggle for our general national needs. . . . The Bundists are devoted sons of only one 'nation,' the proletarian class. They never join with national parties for any common cause. They do not believe in the totality of the Jewish community."[8]

The greatest challenge to Bundist hegemony over Jewish workers was the rise of the labor Zionist movement in 1905. Until 1905 the Bund constituted the only Jewish revolutionary party in the Jewish world.[9] The emergent labor Zionist movement had not concerned the Bund until 1900 and 1901, when the first labor Zionist groups began to organize workers in the Pale. It was at its fourth congress in April 1901 that the Bund first placed Zionism on its agenda, calling for the expulsion of Zionists from the party while characterizing it as a "utopian goal" that inflamed nationalist feeling and hindered the development of class consciousness.[10] At the time, between 1901 and 1904, scattered labor Zionist groups in Russia coalesced into three distinct currents—territorialist, autonomist, and Palestinian-centered—leading to the formation of separate political parties in 1905–6. The first party, founded by territorialists in Odessa in

January–February 1905, organized under the name Zionist Socialist Workers' Party (SS). The SS argued that there was no "organic link" between Zionism and Palestine and called for an immediate territorial solution to the Jewish problem.[11] The SS placed less emphasis on Hebrew than certain other groups in this category and in fact became increasingly Yiddishist in orientation. Some of its followers, such as Shmuel Niger, played major roles in the Yiddish literary revival. Second only to the Bund in popularity among Jewish socialists, the SS claimed 24,210 members by December 1906.[12]

The smallest of the three new parties, the Jewish Socialist Workers' Party (or SERP, the acronym of the Russian name), was founded in April 1906 in Kiev. Known as "Seimists," these autonomists maintained that the Palestinian versus territorialist question should be postponed until a Jewish national parliament in Russia deliberated over such issues. In the meantime, SERP called for recognition of the Jews in Russia as a national body with rights to national autonomy and claimed some thirteen thousand members by the end of 1906.[13]

The third labor Zionist party to form was Ber Borochov's Jewish Social-Democratic Workers' Party-Poale Zion. Poale Zion was founded at a unification congress in Poltava in early 1906 and claimed sixteen thousand members by the end of that year.[14] Borochov called for a Jewish socialist state in Palestine, a solution he derived from what he maintained was a strictly Marxist analysis of the Jewish problem in eastern Europe. His "Program for Proletarian Zionism," which was approved at the founding congress, claimed that Jewish territorial autonomy could only be achieved in Eretz Israel, and that the primary aim of the party was to create conditions for the realization of this aim. Realizing the immediacy of the crisis in Russia, however, the Poale Zion also laid out a "secondary program" of work in the Diaspora. It called for "national political autonomy" for Jews in Russia, including the right to "freedom in national education, national cultural autonomy, linguistic equality," and proportional representation in a national government. Thus, by 1906 four Jewish socialist parties competed for the allegiance of the Jewish working class: the Bund, the SS, the SERP, and Poale Zion.[15]

It should also be noted that the general Zionist movement in Russia, at its conference, which took place in December 1906 in Helsinki, officially revised the principle of negating the Diaspora and acknowledged the need to fight for a Jewish national existence in Russia. In a memorandum sent to local Zionist divisions in Russia, the All-Russian Zionist Organization endorsed a program of *Gegenwartsarbeit*, or "work in the present," to struggle for the national and cultural rights of Jews in Russia.[16]

The revolutionary period also saw the formation of the nonsocialist *Folkspartey*, or Jewish People's Party, in December 1906. The principle theorist behind the party, the Russian-Jewish historian Simon Dubnow, had formulated the idea of autonomism as a prescription for Jewish national survival in the Diaspora in the pages of *Voskhod* between 1897 and 1901.[17] The *Folkspartey* thus called for a program of "national cultural autonomism."[18] The party stood for recognition of Jews as a nation, the right of national autonomy in private and public life, the rights of the Jewish vernacular, and the creation of a Union of Jewish Communities in the Russian Empire that would represent Jewish national interests to the government and administer Jewish institutions.[19] Dubnow envisioned a secularized version of the medieval Council of Four Lands and emphasized the centrality of education. "Freedom of language and autonomy of the school are the most important of all 'national rights,' without which full civic equality before the law is impossible."[20] Although formally neutral on the language question, the *Folkspartey*, as a people's party, became Yiddishist in orientation. Its central organ, *Dos yidishe folk*, made up part of the new Yiddish press.

The 1905 revolution also saw the emergence of the daily Yiddish press in the Pale and Congress Poland. Prior to 1905 the autocratic government had looked upon both the Yiddish press and the Yiddish theater with great suspicion and with few exceptions denied all requests for periodical publications in the Jewish vernacular.[21] But with the new freedoms granted in 1905 and 1906, the Yiddish press flourished. *Der veker*, the Bund's legal daily issued in Vilna in December 1905, was the first Yiddish daily newspaper to be printed in the Pale. After the revolutionary period, when all the socialist party newspapers were suppressed, the center of the Yiddish daily press shifted from Vilna to Warsaw. In January 1908 the Zionist-leaning Yiddish daily *Haynt* appeared in Warsaw. By the following year *Haynt* reached an unprecedented circulation of seventy thousand and was followed in 1910 by a rival Yiddish daily in Warsaw, *Der moment*, which was folkist in orientation.

The emergence of a daily Yiddish press and the concomitant Yiddish cultural revival led to a general shift in the attitude of the Jewish intelligentsia toward Yiddish. These developments culminated in the historic language conference that took place between August 30 and September 4, 1908 in Chernowitz (present-day Chernivtsi). Some seventy people participated, across ideological and party lines, including such figures as I. L. Peretz, Sholem Asch, Chaim Zhitlowski, H. D. Nomberg, as well as the Bundist Ester Frumkin.[22] After five days of deliberations, the Chernowitz Language Conference passed the following historic resolution: "The first conference devoted to the Yiddish language recognizes Yiddish as a national language of the Jewish people and demands for it political, communal and cultural equality. At the same time the Conference feels it necessary to declare that every participant in the Conference and also every member of the future organization retains the freedom to feel toward the Hebrew language as he personally sees fit."[23]

The proposal of Asch, Nomberg, Zhitlovsky, and Frumkin to designate Yiddish as *"the* national language of the Jews" was vetoed, although only Frumkin had favored the exclusion of Hebrew from the resolution.[24] In a draft resolution drawn up by Peretz, the conference also announced the following objectives, among others: the recognition and attainment of equal rights for the Yiddish language; the dissemination of culture and art in Yiddish, the establishment of Yiddish libraries, and the publication of model textbooks; the formation of model Yiddish schools; and the establishment of an authoritative body to deliberate on questions of Yiddish orthography and grammar.[25]

The Chernowitz Language Conference raised the status of Yiddish. Although no practical results followed from the conference, the official recognition of Yiddish as a Jewish national language signaled a change in the attitude of a section of the Jewish educated elite. As a scholar of the history of Yiddish secular schools commented, the Chernowitz conference "immeasurably strengthened the Yiddishist movement in Russia."[26] Henceforth the term *zhargon* would be either placed in quotations marks or dropped altogether in favor of the more respectable term *Yiddish* during the period 1907–14.[27]

## The Bund in the Aftermath
## of the Revolution's Failure, 1907–9

For the Bund the symbol of the revolution's end came in September 1907, when the government shut down *Folkstsaytung*, the party's Vilna-based legal daily since January 1906. A successor Yiddish daily, *Di hofnung*, operated but was closed down in early November of the same year and its editors placed under arrest. The period of the legal Bundist daily press came to an end, accompanied by crackdowns on many freedoms enjoyed during the revolutionary days. Not for another four and one-half years would the Bund develop another legal party press publication.[28]

The Bund was now severely limited to legal activities in trade unions and cultural organizations. Sholom Levin, an important Bundist in Vilna who was on the editorial board of *Folkstsaytung* when it was closed down, recalled that in late 1907 and 1908 "the spirit of the leadership fell and the connection with the masses was severely weakened." Levin recalled that in some cities in the Pale and Congress Poland, nearly the entire Bundist division and the majority of dues-paying members left for America. But even worse, Levin continued, was the situation with the party's intelligentsia, which was overcome by a "pessimistic, depressed, and often cynical mood."[29]

Raphael Abramovitch, a member of the Bund's central committee, recalled the mood among Bundists in May 1908 upon his return to Russia. "I found the party and the Bund, after six months abroad, in a sorry state. The movement had gone into decline. . . . A sharp psychological crisis came over the spirit of the masses and particularly of the intelligentsia."[30] Another member of the Bund's central committee, A. Litvak, similarly recalled: "During the entire summer of 1907, we spoke of a crisis in all our organizations. We discussed and searched for the reasons. Already in 1908 there was nearly no one with whom to talk about the crises. One after another, the organizations had either crumbled or fallen into a deep winter sleep."[31] Vladimir Medem, too, noted the "pervasive weariness" that hung over the party beginning in the second half of 1907. "All of us at the center of the movement could see and feel it in the most varied signs. . . . Finances became exceedingly slim. Organizational life grew weak. The number of people under the sway of our movement had begun to decline. The prevailing mood was one of depression."[32]

Letters from local organizations to the Bund in 1908 and 1909 mirrored the depressed state of the party. A party activist from Dvinsk, writing in 1909, maintained that the local organization had been "totally severed" from the masses. "Former party leaders now keep away from the organization. The spirit of our comrades is very low. From all the trade unions that had once existed (among them, eleven legal ones), only one continues to function." A correspondent from Bobruisk reported that the local organization practically ceased to function.[33]

The Bund's May Day proclamation of 1908, illegally printed and distributed in the Russian Empire, reflected the mood of the postrevolutionary period. "The whole of our country has the appearance of a huge graveyard," the circular stated. Signed by the Central Committee of the Bund, the leaflet disseminated the following May Day message:

> In the ranks of the proletariat there is to be observed a not uncommon and fatal indifference, and it would seem as though history had turned its back on those who have fought for a brighter future, and yet we come to you with the cry, "Long live our bright ideal, Socialism; our method, the struggle; the bearer of the standard, the proletariat!" . . . Comrades, the Jewish proletariat is now living through a particularly heavy time. The great masses of the Jews have sunk to a level of dull despair; their blood, which has been spilt so profusely, has made them blind; the blows that had been dealt them so heavily have made them deaf; and they see not that the national and civil rights of the Jewish people can but grow together with the growth of the forces of those who will fight for them. Indifference and despair have imprisoned the spirit and political will [of the Jewish proletariat] as in an iron vice. . . . By celebrating the first of May we will demonstrate that the great power is not dead which in the days of the self-sacrificing struggle fought for the rights and liberties of all the oppressed.[34]

One symptom of declining membership and morale was the sharp reduction in funds after 1907. The party lost over two-thirds of its income between 1908 and 1910, while its support for professional revolutionaries was reduced by more than a half.[35] A biographical study of 123 party activists who joined the Bund by 1905 reveals that there were three responses to the crises that befell Russia in 1907–10. Bundists emigrated, remained in Russia but withdrew from activity in the Bund, or chose to remain in Russia and continue to be active in the Bund.[36] Those involved in the local and central party press and committees were the least likely to emigrate. And it was precisely this core of dedicated activists who would play a decisive role in shaping the direction of the Bund's ideology in the years of reaction.

Despite the crises the party continued to function. In the summer of 1908 local organizations and committees were active in Pinsk, Gomel, Bobruisk, Grodno, Łódź, and Riga even if severely weakened in both numbers and in morale.[37] The central committee itself visited these remaining active regions with the aim of raising spirits and rebuilding local organizations.[38] But the network of police informants made the plan ineffective and the crises did not abate.[39] Following the failure of the new tactic to rejuvenate the movement, a long discussion began in Bundist circles, which, in turn, mirrored the wider crisis in the Russian Social Democratic movement.

Within the RSDRP a debate took place over the question of legal versus illegal party work. The so-called liquidators (a term Lenin used and which his opponents accepted) favored the elimination of small conspiratorial party circles. They argued that, under current conditions, the most beneficial and worthwhile work involved activity within legally sanctioned trade unions, cultural societies, and cooperatives, a view favored by part of the Menshevik party faction. Most party members, however, favored a combination of both legal and illegal activities. Seizing upon the opportunity to lambaste his opponents, Lenin, until 1914, waged his struggle against the Mensheviks under the banner of saving the party from the "liquidators" even if only a small minority favored eliminating illegal party work altogether.

The leadership of the Bund held similar discussions. In March 1908 a party conference took place in Grodno at which members of the central and local committees were present. Representatives from six cities attended the conference.[40] Participants with voting rights included central committee members Noyakh Portnoy, I. Aizenshtat, V. Medem, M. Liber, R. Abramovitch, and A. Weinstein, while only six leaders of local committees attended, among them Moshe Terman (Mohilev), Victor Shulman (Vilna), Berl Zlotovitski (Vitebsk), and Isaac Alter (Grodno).[41]

The Bund's 1908 conference focused on how to make use of the limited legal possibilities that had remained since 1905.[42] The so-called *legalistn* (legalists), among them Liber, Abramovitch, Weinstein (and, subsequently, P. Rozental), came out in favor of total immersion in legal possibilities. Liber argued that the failed revolution had left behind certain organizational possibilities. Even if Stolypin's regime was a sinister one, it had not liquidated all aspects of the revolution. Thus, under current conditions the party should not begin a new revolutionary spurt of activity but rather focus on a gradual but systematic effort to strengthen existing freedoms through legal possibilities of action.[43] Opponents, or *anti-legalistn*—Aizenshtat, B. Mikhalovitch, A. Litvak, and Y. Koigen—argued that the revolution was not over.[44] The struggle had to be carried on. Legal activities could only influence a tiny part of the working masses.[45] The legalists carried the day, and the conference resolved in favor of "energetic participation in all social movements and institutions that advance directly or indirectly the interests of the proletariat: in the trade union movement, cultural work, and kehillah work, and so on. . . . The conference holds that participation in these local movements, on the bases of the proletariat's daily needs, can strongly contribute to reinforcing and augmenting our organizations . . . as well as their political influence."[46]

The exploitation of all legal forms of communal activity—as a cover for political work—became known as the "new form" of the movement. For the rest of the year discussions around the type and character of this new activity dominated the Bundist press. The first issue of *Di shtime fun bund*, the Bund's illegal organ that first appeared in December 1908, featured polemics on the new form of legal work. Litvak emphasized that the question of legal versus illegal activity was simply a tactical one: "Nobody is maintaining that we must work *only* legally or *only* illegally according to the fundamental principles of Marxism."[47]

In a reply the young Raphael Abramovitch wrote of the new tactic as something more than merely pragmatic. "These days give no basis or possibility of rapidly organizing (politically or economically) the working masses. The task of the moment," Abramovitch wrote, "is to support the living domain of the proletariat. . . . With all our energy, with the full power of our conviction, we must call forth all living and active elements of the working class" within the limited possibilities available. To the question of legal versus illegal work, "we answer: make use of legal possibilities—that is the foundation" of the new tactic.[48] In a Bundist leaflet printed in Geneva and addressed to sympathizers abroad, the party explained the new *kampsformen* (forms of struggle) that would now be employed, including "all legal and semilegal avenues: legal trade unions, cooperatives, educational societies, and evening courses" that would benefit the movement. The leaflet emphasized the party's demand "for the rights of the Yiddish language and culture."[49]

The debate between legalists and antilegalists continued to fill the party press in 1909, when the Bund sank to its lowest ebb in popular support. In an extended reply to Abramovitch, Aizenshtat, thirteen years Abramovitch's senior, warned his fellow Bundists "not to make an idol out of legal possibilities" and thereby abandon the "force of the proletariat struggle." The new form of work should not divert the party from its principle task of developing "the political socialist consciousness" of the proletariat and "raising its revolutionary spirit."[50]

While the discussion over how to respond to the postrevolutionary crises appeared to revolve around a question of tactics, it in fact had wider implications. What was the relation between the Bund and Jewish society as a whole? To what degree would the Bund participate in general Jewish associations that crossed party lines? Precisely how Jewishly involved could the party become without compromising its fundamental principles of international class solidarity?

The split between the legalist and antilegalist wings tended to reflect an older nationalist and internationalist division within the party. It is no coincidence that the antilegalists had earlier been numbered among the party's antinationalist wing during the debates of 1901 and 1903. At the fifth congress of the Bund in 1903, for example, Aizenshtat and Koigen had maintained that submission to the class struggle was at odds with the promotion of national aspirations.[51] On the other hand, the legalist camp leaders such as Marc Liber and Pavel Rozental were instrumental figures in promoting a national program in 1901.

Meanwhile, the central committee struggled to survive financially. Drastically reduced funds forced party leaders to settle down in various cities and assume open legal and half-legal lives to sustain themselves.[52] With the exception of three or four who remained "professionals," the rest of the party leadership retreated from clandestine revolutionary activity and sought employment as teachers, Yiddish writers, journalists, dramatists, and musicians.[53]

In 1908 the party's central committee was dispersed among Vilna, Minsk, and Warsaw.[54] Ester Frumkin, recently coopted into the central committee, as well as Portnoy and Aizenshtat, settled in Warsaw, while Liber, Weinstein, and Abramovitch settled in Vilna. Liber and Abramovitch worked as teachers in local high schools, while Weinstein worked for the publishing house Di velt (officially non-party but Bundist in practice). Other prominent Bundists lived in Vilna at the time, including Pavel Rozental and his wife, Anna Heller, an activist in the local Vilna organization, as well as Arkadi and Pati Kremer, making Vilna the principle center of the movement.[55]

### From Politics to "Cultural Work"

The dramatic developments that followed the 1905 revolutionary days led to a new emphasis in the Bund. Beginning in April 1906, when imperial Russia's first constitution granted freedom of assembly, press, and speech to all imperial subjects, a network of Jewish cultural organizations sprang up in the Pale and Congress Poland.[56] These included theater groups, choirs, literary societies, and evening schools. Because the Bund could not organize cultural activities under its own name, it opted for indirect influence by participating in legal cultural societies. "Until now, our work among the proletariat was confined to two spheres: politics and trade unions," the Bund declared. "Lately a new organizational form has arisen: the cultural societies."[57]

The connection between Jewish socialists and the Yiddish literary revival crystallized during this period. Daniel Charny, the younger brother of Yiddish literary activists Shmuel Niger and Baruch "Vladeck" Charny, recalled how the organs of the Bund, the SS, and Poale Zion began to focus more and more on the new Yiddish cultural movement to delude the censor. To evade the authorities, activists formed cultural, drama, and music societies partly as fronts for political agitation. That is one reason why many party leaders in the Bundist and labor Zionist camps became poets, writers, and literary critics after 1906. The freedom offered to Yiddish literary periodicals—generally suppressed before 1905—was an impetus for the language movement. "Beginning in 1908 and after," Charny wrote, "modern Yiddish literature truly began a wholly new turning point both in Europe and in America."[58]

Warsaw, Vilna, and Łódź became the principal centers for the Bund's cultural activities. This included participation in four main cultural organizations: the Jewish Literary Society, the Yiddish Section of the University for All in Warsaw, the musical-dramatic society in Łódź, Harfe, and the evening schools for Jewish adults in Vilna and Warsaw.

The Jewish Literary Society was first established in Saint Petersburg in 1908. Between 1908 and 1911 the Jewish Literary Society established 120 branches in Russia.[59] Warsaw hosted the most prominent division of the Society. The society's executive council included prominent figures in Yiddish literature, theater, and literary criticism: I. L. Peretz acted as chairman; the popular Yiddish novelist Jacob Dineson (1856–1919) was treasurer; A. Mukdoni (1877–1958), the Yiddish essayist and theater critic, was secretary; while the Bundist Dovid Myer (b. 1888) became assistant secretary.[60] At the time Peretz's home in Warsaw had become "the world address . . . of the newly awakened Yiddish literature," as Daniel Charny characterized it.[61] Peretz was the main speaker at the society's weekly Saturday-evening lectures. Other speakers included the Warsaw Yiddish writer H. D. Nomberg (1876–1927), as well as Yiddish writers and essayists belonging to the Bund, such as A. Veiter (1878–1919) and A. Litvak (1874–1932). According to Dovid Myer, the Warsaw Bund called on its members to join the society, seeing in it a vehicle for conducting cultural activities.[62] The growing influence of the Bund in the society became evident when Bronislav Groser, a member of the Bund's central committee, became head of the organization.[63] By 1911 Bundists became so prominent that the authorities closed down the society and placed its leaders under arrest.[64]

The second cultural institution in which the Bund played an important role was connected with the Polish progressive educational movement. During the 1905 revolutionary period, Polish progressive democrats and socialists established an illegal school of higher education in Warsaw, known as the University for All (Uniwersytet dla Wszystkich).[65] After the April 1906 law on associations, the founders of the University for All, the eminent socialist

Ludwik Krzywicki, the geographer Wacław Nałkowski, and Samuel Dicksztajn, submitted a request for legalization that was granted on November 17 of the same year.[66] As one Polish historian has commented, the University for All became the only institution of higher education in the Russian Empire to apply the principle of complete equality of admissions to all nationalities and faiths.[67]

The University for All opened for its first semester in January 1907 with faculties of science, mathematics, history, economics, and pedagogy.[68] Due to the intervention of Zdzisław Muszkat (1878–1960), a Warsaw Bundist who was a member of the University for All's governing council, a separate Jewish department for Yiddish speakers was established.[69] With the cooperation of the Warsaw Bund, Muszkat became director of the university's so-called Yiddish Section, which opened its doors to aspiring students on 7 February 1907.[70] The University for All, which offered both single-presentation lectures and courses, employed I. L. Peretz, Gershon Levin (1868–1939), a doctor of medicine, and Pesach-Liebman Hersh (1882–1955), a demographer and statistician who had been a member of the Warsaw Bund since 1905.[71] The eight formal lectures offered in the Yiddish Section during the first semester became extraordinarily popular, drawing an average of 758 students per lecture and a total student attendance of 6,064.[72] The Yiddish Section devoted more resources to its courses. It offered twenty-seven courses, employed eighteen teachers, and drew 15,812 students.[73] With an average of four hundred students per course, the Yiddish Section drew more students than any other department in the university.[74]

In the academic year of 1907–8 the University for All's Yiddish Section added the Bundist Shmuel Gozhanski and the demographer and labor Zionist Jacob Lestschinsky to its faculty and offered nineteen courses, with Peretz attracting half of the student body in his courses on Yiddish literature and drama.[75] The courses attracted 8,798 students, a significant drop but still more than any other department.[76] According to Dovid Myer, the University for All "raised the cultural standing" of Jewish workers, who constituted the majority of students, and awakened in them more interest in education.[77]

In Łódź the Polish progressive educational movement operated under the University for All's sister organization, the Society for the

Spread of Education (Towarzystwo Krzewienia Oświaty, TKO). Established in December 1905 under the direction of Dr. Mieczysław Kaufman, the TKO established courses and lectures for workers as well as libraries.[78] One historian estimates that between November 1906 and the end of 1907, the TKO offered 360 lectures that were attended by fifty thousand students.[79] A Bundist, Israel Okun (1877–1941), helped establish a Yiddish division of the TKO's library in 1908, and another Bundist, Roza Eichner (1879–1942), became its director.[80] Eichner, whom the Bund's central committee sent to Łódź in 1905, became active in the TKO around 1907. Under Eichner's directorship the TKO's Yiddish library lent out 22,801 books in 1909. In 1910, 1,118 readers, 90 percent of whom were workers, borrowed 26,643 books.[81] But in 1910 the local Russian authorities arrested Roza Eichner for allegedly housing illegal Yiddish literature.[82]

A third cultural association in which the Bund played an important part was the musical dramatic society Harfe (Harp). Established in Łódź in March 1908, Harfe was officially a legal, non-affiliated group that promoted the dissemination of Yiddish culture and music.[83] In practice, however, it was a militantly Yiddishist workers' organization. In his memoirs the Łódź Jew Isaiah Trunk remarked about Harfe that "[b]ehind this legal cultural organization stood illegally the Bund."[84] The organization sponsored lectures, performed orchestral and choir concerts, staged Yiddish plays, and formed a library. In the first weeks of the organization's activity, Harfe's musical division featured a choir and 120-person orchestra performance, while the dramatics division performed a Sholem Asch play. In addition, Peretz, H. D. Nomberg, and the Bundist Baruch "Vladek" Charny gave a series of evening lectures.[85] The lectures would later include Bundists such as Boris Frumkin, R. Abramovitch, and A. Litvak. According to Litvak, Peretz adored Harfe and is alleged to have said, "There I had my best audience."[86] The tsarist authorities soon got wind of the Bundist role in Harfe. In 1910 the government closed down the organization, arresting eighty of its members.[87]

The Bund in Łódź conducted other cultural activities as well. In late 1907 Roza Levit, a leader of the local Bund who went under the pseudonym "Frieda," was asked to join the party's central committee, to which she agreed.[88] In return she requested that Bundists prominent in the Yiddish literary revival such as Vladeck and A. Veiter offer lectures in Łódź. The central committee conceded to her request. Levit's instinct about the growing interest among Jewish workers in the Yiddish literary revival was correct: Vladeck's first lecture reportedly drew 1,200 people.[89]

Litvak would later comment that of all the cultural organizations he participated in between 1908 and 1911, only two stood out in his memory: the Jewish Literary Society in Warsaw and Harfe in Łódź.[90]

The period 1908–11 also saw the rise of evening adult schools for workers in Warsaw and Vilna. It will be recalled that the Russian government, with few exceptions, did not permit schools in non-Russian languages. Between the two failed Polish insurrections of 1830 and 1863, Russian became the language of instruction in all schools in the western provinces and Congress Poland. The exception was religious schools, such as the heder and the yeshiva, where subjects were taught in Yiddish. Since modern schools in Yiddish were not possible, the idea of evening schools for adults became popular among the secular Jewish intelligentsia, and particularly the Bund, in fin-de-siècle Russia, as a way of providing education to Jewish workers. "The evening school in particular," wrote S. Kazdan, "became an organic part of socialist activity."[91]

The Bund initiated the first attempts to establish evening schools for Jewish adults in Vilna. In 1897 Noyakh Portnoy, along with two young students, applied to the government for permission to open an evening school for Jewish adults in Vilna.[92] Five years later, in 1901, the government granted permission for an adult evening school for women in which Russian was to be the language of instruction.[93] The school adapted its charter to governmental regulations, but with a clause that allowed Yiddish for purposes of clarification. The adult evening school in Vilna, which admitted students age sixteen and above, officially provided three subjects of study: Russian, arithmetic, and Judaism. In the first year the evening school drew 180 students. Permission was granted for a parallel adult evening school for Jewish men in the fall of 1903. Together the two evening schools in Vilna employed thirty-two teachers and drew 300 women and 130 men in 1903–4 and 1904–5.[94] Although licenses to open evening schools were granted in these exceptional cases, new ones were almost impossible to obtain before 1905.[95]

The transformation of Russia in 1905 opened new possibilities for Jewish education in the Pale and Congress Poland. Concessions made to the Polish population raised expectations. For the first time in over forty years, the government announced that the language of instruction in elementary schools in Congress Poland could now be Polish.[96] Moreover, the Polish school movement, under the name Polska Macierz Szkolna (Polish motherland schools), was legalized in the same year at a time when it controlled a network of seventy-seven illegal schools in Congress Poland.

While the right of Jews to open secular Yiddish schools for children was not granted during the revolutionary days, the government did allow the expansion of adult evening schools. Between 1906 and 1911 Yiddish gradually replaced Russian as the language of instruction.[97] In fact, the Vilna evening school was the first in all of Russia to offer systematic courses on the Yiddish language.[98] Such Bundists as Moissaye Olgin, Gershon Pludermakher (1879–1942), Shmuel Gozhanski, and Pavel Rozental played significant roles in establishing the evening school network. Some, like Pludermakher, devoted themselves entirely to secular Jewish education after 1905.[99] The Bund, in fact, was the first to publicly demand the use of Yiddish in the evening schools, while concluding that the worker organizations had to have as much influence as possible over the direction and curriculum of the evening schools.[100] The student body of the adult evening schools in Vilna increased from 430 in 1906–7 to 610 in 1911–12.[101]

Pludermakher, who taught at evening schools in Vilna between 1907 and 1913, recalled the atmosphere of the evening schools. "The socialist intelligentsia—in fact, the Bund—had the greatest influence at the [evening] school," Pludermakher wrote, continuing: "All classes were conducted in Yiddish; that is, illegally. The curriculum was the following: two hours of Russian; two hours of Yiddish, and on Shabbat, instead of courses on Judaism, we gave lectures on science, geography, and history, both general and Jewish."[102]

With the rise of evening schools for Jewish adults as well as Yiddish-language university courses in Warsaw, the demand for instructional materials became acute. Beginning in 1907, a few books appeared specifically designed for use in the secular Yiddish classroom.[103] A group of teachers in the Vilna evening school decided to prepare a multivolume reader of contemporary Yiddish fiction, prose, drama, and poetry. The main initiator was Moshe Olgin (1878–1939), a prominent Bundist who had returned to Russia in 1909 after studying at Heidelberg University for three years.[104] Olgin worked with a pedagogical committee of Vilna evening-school teachers that included the Bundists Gershon Pludermakher and Shmuel Gozhanski, as well as the labor Zionists M. Shalit and I. Tsipkin.[105] The result was the publication, in 1913, of *Dos yidishe vort*, the first Yiddish literary reader designed for the secular Yiddish school. The anthology, published in two volumes, consisted of selections from the most important Yiddish writers, playwrights, poets, and essayists.[106]

The first secular Yiddish schools in Warsaw consisted of evening courses for workers in 1905 and 1906.[107] The establishment of legally sanctioned evening schools for Jewish adults in Warsaw was connected with the organization, the Society to Combat Illiteracy (Di gezelshaft tsu bakempfen dem analfabetizm), established in July 1907. Operating under the auspices of a Polish organization for the spread of adult education, the society opened its first evening school in Warsaw in March 1908.[108] By the summer of 1908 the society had opened six schools with between 450 to 500 students, where Polish, Yiddish, and arithmetic were taught.[109] But the participation of Bund and other socialist party members in the teaching staff led the authorities to shut down the society in late 1908, eight months after the schools were opened.[110]

## Ideological Evolution

All the changes that took place in the wake of the failed 1905 Revolution spilled over into the Bundist press, which itself was recovering from the repressions. From 1908, the Bund began to publish a series of irregular *zamelbikher* (literary anthologies), which were officially literary anthologies in order to evade the censor. Alongside these anthologies was an illegal press that was miniscule in comparison with the prior period, but which nonetheless made an impact. It was in the pages of the legal *zamelbikher*, which frequently changed titles, as well as in the illegal Yiddish and Russian press, that the Bund discussed the principal issues of the national program.[111]

The themes developed in the Bundist press reflected a general shift toward Jewish communal concerns among the Jewish political parties. "We ought to become more deeply involved in the more sober and prosaic questions of daily life," Medem told his colleagues in the party's central committee during this time, "particularly in those questions bearing upon Jewish life."[112] *Di shtime fun bund* echoed the party's shift toward communal affairs. "The cultural needs of the *folk* have begun to grow," stated *Di shtime fun bund* in 1909, giving rise to "a whole array of questions about our culture: the question of the folk school, of adult education, of our literature, our theatre, our art and so on."[113]

The themes in the Bund's press during the period 1908–11 focused on three broad issues: the place of the Yiddish language in secular Jewish life, the nature of the party's national program, and the secularization of Jewish communal life through reform of the kehillah.

### THE STRUGGLE FOR THE RECOGNITION OF YIDDISH

One of the first studies to develop the idea of a Yiddish *folkshul* appeared in the Bundist daily newspaper, *Folkstsaytung*, in 1906.[114] The author, Joseph Becker (b. 1881), drew upon the findings of nineteenth-century pedagogical theories to bolster his argument for the centrality of the mother tongue in the education of children. Paraphrasing the German philologist Karl Wilhelm von Humboldt (1769–1835), the founder of comparative philology, Becker wrote that "language is a tool for reasoning; language is the soul of a people. [It] encloses a distinct sphere around each people. Dismissing one's [native] language," Becker concluded, was tantamount to "renouncing the individual separateness that each people possesses."[115] Becker thus concluded that instruction in a foreign language would undermine the normal development of a child, and that all teachers in the *folkshul* must be fully fluent in the language that the children speak. The future public school thus could not be conducted in anything but the native language, which in the case of Russian Jewry applied solely to Yiddish.

Within the ranks of the Bund, Jewish educators with specialties in pedagogy became more prominent. During Pesach 1907 Bundists helped organize the first nationwide conference of Jewish teachers involved in modern secular schools. Of sixty-seven teachers attending the conference, forty-four were members of the Bund.[116] Among the organizers was the Bundist Boris Levinson (1880–1923).[117] Levinson was born into a traditional Jewish family in the Belarussian town of Lepel, where he completed a traditional Jewish education. In 1895 Levinson entered the Vilna Teacher's Institute, where he studied for four years. At the time he became involved in the "Zhargon Committee," an organization that disseminated literature in Yiddish, and he joined the Bund. Upon completing his studies in Vilna in 1899, Levinson was employed as director of a Talmud Torah in the southern Pale. Afterward Levinson went abroad to study at the universities of Berlin and Berne. In 1905 he returned to Russia to help edit the Bund's legal daily press in Vilna.

In the pages of the Bund's first literary anthology, *Di naye tsayt*, Levinson argued for the importance of a modern school in the Jewish vernacular. Levinson developed his argument with a discussion of the shortcomings of the existing types of Jewish schools in Russia: the heder, the heder metukan (reformed Hebrew school), the community Talmud Torah, and the government-run Crown Jewish elementary schools. Levinson concluded that none satisfied the needs of the Jewish masses for a modern education in their spoken language. "We will have a Yiddish *folkshul*," Levinson wrote, "only when all subjects in a secular school are taught in Yiddish. Russian (in Poland—Polish) will be taught only insomuch as it is required for practical purposes."[118]

In the years 1909 and 1910 the *shprakh-frage* and the *shul-frage* took on increasing importance. Both the conflict between the Jewish Social Democratic Party of Galicia (ŻPS) and its Polish and Austrian counterparts, as well as the Austro-Hungarian census of 1910, in which the state refused to recognize Yiddish as a language, strengthened the Bund's resolve to struggle for the rights of Yiddish. In *Tsayt-fragen*, which appeared in Vilna between November 1909 and September 1910, Ester Frumkin (1880–1943) elaborated her theory of the secular Yiddish school. Frumkin was born into a merchant family of Maskilic parents in Minsk. Her father, who wrote Yiddish poetry and song, was an admirer of I. L. Peretz, taught her biblical and modern Hebrew at home, and introduced her to Hebrew writers of the Russian Haskalah. As a teenager, in the mid-1890s, Frumkin became enamored with modern Yiddish literature and even wrote a novel in Yiddish at the age of fourteen. She recalled that as a teenager, Avram Liesen's poetry made a greater impression on her than the political polemics of the day. "Never," Frumkin wrote, "did I become distant from the Yiddish language and its literature."[119] One of her fondest memories of home was singing Yiddish songs with her father. On graduating from the Minsk gymnasium, Frumkin entered Saint Petersburg University, where she enrolled in courses on pedagogy and education. From 1901, Frumkin became active in the Bund, working in its legal press between 1905 and 1907.[120]

In *Tsayt-fragen* Frumkin developed her theories on "national education," that is, modern schools in the Jewish vernacular, as part and parcel of the party's program of national-cultural autonomy. "In the national school," Frumkin wrote, "the state language can and should be taught . . . but the language of development, the language of instruction can and must only be the language of the *folk*, the mother tongue." Frumkin then proceeded to express the socialist approach to secular Jewish education. The folk school would cultivate class consciousness in the children of Jewish workers by "awaken[ing] in them . . . affection for their class." The folk school would teach those Jewish holidays that "can be largely filled with true proletariat content." But Frumkin emphasized that by educating children in a "proletarian spirit," she did not envision the disappearance of Judaism from the lives of the Jewish masses. "When we speak of education in a proletarian spirit, we do not mean that children should recite part of the Erfurt Program instead of the 'Shema', or a chapter of the Communist Manifesto instead of the 'Modeh Ani' [a morning prayer]. . . . But when we say 'proletariat upbringing' we mean that Marxism is not only a political program but a *weltanschauung* . . . and in such a form it is never too early for a proletarian child. That which a child now feels he will later understand."[121] Henryk Erlich later recalled that Frumkin had spoken about religion as a necessary element in the upbringing of children. "She spoke with great warmth," Erlich remembered, "about the positive educational value of religious customs. She delighted in the custom of blessing the candles, for example. It did not occur to anyone that Ester Frumkin should be expelled from the party for her national-religious 'deviation.'"[122]

Boris Levinson replied to Frumkin, arguing that she had placed too much emphasis on socialism. In a Jewish school Jewish culture and traditions had to be taught first and foremost. Criticizing the socialist Jewish intelligentsia for their attitude to Jewish customs and traditions, Levinson proclaimed the following: "I do not see any sin against progress when a clean cloth covers the table on the Sabbath, when we light candles on a Friday night; or when, during the Passover, the holiday of spring and freedom, our homes are brightened, or when we fill our homes with greenery on Shavuot— or when national mourning is felt on the Nineth of Av."[123]

Levinson continued with a discussion of a program for the new secular Yiddish school. Writing of the near absence of suitable teaching materials in Yiddish, Levin advanced the following programmatic slogan: "To create a Yiddish literature that should embrace all sciences, popularize the whole of Jewish history, to publish original Yiddish and translated works that mirror Jewish life, both contemporary and old, to translate all classic works from world literature, to collect folk songs and melodies, folk tales—this is a program not for a year—but this must become the aim of our community. To accomplish this work, we must begin right now."[124]

Frumkin continued to develop her views in 1909 and 1910. More and more she situated the demand for Yiddish folk schools within the larger issue of minority language rights and national-cultural autonomy.[125] But it was the appearance, in 1910, of Frumkin's full-length study, *On the Question of the Yiddish Folk School*, that made the biggest splash on the socialist scene. In four chapters Frumkin systematically explored the pedagogical theories and socialist basis behind the demand for the Yiddish folk school.[126] Restating the themes she had evolved in the previous two years, Frumkin emphasized the socialist basis underpinning the demand for Yiddish folk schools. "In the name of the class struggle," she wrote, "the Jewish proletariat, with its entire energy, demands a folk school that will give the younger generation access to education and culture—a folk school in the mother tongue."[127]

## THE NATIONAL QUESTION AND "NEUTRALISM"

The increasing emphasis on language rights and secular Yiddish schools led to a further reevaluation of the party's national program. Since 1904 Vladimir Medem had emerged as the most important Bundist theoretician on the national question. In a series of articles in the Bund's Russia-language organ, *Vestnik Bunda*, titled "The National Question and Social Democracy," Medem had constructed a theoretical justification for the Bund's national program based on the principles of Social Democracy. Medem argued that in the debate between assimiliationists and nationalists on the future of the Jewish people and Jewish culture, Social Democrats should remain neutral.[128] Let it be, Medem argued, that the objective course of history led either to assimilation or to the growth and preservation of the Jewish nation in eastern Europe. "We are not opposed to assimilation," Medem wrote. "We are opposed to the *striving* for assimilation, to assimilation as a goal." On the other hand, "we are not opposed to the national character of our culture; we are opposed to *nationalist* politics."[129] While Social Democrats should be officially neutral on the question of the future of Yiddish and Jewish nationality, the state must also remain neutral. State neutrality meant, above all, abstaining from all attempts to impose the dominant culture on a minority nationality. Medem therefore argued that all nations deserved the legal right to full freedom of cultural and national development. The program of national-cultural autonomy for all nationalities thus constituted the only legal safeguard. But one could not simply entrust state institutions to grant minority rights to free cultural development. Cultural services such as public education would have to be removed from the jurisdiction of the state and turned over to each nation's autonomous institutions regardless of territory.[130] Medem's position, known as "neutralism," became the semiofficial Bundist position during the revolutionary period.

But beginning in 1908, neutralism came under scrutiny from within the party. Such publicists as A. Litvak, Ester Frumkin, and M. Olgin took Medem to task. How could the party be officially "neutral" on the question of the future of the Yiddish language and culture, or on the future of the Jewish people, when it was actively promoting that national culture? "One thing is clear," Frumkin wrote in 1908. "Only those who believe in the future of Yiddish can consciously work for its development, enhancement and improvement. How can those who . . . train their children in a language which is alien to the Jewish masses . . . fight for the rights of the mother tongue?"[131]

Medem set about clarifying his position the following year. "We

have long since become alien to the mood of cosmopolitanism,"
Medem wrote in 1909, "but we are also no idolatrous worshippers
of the national idea."[132] But it was A. Litvak's article in the pages of
the Saint Petersburg Yiddish daily, *Der fraynd*, that prompted
Medem to fully respond to his critics. Litvak questioned the suit-
ability of neutralism to the current conditions of the party. What
did it mean, he asked, to be "neutral" on the question of whether
the Jewish nation will flourish or become extinct, or be "neutral" on
the question of the fate of the Yiddish language and culture? Did the
Bund truly have no stand on such issues?[133]

Medem replied to Litvak in a 1910 article titled "Nationalism or
'Neutralism.'"[134] In this piece we observe the beginnings of
Medem's theoretical shift from neutralism to a more positive affirmation of the Jewish future, when he began to acknowledge that the
term *neutralism* itself implied both indifference and inactivity. Thus,
on such questions as language and schools, "one has to come out
one way or another—either for or against a folk school; and in such
questions . . . one has to openly state if one desires a national school
or not. Neutralism is, then, possible only when one does nothing; to
be neutral would mean, in principle, severing one's self from [party]
work."[135] At the same time Medem reiterated his view that a prognosis with regard to the Jewish future was impossible. Therefore,
"our neutralism is a thousand times more honest than mystical
nationalism."[136]

Following the debate between Medem and Litvak, M. Olgin
responded in a forceful antineutralist polemic.[137] Olgin criticized
those Bundist intellectuals who continued to speak Russian or
Polish in their private lives. It was a fact, Olgin wrote, that Yiddish
remained a foreign language to many party intellectuals. "I do not
know a single *intelligent* who speaks Yiddish in the home with his
wife and children." By continuing to speak Russian and Polish in
private life, "we are assimilating our children! In this way, we, the
'leftist' Jewish intelligentsia, are no better than the assimilationists."
The "tragedy" of the Bund's intelligentsia, Olgin maintained, was
that at the same time that it promoted secular Yiddish culture, many
continued to harbor the assumption that to be a man of culture
meant to "to inhabit another cultural world, outside the Jewish
sphere."[138] Neutralism, then, was used to justify such a state of
affairs. The party could no longer afford to philosophize about a

prognosis of the Jewish future. Neutrality on the question of the future of the Jewish people and its culture was no longer viable.

### THE EIGHTH CONFERENCE OF THE BUND
### AND ITS SIGNIFICANCE, 1910

The Bund's involvement in cultural work and programmatic discussions in the years 1907–10 set the stage for its historic party conference. The gathering marked "a moment of recovery and revival" and was meant "to open a new phase of activity."[139] Taking place in October 1910 in Lemberg, the Bund's eighth party conference was attended by twenty-five people, including twelve delegates from local divisions.[140] The participants included a virtual who's who of the Bundist world: Aizenshtat, Portnoy, Koigen, Weinstein, and Litvak from the central committee, as well as Medem, Groser, Henryk Erlich, Ester Frumkin, Kossovsky, Frants Kursky, Pesach-Liebman Hersh, Victor Shulman, and Dovid Myer.[141] For the first time in the Bund's history, Yiddish replaced Russian as the official language of the conference.

The eighth party conference focused its discussions on issues relating specifically to Jewish communal life. First, on the question of *kultur-arbeyt*, the conference called on its local organizations to found cultural societies for workers as well as to join existing associations. Second, the conference passed a resolution on the Saturday and Sunday rest days in Russia, demanding the "legally guaranteed right of the Jewish proletariat to observe the Shabbat." Third, the conference called for the democratization of the kehillah, which it demanded become a democratically elected body.[142] In the most significant resolution on the language and school questions, the Bund issued the following resolution:

> Until the realization of national-cultural autonomy which will transfer responsibility for educational and cultural matters to the nations themselves, it is necessary to work for the establishment of a government school for each national group in the general population in which its own language will be used. All limitations on the use of one's mother tongue in public life, assemblies, the press, business institutions, school, *et cetera*, must be abolished.
>
> In the struggle to achieve these demands, it is necessary to secure the rights of the Yiddish language, which is denied these rights more

than any other language and, moreover, is not even officially recognized, while the other non-dominant languages receive at least partial recognition.[143]

Following the demands for the rights of the Yiddish language, the Bund passed the following resolution on relations with other Jewish parties. "While making clear its reservations about those nationalist trends that turn the struggle for Yiddish into an instrument with which to blunt the class consciousness of the proletariat," the resolution stated, "Jewish Social Democracy . . . must conduct the struggle against the assimilationists and Hebraists so that the Yiddish language will acquire in all areas of Jewish public life— especially, in the schools and cultural institutions—the prominent position it merits as the national language of the Jewish people."[144]

The Bund's eighth party conference was reinforced by a parallel party conference in Galicia. During October 1910 the ŻPS held its fourth congress, also in Lemberg. Inspired by the Bund, the ŻPS issued a five-point resolution on the "struggle for the rights of the Yiddish language," calling for a full program of national-cultural autonomy for Galician Jewry.[145]

The eighth conference of the Bund constituted a significant milestone. According to *Di shtime fun bund*, the conference was meant, above all, to send a message to the Gentile world. "Russian and Polish society . . . [and] the folk masses of all nations should learn that the Jewish people strive for an independent cultural existence; that they cannot become Russified or Polonized; that they are in need of Jewish schools in which the Yiddish language will be recognized as fully equal."[146] The report, which appeared immediately after the conference, concluded: "Rights for our language! . . . We cannot lead our economic and political struggle . . . in a language other than the mother tongue." By the following year, in 1911, the Bund would characterize the eighth conference a landmark event, one that "concretized our national program. The eighth conference has a particular importance: it took place after a long and difficult crisis, at the threshold of a new revival." That the Bund survived the crises and resolved, by near unanimous vote, vital outstanding questions "demonstrates that the Jewish workers' movement lives, and that its guardian and founder—the Bund—lives on."[147] A 1912 May Day leaflet, with a circulation of twenty-five thousand, echoed the party's new emphasis on language rights, advancing the slogan of "equal national rights; the right of our mother tongue in schools, courts, public meetings, trade unions, and in all state institutions." It continued that the Bund vociferously demanded "the legally guaranteed right for the Jewish worker to a Shabbas rest day!"[148] Vladimir Kossovsky, in a detailed article on the conference in the party's Russian organ, *Otkliki Bunda*, remarked that "The responses provided by the conference testify to the deep organic interest in the national needs and requirements of the Jewish proletariat and of the broad popular masses in general, and testify to the readiness to defend with the greatest energy the demands which flow from these needs both externally as well as internally, within the Jewish environment proper."[149]

Historians of the Yiddish language movement have attributed great importance to the Bund's 1910 party conference. Chaim Kazdan (1883–1979), in his study on the history of the modern Yiddish school system in eastern Europe, remarked that the 1910 party conference of the Bund "concretized the language and school demands of the Jewish working class."[150]

This chapter has argued that the period 1907–14 occupies a significant place in the history of the Bund. The involvement in cultural work strengthened the Bund's link to Jewish culture. As Woodhouse and Tobias have commented, these cultural activities "gave substance to the claim to national cultural autonomy through a range of activities which could be pursued at less hazard than strikes and demonstrations."[151] Moreover, the Bund's leading role in the struggle for the rights of Yiddish, the demand for the democratization of the kehillah, and for a legally guaranteed Sabbath rest day reveals a significant evolution in the party's development. As late as 1903 the Bund's left wing vociferously opposed the demand for Jewish national rights. But by 1907 the party's assimilationist wing had disappeared. That the Bund's political program should have a national component was no longer questioned. By 1907–8, the party could no longer remain officially "neutral" on the question of the Jewish nation's future. As Kossovsky commented some years later, "The Bund aided in developing the Yiddish language, Yiddish culture, and Yiddish schools, that is, in [the development] of modern Yiddish culture. . . . In other words, in the period when the Bund held that it was neutral [on the Jewish future] . . . the Bund energetically intervened in the 'objective process' and . . . actively worked against assimilation."[152] It was thus during the last years of the tsarist empire that the Bund became, in practice, a Jewish national party.

# ■ 10.

# The PPS and the Jewish Question on the Eve of the First World War

> *Jewish jargon will never serve the cultural needs of a higher level—it is only a temporary tool, an elementary guide to culture for the unenlightened masses. Together with the growth of culture, above all with the establishment of normal political relations, the language of the country's majority must take on an ever-increasing meaning in the lives of the Jewish masses.*
> PPS REVOLUTIONARY FACTION (1908)

> *We demand legal guarantees for the right of Jews to use Yiddish in all public institutions, schools, and courts of law.*
> PPS LEFT RESOLUTION (1910)

FROM 1906, THREE POLISH SOCIALIST PARTIES competed for the hearts and minds of the working class in Russian Poland: the SDKPiL, the PPS Left, and the PPS Revolutionary Faction (Right). In contrast to a prevailing consensus that Polish socialists— and especially those of Jewish origin—were assimilationists, the attitude of these parties to the Jewish question varied according to political program, the character of the leadership, and the degree of adherence to Marxist principles.[1] On the far left, the SDKPiL's assimilationist stand only became sharper during and after 1905, as it continued to steadfastly oppose the Bund's national program.[2] More subtle and complex, however, were the views of the PPS's two factions during the last years of the tsarist empire.

Prior to 1905 the PPS had regarded itself as the vanguard of the revolutionary movement in imperial Russia. But, as already noted, the 1905 Russian Revolution led to a crisis in Polish socialism over how to respond to the revived Russian revolutionary movement. One faction of the PPS—the Young—favored downgrading the party's demand from independence to autonomy, while struggling alongside other socialist groups for the democratization of Russia. The other faction—the Old—argued that the separation of Poland was a fundamental precondition for democratization and for the achievement of socialism.[3]

Formally established in 1907 and 1908, respectively, the two factions took very different positions on the Jewish question in general and on the Bund in particular. The PPS Right, at its first congress held March 1907 in Vienna, called for an independent Polish republic and a continuation of the armed struggle. Probably due to the opposition of Feliks Perl, who was a committed assimilationist, the congress refused to include a separate point on the rights of Jews to cultural autonomy, something Piłsudski had favored earlier. Instead, the program included a statement guaranteeing "the rights of national minorities in administration, schools, and courts," although this did not necessarily apply to Jews.[4] Fundamental to the PPS Right's ideology was the idea that socialism and Polish independence were integrally linked. The main reason for the lack of democratic and political freedoms, the Revolutionary Faction argued, was national—not social—oppression. For Piłsudski, Perl, and Wasliewski, the term *revolution* referred to a struggle against tsardom for independence. "We are a revolutionary party," Piłsudski wrote in 1910, "and the revolution for which we are preparing is the armed struggle of a people's army with the army of the tsar. . . . To prepare for this revolutionary struggle, two things are needed: an army and weapons."[5] Because the PPS Right maintained that socialism could only be achieved after independence, the emphasis on socialist agitation among workers dramatically diminished after 1908. The party's principle figure, Piłsudski, began a gradual departure from socialism at this time, arguing that the social base of the military organizations had to expand beyond the working classes.

Whereas the PPS Right saw the Russian autocratic government as the working class's main enemy and national freedom as the only solution, the PPS Left looked to the lack of democratic rights as the main cause of the working class's ills in Russian Poland. The immediate goal had to be the democratization of the Russian Empire. The PPS Left's program was thus substantially different with regard to both the national question in general and the Jewish question in particular. At its first congress in January 1908, the PPS Left removed the demand for Polish independence from its minimum program. Instead, the congress demanded "wide autonomy" for Congress Poland based on a legislative Sejm in Warsaw. Some of the party leaders, such as Horwitz, Bielecki, and Sachs, had advocated Jewish autonomous rights in 1905. It is thus not surprising that the PPS Left's platform specifically recognized the rights of Jews to extraterritorial national autonomy, demanding "a guarantee of the rights of national minorities (Jews, Germans, etc.) not separated into autonomous territorial units."[6] Now that it no longer demanded independence, the PPS Left openly sought alliances with the Bund and the SDKPiL.

### Attitude of the PPS Right to the Jewish Question, 1908–13

The crisis that befell socialist parties in Russia in 1907 led to a total reorientation among Polish socialists who remained committed to the struggle for independence. By 1908 the leadership of the PPS Right and party press relocated to Kraków, in Austrian Galicia. The party's dominant figure, Piłsudski, gave up hope of unifying the socialist parties in Russian Poland and instead devoted his energies to building the PPS's Fighting Division (OB). Piłsudski had earlier played a major role in defining the party's attitude to the Bund and to the Jewish question, a position that softened considerably between the late 1890s and 1905. With Piłsudski's withdrawal from intellectual activity after 1907, two figures reshaped the party's stand with regard to the Bund and the Jewish question: Feliks Perl and Leon Wasilewski.

During the period under examination, when socialist activity was severely limited in the Russian Empire, Perl and Wasliewski paid close attention to developments in Austrian Galicia. In particular, it was the conflict between the Jewish Social Democratic Party of Galicia (ŻPS) and the Polish Social Democratic Party of Galicia (PPSD) that would influence the specific debate on the Jewish question among Polish socialists inside tsarist Russia. Let us, then, summarize the developments in Galicia before examining the PPS Right's position.

The ŻPS was founded in May 1905 by a breakaway faction of the PPSD. The PPSD charge of "separatism" found support in Vienna, when the Austrian Social Democrats declared the ŻPS had no right to organizational independence. Social Democratic parties, it was argued, should be divided along territorial lines. But the ŻPS only strengthened its resolve. At its second party congress held in May 1906 in Lemberg, the ŻPS endorsed the program of national cultural autonomy for Galician Jewry, thereby rejecting the territorial principle of nationality passed by the Austrian Social Democrats at Brünn in 1899.[7] In Vienna several Austro-Marxists came out specifically against the ŻPS, particularly two leaders of Jewish origin, Victor Adler and Otto Bauer (1881–1938).

The issue of the right of Galician Jewish workers to organizational independence received heightened interest with the appearance in 1907 of Otto Bauer's seminal study *The Question of Nationalities and Social Democracy*. Drawing on the work of his fellow Austrian Social Democrat, Karl Renner (1870–1950), who had developed the idea of the "personality principle" in national thought, Bauer argued that the nation was not a "territorial corporation" but an "association of persons." The nation, Bauer maintained "is the totality of men bound together through a common destiny into a community of character." From Bauer's and Renner's emphasis on the nation as a "community of character," they arrived at a full-fledged endorsement of the principle of national-cultural autonomy in multinational states. The program called for the creation of a national register of nationalities in which each adult would formally declare membership in a national group. The state would then be divided into nationalities based on an official national registry.[8]

While the principles put forth in *The Question of Nationalities and Social Democracy* appeared to support the ŻPS's program, Bauer in fact rejected outright the application of national cultural autonomy to the Jews. "With the progressive development of capitalism and the modern state, the Jews of the east will also cease to constitute a nation and will be absorbed into other nations just as the Jews of the west have long since been." Bauer acknowledged that Yiddish culture was experiencing a revival, and that it, along with its promoters, such as the Bund, would persist for some decades. This was nonetheless merely a period of transition. "From a historical point of view, the awakening of the eastern Jews to a new cultural life is nothing but a precursor to ultimate assimilation."[9]

Bauer maintained that the principle of national autonomy was fundamentally about the question of education. At a time when the *shprakh-frage* was assuming increasing importance within the Bundist camp, Bauer proclaimed that "Jewish workers in Galicia and in Bukovina cannot, to the extent that they recognize their true interests, demand separate Jewish schools." He continued: "For the Jews, the Jewish school represents first and foremost the artificial preservation of their old cultural specificity, one that limits their freedom of movement and consequently increases their suffering. . . . If we do not want specifically Jewish schools, the national autonomy of Jews makes no sense." Bauer concluded that "national autonomy cannot be a demand of the Jewish workers."[10]

When *The Question of Nationalities and Social Democracy* appeared, Otto Bauer was a youthful twenty-six years old. At the time, in 1907, debates within socialist circles on the Jewish question had long been under way, while the Bund had already endorsed the principle of Jewish nationality (1901) and national-cultural autonomy (1905). Moreover, Bauer's senior colleague, Karl Kautsky (1854–1938), the foremost European socialist theorist on the national question, had taken a much more sympathetic view of the Jewish national idea on several occasions. Just prior to the appearance of Bauer's book, Kautsky had sent a congratulatory letter to the Bund on the occasion of its seventh party congress in August 1906. Although Jews were different from other European nations, Kautsky wrote, "one can manifestly not deny that Jewry is a distinct societal unity with a culture which is peculiar to itself, and that it differentiates itself from the nations of Eastern Europe among which it lives." As Jack Jacobs has argued, Kautsky's position implied a willingness to accept the Bund's national program.[11] Thus, the Bund studiously ignored Bauer's position on the Jewish question.[12] Some European socialists who agreed with Bauer's assimilationist position nonetheless maintained that it was inconsistent with the rest of his book. As Lenin wrote, Bauer's position on the Jewish question "proves more conclusively than lengthy speeches how inconsistent Otto Bauer is and how little he believes in his own idea, for he excludes the *only* extra-territorial . . . nationality from his plan for extra-territorial autonomy!"[13]

Bauer's book appeared at a moment of great transition in Polish socialism. The PPS had just split into two parties, and ideological lines between the two factions were hardening. The defection of the PPS's Jewish Section to the PPS Left in November 1906, as well as the prominence of Jewish Poles in the PPS Left's leadership, left some leaders of the Revolutionary Faction embittered. Jewish loyalty to the Polish national idea was under question. The tense situation put Feliks Perl, the architect of the PPS Right's party platform, on the defensive. From 1908 Perl emerged as the party's most vocal advocate of assimilationism.

One of the earliest translations of Bauer's *The Question of Nationalities and Social Democracy* appeared in Polish in 1908.[14] With Bauer's seminal work now available to Polish readers, it is no surprise that Perl capitalized on Bauer's analysis of the Jewish question. And this was the case despite the fact that Bauer's general position on the national question ran directly counter to the PPS Right's independence platform.

In the pages of *Przedświt*, the Kraków-based organ of the PPS Right, Perl raised serious questions about the practical applicability of the Bund's solution to the general national question in imperial Russia (national-cultural autonomy). How would national cultural autonomy function, Perl asked, in the army, in central state institutions, and in the relations between such institutions and local authorities? If, over the whole of the Russian state, each national language was coequal in these institutions, then the result would be a "virtual Babel of linguistic chaos" that would render such a state of affairs impossible. Besides, Perl wrote, Bauer had proved that the Jews did not constitute a nation in the modern sense of the word, and that the program of national-cultural autonomy would only prolong Jewish separateness.[15] Polish Jewry could thus, Perl maintained, only base its future on immersion "with a territorial nation." He continued, "Both in their material struggle for existence and in their endeavor to achieve a higher spiritual culture, Jews must use the language of the majority, and claim for themselves its intellectual property. They should work to multiply this wealth, and contribute to its growth and excellence. Jewish jargon will never serve the cultural needs of a higher level—it is only a temporary tool, an elementary guide to culture for the unenlightened masses. Together with the growth of culture, above all with the establishment of normal political relations, the language of the country's majority must take on an ever-increasing meaning in the lives of the Jewish masses."[16] Perl concluded with a summary of Bauer's "correct" argument against Jewish national autonomy.[17]

Following the Bund's eighth party conference in 1910, Perl responded in several pieces on the Jewish question. But now that debate would be directed toward the Bund's emergent Polish-Jewish intelligentsia, a group of second-generation Bundists who became prominent after 1905. More than any other figure, it was the Polish-Jewish intellectual Bronislav Groser who represented a trend that Perl found alarming: the defection of Polish-speaking Jews, raised in Polonized families, to the Bund.

Despite their different political views and affiliations, Perl and Groser came from similar backgrounds. Both were raised in middle-class assimilated households in Congress Poland, received a secular education, and held professional degrees from prestigious universities. But while Perl, whose father fought in the 1863 Polish uprising, became passionately devoted to the proindependence socialist movement, Groser, twelve years younger, followed a different path. As a child and teenager, Groser had fully identified as a Pole. Groser's parents, although not converts, had severed their ties to the Jewish community to such an extent that Groser had no knowledge of his Jewish origin until the age of fourteen or fifteen. [18] Upon applying to the Warsaw gymnasium, Groser was shocked to learn that he was being subjected to a special Jewish quota.[19] Accepted into the gymnasium, Groser joined an illegal group of young Polish socialists. But it was in high school that Groser began to wrestle with his identity, gradually moving away from the assimilationist spirit in which he was raised.

After graduating high school in 1902 Groser joined the Warsaw Bund and went abroad to Switzerland for university studies. At the age of nineteen Groser, who now went by the name "Slavek," met Vladimir Medem for the first time in Geneva. "When I first became acquainted with Slavek," Medem recalled, "he knew scarcely a word of Yiddish. He was an artist in the realm of thought . . . enriched by a broad European, scientific, aesthetic, and political culture. But it was that Jewish mind which . . . was like a sensitive instrument that measured and weighed with the precision of a druggist's scale; a mind of steel-like sharpness, capable of penetrating issues and concepts, dissecting and analyzing them, identifying the smallest, most delicate elements. In a word—Slavek's was the mind of a born Marxist." Despite his involvement in the Bund, Groser remained, as Medem observed, "impregnated with Polish culture that he loved."[20] As Beynish Mikhalevitch would later comment, Groser was a true gift to the Bund.[21] He edited the Bund's Polish-language organs, *Głos Bundu* (1904–1905) and *Nasze Hasła* (1906), as well as composed Polish-language circulars.

With the growing popularity of Dmowksi's National Democratic Party, as well as the spread of political anti-Semitism to the Polish political center, Groser felt the need to engage the Polish public. In the pages of *Wiedza*, the Vilna-based organ of the PPS Left and the only legal socialist journal in the Polish language at the time, Groser argued that the Polish debate over the Jewish question was lacking an authentic Jewish voice. Groser began by expressing profound disappointment at the growing wave of anti-Jewish sentiment in the Polish press. But he did agree with Dmowski on one point: assimilation was bankrupt. The mass of Polish Jews spoke Yiddish, came from the lower-middle- and working-class strata of society, and possessed a low level of general culture. The only way to modernize the Jewish masses, to raise their cultural standing and political consciousness, to bring them closer to Polish culture, was through the free development of secular Jewish Yiddish culture. Recognition of this historical process and its inevitability "must be understood as a fundamental point of departure for any solution to the Jewish question."[22]

The combination of Groser's article, which led to further discussion in the Polish press, as well as the Bund's eighth party conference in 1910, led Perl to further reflect on the Jewish problem in Polish lands.[23] In 1911 both Groser and Perl used the pages of their respective sister organizations in Galicia—the ŻPS and the PPSD—to debate the implications of the Bund's program on Polish-Jewish relations. In a reply to Perl, who wrote an article in favor of assimilation and highly critical of the Bund's new program, Groser published an article in *Der sotsial-demokrat* in which he argued the case for extraterritorial national autonomy for the Jews of Russia and Galicia.[24] In this lengthy three-part article, comprising nineteen columns, Groser challenged the positions of Perl and Otto Bauer on the Jewish question. Both Perl and Bauer shared a common belief in the inevitability of complete Jewish assimilation. After summarizing Bauer's position in *The Question of Nationalities and Social Democracy*, Groser shifted the debate from theory to pragmatism. How did Bauer's and Perl's theories of Jewish assimilation measure against the current trends in east European Jewish life? "There is no doubt," Groser stated, "that a revival of Jewish national culture is taking place before our eyes." The Jewish masses, who for centuries led pious lives with little interest in the larger society around them, were now beginning to awaken out of their slumber. They were taking part in the class struggle and showing interest in political and cultural life. According to Groser, the same process of national differentiation that was penetrating the east European Jewish masses had earlier taken place among the Czechs, Ruthenians, Croats, and Slovenes and was concurrently occurring among Lithuanians, Latvians, Belarussians, and others. "Just as with other nations, a national folk culture has arisen among the Jews. A dialect has become a language and the rise of a Yiddish literature and press has developed national self-awareness [*natsionale zelbstgefil*]."[25]

At the same time Groser acknowledged that assimilation continued to make advances side by side with a Jewish cultural revival. "The process of assimilation, which at one time grew strongly among the Jewish bourgeoisie, is today not only being restrained, but we observe its reversal. On the other side, one cannot hide the fact that an assimilatory tendency is having an effect, and it will continue to do so." Groser thus observed what he called "a tendency against a tendency," that is, the emergence of competing currents that marked east European Jewish life.[26] The outcome of these competing tendencies would shape the character of east European Jewry.

It was precisely Perl's and Bauer's pretense of "scientifically showing" the inevitability of one tendency over another that Groser derided. One could not establish the policies of a political party based on a prediction that runs counter to the current realities. The role of Social Democracy, Groser argued, was not to make prophecies "on the natural development of a particular national culture. Just as Social Democracy does not strive to artificially preserve [one national culture], so it similarly does not work to destroy the elements of national distinctiveness. Rather, its aim is to . . . meet the concrete national needs of the worker and to reduce occurrences of national persecution, possible only in the capitalist system, to a minimum." As a supporter of Medem, Groser argued that a dispassionate neutralism should guide Jewish Social Democratic politics: "As a political party, we cannot be concerned with scholastic investigations into the question, 'What is a nation?' . . . As a party of struggle, we try not to predict what we cannot foresee, nor shut our eyes to reality. The Jewish worker today communicates freely only in his own language, something Jewish Social Democrats must repeatedly underline. When, due to natural developments, an epoch arrives when the national needs of Jewish workers have withered away, Social Democracy will accommodate itself to the new situation. But today Jewish Social Democracy must base its demands on current conditions."[27]

Perl responded to Groser in the PPSD's daily in Lemberg, *Głos*, with a blow-by-blow refutation.[28] The problem with the Bund's program, Perl argued, was that it placed Jews, a "tribal-religious group devoid of territory," on the same footing with "modern authentic nations" which, like the Czechs in Austria-Hungary, possessed the objective conditions for independent development. By entirely overlooking the territorial aspirations of subjugated nations, Groser misunderstood the fundamental basis of the national problem in eastern Europe: "In general, when comrade [Groser] speaks at length about nations, about the nationalities question, one has the impression that all these nations . . . exist on air. *Land* disappears from our view. . . . Poland and the Czech lands do not exist; majorities and national minorities do not exist. It is in this mist that Jews appear and demand 'equal political rights for each nation.'"[29]

Perl continued to write on the Jewish question in 1913 following a schism in the PPS Right. Perl, who had opposed the party's increasing emphasis on militarism at the expense of socialist principles, left the party and formed the so-called PPS Opposition. The new faction's platform, drafted in 1913, included an official position on "the Jewish Question and anti-Semitism." Perl's splinter group declared itself opposed to the program of national-cultural autonomy for the following reasons: the Jews lacked territory; autonomy would maintain Jewish isolation from Polish culture and society; and equality for the Yiddish language in schools and administration would interrupt a natural process of Jewish integration into Polish culture. The party's goals regarding the Jews thus included "the removal of Jewish separateness, and joining the Jewish masses with the national-political interests of the country, particularly [in the realm] of proletarian solidarity in Poland without distinction of faith and origin."[30]

Similar arguments against the idea of Jewish national-cultural autonomy were put forward by Leon Wasilewski, a major figure in the PPS Right. In a response to the Bund's eighth party conference, Wasilewski argued that the Bund had undergone a gradual transformation from a revolutionary party of the Jewish working class to a Jewish nationalist party whose demands were "in essence, reactionary." Nowhere was this more evident, Wasilewski argued, then in the Bund's resolution on the Jewish kehillah. What did a socialist party, he asked, have to do with an institution of an exclusively religious character that was a relic of the medieval ghetto? Wasilewski also derided the Bund for taking up the cause of the Sabbath rest day, arguing that it was an improper demand for socialists. If there were a Jewish state, would anyone expect there to be two official rest days, Saturday for the majority and Sunday for the non-Jewish minority, he asked.[31] Last, Wasilewski asked why the Bund, in its lengthy conference report, did not address the separate political and national interests of Poles, Lithuanians, Latvians, and Ukrainians among whom the Jews lived.

In his 1913 study, *The Jewish Question on the Lands of Old Poland*, Wasilewski examined the Jewish question in more detail. Like Perl, Wasilewski argued that the program of national-cultural autonomy was utopian. Either it would require separate schools, courts, post offices, administrative institutions, and health institutions for the Jews, or all personnel in state and local institutions would have to learn Yiddish. In any event, the persistence of Jewish isolation was merely the consequence of Russia's backward economic and social conditions. In particular, two forces interacted with the backward Russian political system to create a formidable barrier to "the only escape for Jews," assimilation: reactionary anti-Semitism and Jewish nationalism. The PPS thus had to struggle against anti-Semitism as a force that retarded Jewish integration and that simultaneously strengthened Jewish nationalism.[32]

While Perl and Wasilewski were united in their positions, alternative views on the Jewish question could be heard within the PPS Right. Piłsudski, for one, had come out in favor of extending autonomous rights to Jews already in 1902. Although he did not write on the Jewish question after 1905, there is nothing to indicate that Piłsudski changed his views on the subject. Moreover, in 1908 the veteran Polish socialist, Bolesław Limanowski, declared his support for the principle of Jewish nationality as long as national identity persisted among the Jews.[33]

Władysław Gumplowicz (1869–1942?), an *intelligent* of the PPS Right active in emigration, was the most vocal opponent of the assimilationist ideas espoused in the party's press. Gumplowicz, active in both the PPS and the PPSD since 1898, was a delegate at the PPS Right's founding convention in March 1907.[34] In the debates there, Gumplowicz put forward the postulate of an "ethnographic Poland," arguing that historic frontiers were no longer viable: the future state should be confined to those areas where a compact majority of ethnic Poles resided, he maintained. Advocates of an ethnic Polish state adopted a much more conciliatory attitude toward minority socialist parties in Lithuania, which, they argued, had the full right to organizational independence.[35] Wasilewski vehemently opposed Gumplowicz's views. The formation of a Polish state based on ethnic frontiers, he said at the convention, would lead "not to the normal development of the Ukrainian, Lithuanian, and Belarussian nationalities, but to the triumph of the tsar and Russification."[36]

The division within the PPS Right over the form of a future Polish state had an impact on the debate over the Jewish question. In a lengthy 1908 study, *Socialism and the Polish Question*, Gumplowicz presented his vision of a future democratic Poland based on ethnic frontiers and full equality before the law. He maintained that the rise of national consciousness among minorities—including the Jews—had to be taken into account in formulating the party's demands. In a chapter devoted to the Jewish problem, Gumplowicz recognized the Jews as a distinct nationality with a separate language, customs and traditions.

Gumplowicz argued that the persistence of Jewish separateness was the product of the peculiar social, economic and political conditions in the Pale. He observed that in America, east European Jewish immigrants maintained a quasi-national identity in terms of language and customs. But the children of these immigrants were entering mainstream society and already identified themselves as Americans. In America, where Jews were safe from persecution, enjoyed equal civil rights, and were drawn to the dominant high culture, assimilation took place. "That is precisely why Lithuania is one of the main centers of the antiassimilationist current,"

Gumplowicz wrote insightfully, "where Jews desiring assimilation essentially find themselves in a dilemma." He continued: "With the emerging Belarussian culture Jews simply have no contact; Belarussians do not live in the cities while Jews do not live in the countryside. Similarly, the young, although quickly developing, Lithuanian culture has been heretofore primarily rural. The Jews, as a people from the cities who see the world through specifically urban lenses, have not felt the impact of this culture. [And] the Poles are a minority and numerically weak."[37]

A second difference between America and Russia was the attitude of the general society to Jewish assimilation. Whereas acculturation in America was looked upon favorably by local non-Jews, in Lithuania-Belarus Russification separated Jews further from their local non-Russian neighbors. All these factors impeded assimilationist tendencies and led to the popularity of Jewish autonomist ideas and to the revival of Jewish folk culture.

Gumplowicz thus argued that Jewish assimilation would proceed only under certain conditions. With the normalization of social, economic, and political life in the Polish lands, Jewish integration would follow the Western pattern. But he differed from Perl and Wasilewski by arguing that the rise of secular Yiddish culture was a positive development. Thus, secular Yiddish culture was a transitional stage that would likely lead, as in America, to eventual assimilation, but through a process that had to be democratic. Gumplowicz thus argued that Jews would acculturate when a free, sovereign Poland granted Jews unrestricted freedom of cultural-national autonomy. That is, "only when Poland genuinely and heartily recognizes Jews as their own."[38]

## The PPS Left and the Jewish Question, 1908–11

During the period 1907–14, the PPS Right gradually withdrew from political work inside Russia. In the entirely different context of Austria-Hungary, where socialist parties operated openly and legally, the PPS Right focused its energy on developing a military wing in anticipation of a Russo-Austrian conflict. Particularly after 1908, when Austria-Hungary's annexation of Bosnia-Herzegovina led to increased tensions in the Balkans, the possibility of armed conflict between the partitioning powers appeared less remote. The PPS Left, on the other hand, largely remained in Russian Poland, where it sought alliances with other socialist parties for the democratization of Russia. Composed of a younger generation of Polish socialists, the PPS Left took a more favorable attitude to Jewish autonomist ideas and, as we have seen, recognized the principle of extraterritorial Jewish nationality in January 1908.

The first PPS Left brochure on the Jewish question appeared in 1908. In a study of the origins of anti-Semitism, Marian Bielecki (1879–1912), a coauthor of the PPS Left's founding program and original central committee member, argued that the "voluntary assimilation" of the Jewish population on Polish lands was desirable. "But *limiting* the rights of Jewish society to autonomous development," Bielecki maintained, "would be politically both foolish and disgraceful."[39] Bielecki's position went to the heart of the party's position. It argued that a distinct Jewish culture based on the Yiddish language was a temporary phenomenon. At the same time the PPS Left opposed any governmental attempts to intervene in the internal process of Jewish affairs by such methods as imposing education in the state language. Thus, although eventual assimilation was desirable, Jews had to be granted legal guarantees for the right to full cultural autonomy. Only in this way would Jewish acculturation proceed on a purely voluntary basis.

The years 1909 and 1910 saw the spread of political anti-Semitism in Congress Poland from the Endecja to a breakaway faction of the Polish progressive camp. In particular, the theme of the "invasion" of Lithuanian Jews (Litvaks) into Congress Poland began to dominate the Polish press. In 1909 Andrzej Niemojewski's journal, *Myśl Niepodległa*, condemned Russian-speaking Jewish immigrants in the Kingdom of Poland as agents of Russification.[40] The increasingly sharp tone of the attacks in both the Endek and "progressive" Polish camps raised grave concern within the PPS Left.

By 1910 the PPS Left began to publicly condemn anti-Semitism in Polish political life. In the pages of its illegal party organ, *Robotnik,* it expressed alarm at the growing popularity of anti-Jewish rhetoric. The PPS Left rejected outright what it called "nationalist demagoguery" of the "anti-Semitic" Polish political parties and called for a two-point program. "From our socialist point of view," *Robotnik* stated, "there are two conclusions to be drawn. First, that the Jewish people should have the possibility of the free development of their culture, to form its language, and to create its own cultural institutions. Second, that a person who speaks only Yiddish must have the same right as those who speak only Polish in all areas of social life." Anti-Semitism, *Robotnik* continued, was a threat to the development of democracy on Polish lands. "If we want the rule of genuine democracy in our country, we cannot deny to Jews the right to develop their culture and cultivate the Yiddish language."[41]

While the PPS Left condemned anti-Semitism and supported the right of Jews to full cultural autonomy, it nonetheless opposed the Bund's program. While the Bund worked for the preservation of Yiddish culture, the PPS Left based its program on the likelihood that "the linguistic and cultural separateness" of Jews was temporary. "We have serious reasons [to assume] that the rise [of Yiddish culture] will be transient and that Jews will, in fact, merge with the surrounding environment." One only had to look at the case of America to gain a glimpse into the probable future of Polish Jewry. There Yiddish literature, Yiddish theater, and the Yiddish press served the first generation of immigrants. But Yiddish usage had practically disappeared among the grandchildren of those immigrants.[42] Despite *Robotnik*'s prognosis for the future of Polish Jewry, it emphatically maintained that it was opposed to assimilationism as a political program, and that it recognized the Jewish population as a nationality as long as such characteristics persisted.

Deliberations on the Jewish question took on a more official character at a PPS Left party conference in October 1910. Twenty-three delegates attended, including members of the central committee, representatives of Warsaw, Łódź, Zagłębie, and Częstochowa, as well from the party's foreign committee.[43] The conference report first harshly condemned "chauvinistic and nationalistic" Polish politics that had attacked the revival of Yiddish and the demand for Jewish autonomous rights. In contrast, the PPS Left evaluated positively the revival of the Yiddish language in Jewish life, which "serves to spread education and culture among the Jewish proletariat." Whatever one's prognosis of its future, the conference report stated, "Yiddish is today the spoken language of [the Jewish] masses . . . [which] plays a large role in education and in lifting these mass's cultural level." Considering the needs of the Jewish working class, the PPS Left reaffirmed its demand for a law guaranteeing the right of Jews to use Yiddish in all public institutions and courts of law.[44]

## The Impact of the Elections
## to the Fourth Duma, 1912

The postrevolutionary crises began to abate in the years before World War I. The year 1912 saw a dramatic revival of strike activity. The number of striking workers in the Russian Empire rose from 725,000 in 1912 to 887,000 in 1913 and to 1.45 million in 1914. The revival was largely sparked by the events at the British-owned Lena gold fields in March 1912, when Russian troops opened fire on demonstrators. More than a hundred workers were killed or wounded.[45] The massacre, which some compared to Bloody Sunday in 1905, provoked angry reactions. An agent of the Moscow Okhrana (the Russian security department responsible for combating subversion) described the reactions of Russian society: "There has never been so much tension. People can be heard speaking of the government in the sharpest and most unbridled tones. Many say that the 'shooting' of the Lena workers recalls the 'shooting' of the workers at the Winter Palace of January 9, 1905. Influenced by questions in the Duma and the speeches which they called forth there, pubic tension is increasing still more. . . . It is a long time since even the extreme left has spoken in such a way, since there have been references in the Duma to the 'necessity of calling a Constituent Assembly and overthrowing the present system by the united strength of the proletariat.'"[46] Sympathy strikes were called for throughout the empire. And on May Day 1912 the first mass demonstrations of Jewish workers since the revolutionary days took place in Warsaw, Vilna, Minsk, and Bobruisk.[47] Moreover, the Bund's legal party press reemerged at this time, with the weekly *Di tsayt* in Saint Petersburg.

The surge in strike activity coincided with the revival of political activity, as Russian subjects prepared for elections to the Fourth Duma. Very soon after election campaigns began, the center-right and right-wing parties in Congress Poland made the Jewish question their main focus. The Endecja and their allies launched a vitriolic anti-Semitic campaign warning the Jews that only Poles should decide who represented the Polish kingdom. At the heart of the issue was a peculiar election regulation in Warsaw. Although Jews constituted 36 percent of Warsaw's population, over half of the forty-five thousand voters in the general curia were Jews.[48] The Endecja thus led an anti-Jewish campaign warning Jews of the dire consequences of acting against Polish interests.[49] In the atmosphere of heightened tension, it was left to the PPS Left to make appeals for intercommunal fraternity.

Meanwhile, the Bund articulated four basic demands: universal suffrage, freedom of assembly, equal civil and national rights for nationalities in Russia, and the abolition of the Pale.[50] At the same time the Bund called for solidarity of the socialist parties in the form of a socialist bloc and appealed to both the PPS Left and the SDKPiL. To the Bund's chagrin, the SDKPiL refused, citing ideological differences. The PPS Left nonetheless agreed, and a formal agreement between the two parties was made.[51] The socialist bloc's committee to oversee the election campaign consisted of Aaron Weinstein and Bronislav Groser from the Bund, as well as Maks Horwitz, Maria Koszutski ("Vera"), and Władysław Kowalski from the PPS.[52] In jointly signed leaflets, distributed in separate Polish and Yiddish versions, the PPS-Bund bloc bitterly condemned the Polish anti-Semitic parties, whose loyalist positions vis-à-vis the autocratic government were "shameful." The socialist bloc demanded the abolition of all restrictions on non-Russian nationalities, equal national rights, legal guarantees for the right of the mother tongue, and the immediate abolition of the Pale.[53]

In a dramatic campaign the only Polish candidate who unambiguously endorsed equal civil rights for Jews was the Polish socialist Eugeniusz Jagiełło, who won the election in Warsaw. Moreover, the PPS-Bund bloc won the majority of electors reserved for the workers' curia in Congress Poland.[54] The bitter reaction of the Polish nationalist bloc to the Fourth Duma elections is well known.[55] Dmowski immediately called for an economic boycott of Jewish businesses throughout the Kingdom of Poland in protest over Jagiełło, a "Jewish-elected" Polish socialist. While it is true that the events of 1912 led to a worsening of Polish-Jewish relations in general, the PPS-Bund alliance represented another side to Polish-Jewish relations on the eve of the First World War. The PPS's official position in favor of Jewish national autonomous rights as well as its unambiguous condemnation of anti-Semitism and the Endecja-led boycott constituted one hopeful sign in a time of sharp ethnic strife.[56] Thus, precisely at that moment when a PPS-Bund alliance helped elect a progressive candidate to office, and progressive parties were attracting wider circles of supporters in central and eastern Europe, the First World War broke out.

Between 1908 and 1914 the PPS's position on the Jewish question crystallized into two camps. On the right, the PPS Revolutionary Faction advanced a classic Marxist assimilationist position. Feliks Perl, one of the PPS Right's main publicists, modeled his views on the French revolutionary idea that offered full civil equality to Jews in exchange for the abandonment of Jewish national identity.[57] The PPS Left, which sought an alliance with the Bund, adopted a more pragmatic approach to the Jewish question. As long as part of the population on Polish lands identified nationally as Jews, the PPS Left argued, then the Poles had an obligation to recognize this fact and to extend to Jews the right of free cultural-national development. To the PPS Left, the Jewish question went much deeper than merely a problem of group versus individual rights in a future Polish state. The attitude of the Polish population toward Jews, it maintained, constituted nothing less than a test of democratic values. The PPS Left publicists thus characterized anti-Semitism as fundamentally antidemocratic.

# ■
# Conclusion

At its historic fourth congress in 1901, the Bund boldly declared that the term *nationality* applied to the Jewish people. This book has argued that the Bund's adoption of a national program was an essentially political decision designed to answer the PPS while ensuring that Jews would be represented as a group in a future federal republic of nationalities. In its polemic with the PPS, the Bund claimed exclusive representation of Jewish workers. Even the PPS's Jewish Section, which produced its own Yiddish press, had no right, according to the Bund, to organize Jewish workers.[1]

This book also maintains that as the Bund propagated its new national program, the PPS gradually abandoned its assimilationist position. Already in early 1902 Józef Piłsudski proposed that the party program include a separate guarantee for the rights of Jews "as a nationality." This shift was reflected in the PPS's Yiddish organ, *Der arbeyter,* which, since 1902, referred to Jews as a "nationality." Its new editor, Feliks Sachs, moved to Vilna in that same year and reported that "people here . . . recognize the complete equality of all nationalities—Poles, Lithuanians, Belarussians, and Jews." By recognizing Jewish nationality, Sachs continued, "we are following the 'spirit of the times.'"[2] This new tendency toward a recognition of Jewish nationality was reinforced in 1903 when the highly respected PPS theorist Kazimierz Kelles-Krauz declared that a future Polish state would grant the Jews full communal and cultural autonomy.[3] Pressure from within its own Jewish Section further drove the PPS toward accepting the principle of Jewish nationality. Constituting about 10 percent of the party membership at its peak, the PPS's Jewish Section produced one of the largest underground Yiddish presses in the Russian Empire. During its existence between the 1890s and 1907, the PPS's Jewish Section constituted the only Jewish workers' organization in tsarist Russia that agitated under the banner of Polish independence.

A full shift in the PPS program came in 1905, when its official platform on the Jewish question became almost indistinguishable from the Bund's. The new position received programmatic expression when, in December 1905, the organ of the party's central committee incorporated autonomous Jewish rights into the official platform. That the PPS officially rejected the ideology of assimilationism in 1905 was reflected in its positive attitude to the Yiddish literary revival. With the Young faction in power, the new program sought individual and collective freedom for Jews while simultaneously addressing the vexing problem of Polish statelessness. The old view that the pre-WWI PPS was opposed to Jewish autonomous rights has to be revised.

The recognition of Jewish nationality marked a decisive phase in the politicization of ethnic markers that began in the 1890s and crystallized in the wake of the 1905 revolution. The emergence of mass electoral politics in 1905 and the struggle between the PPS and right-wing National Democrats for the allegiance of the working class demonstrated that ethnic divisions would henceforth play a central role in Polish politics. As Andrzej Walicki has recently argued, the 1905 revolution forced political parties in Russian Poland to accept in practice the ethnolinguistic conception of the nation.[4]

The schism of the PPS into a left and a right faction in 1906 brought to the surface internal divisions over the Jewish question. With the defection of the Jewish Section to the PPS Left, and its dissolution in 1907, polemics on the Jewish question assumed less importance in general. Yet two positions solidified, largely among the party members of Jewish origin within the two fractions. Representing the PPS Left was Maks Horwitz, the founding editor of *Der arbeyter* in 1898, who argued for the extension of full cultural-national autonomy to Jews in a future Polish state. On the PPS Right was Feliks Perl, who wanted Polish Jewry to follow the west European pattern and argued that the Bund's affirmation of Russia's territorial integrity worked directly counter to Polish national aspirations. A self-assertive Jewish nationality, consciously resistant to acculturation, would only foment anti-Jewish hatred on Polish soil. In an important essay, J. S. Hertz observed insightfully that the dispute between the Bund and Polish socialists in late imperial Russia was to a considerable extent a reflection "of the internal struggle among the various trends in Jewry."[5] With the strengthening of the Bund's national program by the eve of the First World War, the gap between the PPS Right and the Bund widened. Whereas the Bund advocated the socialist transformation of Russia, a condition it believed would bring about civic and national rights for Jews, Piłsudski countered that Jewish interests were best served by supporting the Polish movement for independence. Rooted in a belief that Polish lands constituted the bulwark of Western civilization, Piłsudski maintained that the Jewish question and Polish statelessness were intricately linked. Only a breakaway democratic Polish republic—national in form yet socialist in content—would create the conditions for the achievement of individual and collective Jewish freedom in Eastern Europe. That the Bund remained unsupportive of Piłsudski's vision only underscored the failure of socialism to transcend national barriers in twentieth-century Europe.

**Abbreviations**
**Notes**
**Bibliography**
**Index**

# Abbreviations

## Archives and Depositories

| | |
|---|---|
| AAN | Archiwum Akt Nowych (Archive of New Records, Warsaw) |
| AGAD | Archiwum Główny Akt Dawnych (Archive of Old Records, Warsaw) |
| APW | Archiwum Państwowe we Warszawie (State Archive in Warsaw) |
| Archiwum PAN | Archiwum Polskiej Akademii Nauk (Archive of the Polish Academy of Arts and Sciences, Warsaw) |
| BN DŻS | Biblioteka Narodowa, Zakład Dokumentów Życia Społecznego (National Library, Documents of Public Life, Warsaw) |
| ŻIH | Żydowski Instytut Historyczny (Jewish Historical Institute, Warsaw) |

## Abbreviations Used in the Notes and Text

| | |
|---|---|
| *BŻIH* | *Biuletyn Żydowskiego Instytutu Historycznego* (Bulletin of the Jewish Historical Institute, Warsaw) |
| CKR | Centralny Komitet Robotniczy PPS (Central Committee of the PPS) |
| Endecja | Stronnictwo Narodowo-Demokratyczne (National Democratic Party) |
| *KRRwP* | *Kronika Ruchu Rewolucyjnego w Polsce* (Chronicle of the Revolutionary Movement in Poland, Warsaw, 1935–39) |
| KŻ PPS | Jewish Committee of the Polish Socialist Party |
| LSDP | Lithuanian Social Democratic Party |
| NZR | Narodowy Związek Robotniczy (National Workers' Union, aligned with Endecja) |
| OSB | Oganizacja Spiskowo-Bojowa (Conspiratorial Fighting Division of the PPS) |
| PPS | Polska Partia Socjalistyczna (Polish Socialist Party) |
| PPSD | Polish Social Democratic Party of Galicia |
| *PSB* | *Polski Słownik Biograficzny* (Polish Biographical Dictionary, Kraków-Warsaw, 1935–) |
| RSDRP | Rossiiskaia Sotsialno-Demokraticheskaia Robochaia Partiia (Russian Social Democratic Workers' Party) |

| | |
|---|---|
| *SBDzPRR* | *Słownik Biograficzny Działaczy Polskiego Ruchu Robotniczego* (Biographical Dictionary of Activists in the Polish Worker's Movement, Warsaw, 1978–92) |
| SDKP | Socjaldemokracja Królestwa Polskiego (Social Democracy of the Kingdom of Poland, 1893–99) |
| SDKPiL | Socjaldemokracja Królestwa Polskiego i Litwy (Social Democracy of the Kingdom of Poland and Lithuania, 1899–1918) |
| SERP | Jewish Socialist Workers' Party (autonomists) |
| SS | Zionist Socialist Workers' Party (territorialists) |
| TKO | Towarzystwo Krzewienia Oświaty (Society for the Spread of Education, Łódź) |
| ŻPS | Jewish Social Democratic Party of Galicia |
| ZRP | Związek Robotników Polskich (Union of Polish Workers) |
| ZZSP | Związek Zagraniczny Socjalistów Polskich (Union of Polish Socialists Abroad, London) |

# Notes

## Introduction

1. Cited in Tobias, *The Jewish Bund in Russia*, 217.

2. In the Pale and the Kingdom of Poland, Jews comprised the fourth largest ethnic group and the fifth largest in the Russian Empire as a whole. See table 2.1 as well as Bauer, Kappeler, and Roth, *Die Nationalitäten des Russischen Reiches in der Volkszählung von 1897,* 2:77–78.

3. Piasecki, *Żydowska Organizacja PPS.*

4. Post-WWII studies on the PPS generally omit the subject of the Bund or confine it to a single footnote. See, for example, Andrzej Garlicki, *U źródeł obozu belwederskiego* (Warsaw: Państwowe Wydawn. Naukowe, 1979); Holzer, *PPS: Szkic dziejów PPS*; Michał Śliwa, *Myśl państwowa socjalistów polskich w latach 1918–1921* (Kraków: Wydawn. Nauk. WSP, 1980); and Tomicki, *Polska Partia Socjalistyczna.* Two notable exceptions are Żarnowska, *Geneza rozłamu w Polskiej Partii Socjalistycznej,* and Kancewicz, *Polska Partia Socjalistyczna w latach, 1892–1896,* which contain valuable information about PPS-Bund relations. Since 1989 there has been renewed interest in the topic among Polish scholars. See Piotr Wróbel, "From Conflict to Cooperation: The Bund and the Polish Socialist Party, 1897–1939," in *Jewish Politics in Eastern Europe,* ed. Jack Jacobs (New York: New York University Press, 2001), 155–71; and Kancewicz, "Bund a rosyjski i polski ruch robotniczy," 93–108.

5. In particular, see Pinson, "Arkady Kremer, Vladimir Medem and the Ideology of the Jewish Bund," 233–64; Hertz, Aronson, and Dubnow-Erlich, *Di geshikhte fun bund,* vols. 1–2; and Nora Levin, *While Messiah Tarried: Jewish Socialist Movements, 1871–1917* (New York: Schocken Books, 1977).

6. See in particular Shukman, "Relations between the Jewish Bund and the RSDRP"; Tobias, "Bund and Lenin until 1903," 344–57; Tobias, *The Jewish Bund in Russia*; Mendelsohn, *Class Struggle in the Pale*; Mendelsohn, "Russian Jewish Labor Movement and Others," 87–98; Wildman, "Russian and Jewish Social Democracy," 75–87. Most recently, see Minczeles, *Histoire générale du Bund.*

7. Mishkinsky, "Regional Factors in the Formation of the Jewish Labor Movement in Tsarist Russia," 46; Mishkinsky, "Jewish Labor Movement and European Socialism," 289.

8. Mishkinsky, *Reshit tnuat ha-poalim ha-yehudit be-rusya,* 260–61. Mishkinsky first introduced his argument on the importance of Polish socialism in the early history of the Bund in his doctoral dissertation. See

Mishkinsky, "Yesodot leumiyim be-hithavuta shel tnuat ha-poalim ha-yehudit be-rusya me-reshita ve-ad 1901," chapter 5, as well as his "Tnuat ha-poalim ha-yehudit be rusya ve-hatnuah ha-sotsyalistit ha-polanit," 81–131. The subject was also treated in Z. Asher, "Ben ha-pps ve-habund," 165–84.

9. Mishkinsky, "Regional Factors in the Formation of the Jewish Labor Movement in Tsarist Russia," 47–49.

10. Frankel, *Prophecy and Politics*, 206.

11. Jacobs, *On Socialists and the "Jewish Question,"* 126–27; Ezra Mendelsohn, introduction to *Essential Papers on Jews and the Left*, ed. E. Mendelsohn (New York: New York University Press, 1997), 3.

### Chapter 1. Industrialization and the Rise of the Polish Socialist Party in Tsarist Russia

1. While it is true that *Narodnaia Volia* (People's Will) and other Russian terror-oriented organizations continued to operate inside the empire after the massive repressions of 1881, they did so, until the second half of the 1890s, more as a symbolic focus than as functioning revolutionary parties. On the Russian radical movement in the 1880s and early 1890s, see Naimark, *Terrorists and Social Democrats: The Russian Revolutionary Movement under Alexander III.*

2. Martov, *Zapiski sotsial-demokrata*, 225, cited in Wildman, *Making of a Workers' Revolution*, 39; I. Martov, "Razvitie krupnoy promishlennosti i rabochi dvizhenie do 1892 g.," in *Istoriia Rossii v XIX vieke* (Saint Petersburg: A. I. Granat, 1909), 6:157.

3. *Di geshikhte fun der yidisher arbeyter bavegung in rusland un poyln* (Geneva: Bund, 1900), 9.

4. On Polish positivism and the Jews, see Stanislaus Blejwas, "Polish Positivism and the Jews," *Jewish Social Studies* 46 (1984): 21–36. On Polish Positivism in general, see Blejwas, *Realism in Polish Politics*. Also see Andrzej Jaszczuk, *Spór pozytywistów z konserwatystami o przyszłość Polski, 1870–1903* (Warsaw: Państwowe Wydawn. Naukowe, 1986); and Marcin Król, *Konserwatyści a niepodległość: Studia nad polską myślą konserwatywną XIX wieku* (Warsaw: Instytut Wydawniczy Pax, 1985). For a concise summary in English, see the introduction to Bartoszewski and Polonsky, *Jews in Warsaw.*

5. Roman Szporluk, "Ukraine," 92.

6. Kula, *Historia gospodarcza Polski w dobie popowstaniowej,* 44.

7. Rosa Luxemburg, *The Industrial Development of Poland,* trans. Tessa DeCarlo (Zurich, 1898; reprint, New York: Campaign Publications, 1977), 114. For a concise summary and analysis of economic development in the Kingdom of Poland, see Blobaum, *Rewolucja*, 18–28.

8. A. Jezierski, *Handel zagraniczny Królestwa Polskiego, 1815–1914* (Warsaw: Państwowe Wydawn. Naukowe, 1967), 66.

9. Blobaum, *Rewolucja*, 16. Also see Kieniewicz, *Emancipation of the Polish Peasantry*, 182; Kieniewicz, *Historia Polski*, 333; Piltz, *Poland*, 245.

10. *Evreiskaia Entsiklopediia* (Saint Petersburg, 1911), 11:538. Despite popular usage that equates "the Pale" with the entire region of the Russian partition of Poland, the Pale of Settlement and the Kingdom of Poland were in fact two distinct regions between 1815 and 1917.

11. Bauer, Kappeler, and Roth, *Die Nationalitäten des Russischen Reiches in der Volkszählung von 1897*, 1:200.

12. Bauer, Kappeler, and Roth, *Die Nationalitäten des Russischen Reiches,* 2:77, table 6. Among Polish-speaking Jews, over half (29,564) lived in Warsaw. See Shatski, "Di yidn in poyln fun 1772 biz 1914," 714.

13. Lestschinsky, *Dos yidishe folk in tsiferen,* 45.

14. *Pervaia vseobshchaia perepis' naseleniia Rosiiskoi Imperii 1897 g.* (Saint Petersburg: Tsentralnii statisticheskii komitet, 1905), 7:5–6.

15. Paul Robert Magocsi, *Historical Atlas of East Central Europe* (Seattle: University of Washington Press, 1993), 108.

16. On the social and economic conditions of the Jewish working class in Lithuania-Belarus, see Mendelsohn, *Class Struggle in the Pale,* 6–26.

17. On the artisan nature of the Jewish working class, see in particular Mendelsohn, "Russian Jewish Labor Movement and Others," 90.

18. *Recueil de matériaux sur la situation économique des Israélites de Russie,* 2:118.

19. Paweł Korzec, "Dwa bunty Łódzkie (1891 i 1892)," in *Z dziejów ruchu robotniczego w Łodzi* (Łódź: Wydawnictwo Łódzkie, 1967), 64–65. For the standard account of the 1892 strike, see Adam Próchnik, *Bunt łódzki w roku 1892: Studium historyczne* (Warsaw: Książka i Wiedza, 1950). For recent studies, based on new archival sources, see Mieczysław Bandurka, "Dokumenty buntu łódzkiego 1892 roku," *Rocznik Łódzki* 31 (1982): 203–37; and Paweł Samuś, ed., *"Bunt łódzki" 1892 roku: Studia z dziejów wielkiego konfliktu społecznego* (Łódź: Wydawnictwo Uniwersytetu Łódzkiego, 1993).

20. *Przedświt,* no. 8 (22 Aug. 1891): 2, 3.

21. Perl, "Szkic dziejów PPS." For a longer discussion on the background to the Paris congress, see Perl [Res], *Dzieje ruchu socjalistycznego,* 350–401.

22. For the most important scholarly treatment of the life of Mendelson, who left the PPS in 1893 and became a Zionist, see Guttermann, "Manhigei tnuat ha-poalim ha-polanit mi-motsa yehudi," 35–60. Also see Wiesław Bieńkowski, "Mendelson, Stanisław," in *PSB* 20, no. 3 (1975): 421–27.

23. For sources on the Paris congress, see Wasilewski, "Dokumenty do historii zjazdu paryskiego 1892," 107–52; Kancewicz, "Zjazd Paryski socjalistów polskich," 3–34; Perl [Res], *Dzieje ruchu socjalistycznego,* 378–401;

Malinowski, *Materiały do historyi PPS,* 1:1–20; and Tych, *Polskie programy socjalistyczne,* 216–60.

24. Limanowski, *Pamiętniki,* 2:439–40; Perl [F. P.], "Wspomnienia ze zjazdu paryskiego," 2–3.

25. The eighteen participants were as follows: Stanisław Mendelson, Maria Jankowska-Mendelson, Bolesław Jędrzejowski, Aleksander Dębski, Witold Jodko-Narkiewicz, Feliks Perl, Aleksander Sulkiewicz, Wacław Skiba, Edward Abramowski, Jan Strożecki, Stanisław Tylicki, Stanisław Wojciechowski, Stanisław Grabski, Jan Lorentowicz, Władysław Ratuld, Maria Szeliga, Bolesław Limanowski, and Wacław Podwiński. See Wasilewski, "Dokumenty do historii zjazdu paryskiego 1892," 118–19.

26. Kancewicz, *Polska Partia Socjalistyczna w latach 1892–1896,* 45.

27. For biographical materials other than those previously cited, see Tadeusz Sterocki, "Abramowski, Edward (1868–1918)," *SBDzPRR,* 1:41–42; Jan Tomicki, "Dębski, Aleksander (1857–1935)," *SBDzPRR,* 1:572–73; M. Drozdowski, *Aleksander Dębski* (Warsaw: Iskry, 1986); Feliks Tych, "Grabski, Stanisław (1871–1949)," *SBDzPRR,* 2:349–51; Redakcja, "Jędrzejowski, Bolesław Antoni (1867–1914)," *SBDzPRR,* 2:718–21; W. H. Melankowski, "Jodko-Narkiewicz, Witold (1864–1924)," *PSB* 11 (1964–65): 252–53; Alicja Pacholczykowa, "Ratuld, Władysław," *PSB* 30 (1987): 641–43; Władysław Zieliński, "Podwiński, Wacław (1872–?)," *PSB* 27 (1982): 193–94; "Sulkiewicz, Aleksander," *Wielka Encyklopedia Powszechna* (Warsaw: Państwowe Wydawn. Naukowe, 1968), 11:55. For Strożecki, see the biographical preface to Jan Kancewicz and Feliks Tych, eds., "Wspomnienia Jana Strożeckiego," in *Archiwum ruchu robotniczego* (Warsaw: Książka i Wiedza, 1977), 4:37–39.

28. Tomicki, *Polska Partia Socjalistyczna,* 22–23.

29. Kancewicz, *Polska Partia Socjalistyczna,* 46. For the full text of the Paris congress protocols, which is preserved in handwritten form in the PPS Archive in Warsaw, see Wasilewski, "Dokumenty do historii zjazdu paryskiego 1892," 119–41.

30. Malinowski, *Materiały do historyi PPS,* 1:20; Feliks Perl, "Szkic dziejów PPS," 4; Wasilewski, *Zarys dziejów Polskiej Partii Socjalistycznej,* 33; Wereszycki, *Historia polityczna Polski,* 121; Tomicki, *Polska Partia Socjalistyczna,* 24.

31. Wasilewski, "Dokumenty do historii zjazdu paryskiego 1892," 121. The protocol records that "in a long speech Mieczysław [Mendelson] declared he was opposed to Józef's [Abramowski's] presentation and treatment of the [national] question."

32. Limanowski, *Pamiętniki,* 2:440.

33. Limanowski, "Z moich wspomnień o narodzinach PPS," 25.

34. Wasilewski, "Dokumenty do historii zjazdu paryskiego 1892," 137.

35. "Listy z Rosyi," *Przedświt,* no. 11 (12 Sept. 1891): 6.

36. Authorship of the program is confirmed in Perl [Res], *Dzieje ruchu socjalistycznego w zaborze rosyjskim,* 385; and Tych, *Polskie programy socjalistyczne,* 224. The outline program with Mendelson's preface first appeared as "Szkic programu Polskiej Partyi Socjalistycznej," *Przedświt,* no. 5 (May 1893): 2–7. The program is reprinted in Mazowiecki [Ludwik Kulczycki], *Historya ruchu socjalistycznego w zaborze rosyjskim,* 243–54; Malinowski, ed., *Materiały do historyi PPS,* 1:8–20; Perl [Res], *Dzieje ruchu socjalistycznego,* 385–99; and Tych, *Polskie programy socjalistyczne,* 242–60. For a partial translation in English, see Krystyna Olszer, ed., *For Your Freedom and Ours* (New York: F. Ungar, 1981), 150–51.

37. [S. Mendelson], "Szkic programu Polskiej Partyi Socjalistycznej," reprinted in Tych, *Polskie programy socjalistyczne,* 253–54.

38. Ibid., 259, 258. In the absence of a state, the term "our country," used repeatedly throughout PPS publications, referred in general to the prepartition borders of Poland.

39. Ibid., 259.

40. Mendelson's proposal is recorded in the congress protocols. See Wasilewski, "Dokumenty do historii zjazdu paryskiego 1892," 137.

41. "The French National Assembly: Debate on the Eligibility of Jews for Citizenship (December 23, 1789)," in *The Jews in the Modern World,* ed. J. Reinharz and P. Mendes-Flohr (New York: Oxford University Press, 1995), 115.

42. Wasilewski, "Dokumenty do historii zjazdu paryskiego 1892," 148. The fifth and sixth members were Lorentowicz and Ratuld.

43. Kancewicz, *Polska Partia Socjalistyczna,* 53.

44. Wasilewski, introduction to Piłsudski, *Pisma-Mowy-Rozkazy,* xvi.

45. For a contemporary account of the establishment of the PPS in Warsaw by a participant, see Leon Falski's memoirs, "Wspomnienia z dwóch lat (1892–1893)," in *Z pola walki: zbiór materiały tyczących się polskiego ruchu socjalistycznego* (London: PPS, 1904), 28–32. For secondary accounts, see Malinowski, *Materiały do historyi PPS,* 1:24; Kancewicz, *Polska Partia Socjalistyczna,* 47; Tomicki, *Polska Partia Socjalistyczna,* 32; Wacław Jędrzejewicz and Janusz Cisek, *Kalendarium życia Józefa Piłsudskiego 1867–1935* (Wrocław: Zakład Narodowy im. Ossolińskich, 1994), 1:46–47; and Garlicki, *Józef Piłsudski,* 40.

46. Garlicki, *Józef Piłsudski,* 42.

47. Józef Piłsudski, "Jak się stałem socjalistą," in *Pisma zbiorowe,* 2:46.

48. Piłsudski, *Joseph Pilsudski: The Memories of a Polish Revolutionary and Soldier,* ed. and trans. D. R. Gillie (London: Faber and Faber, 1931; reprint, New York: AMS Press, 1977), 12, 13.

49. Jędrzejewicz, *Piłsudski*, 7.

50. Wapiński, *Pokolenia Drugiej Rzeczypospolitej,* 99.

51. The two firsthand accounts of this meeting are contradictory on the language question. According to Kopelzon, Piłsudski urged the Jewish Social Democratic group to switch to Polish. Piłsudski, however, maintained he urged them to abandon Russian for Yiddish. See T. Kopelzon, "Evreiskoe rabochee dvizhenie kontsa 80-kh i nachala 90-kh godov," in Dimanshtein, *Revoliutsionnoe dvizhenie sredi evreev,* 72–73; and Piłsudski, London, to W. Gumplowicz, Zurich, 16 Jan. 1902, in Piłsudski, *Pisma zbiorowe: Uzupełnienia,* 2:92–93. Also see Wojciechowski, *Moje Wspomnienia,* 1:111, in which he also claimed the PPS urged Kremer to adopt Yiddish as the language of agitation in early 1893. Wasilewski recalled a conversation with Piłsudski about the 1893 meeting and claimed Piłsudski referred to his relations with Jews often during his visits to London in the 1890s. See Wasilewski, *Józef Piłsudski jakim go znałem,* 29–30.

52. In a series of articles on the national and Jewish questions in 1892, Mendelson criticized the Jewish socialist intelligentsia in Vilna for contributing to the "Russification" of "occupied" Polish lands, as well as for their ties to the Russian—as opposed to the Polish—revolutionary movement. See [S. Mendelson], "Wobec grożącego u nas antisemityzmu," *Przedświt,* nos. 39–40 (26 March 1892): 6. For a full examination of the attitude of Polish socialists to the Jewish question in the early 1890s, see Mishkinsky, "Polish Socialism and the Jewish Question," 250–72.

53. Rom [Józef Piłsudski], "Wilno, 4 marca 1893," *Przedświt,* no. 4 (Apr. 1893), reprinted in Piłsudski, *Pisma zbiorowe,* 1:25–27.

54. [Józef Piłsudski], "Do towarzyszy socjalistów Żydów w polskich zabranych prowincjach," *Przedświt,* no. 5 (May 1893), reprinted in Piłsudski, *Pisma zbiorowe,* 1:28–29.

55. Ibid., 30.

56. Wojciechowski, *Moje wspomnienia,* 1:63.

57. Garlicki, *Józef Piłsudski,* 42.

58. Falski, "Wspomnienia z dwóch lat (1892–1893)," 34; Wojciechowski, *Moje wspomnienia,* 1:62.

59. The only firsthand account of the meeting is to be found in Wojciechowski, *Moje wspomnienia,* 66–67.

60. Wasilewski, *Józef Piłsudski jakim go znałem,* 60–61.

61. [Józef Piłsudski], "Stosunek do rewolucjonistów rosyjskich," *Przedświt,* no. 8 (Aug. 1893), reprinted in Piłsudski, *Pisma zbiorowe,* 1:42–45.

62. Wasilewski, "Kierownictwo PPS zaboru rosyjskiego (1893–1918)," 353; Garlicki, *Józef Piłsudski,* 46–47.

63. Piłsudski, Vilna, to the Union of Polish Socialists Abroad (ZZRP), London, 29 Apr. 1894, in Piłsudski, *Pisma zbiorowe: Uzupełnienia,* 1:89.

64. Frants Kursky, "Di 'tsukunft' in untererdishn rusland," in *Gezamelte shriftn*, 253.

65. Malinowski, *Materiały do historyi PPS*, 1:46, 91, 101.

66. Piłsudski, Vilna, to the ZZRP, London, [?] May 1894, in Piłsudski, *Pisma zbiorowe: Uzupełnienia*, 1:93.

67. *25 yor: zamlbukh* (Warsaw: Di velt, 1922), 112. Piłsudski remarked in a letter that the mimeograph had arrived from London. See Piłsudski, Vilna, to ZZRP, London, [?] July 1894, in Piłsudski, *Pisma zbiorowe: Uzupełnienia*, 1:97.

68. Czasowy [J. Piłsudski], "Wilno we wrześniu," *Przedświt*, no. 9 (Sept. 1894), reprinted in Piłsudski, *Pisma zbiorowe*, 1:63, quoted in Frankel, *Prophecy and Politics*, 199.

69. [Józef Piłsudski], "Rosja," *Robotnik* (special issue, Apr. 1895), in Piłsudski, *Pisma zbiorowe*, 1:80, 91, emphasis mine. In Mendelson's articles from 1891–92, use of the term "Polish democratic republic" was consciously avoided. Instead, Mendelson called for a breakaway federal republic of equal nations: Poles, Lithuanians, and Ukrainians, with special emphasis on the suppression of the latter two cultures under Russian rule. For a discussion of Mendelson's writings on the national question, see Joshua D. Zimmerman, "Poles, Jews and the Politics of Nationality: Relations between the Polish Socialist Party and the Jewish Labor Bund, 1892–1905" (Ph.D. Diss., Brandeis University, 1998), 60–65.

70. [Józef Piłsudski], "Na posterunku," *Robotnik* (June 1895), in Piłsudski, *Pisma zbiorowe*, 1:92–95.

71. Wojciechowski, *Moje wspomnienia*, 100–101. Resolutions of the third party congress are reprinted in Malinowski, *Materiały do historyi PPS*, 1:144–50.

72. [W. Jodko-Narkiewicz], "Etapy," *Przedświt*, no. 8 (Aug. 1894): 1–4.

73. [W. Jodko-Narkiewicz], "Etapy III," *Przedświt*, no. 10 (Nov. 1894): 6.

74. Tych, *SDKPiL*, vol. 1, bk. 1, vi.

75. The first issue spelled out the SDKP platform in its lead article. See "Zadania polityczne polskiej klasy robotniczej," *Sprawa Robotnicza*, no. 1 (July 1893), reprinted in Szmidt, *Socjaldemokracja Królestwa Polskiego i Litwy*, 9.

76. Nettl, *Rosa Luxemburg*, 1:71.

77. Cited in ibid. The original German text has not survived. It was printed in Polish translation in *Kwestia polska a ruch socjalistyczny* (Kraków, 1905) and has been reprinted in Tych, *SDKPiL*, vol. 1, bk. 1, 23–29.

78. Quoted in Paul Frölich, *Rosa Luxemburg: Her Life and Work*, trans. Edward Fitzgerald (London: V. Gollancz, 1940), 51–52.

79. *Sprawa Robotnicza*, no. 2 (Aug. 1893), in Tych, *SDKPiL*, vol.1, bk. 1, 30.

80. Tych, *Polskie programy socjalistyczne*, 262.

81. Perl [Res], *Dzieje ruchu socjalistycznego,* 358.

82. F. P. [Feliks Perl], "Geneza naszego programu politycznego," *Przedświt,* no. 10 (Oct. 1894): 7–11.

## Chapter 2. The First Sproutings of the Jewish Socialist Movement

1. Mendelsohn, "Note on Jewish Assimilation in the Polish Lands," 141–42.

2. Mendelsohn's findings are reflected in Allan Wildman's study, which observes that Russian Jewish socialists in the southwestern provinces were active in exclusively Russian organizations, and with few exceptions, remained in the Russian movement. See Wildman, "Russian and Jewish Social Democracy," 75–76.

3. Mishkinsky, "Regional Factors in the Formation of the Jewish Labor Movement in Tsarist Russia," 47–49.

4. Mendelsohn, "Note on Jewish Assimilation in the Polish Lands," 141.

5. Chaim Zhitlovsky, *Zikhroynes fun mayn lebn* (New York: Dr. Hayim zhitlovski yubiley komitet, 1940), 3:184–94; and Kursky, *Gezamelte shriftn,* 355–56, both cited in Mishkinsky, "Regional Factors in the Formation of the Jewish Labor Movement in Tsarist Russia," 43.

6. Mill, "Di pionern epokhe fun der yidisher arbeyter bavegung," 3:375–76; Mill, "Arkadi un der ershter tsuzamenfor," 148–49; Kopelzon, "Evreiskoe rabochee dvizhenie kontsa 80-kh i nachala 90-kh godov," 74; and Tobias, *The Jewish Bund in Russia,* 11.

7. For biographical information on the Vilna Group leaders, see "Kopelzon, Tsemakh," in *Leksikon fun der nayer yidisher literatur* (New York: Congress for Jewish Culture, 1981), 8:105–6; Israel Figa, "Arkadi Kremer," in *Leksikon,* 8:270; John Mill, "Pati Kremer," in *Doyres Bundistn* (New York: Uzner tsayt farlag, 1956), 1:130–37; Yitzkhak Kharlash, "Gozhanski, Shmuel," in *Leksikon fun der nayer yidisher literatur* (New York: Congress for Jewish Culture, 1958), 2:7–8; Mordkhe Velvl Bernshtein, "Mill, John," *Leksikon fun der nayer yidisher literatur* (New York: Congress for Jewish Culture, 1963), 5:624–26; Grigoray Aronson, "Isai Aizenshtat," in *Doyres bundistn,* 1:137–54; J. S. Hertz, "Liuba Levinson-Aizenshat," in *Doyres bundistn,* 1:154–56; J. S. Hertz, "Vladimir Kossovsky," in *Doyres bundistn,* 1:11–67; J. S. Hertz, "Avrom Mutnik," in *Doyres bundistn,* 1:122–30; C. Kazdan, "Noyakh Portnoy," in *Doyres bundistn,* 1:68–122; Dina Blond, "Dr. Pavel Rozental," in *Doyres bundistn,* 1:157–79; Dina Blond, "Ana Rozental," in *Doyres bundistn,* 1:180–92; J. S. Hertz, "Pavel Berman," in *Doyres bundistn,* 1:241–43.

8. For studies on the impact of the government-run schools and rabbinical seminaries, first established under Tsar Nicholas I, see Michael Stanislawski, *Tsar Nicholas I and the Jews: The Transformation of Jewish Society*

*in Russia, 1825–1855* (Philadelphia: Jewish Publication Society of America, 1983); and Eli Lederhendler, *The Road to Modern Jewish Politics: Political Tradition and Political Reconstruction in the Jewish Community of Tsarist Russia* (New York: Oxford University Press, 1989).

9. *Pervaia vseobshchaia perepis' naseleniia Rosiiskoi Imperii 1897 g.: Naseleniia mesta Rosiiskoi Imperii v 500 i bolie zhitelei* (Saint Petersburg, 1905), 11.

10. Peskin, "Di 'grupe yidishe sotsyal-demokratn' in rusland un arkadi kremer," 3:547. For a detailed description of Kremer's father, see the account of Kremer's wife in P. Kremer, "Zikhroynes vegen arkadi," 23–28.

11. Peskin, "Di 'grupe yidishe sotsyal-demokratn' in rusland," 547–48. For the fullest biographical account, see P. Kremer, "Zikhroynes vegen arkadi," 22–72.

12. Abram Liessin, *Zikhroynes un bilder*, quoted in Lucy Dawidowicz, ed., *The Golden Tradition* (New York: Schocken, 1967), 423–24.

13. Quoted in Pinson, "Arkady Kremer, Vladimir Medem, and the Ideology of the Jewish Bund," reprinted in *Emancipation and Counter-Emancipation*, ed. A. Duker (New York: Ktav Publishing House, 1974), 294.

14. Mill, *Pionern un boyer*, 1:88.

15. Moshe Mishkinsky, "Mill, Joseph Solomon," in *Encyclopaidea Judaica* (Jerusalem: Keter Publishing House, 1971), 11:1577–78.

16. Kursky, *Gezamelte shriftn*, 105.

17. *Naselennyia mesta Rossiiskoi Imperii v 500 i boliee zhitelei . . . : Po dannym Pervoi Vseobshchei perepisi naseleniia 1897 g.* (Saint Petersburg, 1905), 91.

18. Mill, *Pionern un boyer*, 1:13, 18.

19. Ibid., 1:19–20, 35.

20. Ibid., 1:35.

21. Mill, "Di pionern epokhe," 370.

22. Mill, *Pionern un boyer*, 1:41.

23. Mill, "Di pionern epokhe," 371.

24. Mill, *Pionern un boyer*, 1:50–51. For an extended discussion of the socialist circle with which Mill became involved, see 1:45–51.

25. Ibid., 1:38.

26. Frankel, *Prophecy and Politics*, 186.

27. Kopelzon, "Evreiskoe rabochee dvizhenie kontsa 80-kh i nachala 90-kh godov," 71–72.

28. Arkadi Kremer, "Mit 35 yor tsurik," in *Arkadi: zamlbukh tsum ondenk fun grinder fun "bund" arkadi kremer* (New York: Unzer tsayt, 1942), 395; partially cited in Frankel, *Prophecy and Politics*, 187.

29. Wildman, *Making of a Workers' Revolution*, 40–41.

30. *Leksikon fun der nayer yidisher literatur* (New York: League for Jewish Culture, 1958), 2:7–8.

31. Hersz Abramowicz, *Profiles of a Lost World* (Detroit: Wayne State University Press, 1999), 124–25.

32. Kopelzon, "Evreiskoe rabochee dvizhenie kontsa 80-kh i nachala 90-kh godov," 70; Menes, "Di groyse tsayt," 11.

33. Menes, "Di groyse tsayt," 11.

34. The four speeches, three of which were given in Russian and one in Yiddish, were published in Russian as *Pervoe maia 1892: Chetyre rechi evreiskikh rabochikh,* with a foreword by L. Jogiches (Geneva: Tip. "Sotsialdemokraticheskoi biblioteki," 1893). Nettl, in his *Rosa Luxemburg* (1:68), maintains that the speeches were in fact first published in Polish with an introduction by Rosa Luxemburg, her first known publication, under the pseudonym of Kruszyńska, *Święto Maja* (Paris, 1892). Mishkinsky, however, claims that the Polish edition was something altogether different. See his review of Nettl's book in *Soviet Studies* 19, no. 3 (1968): 453–57. In 1894 Jogiches also published excerpts from the 1892 speeches in *Sprawa Robotnicza,* the SDKP organ. See Tych, *SDKPiL,* 1:146–52. I am grateful to Jack Jacobs for bringing Mishkinsky's review to my attention.

35. For an important analysis of the speeches, see Peled, *Class and Ethnicity in the Pale,* 32–34.

36. "Fir redes fun yidishe arbeyter oyf der ershte mai-feyerung in 1892 yor," in Agursky, *Di sotsyalistishe literatur oyf yidish in 1875–1897,* 2:103. For a Hebrew translation, with an important introduction by Moshe Mishkinsky, see *Arbaha neumim shel poalim yehudim,* trans. T. Dolzhansky and M. Mishkinsky (Jerusalem: Ha-hug le-historyah shel am yisrael, 1967).

37. Mishkinsky, "Jewish Labor Movement and European Socialism," 288.

38. "Fir redes fun yidishe arbeyter oyf der ershte mai-feyerung in 1892 yor," in Agursky, *Di sotsyalistishe literatur oyf yidish,* 2:114.

39. P. Kremer, "Zikhroynes vegn arkadin," 51; *Historya żydowskiego ruchu robotniczego,* 2nd ed. (London: Bund, 1902), 12; Frankel, *Prophecy and Politics,* 185.

40. For an analysis of *On Agitation* and *A Letter to Agitators,* see Peled, *Class and Ethnicity in the Pale,* 34–49; and Frankel, *Prophecy and Politics,* 187–89. According to the editors of *Historishe shriftn,* vol. 3, both *On Agitation* and *A Letter to Agitators* were printed together as one brochure at the end of 1893. See *Historishe shriftn* 3 (1939): 626.

41. For the text of *On Agitation,* see *Arkadi: zamlbukh,* 293–321.

42. Menes, "Di yidishe arbeyter-bavegung in rusland fun onheyb 70-er bizn sof 90-er yorn," 44–45.

43. Frankel, *Prophecy and Politics,* 188.

44. Tobias, *The Jewish Bund in Russia,* 28.

45. Wildman, "Russian and Jewish Social Democracy," 78–79.

46. Although only a hand-written copy in Russian is preserved in the Bund Archive, Gozhanski claimed he wrote *A Letter to Agitators* in Yiddish. See Gozhanski, "Evreiskoe rabochee dvizhenie nachala 90-kh godov," 91.

47. For the most thorough discussion of *A Letter to Agitators,* see Frankel, *Prophecy and Politics*, 187–90; also see Tobias, *The Jewish Bund in Russia,* 28; and Mishkinsky, "Jewish Labor Movement and European Socialism," 289. The full text is reprinted in S. Gozhanski, "A briv tsu agitatorn," *Historishe shriftn* 3 (1939): 629–48. For a Hebrew translation, see Shmuel Gozhanski, *Mikhtav al ha-agitatorim,* trans. N. Ginton (Jerusalem, 1967).

48. Gozhanski, "A briv tsu agitatorn," 629.

49. Mishkinsky, "Regional Factors in the Formation of the Jewish Labor Movement in Tsarist Russia," 46.

50. Gozhanski, "A briv tsu agitatorn," 629.

51. Ibid., 630, 631.

52. Ibid., 645, 646–47.

53. Ibid., 647.

54. Peled, *Class and Ethnicity in the Pale*, 39.

55. Frankel, *Prophecy and Politics,* 190.

56. Mill, *Pionern un boyer,* 1:215. The participants included Mill, Arkadi and Pati Kremer, Liuba and Isai Aizenshtat, Mutnik, Martov, Liachovsky, Leon Goldman, Gozhanski, and Solomon Menaker.

57. Ibid., 1:216, cited in Frankel, *Prophecy and Politics*, 190.

58. The speech was given, and subsequently printed, in Russian. In 1900 a Yiddish version was printed in *Der yidisher arbeyter*, the Geneva-based organ of the Bund. Then in 1939 the editors of *Historishe shriftn*, claiming the 1900 translation was poor, printed a more precise Yiddish translation of Martov's 1895 speech. Ironically, Martov would later leave the Bund and, as an influential Menshevik, denounce the Bund for its "separatist" and "nationalist" tendencies. On Martov's 1895 speech, see Pinson, "Arkady Kremer, Vladimir Medem, and the Ideology of the Jewish Bund," 292; Peled, *Class and Ethnicity in the Pale*, 45–49; and Frankel, *Prophecy and Politics,* 192–93.

59. Iu. Martov, "Der vendpunkt in der geshikhte fun der yidisher arbeyter-bavegung (1895)," *Historishe shriftn* 3:650. For a Hebrew version, see Iu. Martov, *Nekudat ha-mifneh be-toledot tnuat ha-poalim ha-yehudit,* trans. M. Moyal (Jerusalem: The Hebrew University, 1968).

60. Martov, "Der vendpunkt in der geshikhte fun der yidisher arbeyter-bavegung (1895)," 650, 651, emphasis mine.

61. Ibid., 652

62. On Martov's speech, see Menes, "Di groyse tsayt," 3–21; Trunk, "Di onheybn fun der yidisher arbeyter-bavegung," in Hertz, Aronson, and

Dubnow-Erlich, *Di geshikhte fun bund,* 1:73–75; Tobias, *The Jewish Bund in Russia,* 55–56; and Frankel, *Prophecy and Politics,* 192–93.

63. Mill, *Pionern un boyer,* 1:175. Mill's unfavorable impression of Perl may have been a reflection of the generally negative relations between Litvaks and Polish Jews. Consider the disdainful description of Mill by a PPS Jew, Mojżesz Kaufman, who described Mill as "an ill-tempered, argumentative, and nervous fellow who never found it in himself to express a single positive word." See Kaufman, "Początki roboty żydowskiej PPS," 342.

64. Mill, *Pionern un boyer,* 1:223.

65. Mill, *Pionern un boyer,* 1:224–25; also see Frankel, *Prophecy and Politics,* 198.

66. Mill, *Pionern un boyer,* 1:225.

## Chapter 3. Into the Polish Heartland

1. Śliwa, *Feliks Perl,* 13; Piasecki, "Feliks Perl," 60. Also see Alexander Gutterman's comments on Perl's family background in his "Assimilated Jews as Leaders of the Polish Labour Movement between the Two World Wars," 63–65.

2. Piasecki, *Żydowska Organizacja PPS,* 13–21, where the names of the first circle of PPS Jewish workers is found; I checked this source against information found in Polish biographical dictionaries.

3. Michał Szulkin, "Maksymilian Heilpern—Działacz socjalistyczny i pedagog (w 50-lecie śmierci)," *BŻIH* 74 (Oct.–Dec. 1974): 3–5.

4. Memoirs of Leon Gottlieb (Yiddish, handwritten), p. 2, bk. 2, RG108.162, Yivo Archives. The artisan school for Jewish youth in Warsaw was established in 1886 by Józef Poznański.

5. Shatzky, *Geshikhte fun yidn in varshe,* 3:392.

6. Ibid., 3:398.

7. Alicja Pacholczykowa, "Faterson, Izador (Israel)," in *SBDzPRR,* 60–61.

8. Kaufman, "Początki roboty żydowskiej PPS," 337; and Król, "Żydowska Organizacja Polskiej Parii Socjalistycznej (1893–1903)," 134. Members of Faterson's first circle included the carpenter Saul Degenfisz, the sculptor Srul Auerbach, the metalworker Maurycy Montlak, Henryk Bassel, Abraham Blumowicz, David Perlmutter, the sculptor Kadish Altglas, I. Kornblit, Mendel Rubinstein, and his brother.

9. Kaufman, "Początki roboty żydowskiej PPS," 337.

10. Kancewicz, *Polska Partia Socjalistyczna,* 138.

11. Kaufman, "Początki roboty żydowskiej PPS," 338; Piasecki, *Żydowska Organizacja PPS,* 16–17.

12. Kaufman, "Początki roboty żydowskiej PPS," 338–39. For a biographical entry on Róg, see the note in Kelles-Krauz, *Listy,* 2:447.

13. The nine new members were the house painter Leyb Burgin, Natan Nadelman, Sonia Dawidowska (subsequently Burgin's wife), her brother Judel Dawidowski, Salomon Rowinski, Naftali Shatz, Hersh Minoga, Chaya Minoga, and Hersh Kohn. See Kaufman, "Początki roboty żydowskiej PPS," 338.

14. Piasecki, *Żydowska Organizacja PPS*, 18, 17.

15. Mention of the circular can be found in the memoirs of Yitzkhok Pesakhzon. See An alter bakanter [Y. Pesakhzon], "In varshe erev 'bund,'" in *25 yor: zamlbukh* (Warsaw: Di velt, 1922), 41. Also see An alter bakanter [Y. Pesakhzon], "Der onfang fun der yidisher arbeyter bavegung in varshe (zikhroynes fun a yidishen sotsialist)," *Der yidisher arbeyter,* no. 10 (1900): 28; Mill, *Pionern un boyter,* 1:237. The proclamation is also mentioned in A. Cherikover, "Di onheybn fun der umlegaler literatur in yidish," 3:587; "Proklamatsya in yidish erev dem 'bund,'" *Historishe shriftn,* 3:750; and P. Shvarts, "Di ershte yidishe oysgabes fun der pps," 3:528.

16. See the introductory remarks in P. Shvarts, "Di ershte yidishe oysgabes fun der pps," 3:527–28. For a discussion of the pioneering role of the Polish socialist movement in tsarist Russia, see Wildman, *Making of a Workers' Revolution*, chapter 2.

17. Tobias, *The Jewish Bund in Russia,* 39–40.

18. Pavel Berman was sent to Minsk, Kopelzon and Aizenshtat to Odessa, while L. Zalkind, Avram Baskin, Gozhanski, Liuba Levinson, and N. Lipshitz established a center in Białystok. See Mill, "Arkadi un der ershte tsuzamenfor," 159–60; An alter bakanter [Y. Pesakhzon], "In varshe erev 'bund,'" 46.

19. Mill, "Arkadi un der ershte tsuzamenfor," 160.

20. Mishkinsky, "Al hug sotsialisti yehudi be-varsha be-shnat 1893–1894," 333–39; and Mill, "Di pionern epokhe," 382.

21. Isaiah Trunk, "Di onheybn fun der yidisher arbeyter-bavegung," in Hertz, Aronson, and Dubnow-Erlich, *Di geshikhte fun bund,* 1:80. See also the entry on Hurvitsh by J. S. Hertz in *Doyres bundistn* (New York: Unzer Tsayt, 1956), 1:228–31.

22. Mill, *Pionern un boyer,* 1:227.

23. The full text of the 1895 circular can be found in P. Shvarts, "Di ershte yidishe oysgabes fun der pps," 3:529–30.

24. Mill, "Di pionern epokhe," 383.

25. It is not clear exactly when Mill's organization was established. In his own writings he did not mention a date. According to Pesakhzon, who worked closely with Mill's group but did not join until January 1897, "the Jewish Social Democratic group appeared in Warsaw in the beginning of 1896." Piasecki, however, argues for 1895. See An alter bakanter [Y.

Pesakhzon], "Der onfang fun der yidisher arbeyter bavegung in varshe," 31; Piasecki, *Żydowska Organizacja PPS,* 23. Two secondary sources mistakenly maintain that Mill's organization was founded in 1894, when Mill was in Zurich. See Shatzky, *Geshikhte fun yidn in varshe,* 3:398; and Hertz Burgin, *Di geshikhte fun der yidisher arbeyter bavegung in amerike, rusland, un england* (New York: Fareynigte yidisher geverkshaften, 1915), 209.

26. Kaufman, "Początki roboty żydowskiej PPS," 340–41.

27. Jewish members of the PPS, Warsaw, to the Central Committee of the PPS, Vilna [?], Dec. 1895, reprinted in Aleksander Malinowski, ed., *Materiały do historyi PPS,* 1:163.

28. Ibid.

29. Wojciechowski, *Moje Wspomnienia,* 1:112; [Wojciechowski], *Polska Partya Socyalistyczna w ostatnich pięciu latach* (London: PPS, 1900), 30.

30. P. Shvarts, "Di ershte yidishe oysgabes fun der pps," 3:528; A. Cherikover, "Di onheybn fun der umlegaler literatur in yidish," 3:587; and "Proklamatsya in yidish erev dem 'bund,'" *Historishe shriftn,* 3:750.

31. P. Shvarts, "Di ershte yidishe oysgabes fun der pps," 3:528–30. An original copy of the historic 1895 May Day proclamation is preserved in the PPS archive. See AAN, sygn. 305/III/34, fol. 11.

32. An alter bakanter [Y. Pesakhzon], "Der onfang fun der yidisher arbeyter bavegung in varshe," 29; Mill, "Di pionern epokhe," 385.

33. An alter bakanter [Y. Pesakhzon], "In varshe erev 'bund,'" 43.

34. Pesakhzon was born in the town of Shklov, near the Dnieper, and far from Congress Poland. See J. S. Hertz, "Yitzkhok Mordechai Pesakhzon," in *Doyres bundistn* (New York: Unzer tsayt, 1956), 1:262–69.

35. An alter bakanter [Y. Pesakhzon], "In varshe erev 'bund,'" 44.

36. Jewish members of the PPS, Warsaw, to the Central Worker's Committee, Vilna [?], Sept. 1896, reprinted in Malinowski, *Materiały do historyi PPS,* 1:218.

37. Ibid., 219.

38. Ibid., 220–21.

39. J. Piłsudski, Vilna, to the ZZSP, London, 6 Oct. 1896, in Piłsudski, *Pisma zbiorowe: Uzupełnienia,* 1:272.

40. Józef Piłsudski, Vilna, to the ZZSP, London, 12 Dec. 1896, in Piłsudski, *Pisma zbiorowe: Uzupełnienia,* 1:280.

41. It is not clear who initiated the negotiations. Mill claimed the PPS group, represented by Róg, approached him. According to Mojżesz Kaufman, however, Mill came to the PPS with a request for cooperation. See Mill, "Di pionern epokhe," 385; and Kaufman, "Początki roboty żydowskiej PPS," 344.

42. Mill, "Di pionern epokhe," 385; An alter bakanter [Y. Pesakhzon], "Der onfang fun der yidisher arbeyter bavegung in varshe," 33; Shvarts,

"Di ershte yidishe oysgabes fun der pps," 3:530; Trunk, "Di onheybn fun der yidisher arbeyter-bavegung," 1:80; Piasecki, *Żydowska Organizacja PPS,* 31.

43. An alter bakanter [Y. Pesakhzon], "Der onfang fun der yidisher arbeyter bavegung in varshe," 33.

44. Piłsudski, Vilna, to the ZZSP, London, 12 Feb. 1897, in Piłsudski, *Pisma zbiorowe: Uzupełnienia,* 1:292.

45. For the text of the 1897 May Day proclamation, see "Proklamatsya in yidish erev dem 'bund,'" 3:753–54.

46. "A briv in redaktsye," *Der yidisher arbeyter,* nos. 4–5 (Nov. 1897): 45–46.

47. Mill, "Di pionern epokhe," 385–86.

48. The sources are contradictory on the question of the new organization's name. Trunk utilizes the name employed in the text, which is supported by the fact that the letter of June 1897 printed in *Der yidisher arbeyter* was signed "The Jewish Social Democratic Workers' Bund in Warsaw." Writing some forty years later, Mill referred to the organization in his memoirs as "The Jewish Workers' Bund in Warsaw." See "A briv in redaktsye," 46; Trunk, "Di onheybn fun der yidisher arbeyter-bavegung," 1:84; Mill, *Pionern un boyer,* 1:240; and Burgin, *Di geshikhte fun der yidisher arbeyter bavegung,* 203.

49. Piłsudski, Vilna, to the ZZSP, London, 24 July 1897, in Piłsudski, *Pisma zbiorowe: Uzupełnienia,* 1:304.

50. Piłsudski, Vilna, to the ZZSP, London, 30 May 1897, in Piłsudski, *Pisma zbiorowe: Uzupełnienia,* 1:300.

51. Ibid.

52. Secretary of Union Abroad, London, to Jewish Socialist Post from America to Poland, 27 July 1897, New York, fol. 128, vol. 8, sygn. 305/II/22, AAN.

53. Mishkinsky, *Reshit tnuat ha-poalim ha-yehudit be-rusya,* 260–61.

**Chapter 4. Organizational Breakthrough**

1. Arkadi [Kremer], "Di grindung fun bund," *Arbeter-luakh* (Warsaw, 1922), reprinted in *Arkadi: zamlbukh tsum ondenk fun grinder fun "bund" arkadi kremer* (New York: Unzer tsayt, 1942), 358, 359.

2. Mill, *Pionern un boyer,* 1:261.

3. Kremer, "Di grindung fun bund," 360.

4. Mill, *Pionern un boyer,* 1:268.

5. Ibid., 270, 271.

6. Kremer, "Di grindung fun bund," 361; Hertz, Aronson, and Dubnow-Erlich, *Di geshikhte fun bund,* 1:114; and Frants Kursky, "Arkadi un zayn tkufe," in *Arkadi: zamlbukh,* 86.

7. The earliest source to put the delegate count at thirteen was Hertz Burgin, *Di geshikhte fun der yidisher arbeyter bavegung in amerika, rusland, un england* (New York, 1915), 214. Two subsequent sources, however, wrote that eleven delegates were present. These sources include Mill, "Der ershter tsuzamenfor fun 'bund," 31; and Bukhbinder, *Di geshikhte fun der yidisher arbeyter bavegung in rusland*, 78–79. Tobias points out that Mill then revised that figure to thirteen in *Pionern un boyer*, 1:272. The figure of thirteen delegates accords with the accounts of Kremer and Dovid Katz, both of whom were present at the congress. See Dovid Katz, "Pervyi sezd Bunda," in Dimanshtein, *Revoliutsionnoe dvizhenie sredi evreev*, 139; and Kremer, "Di grindung fun bund," 361. Also see Tobias, *The Jewish Bund in Russia*, 66; C. Kazdan, "Der 'bund' biz dem finftn tsuzamenfor," in Hertz, Aronson, and Dubnow-Erlich, *Di geshikhte fun bund*, 1:113; Kursky, "Arkadi un zayn tkufe," 89; and Kursky, *Gezamelte shriftn*, 129.

8. Mill, "Arkadi un der ershter tsuzamenfor," 161.

9. *Di arbeyter shtimme*, no. 6 (17 Oct. 1897): 1–2.

10. Mill, "Arkadi un der ershter tsuzamenfor," 164.

11. Ibid., 164, 165; also see C. Kazdan, "Der 'bund' biz dem finftn tsuzamenfor," 1:116.

12. *Di geshikhte fun der yidisher arbeyter bavegung in rusland un poyln* (Geneva: Bund, 1900), 38.

13. Mill, *Pioner un boyer*, 1:276–78; Mill, "Arkadi un der ershter tsuzamenfor," 161; and C. Kazdan, "Der 'bund' biz dem finftn tsuzamenfor," 1:117–19.

14. Mishkinsky, "Regional Factors in the Formation of the Jewish Labor Movement," 34–35.

15. Arkadi Kremer, "Ershter ts. k. fun 'bund,'" *Naye folkstsaytung* (17 Oct. 1927): 6. Issues 1 through 5 of *Di arbeyter shtimme* had appeared in the spring and summer of 1897 as a general Jewish social democratic organ. Issue number 6 (17 Oct. 1897) was the first to appear under the banner of the Bund. See A. Kirzhnits, *Di yidishe prese in der gevezener ruslendisher imperie*, 12.

16. Postwar histories of the PPS and biographies of Piłsudski characteristically ignore the question of the Jews altogether, and Jan Tomicki's standard monograph of the PPS, written in 1983, is no exception. It nonetheless does mention the founding of the Bund as a momentous event in the early history of the PPS. Because it fails to make a single reference to Jewish social democratic centers operating in Vilna and Warsaw before 1897, however, the reader is left without any context. "The PPS's monopoly as the only socialist party in the Russian partition," Tomicki writes, "was broken in 1897 with the founding of the General Jewish Workers' Union—the Bund." See Jan Tomicki, *Polska Partia Socjalistyczna 1892–1948*, 65.

17. Józef Piłsudski, Vilna, to the ZZSP, London, 30 May 1897, in Piłsudski, *Pisma zbiorowe: Uzupełnienia,* 1:300.

18. The figure of thirteen participants is given by Aleksander Malinowski in his subsequently published *Materiały do historyi PPS,* 1:295, and accords with the account in Wacław Jędrzejewicz and Janusz Cisek, *Kalendarium życia Józefa Piłsudskiego 1867–1935* (Wrocław: Zakład Narodowy im. Ossolińskich, 1994), 186–87. Besides Jodko-Narkiewicz and the three CKR members, identification of the other nine delegates, referred to in the protocols by one- or two-letter pseudonyms, is not noted in the sources.

19. [J. Piłsudski], "Czwarty zjazd naszej partii," *Robotnik,* no. 26 (13 Feb. 1898), in Piłsudski, *Pisma zbiorowe,* 1:201.

20. Malinowski, *Materiały do historyi PPS,* 1:301.

21. *Robotnik,* no. 26 (13 Feb. 1898), in Piłsudski, *Pisma zbiorowe,* 1:200.

22. Reprinted in Malinowski, *Materiały do historyi PPS,* 1:302. It is interesting to note that, despite its emphasis in party histories, accounts of the PPS fourth congress in postwar Polish historiography wholly omit the resolution's section on the Bund. See Tomicki, *Polska Partia Socjalistyczna,* 62–63; Holzer, *PPS: Szkic dziejów,* 20–21; Żychowski, *Polska myśl socjalistyczna,* 250–51; and Jędrzejewicz and Cisek, *Kalendarium życia Józefa Piłsudskiego,* 1:86–87. In contrast to postwar historians who emphasize the resolution on relations with Russians, Leon Wasilewski, writing in the interwar period, places chief emphasis on the congress's resolution on the Bund, while clearly delineating the PPS position on the Lithuanian socialists. See Wasilewski, *Zarys dziejów Polskiej Partji Socjalistycznej,* 58–60; and Wasilewski, "Polska Partja Socjalistyczna w pierwszym okresie jej rozwoju," 54.

23. Piłsudski, *Pisma zbiorowe,* 1:201.

24. These included *Robotnik Litewski* (1896–99), *Lietuvos Darbininkas* (1896–99), *Echo życia robotniczego* (1897–98), and *Kowieński Robotnik* (1897). See Sabaliunas, *Lithuanian Social Democracy in Historical Perspective,* 155.

25. Sabaliunas, *Lithuanian Social Democracy in Historical Perspective,* 340.

26. *Robotnik Litewski* 1 (May 1896), quoted in Römer, *Litwa,* 277.

27. *Robotnik,* no. 26 (13 Feb. 1898), in Piłsudski, *Pisma zbiorowe,* 1:202.

28. Writing in 1904, Ludwik Kulczycki, who broke with the PPS in 1900 to form the PPS Proletariat, pointed to the fourth congress resolution on Lithuanians and Jews as a mark of chauvinism. One element of this chauvinism, he maintained, was the implied association of nation with language, something which the case of Ireland disproved. "If, for whatever reason, socialists in Lithuania who speak Polish in everyday affairs regard themselves as Lithuanians and want to form a separate political party," Kulczycki wrote in 1904, "then no one can deny them this right." See Mazowiecki [Kulczycki], *Historya ruchu socyalistycznego w zaborze rosyjskim,* 349.

29. Tomicki, *Polska Partia Socjalistyczna,* 62; also see Żychowski, *Polska myśl socjalistyczna,* 250, who also restates the fourth congress resolution on Lithuanians without including the language qualification.

30. Żychowski, *Polska myśl socjalityczna,* 250.

31. Piłsudski, *Pisma zbiorowe,* 1:202.

32. A. Wr. [Witold Jodko-Narkiewicz], "Ruch robotniczy na Litwie," *Przedświt,* no. 8 (Aug. 1898): 11.

33. See [J. Piłsudski], "Czwarty zjazd naszej partii," *Robotnik,* no. 26 (13 Feb. 1898), in Piłsudski, *Pisma zbiorowe,* 1:199–202

34. [Józef Piłsudski], "W kwestyi żydowskiej," *Robotnik,* no. 26 (13 Feb. 1898): 3.

35. Ibid.

36. Shvarts, *Yuzef pilsudski,* 149.

37. Since the party aimed to represent workers throughout the empire and not just ethnic Russians, Bundist participants insisted on the use of "rossiiskaia" (of Russia) in the title instead of the ethnically based "russkaia," to which the party agreed. Thus the "Rossiiskaia Sotsialno-Demokraticheskaia Robochaia Partiia" was born.

38. "Sprawa proletaryatu żydowskiego," *Przedświt,* no. 4 (Apr. 1898): 1.

39. Żyd [Kazimierz Róg], "Z ruchu żydowskiego," *Przedświt,* no. 6 (June 1898), 21.

40. Jan Kacewicz, "Goldberg, Władysław," *SBDzPRR,* 2:284.

41. Quoted in Cała, *Asimilacja Żydów w Królestwie Polskim,* 307.

42. Arkadi Kremer, "Ershter ts. k. fun bund: Epizod—Zubatov," *Di naye folkstsaytung* (17 Oct. 1927): 6. The article was reprinted in *Arkadi: zamlbukh,* 380–94.

43. Vl. Kossovsky, "Di ershte 'likvidatsye' (zikhroynes vegn 'bund')," *Di naye folkstsaytung* (17 Oct. 1927): 7. A different version of these memoirs was reprinted in *Arkadi: zamlbukh,* 175–207.

44. Ibid.

45. Referred to in Tobias, *The Jewish Bund in Russia,* 83.

46. Arkadi Kremer, "Ershter ts. k. fun bund," 6.

47. L. Men'shchikov, *Okhrana i Revoliutsiia,* vol. 2, bk. 1 (Moscow: Izd-vo Vsesoiuznogo Ob-va Polit. Katorzhan, 1930), 112–13.

48. Tobias, *The Jewish Bund in Russia,* 80–83.

49. For the Okhrana report on the raid of Bundists, which includes a full list of seized illegal literature, see Men'shchikov, *Okhrana i Revoliutsiia,* vol. 2, bk. 1:112–13.

50. [Vladimir Kossovsky], *Di milkhome fun der poylisher sotsyialistisher partay gegn dem yidishn arbeyter-bund* (July 1898, n.p.). Kossovsky's brochure on the PPS was printed together with the statement of aims from *Der arbeyter shtimme,* nos. 9–10, which was most likely authored by Kremer.

"Our Aims" was later printed in December 1898 in issue 11 of *Der arbeyter shtimme,* thus making it available to the rank and file Jewish worker. According to the editors of *Arkadi: zamlbukh,* the brochure was published in Yiddish, Russian, and Polish. However, neither the PPS nor the Bund archive contain a Polish edition, nor is there any reference to one in the secondary literature.

51. "Unzer tsiln (ibergedrikt fun 'arbeyter shtimme' no. 9–10)," in *Di milkhome fun der poylisher sotsyialistisher partay,* 2.

52. This quote is taken from the Yiddish text of the manifesto. See ibid., 3.

53. Ibid., 5–8.

54. Ibid., 15.

55. [Kossovsky], *Di milkhome fun der poylisher sotsyialistisher partay,* 21.

56. Ibid., 26. For the part of the PPS resolution referred to by Kossovsky, see [Piłsudski], "Czwarty zjazd naszej partii," 2.

57. [Kossovsky], *Di milkhome fun der poylisher sotsyialistisher partay,* 27.

58. Ibid., 46–47.

59. "Sprawa proletaryatu żydowskiego," *Przedświt,* no. 4 (Apr. 1898): 1–5.

60. [Kossovsky], *Di milkhome fun der poylisher sotsyialistisher partay,* 50–51.

61. Ibid., 52.

## Chapter 5. Ideological Transformation

1. Tobias, *The Jewish Bund in Russia,* 86–90.

2. *Di arbeyter shtimme,* no. 11 (2/15 Dec. 1898).

3. Tobias, *The Jewish Bund in Russia,* 92–93.

4. Frankel, *Prophecy and Politics,* 217.

5. John Mill, "Tsvantsik yor 'bund,'" *Di tsukunft* 1 (Jan. 1918): 50.

6. Khayim [John Mill], "'Der arbeyter' numer 1," *Der yidisher arbeyter,* no. 6 (March 1899): 44–45.

7. For a discussion of Kautsky's position on the national question in general and the Jewish question in particular, see Jacobs, *On Socialists and the "Jewish Question,"* 5–43.

8. Khayim [John Mill], "'Der arbeyter' numer 1," 46.

9. Khayim [John Mill], "'Der arbeyter' numer 1," quoted in Frankel, *Prophecy and Politics,* 217–18.

10. Mill, *Pionern un boyer,* 2:53; also see Jacobs, *On Socialists and the "Jewish Question,"* 124.

11. Karl Kautsky, "Der kampf fun di natsionen in estraykh," *Der yidisher arbeyter,* no. 8 (Dec. 1899): 11–12. Kautsky's article is summarized in Jacobs, *On Socialists and the "Jewish Question,"* 125.

12. Mill, *Pionern un boyer,* 2:54.

13. The PPS context was generally ignored in the old school of Bundist historiography. See, for example, Pinson, "Arkady Kremer, Vladimir Medem, and the Ideology of the Jewish 'Bund,'" 250; and Mishkinsky, "Jewish Labor Movement and European Socialism," 291. The corrective is provided in Jacobs, *On Socialists and the "Jewish Question,"* 125–26.

14. Zhitlovsky had made similar arguments in an 1892 brochure in which he advocated a synthesis of socialism and Diaspora nationalism for European Jewry. For a summary of that brochure, see Goldsmith, *Modern Yiddish Culture,* 164–65.

15. Ben Ehud [Chaim Zhitlovsky], "Tsionizm oder sotsyalizm?" *Der yidisher arbeyter,* no. 6 (Mar. 1899): 12–14.

16. Frankel, *Prophecy and Politics,* 217. On Zhitlovsky's early writings, also see Goldsmith, *Modern Yiddish Culture,* 161–82.

17. *Der yidisher arbeyter,* no. 6 (Mar. 1899): 11, quoted in Frankel, *Prophecy and Politics,* 217.

18. "Di litvishe (khristlikhe) arbeyter bavegung," *Der yidisher arbeyter,* no. 6 (Mar. 1899): 25–26.

19. "Der protest fun der litvisher sotsialdemokratisher partay gegn der poylisher sotsialistisher partay," *Der yidisher arbeyter,* no. 6 (Mar. 1899): 27–28.

20. See Rosa Luxemburg, "Der sotsyalizmus in poyln," *Der yidisher arbeyter,* no. 8 (Dec. 1899): 15–18, originally published October 1897 in German and reprinted in *Kwestja polska a ruch socjalityczny* (Kraków, 1905), 101–8.

21. Arthur G. Kogan, "The Social Democrats and the Conflict of Nationalities in the Habsburg Monarchy," *Journal of Modern History* 21, no. 3 (Sept. 1949): 208–10.

22. *Protokoll über die Verhandlungen des Gesamtparteitages der Sozialdemokratischen Arbeiterpartei in Oesterreich* (Vienna: Verlag der Wiener Volksbuchhandlung Brand, 1901), 85, cited in Kogan, "Social Democrats and the Conflict of Nationalities in the Habsburg Monarchy," 209.

23. Kogan, "Social Democrats and the Conflict of Nationalities in the Habsburg Monarchy," 210.

24. Ibid., 213.

25. [Mill], "Di natsyionale frage oyf dem kongres fun der estraykher sotsyal-demokratye in brin," *Der yidisher arbeyter,* no. 8 (Dec. 1899): 25.

26. Ibid., 27. Also see Frankel, *Prophecy and Politics,* 218–19.

27. Mill, *Pionern un boyer,* 2:54.

28. See "Protest," *Przedświt,* no. 11 (Nov. 1899): 21.

29. Memoirs of participants have given conflicting numbers of between fifteen and twenty delegates. Those whose presence has been confirmed include Dovid Katz and Sender Zeldov from the central committee, Mill

from Geneva, Albert Zalkind from Minsk, Pavel Rozental and B. Levin from Białystok, B. Klevanski from Kovno, A. Weinstein and Khaym Zakan from Warsaw, S. Weissenblum from Łódź, Tsivia Hurvitsh and S. Yakavi from Warsaw and Łódź, Boris Tseytlin from Vitebsk, Zalman Singer from the Bershter Bund, and Pati Srednitski-Kremer, who represented *Di arbeyter shtimme.* For a list of participants, see Hertz, Aronson, and Dubnow-Erlich, *Di geshikhte fun bund,* 1:147.

30. "Der driter tsuzamenfor fun dem algemaynem yidishen arbeyter bund in rusland un poyln," *Der yidisher arbeyter,* no. 9 (1900): 6.

31. Mill, *Pionern un boyer,* 2:66.

32. "Der driter tsuzamenfor," 6–7.

33. Mill, *Pionern un boyer,* 2:66–67.

34. Katz-Blum, *Zikhroynes fun a bundist*, 184.

35. Cited in Wildman, "Russian and Jewish Social Democracy," 84–85.

36. Mill, "Di natsyonale frage un der 'bund,'" 117.

37. "Der driter tsuzamenfor," 7.

38. Ibid.

39. Mill, *Pionern un boyer,* 2:81; Frankel, *Prophecy and Politics,* 224.

40. Mill, *Pionern un boyer,* 2:93.

41. Tobias, *The Jewish Bund in Russia,* 115.

42. Mill, *Pionern un boyer,* 2:94; Frankel, *Prophecy and Politics,* 224.

43. Mill, *Pionern un boyer,* 2:93; Tobias, *The Jewish Bund in Russia,* 115; Frankel, *Prophecy and Politics,* 224.

44. Mill, *Pionern un boyer,* 2:81.

45. Mill, *Pionern un boyer,* 2:80–81.

46. Mill, "Di natsyonale frage un der bund," 118.

47. Authorship of "From the Press" columns is confirmed in Mill, "Di pionern-epokhe fun der yidisher arbeter-bavegung," 3:387.

48. [John Mill], *Der yidisher arbeyter*, no. 7 (Aug. 1899): 47.

49. The delegate count is given in the congress report, "Der ferter kongres fun algemaynem yidishen arbeyter-bund in rusland un poyln," *Der yidisher arbeyter*, no. 12 (1901): 97. The fourth congress resolutions were the first to be published as separate brochures in both Polish and Russian. See *Czwarty zjazd ogólnego żydowskiego związku robotniczego na Litwie, w Polsce i Rosyi* (London, 1901); and *Chetvertyi sezd vseobshchego evreiskogo rabochego soiuza v Litve, Polshe i Rossii* (Geneva: Tip. Soiuza russkich sotsialdemokra-tov, 1901). For a complete Hebrew translation, see *Din ve-heshbon ha-vaadah ha-reviit shel ha-bund,* trans. T. Dolzhansky (Jerusalem: The Hebrew University, 1971).

50. *Czwarty zjazd,* 9.

51. "Der ferter kongres," 99. For a partial translation in English, see Paul R. Mendes-Flohr and Jehuda Reinharz, eds., *The Jew in the Modern World*

(Oxford: Oxford University Press, 1980), 340–41; and Frankel, *Prophecy and Politics,* 220.

52. "Der ferter kongres," 100; Frankel, *Prophecy and Politics,* 220–21. For a full reprint of the Bund's fourth congress resolutions and protocols, see *Materialy k istorii evreiskago rabochego dvizheniia,* 111–28; Bukhbinder, *Di geshikhte fun der yidisher arbeter-bavegung in rusland,* 104–12.

53. Mill, *Pionern un boyer,* 2:94; Frankel, *Prophecy and Politics,* 224.

54. Frankel, *Prophecy and Politics,* 224.

55. Authorship of the published congress report is confirmed by Frants Kursky in his *Gezamelte shriftn,* 234.

56. P. An-man [Pavel Rozental], "Der bialistoker period in lebn fun tsentraler-komitet fun 'bund' (1900–1902)," *Royter Pinkes* 1 (1921): 59–60; *Czwarty zjazd,* 9. Also see the account of another delegate, Blekhman [Avram der Tate], *Bleter fun mayn yugent,* 106, who similarly stresses the importance of the Brünn program.

57. *Czwarty zjazd,* 9.

58. Ibid., 10–11; "Chetverty zezd," in *Materialy k istorii evreiskago rabochego dvizheniia,* 115. Liber's speech is quoted in Frankel, *Prophecy and Politics,* 221, as "we must become nationalists." A more accurate translation of *natsionalnii,* however, would be "national," given that the Russian word for "nationalist" is *natsionalist,* as well as the negative association of "nationalist" with chauvinism. The Polish version similarly uses the term *nacyonaly* ("national").

59. [Rozental], "Der bialistoker period in lebn fun tsentraler-komitet fun 'bund,'" 60.

60. According to *Czwarty zjazd,* 10, no adherents of a territorial solution were present, while Rozental implied by omission that no such discussion took place.

61. Avram der Tate [Leyb Blekhman], "Der ferter tsuzamenfor fun 'bund'," in Blekhman, *Bleter fun mayn yugent,* 106.

62. *Czwarty zjazd,* 10.

63. "Der ferter kongres," 100.

64. *Czwarty zjazd,* 13.

65. Mishkinsky, "Regional Factors in the Formation of the Jewish Labor Movement in Tsarist Russia," 35–36.

66. Perl became editor of *Robotnik* in 1900 after Piłsudski's arrest.

67. [Perl], "Bund o niepodległość Polski," *Robotnik,* no. 41 (17 Sept. 1901): 2.

68. Ibid.

69. "Di diskusye vegn der natsyonaler frage oyfn v tsuzamenfor fun bund yuni 1903 tsirikh (fun di protokaln fun tsuzamenfor)," *Unzer tsayt* 3 (20 Dec. 1927): 87.

70. Jacobs, *On Socialists and the "Jewish Question,"* 126–27.

## Chapter 6. Polish Socialism Responds

1. Although Henryk Piasecki's pioneering work *Żydowska Organizacja PPS* makes use of the PPS Yiddish press, no general analysis is offered.

2. "Pamiętniki Bolesława Miklaszewskiego" (Warsaw, 1928), p. 153, sygn. 61, Archive of the Polish Academy of Arts and Sciences, Warsaw (henceforth: Archiwum PAN).

3. Alicja Pacholczykowa, "Feigenbaym, Benjamin," in *Słownik Biograficzny Działaczy Polskiego Ruchu Robotniczego*, 2:65–66; and "Feigenbaum, Benjamin," in *Leksikon fun der yidisher literatur un prese*, ed. Zalman Reisen (Warsaw: Tsentral, 1914), 466–67.

4. Bolesław Miklaszewski, New York, to the Union of Polish Socialists Abroad, London, 5 Apr. 1896, reprinted in *Niepodległość* 14 (July–Dec. 1937): 450–52. Also see Pobóg-Malinowski, *Józef Piłsudski, 1864–1901*, 297–98. For an account of Miklaszewski's activities in 1896 linking the PPS with Polish socialist émigrés in U.S. cities, see Danuta Piątkowska-Koźlik, *Związek Socjalistów Polskich w Ameryce 1900–1914* (Opole: Wyższa Szkoła Pedagogiczna, 1992), 24–30.

5. Archiwum PAN, sygn. 61, p. 72.

6. Józef Piłsudski, London, to Bolesław Miklaszewski, New York, 24 Apr. 1896, in Piłsudski, *Pisma zbiorowe: Uzupełnienia*, 1:176.

7. See "Z emigracyi z Ameryki," *Przedświt*, no. 5 (May 1896): 18.

8. Regarding the number of members, see Maurycy Montlak, New York, to ZZSP, London, 27 July 1896, folder 1, sygn. 305/VII/29, AAN.

9. Józef Piłsudski, London, to CKR PPS, Congress Poland, 9 June 1896, in Piłsudski, *Pisma zbiorowe: Uzupełnienia*, 1:223. The use of such terms as *Żydy, Żydek* ("the little Jew"), and *parchy wileńskie* ("the Vilna scabs") in Piłsudski's private correspondences revealed commonly held anti-Jewish prejudices during that time period. While clearly not an anti-Semite, as his contemporaries have attested, Piłsudski did revert to old stereotypes in his exchanges with Jewish political opponents. In fact, Piłsudski also used such derogatory language in his private letters for Russians, to whom he referred as *kacapy* and *mochy*, two strongly anti-Russian terms used at the time in Polish.

10. Al. Dębski [Józef Piłsudski], London, to the Jewish Socialist Post from America to Poland, New York, 10 June 1896, in Piłsudski, *Pisma zbiorowe: Uzupełnienia*, 1:227–28. Garlicki and Świętek confirm that the letter, although signed with Dębski's name, was written in Piłsudski's hand.

11. Józef Piłsudski, London, to Bolesław Miklaszewski, New York, 24 June 1896, in Piłsudski, *Pisma zbiorowe: Uzupełnienia*, 1:231–32.

12. Benjamin Feigenbaum, *Di sotsyalistishe bavegung in rusland un di dortige iden: A propogande-broshur, ekstra geshriben tsu farteyln tsvishn di yidishe*

*arbeyter in rusland in algemeyn un in rusish-poyln bazunders* (New York, 1896), Sejm Library, Warsaw.

13. Ben N. [B. Feigenbaum], *Dos gan-eydn hatakhton: A vunderlikhe emese mayse, vi men is dergangen dem veg tsum gan-eydn oyf der velt, un vi menshen foren ahin* (Warsaw, 1875). The date 1875 was given to elude the censors, even though it was published in New York in 1896. According to one source, the PPS provided the funds for the labor and printing of Feigenbaum's brochure. See Cherikover, "Di onheybn fun der umlegaler literaur in yidish," 599, which includes a reproduction of the falsified title page.

14. Feigenbaum, *Dos gan-eydn,* 14–15, 27, 31.

15. Maurycy Montlak, New York, to Union Abroad, London, 24 Sept. 1897, fol. 51, folder 1, sygn. 305/VII/29, AAN.

16. Piątkowska-Koźlik, *Związek Socjalistów Polskich w Ameryce*, 77.

17. Maurycy Montlak, New York, to the Union of Polish Socialists Abroad, London, 29 July [?] 1897, fol. 3, folder 1, sygn. 305/VII/29, AAN.

18. H. Müntz [Maurycy Montlak], New York, to the Union of Polish Socialists Abroad, London, 12 Apr. 1898, fol. 20, folder 1, sygn. 305/VII/29, AAN. A subsequent letter suggests the Aid Alliance had been first formed in November 1897. See H. Müntz [Maurycy Montlak], New York, to the Union Abroad, London, 16 July 1898, fol. 31, folder 1, sygn. 305/VII/29, AAN, where Montlak wrote of "the nine-month old Aid Alliance."

19. AAN, sygn. 305/II/12, fol. 205, folder 6.

20. H. Müntz [Maurycy Montlak], New York, to the ZZSP, London, 12 Apr. 1898, fol. 21, folder 1, sygn. 305/VII/29, AAN.

21. "List członków Związku Pomocy w Nowym Jorku," fols. 211–13, folder 6, sygn. 305/II/12, AAN.

22. "Nasze Zadanie," fols. 207–10, folder 6, sygn. 305/II/12, AAN. The handwritten program statement is undated. However, its approximate date is revealed in a July letter to London in which Montlak wrote he was enclosing a membership list and "our program." See H. Müntz [Maurycy Montlak], New York, to the Union Abroad, London, 10 July 1898, fol. 205, folder 6, sygn. 305/II/12, AAN.

23. Mojżesz Kaufman, "Początki roboty żydowskiej PPS," 347; Piasecki, *Żydowska Organizacja PPS,* 48.

24. Malinowski, *Materiały do historyi PPS*, 2:153–54.

25. Goldsmith, *Modern Yiddish Culture*, 132. The arrested included Saul Degenfisz, Leyb Burgin, Kadish Altglas, and Mendel Rubinstein in Warsaw; and Abram Blumowicz, I. Kornblit, David Perlmutter, Naftali Shatz, and Srul Auerbach in Białystok. See Kaufman, "Początki roboty żydowskiej PPS," 349–50; Piasecki, *Żydowska Organizacja PPS,* 51.

26. Kaufman, "Początki roboty żydowskiej PPS," 349.

27. Regarding the second wave of emigration, see Piasecki, *Żydowska Organizacja PPS,* 52. Regarding the release of prisoners in 1900, see Feliks Sachs, Vilna [?], to Union Abroad, London, 31 Oct. 1900, folder 1, sygn. 305/VII/34, AAN; Sachs's letter is used in Piasecki, *Żydowska Organizacja PPS,* 52. The information in Sachs's letter accords with police reports on PPS Jews. See entries for the persons cited in the text in Archive of the Biographical Dictionary of Polish Revolutionaries in Warsaw (Henceforth: Archiwum SBDzPRR).

28. AAN, sygn. 305/III/5.

29. Wasilewski, "Polska emigracja londyńska," 256.

30. Leon Wasilewski, "Ze wspomnień (1896–1899)," *Z Pola Walki,* nos. 2–3 (1973): 223.

31. The first document bearing the official stamp of the Polish Socialist Party Aid Alliance, Branch of New York is an August 1900 letter by Montlak. See Maurycy Montlak, New York, to the Union Abroad, London, 8 Aug. 1900, fol. 215, folder 6, sygn. 305/II/12, AAN. For a secondary source on the Aid Alliance, see Piątkowska-Koźlik, *Związek Socjalistów Polskich w Ameryce,* 76–77.

32. "Ustawa oddziału Polskiej Partyi Socyalistycznej pod nazwą 'Związek Pomocy' w New-Yorku," 29 July 1900, fols. 214–15, folder 6, sygn. 305/II/12, AAN.

33. Regarding the scope of circulation in Congress Poland, see the papers of Mojżesz Kaufman, pt. 2, fol. 3, sygn. 1183, Ringelblum Archive I, ŻIH; Kormanowa, *Materiały do bibliografii druków socjalistycznych,* 1. Shvarts claimed issue 1 of *Der arbeyter* had a print run of five thousand, relying on the figure presented in Pobóg-Malinowski's work. Because Pobóg-Malinowski did not cite a source for this figure, I rely on Kormanowa's authoritative account of Polish socialist publications. See Shvarts, *Yuzef pilsudski,* 169; and Pobóg-Malinowski, *Józef Piłsudski,* 1:297.

34. [Leon Gottlieb], London, to the PPS Foreign Committee, London, 9 Jan. 1901, fol. 5, folder 23, Bund Archive ME21.

35. *Der arbeyter,* no. 1 (Dec. 1898): 1, in the Bund Archive (New York), microfilm division.

36. Authorship is confirmed in the papers of Mojżesz Kaufman, pt. 5, fol. 1, sygn. 1183, Ringelblum Archive I, ŻIH.

37. [Mendel Rubinstein], "Di tsarishe regirung und di arbeyter," *Der arbeyter,* no. 1 (Dec. 1898): 2–3.

38. Ibid., 6–7.

39. Adam Próchnik, "Teresa Perlowa," *KRRwP* 5, no. 3 (July–Sept. 1939): 17–18; and Jerzy Holzer, "Perlowa z Reznikowskich, Teresa (1871–1939)," *PSB* 25, no. 4 (1980): 631.

40. "Gottlieb, Leon," *Leksikon fun der yidisher literatur, prese un filologia*

(Vilna: B. Kletskin, 1928), 1:461–62; "Gottlieb, Leon," *Leksikon fun der nayer yidisher literatur* (New York, 1958), 2:19–20; and Barbara Winnicki, "Gottlieb, Leon Aron," *SBDzPRR*, 2:323–24.

41. [Leon Gottlieb], London, to the PPS Foreign Committee, London, 9 Jan. 1901, fol. 4, folder 23, Bund Archive ME21.

42. Winnicki, "Gottlieb, Leon Aron," 324.

43. Wasilewski, "Z roboty zagranicznej PPS," 177. Shvarts acknowledges that the Yiddish in *Der arbeyter* number 2 was superior. See Shvarts, *Yuzef pilsudski*, 201.

44. Authorship is confirmed in internal party correspondence. See B. A. Jędrzejowski, London, to the PPS Aid Alliance, New York, 5 Mar. 1901, fol. 295, vol. 4, sygn. 305/II/25, AAN. For information on Gottlieb's role as translator, see B. A. Jędrzejowski, London, to C. Jakubowicz [Henoch Kowalski], Karlsruhe, 15 Jan. 1901, fol. 1, folder 23, Bund Archive ME21.

45. [Feliks Perl], "Di politik fun der rusisher regirung vegen yuden," *Der arbeyter*, no. 2 (Dec. 1900): 1.

46. Ibid., 2.

47. Ibid., 2, 3.

48. Ibid., 18, emphasis mine.

49. C. Jakubowicz [Henoch Kowalski], Karlsruhe (Germany), to the PPS Foreign Committee, London, 5 Jan. 1901, fols. 1–6, folder 5, sygn. 305/VII/21, AAN. I am thankful to Dr. Alicja Palchoczykowa in Warsaw for providing me with a copy of Kowalski's letter.

50. B. A. Jędrzejowski, London, to C. Jakubowicz [Henoch Kowalski], Karlsruhe, 15 Jan. 1901, fol. 1, folder 23, Bund Archive ME21.

51. Established in London in 1898, *Światło* was a popular-scientific quarterly journal published under PPS auspices. It featured theoretical articles by west European and Austrian socialists as well as historical pieces on Poland.

52. B. A. Jędrzejowski, London, to C. Jakubowicz [Henoch Kowalski], Karlsruhe, 15 Jan. 1901, p. 1v, folder 23, Bund Archive ME21.

53. Ibid., 2.

54. Ibid.

55. PPS Aid Alliance (Maurycy Montlak), New York, to the PPS Foreign Committee, London, 2 Feb. 1901, fols. 251–52, folder 6, sygn. 305/II/12, AAN.

56. Ibid., fols. 254–55.

57. B. A. Jędrzejowski, London, to E. Bruzel, New York, 15 Mar. 1901, fol. 294, vol. 4, sygn. 305/II/25, AAN.

58. Alicja Pacholczykowa, "Sachs Feliks," *PSB* 36, no. 2 (1992): 265.

59. Wasilewski, "Z roboty zagranicznej PPS," 177.

60. B. A. Jędrzejowski, London, to H. F. Mins [Maurycy Montlak], New York, 15 Mar. 1901, fol. 296, vol. 4, sygn. 305/II/25, AAN.

61. "Der ershter may!" *Der arbeyter,* no. 3 (Apr. 1901): 1, in the Bund Archive, microfilm division.

62. [Feliks Sachs?], "Vos zolen ton di yidishe arbeyter in poyln," *Der arbeyter,* no. 4 (Aug. 1901): 1, in the Bund Archive, microfilm division.

63. Papers of Mojżesz Kaufman, pt. 2, fol. 3, sygn. 1183, Ringelblum Archive 1, ŻIH.

64. Mojżesz Kaufman, "Przyczynki do historji Żydowskiej Organizacji PPS," 31.

65. "Vos zolen ton di yidishe arbeyter in poyln," *Der arbeyter,* no. 4 (Aug. 1901): 2.

66. According to Piasecki, the PPS in Łódź was not able to organize a Jewish division until the spring of 1901. See Piasecki, *Żydowska Organizacja PPS,* 55.

67. Bronisław Szuszkiewicz, "Organizacja Grodzieńska PPS w latach 1898–1910," *Niepodległość* 16 (July–Dec. 1937): 513–19; Monachim Wajner, "Do historji PPS na Litwie," 221–23; and Adam Puszkiewicz, "Z dziejów walki socjalistyczno-niepodległościowej w Grodnia," *KRRwP* 4 (1935): 211–26.

68. Szuszkiewicz, "Organizacja Grodzieńska PPS w latach 1898–1910," 519–20.

69. [Mill], *Der yidisher arbayter,* no. 10 (1900): 78–79.

70. PPS Aid Alliance [M. Montlak], New York, to the PPS Foreign Committee, London, 10 Dec. 1900, fol. 225, folder 6, sygn. 305/II/12, AAN, in which the following eight titles were proposed: (1) E. Abramowski's 1892 brochure, *The Workers' Question (Sprawa Robotnicza);* (2) Jodko-Narkiewicz's article, "The Jews in Poland"; (3) Feliks Perl's brochure, *A Brief History of the Great French Revolution;* (4) K. Kautsky's *The Independence of Poland;* (5) Wilhelm Liebknecht's 1871 speech, *In the Defense of Truth;* (6) [not legible]; (7) Wojciechowski's 1900 brochure, *The Evolution of the PPS in the Last Five Fears;* and (8) Szymon Dickstein's 1881 classic, *What Do People Live By?*

71. PPS Yiddish brochures in 1901 were Karl Kautsky, *Di unobhengigkeyt fun poyln,* trans. Leon Gottlieb (London: PPS, 1901); B. Feigenbaum, *Vi kumt a yid tsu sotsyialismus?* 2nd. ed. (London: PPS, 1901); Aleksander Vronski [Witold Jodko-Narkiewicz], *Di yidn in poyln* (London: PPS & New York Aid Alliance, 1901); and S. Dickstein, *Fun vos eyner lebt,* trans. Feliks Sachs (London: PPS, 1901). Between the Sejm Library (Warsaw) and the Bund Archive (New York), a complete set of PPS Yiddish brochures is preserved.

72. Aid Alliance membership included Maurycy Montlak ("H. F. Mins"), Henry Bassel, Saul Degenfisz ("Robert Baumert"), and Leyb Burgin ("L. Wittig") as well as Leon Gottlieb ("J. Hartman") and the veteran Polish socialist Aleksander Dębski. See Report of the PPS Aid Alliance, Jan. 1 to Dec. 1, 1901, fols. 291–92, folder 6, sygn. 305/II/25, AAN; and Aid Alliance Membership List for 1901, fols. 287–89, folder 6, sygn. 305/II/25, AAN.

73. "Feigenbaum, Benjamin," in *Leksikon fun der yidisher literatur un prese,* ed. Zalman Reisen (Warsaw: Tsentral, 1914), 466–67.

74. B. A. Jędrzejowski, London, to E. Bruzel, New York, 30 Jan. 1901, fols. 156–57, vol. 4, sygn. 305/II/25, AAN.

75. B. A. Jędrzejowski, London, to B. Feigenbaum, Brooklyn, New York, 15 Mar. 1901, fol. 289, vol. 4, sygn. 305/II/25, AAN.

76. B. A. Jędrzejowski, London, to H. F. Mins [M. Montlak], Brooklyn , New York, 15 Mar. 1901, fol. 296, vol. 4, sygn. 305/II/25, AAN.

77. B. A. Jędrzejowski, London, to B. Feigenbaum, Brooklyn, New York, 26 Apr. 1901, fol. 435, vol. 4, sygn. 305/II/25, AAN.

78. J. Hartman [Leon Gottlieb], New York, to the PPS Foreign Committee, London, 7 May 1901, folder 5, sygn. 305/VII/12, AAN.

79. For circulation figures, see Malinowski, *Materiały do historyi PPS,* 2:297.

80. Feigenbaum, *Vi kumt a yid tsu sotsyialismus?* 3, 30–31. A copy is preserved in the Sejm Library, Warsaw.

81. English translation from "Aims of the Polish Socialist Party," reprinted in *For Your Freedom and Ours: The Polish Progressive Spirit from the Fourteenth Century to the Present,* ed. Krystyna M. Olszer, 2nd ed. (1943; New York: F. Ungar, 1981), 150, which has been checked against the original pamphlet, *Program Polskiej Partii Socjalistycznej* (Lublin, 1905); emphasis is mine.

82. "Dos program fun der poylisher sotsyialistisher partay," in Feigenbaum, *Vi kumt a yud tsu sotsyialismus?* 32–33. It will be recalled from chapter 2 that several delegates at the 1892 founding congress had put forward a motion to replace the word "democratic" with "socialist" in the party's national demands, but the majority voted in favor of the former.

83. Aleksander Vronski [Witold Jodko-Narkiewicz], *Di yidn in poyln* (London: PPS & New York Aid Alliance, 1901), adapted from Al. Wroński [Witold Jodko-Narkiewicz], "Żydzi w Polsce," *Światło,* no. 8 (1900): 160–68, under Feliks Perl's editorship. *Di yidn in poyln* was printed with a circulation of two thousand copies, according to Malinowski, *Materiały do historyi PPS,* 2:287.

84. Vronski [Jodko-Narkiewicz], *Di yidn in poyln,* i.

85. Wasilewski, "Polska emigracja londyńska," 247.

86. Jan Kancewicz, "Jodko-Narkiewicz Witold," *SBDzPRR,* 2:725–26.

87. Wasilewski, "Polska emigracja londyńska,"247.

88. Al. Wroński [Witold Jodko-Narkiewicz], "Żydzi w Polsce," *Światło,* no. 8 (1900): 160, 161.

89. Ibid., 168

90. [Edward Abramowski], *Vos yeder arbeyter darf visn un gedenken* (London: PPS, 1902). The Yiddish version was translated from [E.

Abramowski], *Sprawa Robotnicza: O tem, co każdy robotnik wiedzieć i pamiętać powinien,* 2nd. ed., rev. (London: PPS, 1898). According to Malinowski, *Materiały do historyi PPS,* 2:287, the Yiddish version was printed with a circulation of three thousand copies for transport to Russian Poland.

91. [E. Abramowski], *Sprawa Robotnicza,* 44–49, quotation from page 49.

92. Ibid., 48; and [E. Abramowski], *Vos yeder arbeyter darf visn un gedenken,* 36, emphasis mine.

93. [E. Abramowski], *Sprawa Robotnicza,* 48–49.

94. [E. Abramowski], *Vos yeder arbeyter darf visn un gedenken,* 37.

95. J. Piłsudski, Vilna, to ZZSP, London, 2 Feb. 1898, in Piłsudski, *Pisma zbiorowe: Uzupełnienia,* 2:21.

96. See Wasilewski, "Ze wspomnień," 223, on Yiddish leaflets. The author of the April 1898 leaflet was Mojżesz Kaufman, whose handwritten copy, checked against the printed version, is included in his private papers. See Mojżesz Kaufman, pt. 4, fol. 5, sygn. 1185, Ringelblum Archive 1, ŻIH. For copies of the original leaflets, see fols. 10–19, folder 1, sygn. 305/III/37, AAN.

97. "Brider arbeyter!" Central Committee of the PPS, Apr. 1899, in Yiddish Leaflets of the PPS, 1897–1900, fol. 16, folder 1, sygn. 305/III/37, AAN.

98. See, for example, the leaflets of the local workers' committee in Łódź for 1904–1906 in folder 7, sygn. 305/III/35, AAN.

99. Jewish Section of the PPS, leaflets (1901–3), fols. 2–3, folder 2, sygn. 305/III/37, AAN.

100. "Brider un shvester!" Apr. 1901, CKR PPS, in Jewish Section of the PPS, leaflets (1901–3), fol. 3, folder 2, sygn. 305/III/37.

101. "Towarzysze i Towarzyszki!" 7 Mar. 1901, Białystok Committee of the PPS, in Leaflets of Białystok Workers' Committee, 1895–1906, folder 2, sygn. 305/III/35, AAN.

102. "Arbeyter genosen!" Warsaw (Apr. 1902), Warsaw Workers' Committee of the PPS (WKR PPS), in fol. 6, folder 2, sygn. 305/III/37, AAN.

103. Prokurator Warszawskiej Izby Sądowej, sygn. 2907, Archiwum Główny Akt Dawnych (AGAD).

104. B. A. Jędrzejowski, London, to C. Jakubowicz [Henoch Kowalski], Karlsruhe, 15 Jan. 1901, fol. 1, folder 23, Bund Archive ME21.

## Chapter 7. Toward a Recognition of Jewish Nationality

1. Wasilewski, *Józef Piłsudski jakim go znałem,* 65.

2. Piłsudski, London, to Władysław Gumplowicz, Zurich, 16 Jan. 1902, in Piłsudski, *Pisma zbiorowe: Uzupełnienia,* 2:93–94.

3. Piłsudski, London, to Witold Jodko-Narkiewicz, Lwów, 12 Feb. 1902, in Piłsudski, *Pisma zbiorowe: Uzupełnienia,* 2:105.

4. Kazimierz Kelles-Krauz, Vienna, to the PPS Foreign Committee, London, 12 Feb. 1902, in Kelles-Krauz, *Listy,* 2:601–2. Kelles-Krauz became an anomaly in the PPS by April 1902, when, partly under the influence of Piłsudski's new position on the Jews, he praised Zionism as the symbol of modern Jewish nationhood. For Kelles-Krauz's position on the Jewish question, see Sobelman, "Polish Socialism and Jewish Nationality," 47–55, as well as Snyder, *Nationalism, Marxism, and Modern Central Europe,* 191–201. For the best biography in Polish, see Wiesław Bieńkowski, *Kazimierz Kelles-Krauz: Życie i dzieło* (Wrocław: Zakład Narodowy im. Ossolińskich, 1969).

5. Piłsudski, London, to Kazimierz Kelles-Krauz, Vienna, 17 Feb. 1902, in *Niepodległość* 13 (1980): 9–10, emphasis mine.

6. Piłsudski, London, to Władysław Gumplowicz, Zurich, 17 Feb. 1902, in Piłsudski, *Pisma zbiorowe: Uzupełnienia,* 2:108, 109, emphasis mine.

7. Jędrzejewicz, *Piłsudski,* 32.

8. See Wasilewski, "Kierownictwo PPS zaboru rosyjskiego (1893–1918)," 355–56; Piłsudski, *Pisma zbiorowe: Uzupełnienia,* 2:141; and Alicja Pacholczykowa, "Sachs, Feliks," *SBDzPRR,* 265. The other four delegates were Adam Buyno (Warsaw province), Bolesław Czarkowski (Piotrków region), Walery Sławek (Zagłębie Dąbrowskie and Częstochowa), and Jan Rutkiewicz (Kielce, Lublin, and Radom provinces).

9. "VI zjazd PPS," *Przedświt,* no. 8 (Aug. 1902): 281–85; "Szósty zjazd PPS," *Robotnik,* no. 46 (5 Aug. 1902): 1–3. Despite the conspicuous resolutions on the Jews, this aspect of the sixth congress resolution has been virtually ignored in Polish historiography. See Garlicki, *Józef Piłsudski, 1867–1935*; Włodzimierz Suleja, *Józef Piłsudski* (Wrocław: Zakład Narodowy im. Ossolińskich, 1995); Jędrzejewicz, *Piłsudski*; Tomicki, *Polska Partia Socjalistyczna, 1892–1948*; and Holzer, *PPS,* all of whom wholly omit the resolution's points on Jews in their accounts. The exception in postwar historiography is Żychowski, *Polska myśl socjalistyczna XIX i XX wieku,* 255, which includes a remark that the sixth party congress had called upon Jewish socialists to agitate under the PPS banner. For a summary of the sixth congress, see Pobóg-Malinowski, *Józef Piłsudski, 1901–1908,* 25–26. For a polemical account by an ex-PPS member, see Mazowiecki [Ludwik Kulczycki], *Historya ruchu socyalistycznego w zaborze rosyjskim,* 465–66, who condemns the PPS for its "chauvinist" resolution on the Jews.

10. "VI zjazd PPS," 281–82.

11. Ibid., 283–84.

12. Ibid., 283.

13. AAN, sygn. 305/III/1, folder 2, fol. 24, cited in Piasecki, *Żydowska*

*Organizacja PPS,* 64. For the founding of the Jewish Committee, also see Kaufman, "Przyczynki do historji Żydowskiej Organizacji PPS," 38; and Król, "Żydowska Organizacja Polskiej Partii Socjalistycznej (1893–1903)," 135.

14. Feliks Sachs, Vilna, to the PPS Foreign Committee, London, 21 June 1902, fols. 36–37, folder 1, sygn. 305/VII/34, AAN.

15. [Feliks Sachs], "Tsu unzere lezer," *Der arbeyter,* no. 6 (July 1902): 1. Both numbers 6 and 7, which Sachs edited, were produced with an illegal party printing press in Brześć Litewski. See Memoirs of Mojżesz Kaufman, pt. 5, fol. 17, sygn. 1183, Ringelblum Archive 1, ŻIH.

16. In Feliks Sachs, Vilna, to the PPS Foreign Committee, London, 4 July 1902, fols. 43–44, folder 1, sygn. 305/VII/34, AAN; Sachs referred to the negative image of the PPS in Lithuania, as an organization that sought to incorporate Lithuania into a future state.

17. [Feliks Sachs], "Unzer shtrebungen," *Der arbeyter,* no. 6 (July 1902): 2, emphasis mine.

18. Ibid.

19. Feliks Sachs, Vilna, to the PPS Foreign Committee, London, 7 Aug. 1902, fol. 52, folder 1, sygn. 305/VII/34, AAN, emphasis mine.

20. Ibid., fols. 59–60.

21. Ibid., fol. 60.

22. Ibid., fol. 61.

23. The accusation can be found in point five of the PPS's party resolution. See "VI zjazd PPS," *Przedświt,* no. 8 (Aug. 1902): 282.

24. "An alte lid oyfn alten nigun," *Di arbeyter shtimme,* no. 28 (Aug. 1902): 10.

25. Feliks Sachs, Vilna, to the PPS Foreign Committee, London, 23 Nov. 1902, fol. 67, folder 1, sygn. 305/VII/34, AAN.

26. [F. Sachs], "In entfer oyf a frage," *Der arbeyter,* no. 7 (Nov. 1902): 5.

27. [Marc Liber?], "Pps vegn der yidisher arbeyterbavegung," *Di arbeyter shtimme,* no. 30 (Oct. 1902): 1–8, which was translated into Polish and Russian and printed separately as *Polska Partja Socjalistyczna o żydowskim ruchu robotniczym* (London: Bund, 1903), and *Pol'skaia Sotsialisticheskaia Partiia o evreiskom rabochem dvizhenii* (London: Bund, 1903). Sachs responded to the Bund's brochure in [Feliks Sachs], "Odpowiedź Bundowi," *Przedświt,* no. 8 (Aug. 1903): 313–28. A Yiddish version was appended to *Der arbeyter,* no. 8 (Oct. 1903), and then made into a party brochure as [Feliks Sachs], *A klorer entfer* (London: PPS, 1904).

28. "Pps vegn der yidisher arbeyterbavegung," *Di arbeyter shtimme,* no. 30 (Oct. 1902): 1.

29. Ibid., 3.

30. Ibid.

31. Ibid.

32. Literally, "in gypsy language." See ibid., 5.

33. Ibid.

34. Ibid., 6.

35. Ibid., 7.

36. Feliks Sachs, Vilna, to the PPS Foreign Committee, London, 3 Jan. 1903, fol. 78, folder 1, sygn. 305/VII/34, AAN.

37. Report of the PPS Conference, 6–8 Nov. 1902, Warsaw, folder 2, sygn. 305/VII/1, AAN, reprinted in Piłsudski, *Pisma zbiorowe: Uzupełnienia,* 2:146–54.

38. Protocols of the PPS Conference, 22 Dec. 1902, cited in Piasecki, *Żydowska Organizacja PPS,* 69–70.

39. A. Wr. [W. Jodko-Narkiewicz], "'Bund,'" *Przedświt,* no. 6 (June 1903): 228–29.

40. Ibid., 235.

41. Kaufman, "Przyczynki do historji Żydowskiej Organizacji PPS," 38–39. Also see Jan Kancewicz, introduction to *Wybór pism,* by Henryk Walecki, 1:6–7. Other delegates included David Perlmutter, I. Kornblit, T. Nadelman, Gershon Halper, S. Kapulski, and probably M. Kaufman. Perlmutter and Kornblit, it will be recalled, were original members of the first Polish Jewish socialist circle in 1891. Szuszkiewicz, "Organizacja grodzieńska PPS w latach 1898–1910," *Niepodległość* 16 (July–Dec. 1937): 522–23, erroneously dates the Jewish Section's first conference in 1902. It is possible, however, that he was referring to an informal meeting of Jewish representatives that had taken place sometime in the late summer or early fall of 1902 (Piłsudski, *Pisma zbiorowe: Uzupełnienia,* 2:149).

42. AAN, sygn. 305/VII/34, folder 1, fol. 99.

43. "Sprawozdanie z konferencji CKR. odbytej w Wilnie 4, 5, i 6 czerwca 1903 roku," fols. 1–11, folder 3, sygn. 305/III/3, AAN. For the identity of participants, all of whom appeared in the report under pseudonyms, see the list of pseudonyms in Kormanowa, *Materiały do bibliografii druków socjalistycznych,* 223–83, as well as *Niepodległość* 20 (July–Aug. 1939): 89–90.

44. "Sprawozdanie z konferencji CKR odbytej w Wilnie 4, 5, i 6 czerwca 1903 roku," fol. 6, folder 3, sygn. 305/III/3, AAN.

45. Ibid., fol. 7.

46. Ibid., fol. 8.

47. [Feliks Sachs], "Odpowiedź Bundowi," *Przedświt,* no. 8 (Aug. 1903): 313–28.

48. Ibid., 314–15, 321.

49. Ibid., 322.

50. Ibid.

51. Ibid., 324. Official Bundist historiography dismisses Sachs's views as an articulation of the Polish view, not to be taken seriously. See Hertz, Aronson, and Dubnow-Erlich, *Di geshikhte fun Bund,* 2:134.

52. AAN, sygn. 305/III/3, folder 7, fol. 1.

53. Ibid., fols. 1–2.

54. Wajner, "Do historji PPS na Litwie," 228.

55. M. Luśnia [Kazimierz Kelles-Krauz], "Program narodowościowy socjalnej demokracyi austryackiej a program PPS II," *Przedświt,* no. 8 (Aug. 1903): 340–41.

56. J. Piłsudski, Rytro, to London, 14 Aug. 1903, in *Niepodległość* 12 (New York, 1979): 24.

57. [J. Piłsudski], "Wilno, październik 1903 r.," *Walka,* no. 3 (Nov. 1903), in Piłsudski, *Pisma zbiorowe,* 2:217.

58. J. Piłsudski, Rytro, to London, 14 Nov. 1903, in *Niepodległość* (New York, 1986) 19: 47–48, 54.

59. Piłsudski, *Memoires of a Polish Revolutionary and Soldier,* 80.

60. [J. Piłsudski], "Nasze stanowisko na Litwie," *Walka,* no. 3 (Nov. 1903), in Piłsudski, *Pisma zbiorowe,* 2:219–23.

61. [J. Piłsudski], "Kwestia żydowska na Litwie," *Walka,* no. 3 (Nov. 1903), in Piłsudski, *Pisma zbiorowe,* 2:226.

62. Tobias, *The Jewish Bund in Russia,* 288.

63. Sobelman, "Polish Socialism and Jewish Nationality," 47.

64. K. Kelles-Krauz, "Z powodu kongresu syonistów," *Prawda* 22 (1902), cited in Snyder, *Nationalism, Marxism, and Modern Central Europe,* 195.

65. K. Kelles-Krauz, "W kwestii narodowości żydowskiej," *Krytyka* (1904), reprinted in Kelles-Krauz, *Pisma wybrany* (Warsaw: Książka i Wiedza, 1962), 2:319–41.

66. T. Wilenski [Józef Kwiatek], *Kwestya Żydowska* (Kraków: Nakł. Administracyi "Prawa Ludu" i "Naprzodu," 1904), 15, 28, 33, 34. Translation of this final passage, checked against the original, is partly taken from M. Śliwa, "The Jewish Problem in Polish Socialist Thought," *Polin* 9 (1996): 23.

## Chapter 8. The 1905 Revolution in Russia and the Transformation of PPS-Bund Relations

1. See Corrsin, "Polish-Jewish Relations before the First World War," 35–36; and Shlomo Netzer's comments on the pre-WWI period in his "Polish-Jewish Political Confrontation, 1918–1921," *Shvut* 4 (1996): 130. More generally, see H. H. Ben-Sasson, ed., *A History of the Jewish People* (Cambridge, Mass.: Harvard University Press, 1976), 950, where we read that "despite the unanimity of opinion of Jewish political parties and organizations on this question, the principle of Jewish national autonomy

was nowhere accepted before 1918." The lack of literature on the PPS in English, and the fragmentary treatment of the PPS in studies on the Bund, has led to facile generations. See [Vladimir Kossovsky], *Di geshikhte fun der yiddisher arbeyter bavegung in rusland un poyln* (Geneva: Bund, 1900), 11–12, which characterized the PPS as entirely unresponsive to the needs of the Jewish working masses. Such a view found its way into several studies by professional historians although with harsher language. Nora Levin (*While Messiah Tarried: Jewish Socialist Movements, 1871–1917* [New York: Schocken Books, 1977], 262) wrote of the PPS as "vehemently hostile" to the Bund, while Jacob Shatzky (*Geshikhte fun yidn in varshe* [New York: Yivo, 1953], 3:395) lumped the PPS and SDKPiL together as parties who "denied the existence of a specific Jewish proletariat, nor did they recognize the need for . . . special and systematic agitation among Jewish workers." Recently, Henri Minczeles (*Histoire générale du Bund: Un mouvement révolutionnaire juif* [Paris: Éditions Austral, 1995], 53) argued that the PPS "was simply opposed to Jewish national rights" prior to WWI. Similarly, David Vital (*A People Apart: The Jews in Europe, 1890–1939* [Oxford University Press, 1999], 424–25) maintained that the PPS's "ferocious denunciation" of the Bund in 1897 contained an "unmistakably anti-Semitic touch" while providing the factually inaccurate statement that the PPS was founded in 1897 (the PPS was established in 1892). In the works above, the story of the PPS begins and ends with its opposition to the Bund's formation in 1897. In those Jewish works that have taken serious interest in the PPS, such as those of Moshe Mishkinsky, Asher Zeira, and Jonathan Frankel, references to the PPS stop after 1901. Thus, the reader is left with the impression that the PPS, which had initially opposed the formation of a separate Jewish worker's party, remained unchanged throughout the pre-WWI period. This is particularly pronounced in Zeira's scholarly treatment of the subject, where he concludes, "The organizational problem was a distraction from the main thing that divided [the Bund and PPS]: the national consciousness of the Jewish workers. The PPS denied this national aspect to the Jewish working class . . . and therefore did not see any need for the rise of a separate Jewish worker's movement." See Zeira, "Ben ha-pps ve-habund," 181–82.

2. Tobias, *The Jewish Bund in Russia*, 140. All official membership figures of underground political parties were inflated, probably by a factor of at least one-third.

3. Tomicki, *Polska Partia Socjalistyczna, 1892–1948*, 79.

4. Ascher, *Revolution of 1905*, 1:52–53.

5. Ibid., 53.

6. Governer K. Miller, Łódź, to Warsaw Governor-General, 24 Aug. 1904, reprinted in Gąsiorowska, *Źródła do dziejów rewolucji 1905–1907 w okręgu łódzkim*, vol. 1, bk. 1, 126–27.

7. Wandycz, *Lands of Partitioned Poland, 1795–1918*, 308.

8. Blobaum, *Rewolucja*, 46–47.

9. Regarding overall number of demonstrations, see Żarnowska, *Robotnicy Warszawy na przełomie XIX i XX wieku*, 245, cited in Blobaum, *Rewolucja*, 43. Regarding demonstrations organized by the PPS, see Żarnowska, *Geneza rozłamu w Polskiej Partii Socjalistycznej 1904–1906*, 18–20; Tych, *Rok 1905*, 14; Blobaum, *Rewolucja*, 48.

10. Żarnowska, *Geneza rozłamu*, 20.

11. Cited in Frankel, *Prophecy and Politics*, 158.

12. "Sprawa reprezentacji na międzynarodowym kongresie socjalistycznym w Amsterdamie," *Głos Bundu*, no. 3 (Nov. 1904): 28.

13. Żarnowska, *Geneza rozłamu*, 13, 46; Karwacki, *Łódzka orgnizacja PPS Lewicy, 1906–1918*, 42; Blobaum, *Rewolucja*, 48.

14. For the full text of Father Gapon's petition, see Ascher, *Revolution of 1905*, 1:87–89.

15. Ibid., 91, 94.

16. Lewis, "Labor Movement in Russian Poland," 100–102.

17. Regarding the SDKPiL leaflet, see "Strajk powszechny i rewolucja w Petersburgu!" 10/23 Jan. 1905, SDKPiL; reprinted in Daniszewski, *SDKPiL w rewolucji 1905 roku*, 65–67.

18. Tych, *Rok 1905*, 18.

19. For the text of "Our Political Declaration," see "Nasza deklaracja polityczna," Warszawski Komitet Robotniczy PPS, 28 Jan. 1905; reprinted in Tych, *PPS-Lewica, 1906–1918*, 1:3–4.

20. Karwacki, *Łódzka orgnizacja PPS Lewicy*, 44.

21. Żarnowska, *Geneza rozłamu*, 170.

22. "Nasza deklaracja polityczna," in Tych, *PPS-Lewica, 1906–1918*, 1:3.

23. Karwacki, *Łódzka orgnizacja PPS Lewicy*, 44; Żarnowska, *Geneza rozłamu*, 171.

24. Tobias, *The Jewish Bund in Russia*, 299.

25. Cited in Leslie, *History of Poland since 1863*, 78.

26. Tych, *Rok 1905*, 79.

27. Ascher, *Revolution of 1905*, 1:138.

28. Żarnowska, *Geneza rozłamu*, 172.

29. Ibid., 176.

30. Alicja Pacholczykowa, "Kwiatek, Józef," in *SBDzPPR*, 3:599–600; Alicja Pacholczykowa, "Sachs, Feliks," *PSB* 34, no. 2 (1992): 266.

31. Feliks Tych, *PPS Lewica, 1906–1918*, 1:5. Besides Malinowski and Stanisław Jędrzejewski, who represented the Old faction, Young faction participants included Adam Bujno, Feliks Kon, Szymon Posner, Piotr Szumow, Jan Rutkiewicz, Jan Strożecki, Stefan Królikowski, and Zofia Wortman-Posnerowa. For a full list of participants, see Żarnowska, *Geneza rozłamu*, 178.

32. Wasilewski, "Kierownictwo PPS zaboru rosyjskiego (1893–1918)," 357–58; Żarnowska, *Geneza rozłamu*, 184–85.

33. For the text of the seventh congress resolutions, see "Uchwały VII Zjazdu PPS," reprinted in Tych, *PPS Lewica, 1906–1918*, 1:4–5.

34. Ibid.; Pająk, *Organizacje bojowe partii politycznych w Królestwie Polskim, 1904–1911*, 55–56; Żarnowska, *Geneza rozłamu*, 211

35. "Sprawozdanie 3-ej Konferencyi Żyd. PPS," fol. 18, folder 7, sygn. 305/III/3, AAN. Two of the three Jewish Committee members were imprisoned at the time. Sachs had been in a Vilna jail since July 1904, while Kwiatek had been incarcerated since January 29 in the Warsaw Citadel, where he would remain until November. The Jewish Committee member present at the third conference thus had to be Piotr Szumow, who was active in Warsaw at the time. See Pacholczykowa, "Kwiatek, Józef," in *SBDzPPR*, 3:599–600; Pacholczykowa, "Sachs, Feliks," *PSB* 34, no. 2 (1992): 266; and M. K. [Mojżesz Kaufman], "Piotr Szumow (1872–1936)," *KRRwP* 2, no. 3–4 (July–Dec. 1936): 104–5.

36. AAN, sygn. 305/III/3, folder 7, fol. 18.

37. Ibid., fols. 20–21.

38. Ibid., fols. 22–23.

39. For a list of the June council participants, see Tych, *PPS Lewica, 1906–1918*, 1:10; Pacholczykowa, "Sachs, Feliks," 266.

40. Żarnowska, *Geneza rozłamu*, 214.

41. Tomicki, *Polska Partia Socjalistyczna*, 102–3.

42. "Wnioski i rezolucje przyjęte przez Radę Czerwcową PPS," 15–18 June 1905, reprinted in Tych, *PPS Lewica, 1906–1918*, 1:11–12, 18.

43. Żarnowska, *Geneza rozłamu*, 229–30; Wasilewski, "Kierownictwo PPS zaboru rosyjskiego," 358.

44. Wasilewski, "Kierownictwo PPS zaboru rosyjskiego," 358; Tomicki, *Polska Partia Socjalistyczna*, 104.

45. Wasilewski, "Kierownictwo PPS zaboru rosyjskiego," 358; Żarnowska, *Geneza rozłamu*, 273.

46. Blobaum, *Rewolucja*, 204–5; Żarnowska, *Geneza rozłamu*, 273.

47. Blobaum, *Rewolucja*, 205.

48. Wereszycki, *Historia polityczna Polski*, 216. For a history of the NZR, see Teresa Monasterska, *Narodowy Związek Robotniczy*.

49. Blobaum, *Rewolucja*, 193–94, 106.

50. Ascher, *Revolution of 1905*, 1:213.

51. Lewis, "Labor Movement in Russian Poland," 226, 235.

52. Ibid., 237, 238.

53. Wereszycki, *Historia polityczna Polski*, 219.

54. Lewis, "Labor Movement in Russian Poland," 240–41.

55. Ibid., 262.

56. Medem, *Life and Soul of a Legendary Jewish Socialist*, 348.

57. "Vos toren mir itst nit fargesen?" n.p., Dec. 1904, Central Committee of the Bund, File MG7/20, Bund Archive.

58. Medem, *Life and Soul of a Legendary Jewish Socialist,* 349.

59. J. S. Hertz, "Di ershte ruslender revolutsye," in Hertz, Aronson, and Dubnow-Erlich, *Di geshikhte fun bund,* 2:253.

60. "Fun partey-lebn: der VI tsuzamenfor fun algemaynem yidishn arbeyter bund in lite, poyln un rusland," *Der veker*, no. 1 (3 Jan. 1906/25 Dec. 1905): 4.

61. "Di poyln frage," *Der bund*, no. 11 (1 Dec./18 Nov. 1905): 4.

62. Ibid., 5.

63. Hertz, "Di ershte ruslender revolutsye," 250; *Doyres bundistn* (New York: Unzer Tsayt, 1956), 1:327.

64. Hertz, "Di ershte ruslender revolutsye," 250. The Polish Regional Committee was formed in February 1905 to represent local Bundist divisions in Congress Poland outside Warsaw and Łódź.

65. "Fun partey-lebn," 4.

66. Medem, *Life and Soul of a Legendary Jewish Socialist*, 350–51.

67. "Fun partey-lebn," 4.

68. For examples of Old Guard condemnation, see Al. Wroński [Witold Jodko-Narkiewicz], "Wrogowie konstytuanty warszawskiej," *Nowe Życie*, no. 2 (23 Nov. 1905): 1–2; and Al. Wroński [Jodko-Narkiewicz], "Czy samorząd krajowy jest żądaniem proletaryackiem?" *Nowe Życie*, no. 3 (29 Nov. 1905): 2. For refutation of the national-cultural autonomy argument, see "Zjazd 'Bundu,'" *Nowe Życie,* no. 6 (27 Jan. 1906): 4.

69. [B. Groser], "Autonomja terytorjalna, a autonomja kulturalno-narodowościowa," *Nasze Hasła* 1 (Jan. 1906): 5–6, in the Sejm Library, Warsaw, microfilm division.

70. See Hertz, Aronson, and Dubnow-Erlich, *Di geshikhte fun bund*, 2:342–46.

71. Quoted in Hertz, Aronson, and Dubnow-Erlich *Di geshikhte fun bund,* 2:345–46.

72. Jan Kancewicz, introduction to Henryk Walecki, *Wybór pism*, 1:11.

73. [M. Horwitz], "W sprawie żydowskiej," *Kuryer Codzienny*, no. 2 (6 Dec. 1905): 2–4.

74. [M. Horwitz], "Di batsyung fun der poylisher sotsyalistisher partay tsu der yidisher frage," *Der arbeyter,* no. 12 (15 Dec. 1905): 1–4.

75. [M. Horwitz], "W sprawie żydowskiej," 2.

76. Ibid.

77. Ibid.

78. Ibid. It is important to note here the clear departure from the right wing's view. *Kurjer Codzienny* confined the party's territorial ambition to ethnographic borders.

79. Ibid., 3.

80. Contrary to Piasecki's claim in *Żydowska Organizacja PPS,* 221, that no information is available on the Jewish Section's fourth conference, the conference report was reprinted in *Der arbeyter.* This discussion is based on that reprint.

81. "Di ferte konferents fun di yidishe organizatsyonen fun pps," *Der arbeyter,* no. 18 (16 Mar. 1906): 7. Copies of *Der arbeyter* from 1905 and 1906 are preserved in the microfilm division of the Sejm Library, Warsaw.

82. Tomicki, *Polska Partia Socjalistyczna,* 111; Blobaum, *Rewolucja,* 205–6.

83. Blobaum, *Rewolucja,* 206.

84. Ibid., 206.

85. Wojtasik, *Idea walki zbrojnej o niepodległość Polski, 1864–1907,* 216; Blobaum, *Rewolucja,* 207.

86. For a discussion of the Rogów attack and its political repercussions, see the account by participant J. Kwapiński in his *Pod Rogowem: Ze wspomnień bojowca* (Warsaw, 1922), as well as a secondary study by Adam Próchnik, "Akcja bojowa pod Rogowem," in Próchnik, *Studia z dziejów polskiego ruchu robotniczego,* 408–48.

87. *Sprawozdanie z IX zjazdu PPS.* (Kraków: PPS, 1907), 40–41; Tych, *PPS-Lewica,* 1:145–46.

88. Tomicki, *Polska Partia Socjalistyczna,* 120.

89. "Deklaracja delegatów ustępujących z IX zjazdu Polskiej Partii Socjalistycznej," *Robotnik,* no. 200 (30 Nov. 1906): 1; quoted in Żychowski, *Polska myśl socjalistyczna,* 339. Also see Tomicki, *Polska Partia Socjalistyczna,* 120.

90. "Program Polskiej Partii Socjalistycznej [Frakcji Rewolucyjnej]," reprinted in Tych, *Polskie programy socjalistyczne,* 469–71. For Perl's attitude to the Jewish question, see chapter 10.

91. [PPS Lewica], *Dziesiąty zjazd PPS: program, taktyka, organizacja* (Kraków: Nakł. Myśli Socjalistycznej, 1908), 8. For a reprint of the program with editorial commentary, see Tych, *Polskie programy socjalistyczne,* 474–88.

92. *Sprawozdanie z IX zjazdu PPS,* 8; and Żarnowska, *Geneza rozłamu,* 457.

93. "V Konferencja organizacji żydowskiej," *Robotnik,* no. 194 (20 Oct. 1906): 7; *Sprawozdanie z IX zjazdu PPS,* 7–8; Żarnowska, *Geneza rozłamu,* 460.

94. Anna Żarnowska, "Rewolucja 1905–1907 a kultura polityczna społeczeństwa Królestwa Polskiego," 2.

95. "Der 7-ter tsuzamenfor fun bund," in Hertz, Aronson, and Dubnow-Erlich, *Di geshikhte fun bund,* 2:362–63; Woodhouse and Tobias, "Primordial Ties and Political Process in Pre-Revolutionary Russia," 343.

96. Monasterska, *Narodowy Związek Robotniczy*, 40; Żarnowska, "Rewolucja 1905–1907 a kultura robotników," 25.

97. Tych, *Rok 1905*, 73; Żarnowska, "Rewolucja 1905–1907 a kultura polityczna społeczeństwa Królestwa Polskiego," 2; Lewis, "Labor Movement in Russian Poland," 450; Ascher, *Revolution of 1905*, 1:185.

98. Howard D. Mehlinger and John M. Thompson, *Count Witte and the Tsarist Government in the 1905 Revolution* (Bloomington: Indiana University Press, 1972), 123, cited in Ascher, *Revolution of 1905*, 1:302.

99. Adam B. Ulam, *The Bolsheviks* (New York: Collier Books, 1965), 251; Seton-Watson, *The Russian Empire, 1801–1917*, 620.

100. Seton-Watson, *The Decline of Imperial Russia*, 247–50.

101. Corrsin, "Polish-Jewish Relations before the First World War," 33–34.

102. Tracey L. Trenam, "Polish Liberals and the Jewish Vote: The Duma Elections of 1906" (paper presented at the annual meeting of the America Association for the Advancement of Slavic Studies, Boston, Nov. 1996), 1–2.

103. Stegner, "Na pograniczu dwóch obyczajów politycznych," 75. For a full treatment of the Polish liberal camp in the pre-WWI period, see Stegner, *Liberałowie Królestwa Polskiego 1904–1914*.

104. Stegner, "Na pograniczu dwóch obyczajów politycznych," 76.

105. Corrsin, *Warsaw before the First World War*, 86.

106. Leaflets of the National Democratic Party, "Rodacy!" n.p., 25 Apr. 1906, National Democratic Party, sygn. IJ1e, Biblioteka Narodowa, Zakład Dokumentów Życia Społecznego (henceforth: BN DŻS).

107. "Do żydów polskich," n.p., not later than 25 Apr. 1906, National Democratic Party, sygn. IJ3, BN DŻS.

108. "Rodacy Obywatele Woli!" n.p., 24 Apr. 1906, National Democratic Party, sygn. IJ3, BN DŻS.

109. "Rodacy!" Warsaw, 20 Apr. 1906, National Democratic Party, sygn. IJ1e, BN DŻS.

110. "Baczność, Obywatele—Rodacy! Haniebny podstęp PD-cyi," n.p., no later than 24 Apr. 1906, National Democratic Party, sygn. IJ1e, BN DŻS.

111. "Odpowiedź na odezwę socyalistów," n.p., Mar. 1906, National Democrats, sygn. IB8, BN DŻS.

112. "Proletarjusze wszystkich krajów, łączcię się! Narodowi chuligani przy robocie," 27 Apr. 1906, Łódź Workers' Committee of the PPS, file 7, sygn. 305/III/35, AAN.

113. "Precz z antysemityzmen!" Apr. 1906, Częstochowa Workers' Committee of the PPS, file 3, sygn. 305/III/35, AAN.

114. Corrsin, *Warsaw before the First World War*, 86.

115. *Goniec Poranny* (Warsaw), 18 Feb. 1907, quoted in Corrsin, *Warsaw before the First World War*, 88.

116. Corrsin, *Warsaw before the First World War,* 88.

117. For an examination of the Stolypin-led coup, see Hosking, *Russian Constitutional Experiment,* 14–55.

118. Hertz, "Bund's Nationality Program and Its Critics in the Russian, Polish and Austrian Socialist Movements," 62.

119. Holzer, "Relations between Polish and Jewish Left Wing Groups in Interwar Poland," 141.

### Chapter 9. From Politics to the New Yiddish Culture

1. *Barikht fun der VIII konferents fun bund* (1910), 3–4; Woodhouse and Tobias, "Political Reaction and Revolutionary Careers," 377.

2. The five principal scholarly monographs on the pre-WWI Bund cover the period to 1905. See Mendelsohn, *Class Struggle in the Pale;* Tobias, *The Jewish Bund in Russia;* Mishkinsky, *Reshit tnuat ha-poalim ha-yehudit be-rusya;* Frankel, *Prophecy and Politics;* and Peled, *Class and Ethnicity in the Pale.* Studies in Yiddish are similarly sparse on the period between 1905 and 1918. The Bund's official five-volume history of the party allots 898 pages to the origins and development of the Bund to the 1905 Revolution, and 90 pages to the period 1907–14. See Hertz, Aronson, and Dubnow-Erlich, *Di geshikhte fun bund,* vols. 1–2. Another Yiddish monograph, Bukhbinder's *Di geshikhte fun der yidisher arbeter-bavegung in rusland,* devotes 21 of 432 pages to the period 1907–14. Monographs on the subsequent history of the Bund include Bernard Johnpoll, *The Politics of Futility: The General Jewish Workers Bund of Poland, 1917–1943* (Ithaca: Cornell University Press, 1967), which has been succeeded by the excellent new study by Gertrud Pickhan, *"Gegen den Strom": Der Allgemeine Jüdische Arbeiterbund "Bund" in Polen, 1918–1939* (Stuttgart: Deutsche Verlag-Anstalt, 2001); and Daniel Blatman, *Lemaan herutenu ve-herutkhem* (Jerusalem: Hebrew University Press, 1996), on the Holocaust period.

3. Peled, *Class and Ethnicity in the Pale,* 68, my emphasis. Another historian observed that with the decline of political activity and party membership after 1905, the Bund devoted more time to the theoretical development of its program. See Zvi Y. Gitelman, *Jewish Nationality and Soviet Politics: The Jewish Section of the CPSU, 1917–1930* (Princeton, N.J.: Princeton University Press, 1972), 55.

4. Litvak, *Vos geven,* 285–86.

5. Sophia Dubnow-Erlich, "In di yorn fun reaktsye," in Hertz, Aronson, and Dubnow-Erlich, *Di geshikhte fun bund,* 2:554.

6. Woodhouse and Tobias, "Primordial Ties and Political Process in Pre-Revolutionary Russia," 354.

7. Frankel, *Prophecy and Politics,* 252–54.

8. S. Dubnow, "The Moral of Stormy Days," *Voskhod* (Dec. 1905), reprint-

ed in S. Dubnow, *Nationalism and History: Essays on Old and New Judaism,* ed. Koppel S. Pinson (Philadelphia: Jewish Publication Society of America, 1958), 208–9.

9. On this point, see Frankel, *Prophecy and Politics*, 158.

10. For the text of the Bund's 1901 resolution on Zionism, see P. Mendes-Flohr and J. Reinharz, eds., *The Jew in the Modern World,* 2nd ed. (Oxford: Oxford University Press, 1995), 421.

11. M. M. [Moshe Mishkinsky], "Zionist Socialist Workers' Party," *Encyclopaedia Judaica,* 16, cols. 1179–81.

12. Alexander Guterman, *Ha-miflagah ha-tsionit-sotsialistit be-rusya (ss) ba-shanim 1905–1906* (Tel Aviv: I. L. Peretz, 1985), 102.

13. M. M [Moshe Mishkinsky], "Jewish Socialist Workers' Party," *Encyclopaedia Judaica,* 10, cols. 90–92; David Vital, *A People Apart: The Jews of Europe, 1789–1939* (Oxford: Oxford University Press, 1999), 577 n. 161.

14. Frankel, *Prophecy and Politics*, 154.

15. Ber Borochov, "The Program of Proletarian Zionism (1906)," in Mendes-Flohr and J. Reinharz, *The Jew in the Modern World*, 552–53. Both the Poale Zion and SS parties issued Yiddish-language propaganda brochures against the Bund in 1906. See *Der bund un der poale-tsionizm* (Kraków: Poale Zion, 1906) and the SS's *Bund un s"s* (Vilna: S. S., 1906).

16. See "Helsingfors Conference: *Gegenwartsarbeit* (Dec. 1906)," in Mendes-Flohr and J. Reinharz, *The Jew in the Modern World,* 555–56.

17. For a complete English translation of Dubnow's four "Letters on Old and New Judaism," which outline his theory of autonomism, see Dubnow, *Nationalism and History*, 76–142.

18. S. M. Dubnow, "On the Tasks of the Folkspartey," *Voskhod* (Dec. 1906), in Dubnow, *Nationalism and History*, 224–32; Dubnow, *History of the Jews in Russia and Poland* (Philadelphia: Jewish Publication Society of America, 1920), 3:147. On the Russian *Folkspartay*, also see *Encyclopaedia Judaica* 6, cols. 1411–12.

19. "Di yidishe folks-partey" (1907), reprinted in Menes, *Der yidisher gedank in der nayer tsayt*, 180–82.

20. S. Dubnow, "On the Tasks of the Folkspartey," *Voskhod* (Dec. 1906), in Dubnow, *Nationalism and History*, 229–30.

21. On the status of the Yiddish press and theater in late imperial Russia, see David Fishman, "The Politics of Yiddish in Tsarist Russia," in *Essays in Honor of Marvin Fox*, ed. Jacob Neusner, et. al. (Atlanta: Scholars Press, 1989), 4:155–71.

22. Goldsmith, *Modern Yiddish Culture*, 186; and Joshua A. Fishman, "Attracting a Following to High-Culture Functions for a Language of Everyday Life: The Role of the Tshernovits Language Conference in the 'Rise of Yiddish,'" in *Never Say Die! A Thousand Years of Yiddish in Jewish Life*

*and Letters,* ed. Joshua A. Fishman (New York: Mouton Publishers, 1981), 378.

23. M. Weinreich, ed., *Di ershte yidishe shprakh-konferents* (Vilna: Yivo, 1931), 76, cited in Halevy, *Jewish Schools under Czarism and Communism*, 76.

24. Goldsmith, *Modern Yiddish Culture,* 211, 215–16.

25. *Di ershte yidishe shprakh-konferents,* 83, cited in Goldsmith, *Modern Yiddish Culture,* 195–96.

26. Halevy, *Jewish Schools under Czarism and Communism*, 76.

27. The year 1908 also saw the appearance of the Yiddish literary journal *Literarishe monatshriftn* in Vilna. Edited by Shmuel Niger, a labor Zionist; A. Veiter, a Bundist; and Gorelick, its inaugural issue shunned the term *zhargon* in favor *Yiddish*, which it claimed was now going through a renaissance. See the first issue, pages 1–2.

28. Sixty issues of the Bundist weekly *Di tsayt* appeared in Saint Petersburg in 1913–14.

29. Levin, *Untererdishn kempfer*, 314.

30. Abramovitch, *In tsvey revolutsies*, 1:314.

31. Litvak, *Vos geven*, 244.

32. Medem, *Life and Soul of a Legendary Jewish Socialist*, 440.

33. *Di shtime fun bund*, no. 2 (Sept. 1909): 19, 20.

34. "Der 1-der may," Central Committee of the Bund, May 1908, folder 20, MG7, RG 1400, Bund Archive.

35. *Barikht fun der VIII konferents fun bund,* 19–20.

36. Woodhouse and Tobias, "Political Reaction and Revolutionary Careers," 385.

37. Abramovitch, *In tsvey revolutsies*, 1:317; Litvak, *Vos geven*, 271.

38. Abramovitch, *In tsvey revolutsies*, 1:318.

39. Dubnow-Erlich, "In di yorn fun reaktsye," 2:543.

40. *Fun partey-lebn,* no. 1 (Mar. 1908): 1.

41. *25 yor: zamlbukh* (Warsaw: Di velt, 1922), 118; Dubnow-Erlich, "In di yorn fun reaktsye," 2:543.

42. *Fun partey-lebn,* no. 1 (Mar. 1908); Levin, *Untererdishn kempfer*, 317; Dubnow-Erlich, "In di yorn fun reaktsye," 2:545.

43. Liber's *referat* is summarized in Litvak, *Vos geven*, 281, as well as in Dubnow-Erlich, "In di yorn fun reaktsye," 2:545.

44. Levin, *Untererdishn kempfer*, 317; Dubnow-Erlich, "In di yorn fun reaktsye," 2:546.

45. Dubnow-Erlich, "In di yorn fun reaktsye," 2:545.

46. *Fun partey-lebn,* no. 1 (Mar. 1908): 3.

47. Halevi [A. Litvak], "Vegen unzer arbeyt," *Di shtime fun bund*, no. 1 (Dec. 1908): 4. The identity of the author is confirmed in Litvak, *Vos geven*, 284, and in Dubnow-Erlich, "In di yorn fun reaktsye," 2:546.

48. M. Abr [R. Abramovitch], "Tu der frage 'vegen der arbeyt,'" *Di shtime fun bund,* no. 1 (Dec. 1908): 10.

49. "Tsu ale mitglider un fraynd fun bund in oysland," Foreign Committee of the Bund, Feb. 1909 (Geneva), folder 20, MG7, RG 1400, Bund Archive.

50. Y. Din [I. Aizenshtat], "Tsu der frage vegen unzer arbeyt," *Di shtime fun bund,* no. 2 (Sept. 1909): 8.

51. Tobias, *The Jewish Bund in Russia,* 166–67.

52. Medem, however, went abroad in May 1908 and would not return to Russia until 1912.

53. Litvak, *Vos geven,* 275; Medem, *Life of a Revolutionary Soldier,* 455.

54. Dubnow-Erlich, "In di yorn fun reaktsye," 2:543.

55. Abramovitch, *In tsvey revolutsies,* 1:318, 319–23.

56. For the text of the Russian constitution, known as the Fundamental Laws, see Basil Dmytryshyn, ed. *Imperial Russia: A Source Book, 1700–1917* (New York: Holt, Rinehart & Winston, 1967), 316–24.

57. *Di shtime fun bund,* no. 2 (Sept. 1909): 10.

58. Charny, *Vilne,* 137, 139, 188. I am grateful to Avram Nowersztern of the Hebrew University for bringing this memoir to my attention.

59. Dubnow, *History of the Jews in Russia and Poland,* 3:161.

60. Dovid Myer, "'Yidishe literarishe gezelshaft' in varshe," *Unzer tsayt* 11–12 (Nov.–Dec. 1957): 105.

61. Charny, *Vilne,* 178.

62. Myer, "'Yidishe literarishe gezelshaft' in varshe," 104.

63. Dubnow-Erlich, "In di yorn fun reaktsye," 2:556.

64. Woodhouse and Tobias, "Primordial Ties and Political Process in Pre-Revolutionary Russia," 349.

65. *Nowa Encyklopedia Powszechna* (Warsaw: PWN, 1998), 6:429.

66. Miaso, *Uniwersytet dla Wszystkich,* 33; Andrzej Chwalba, *Historia Polski 1795–1918* (Kraków: Wydawnictwo Literackie, 2000), 377; Tych, *Rok 1905,* 52–53.

67. Miaso, *Uniwersytet dla Wszystkich,* 44.

68. Ibid., 34; P. Libma [Pesach-Libman Hersh], "Der 'universitet far alemen' in varshe," *Di naye tsayt,* no. 2 (1908): 84; *Nowa Encyklopedia Powszechna,* 6:429.

69. Miaso, *Uniwersytet dla Wszystkich,* 34. On Muszkat, see *Doyres bundistn* (New York: Unzer Tsayt, 1956), 3:50–56.

70. On Muszkat's role in establishing the University for All's Yiddish Section, see Miaso, *Uniwersytet dla Wszystkich,* 63.

71. Regarding lecture and course offerings, see P. Libma [Pesach-Libman Hersh], "Der 'universitet far alemen' in varshe," *Di naye tsayt,* no. 2 (1908): 83–84. Regarding noted faculty members, see *Leksikon fun der nayer yidish-*

*er literatur* (New York: Congress for Jewish Culture, 1960), 3:220–26; *Doyres bundistn*, 2:32–40; and *Encyclopaedia Judaica*, 8:393–94.

72. Libma [Pesach-Libman Hersh], "Der 'universitet far alemen' in varshe," 87.

73. Miaso, *Uniwersytet dla Wszystkich*, 63 n. 2.

74. Libma [Pesach-Libman Hersh], "Der 'universitet far alemen' in varshe," 88–89; Kazdan, *Di geshikhte fun yidishn shulvezn in umophengikn poyln*, 19–20; Kazdan, *Fun kheder un "shkoles" biz tsisho*, 176–77; and Dubnow-Erlich, "In di yorn fun reaktsye," 2:557.

75. Dovid M. [Dovid Myer], "Di kulturele tetikeyt in varshe," *Di naye tsayt*, no. 5 (1909): 120–21.

76. Miaso, *Uniwersytet dla Wszystkich*, 63.

77. Dovid M. [Dovid Myer], "Di kulturele tetikeyt in varshe," 118.

78. Miaso, *Uniwersytet dla Wszystkich*, 41.

79. W. Karwacki, *Łódzka organizacja Polskiej Partii Socjalistycznej-Lewicy, 1906–1918*, 140.

80. Dubnow-Erlich, "In di yorn fun reaktsye," 2:557. For biographies of Okun, see *Leksikon fun der nayer yidisher literatur*, 1:156–57; and *Doyres bundistn*, 1:468–70. For Eichner see *Doyres bundist*, 2:163–64; and *Leksikon fun der nayer yidisher literatur*, 1:69.

81. "Berikht fun der yidisher sektsie fun tko far yor 1910," Bund Archive, cited in Hertz, *Di geshikhte fun bund in lodz*, 216.

82. Dubnow-Erlich, "In di yorn fun reaktsye," 2:557; Hertz, *Di geshikhte fun bund in lodz*, 214; *Doyres bundistn*, 2:163–64.

83. Hertz, *Di geshikhte fun bund in lodz*, 209.

84. Isaiah Trunk, *Poyln* (New York: Farlag medem-klub, 1949), 5:211.

85. "Harfe: Muzikalish-dramatishe gezelshaft," in *Lodzer gezelshaftlekhkeyt almanakh* (Łódź: Aygener farlag, 1938), 1:58. I am grateful to Leo Greenbaum of the Yivo Institute for bringing this source to my attention.

86. Litvak, *Vos geven*, 70.

87. "Harfe: Muzikalish-dramatishe gezelshaft," 1:58.

88. *Doyres bundistn*, 1:335–41.

89. Dubnow-Erlich, "In di yorn fun reaktsye," 2:556–57.

90. Litvak, *Vos geven*, 269.

91. Kazdan, *Fun kheder un "shkoles" biz tsisho*, 173.

92. G. Pludermakher, "Di ovent-shul oyfn nomen fun I. L. Peretz," in *Shul-pinkas: finf yor arbet fun tsentraln bildungs-komitet, 1919–1924* (Vilna: Ts. B. K., 1924), 223.

93. In the same year, 1901, evening and Shabbat schools also began operating in Grodno, Gomel, Ekaterinoslav (present-day Dnipropetrovs'k), Koshinev, Kovno, Łódź, Tomsk, Kharkov, Kherson, Ackerman, Kerch,

Mariopol, and Deodosia. See Halevy, *Jewish Schools under Czarism and Communism*, 79.

94. Pludermakher, "Di ovent-shul oyfn nomen fun i. l. peretz," table on page 235; Kazdan, *Fun kheder un "shkoles" biz tsisho*, 173.

95. Schulman, *History of Jewish Education in the Soviet Union*, 22.

96. Blobaum, *Rewolucja*, 181–82.

97. "Dos yidishe shulvezn," in *Algemayne entsiklopedie* (New York: Farlag "undzer epokhe," 1942), 3:385.

98. Pludermakher, "Di ovent-shul oyfn nomen fun i. l. peretz," 228; *Doyres bundistn*, 3:133.

99. See *Doyres bundistn*, 3:131–36; and *Leksikon fun der nayer yidisher literatur*, 7:164–65.

100. "Tsu der bildungs-frage," *Di hofnung* (25 Sept./8 Oct. 1907): 1.

101. Pludermakher, "Di ovent-shul oyfn nomen fun i. l. peretz," 235.

102. Ibid., 226.

103. Between 1907 and 1911, five textbooks were published in Russia for use in secular Yiddish schools: M. Krinski, *Der yidish lehrer* (Warsaw: Bikher-far-ale, 1907 or 1908); Zalman Reisen, *Yudishe gramatik* (Warsaw: Ferlag progres, 1908); M. Birenbaum, *Khrestomatye far dervaksene* (Warsaw, 1907; reprint, 1912); Abraham Reisen, *Yudishe khrestomatye: A leze-bukh far shul un hoyz; gezamelt fun di beste literarishe un visenshaftlikhe kveln, nokh di nayste metodes* (Warsaw: Progres, 1908); and L. H. Yafeh, *Di yudishe shul: A zamlung fun shriftlikhe ibungen tsum erlernen di yudishe orthografye un tsum oyslegen gedanken* (Vilna, 1911).

104. *Leksikon fun der nayer yidisher literatur*, 1:89.

105. Pludermakher, "Di ovent-shul oyfn nomen fun i. l. peretz," 229.

106. M. Olgin, ed., *Dos yidishe vort: A literarishe khrestomatye tsum lezen in di eltere grupen fun abend-shulem in un der heym* (Vilna: B. A. Keltskin, 1913). According to Chaim Kazdan, *Dos yidishe vort* was first published in 1911. See *Doyres bundistn*, 3:133. *Dos yidishe vort* went through at least six editions and was used in Yiddish schools in interwar Poland. A copy of the fourth edition (Vilna, 1919) is preserved in the Yivo library.

107. S. Gilinski, "Tsu der geshikhte fun yidishn shul-vezn in varshe," *Shul un lebn* 1–2 (20 Jan. 1922): 68.

108. Cohn, "The Bund and Its Contribution to Cultural Life in Poland between the Two World Wars," 113.

109. Dovid M. [Dovid Myer], "Di kulturele tetigkeyt in varshe," *Di naye tsayt*, no. 5 (1909): 122.

110. Kazdan, *Fun kheder un "shkoles" biz tsisho*, 178.

111. The main legal periodicals in the year 1908–12 were *Di naye tsayt* (7 issues; Vilna, 1908–9), *Tsayt-fragen* (5 issues; Vilna, Nov. 1909–Sept. 1910);

*Fragen fun lebn* (3 issues; Saint Petersburg, 1911–12); and *Lebens-fragen* (2 issues; Warsaw, 1912). The principal illegal organs were *Di shtime fun bund* (4 issues; 1908–11), *Otkliki Bunda* (5 issues; Geneva, Mar. 1909–Feb. 1911), and *Informatsionnyi listok* (5 issues; Geneva, 1911–13). For these and other titles, see Greenbaum, *Periodical Publications of the Jewish Labour and Revolutionary Movements in Eastern and Southeastern Europe, 1877–1916.*

112. Medem, *Life and Soul of a Legendary Jewish Socialist,* 444.

113. *Di shtime fun bund,* no. 2 (Sept. 1909): 11.

114. M. Beker [Joseph Becker], "Folks-shprakhen un folks-shuln," *Folkstsaytung,* no. 18 (12/25 Mar. 1906): 1–2; *Folkstsaytung,* no. 21 (15/28 Mar. 1906): 1–2; *Folkstsaytung,* no. 24 (19 Mar./1 Apr. 1906): 2; *Folkstsaytung,* no. 27 (22 Mar./4 Apr. 1906): 2.

115. M. Beker [Joseph Becker], "Folks-shprakhen un folks-shuln," *Folkstsaytung,* no. 21 (15/28 Mar. 1906): 1.

116. Cohn, "The Bund and Its Contribution to Cultural Life in Poland between the Two World Wars," 113.

117. *Leksikon fun der nayer yidisher literatur,* 5:312–14.

118. B. B-ski [Boris Levinson], "Di yidishe folks-shul," *Di naye tsayt,* no. 1 (1908): 39.

119. Cited in Gelbard, "Ester frumkin," 61.

120. *Leksikon fun der yidisher literatur, prese un filologye* (Vilna: B. Kletskin, 1924), 1:143–45; and Moshe Mishkinsky, "Ester," in *Encyclopaedia Judaica,* CD-ROM edition.

121. E.-R. [Ester Frumkin], "Vegen natsionaler ertsiung," *Tsayt-fragen,* no. 1 (Nov. 1909): 17, 28–29, 24. The translation of this final passage is taken from Gitelman, *Jewish Nationality and Soviet Politics,* 61.

122. H. Erlich, "Ester frumkin," *Der veker* (27 Dec. 1930), cited in Gitelman, *Jewish Nationality and Soviet Politics,* 62.

123. B. B-ski [Boris Levinson], "Eynige bamerkungen tsum artikel fun e.-r. vegen natsionaler ertsiung," *Tsayt-fragen,* no. 2 (1909), cited in Schulman, *History of Jewish Education in the Soviet Union,* 6.

124. Ibid.

125. Ester, "Glaykhberekhfigung fun shprakhen," *Tsayt-fragen,* nos. 3–4 (1910): 25–47; *Tsayt-fragen,* no. 5 (1910): 1–30.

126. For a summary of Frumkin's study, see Schulman, *History of Jewish Education in the Soviet Union,* 7–11; and Kazdan, *Fun kheder un "shkoles" tsu tsisho,* 284–86.

127. Ester [Ester Frumkin], *Tsu der frage vegen der yidisher folkshul* (Vilna: Di velt, 1910), 29.

128. For a summary of Medem's theory of neutralism, see Koppel S. Pinson, "Arkady Kremer, Vladimir Medem, and the Ideology of the Jewish Bund," in *Emancipation and Counter-Emancipation,* ed. A. Duker et. al. (New York: Ktav, 1974): 298–313; and Peled, *Class and Ethnicity in the Pale,* 58–61.

129. "Di sotsial-demokratie un di natsionale frage," in Medem, *Vladimir medem tsum tsvantsigstn yortsayt*, 189–90.

130. For a concise summary of Medem's position, see Peled, "Concept of National Cultural Autonomy," 225–58.

131. E.-R. [Ester Frumkin], *Di naye tsayt* (1908): 86–87, cited in Goldsmith, *Modern Yiddish Culture*, 216.

132. *Di naye tsayt,* no. 7 (1909): 47, cited in Pinson, "Arkady Kremer, Vladimir Medem, and the Ideology of the Jewish Bund," 302.

133. *Der fraynd* 139 (1910), reprinted in Menes, *Der yidisher gedenk in der nayer tsayt*, 127.

134. V. Medem, "Natsionalizm oder 'neytralizm'," *Tsayt-fragen,* nos. 3–4 (1910): 15–25; reprinted in Medem, *Zikhroynes un artiklen*, 112–34.

135. Medem, *Zikhroynes un artiklen*, 123.

136. Ibid., 113, cited in Pinson, "Arkady Kremer, Vladimir Medem, and the Ideology of the Jewish Bund," 306.

137. It was in fact Bronislav Groser's defense of Medem, in Zeltser [B. Groser], "Tsu di shtrayt-frage," *Tsayt-fragen,* no. 5 (1910): 68–83, that prompted Olgin's reply.

138. Olgin, "Di yidishe shprakh in unzer privat-leven," *Fragen fun lebn,* no. 1 (July 1911): 40, 41, 43.

139. Medem, *Life and Soul of a Legendary Jewish Socialist*, 471.

140. *Barikht fun der VIII konferents fun bund*, 3–4.

141. *25 yor: zamlbukh*, 118; Dubnow-Erlich, "In di yorn fun reaktsye," 2:576.

142. *Barikht fun der VIII konferents fun bund*, 74, 76.

143. Rafes, *Ocherki po istorii Bunda*, cited in Reinharz and Mendes-Flohr, *The Jew in the Modern World*, 421.

144. Ibid.

145. *Przed spisem ludności* (Dec. 1910): 4, file IB53, Zakład Dokumentów Życia Społecznego, Biblioteka Narodowa.

146. *Di shtime fun bund,* no. 3 (1910): 3.

147. *Di shtime fun bund,* no. 4 (Apr. 1911): 4.

148. May Day leaflet, 1912, Central Committee of the Bund, folder 20, RG1400 MG7, Bund Archive.

149. *Otkliki Bunda* 5 (1911), cited in Medem, *Life and Soul of a Legendary Jewish Socialist*, 474 n.

150. Kazdan, *Fun kheder un "shkoles" biz tsisho*, 281. Also see Goldsmith, *Modern Yiddish Culture*, 83; and Schulman, *History of Jewish Education in the Soviet Union*, 12.

151. Woodhouse and Tobias, "Primordial Ties and Political Process in Pre-Revolutionary Russia," 347.

152. V. Kossovsky, "Di teorie fun neytralizm inem likht fun der geshikhte," in Menes, *Der yiddisher gedank in der nayer tsayt*, 123.

## Chapter 10. The PPS and the Jewish Question on the Eve of the First World War

1. See chapter 8, note 1.

2. Although the SDKPiL supported the Bund's right to organizational independence, from 1902, it came out unambiguously against the Bund's national program. See *Przegląd socjaldemokratyczny* 3 (July 1902): 17–18, 23–24. For the SDKPiL's position after 1907, see "W kwestji żydowskiej," *Trybuna* 8 (21 May 1908): 1–3; "Dyskusja," *Młot* 14 (5 Nov. 1910): 5–7; and A. Warski, "W sprawie żydowskiej," *Nasza Sprawa* 4 (4 Mar. 1911): 1–2. For a discussion of Luxemburg's attitude to the Bund and the Jewish question, see Robert S. Wistrich, "Rosa Luxemburg, Leo Jogiches and the Jewish Labour Movement, 1893–1903," in *Jewish History: Essays in Honour of Chimen Abramsky,* ed. A. Rapoport-Albert and S. Zipperstein (London: Peter Halban, 1988): 529–45.

3. Among studies on the PPS Right and PPS Left, the two standard monographs are Kasprzakowa, *Ideologia i polityka PPS-Lewicy w latach 1907–1914,* and Ładyka, *Polska Partia Socjalistyczn (Frakcja Rewolucyjna) w latach 1906–1914.* For more concise discussions of the ideological evolution of the two factions, see Grunberg, *Polskie koncepcje federalistyczne, 1864–1918,* chapters 5–6; Michalski, *Socjalizm a niepodległość w polskiej myśli socjalistycznej, 1878–1918,* chapter 3; and the introductory chapter in Eugeniusz Koko, *W nadziei na zgodę: Polski ruch socjalistyczny wobec kwestii narodowościowej w Polsce, 1918–1939* (Gdańsk: Wydawn. Uniwersytetu Gdańskiego, 1995).

4. "Program Polskiej Partii Socjalistycznej [Frakcji Rewolucyjnej]," reprinted in Tych, *Polskie programy socjalistyczne,* 469–71.

5. J. Piłsudski, *Zadanie praktyczne rewolucji w zaborze rosyjskim* (Kraków, 1910), reprinted in Piłsudski, *Pisma zbiorowe,* 3:5, 14.

6. [PPS Lewica], *Dziesiąty zjazd PPS: Program, taktyka, organizacja* (Kraków: Nakł. Myśli Socjalistycznej, 1908), 8.

7. On the origins and establishment of the ŻPS, see Kuhn, "Jewish Social Democratic Party of Galicia and the Bund," 133–54.

8. Otto Bauer, *The Question of Nationalities and Social Democracy,* ed. Ephraim J. Nimni, trans. Joseph O'Donnell (Minneapolis: University of Minnesota Press, 2000), 281, 117, 283.

9. Ibid., 302, 303.

10. Ibid., 306.

11. Karl Kautsky, "Brif tsum 7nt tsuzamenfor fun 'bund,'" *Folkstsaytung,* no. 159 (13–26 Sept. 1906), cited in Jacobs, *On Socialists and the "Jewish Question" after Marx,* 31–32.

12. The only response in the Bundist press to Bauer was by Shimen Dobin who, at the time, was a member of the SS until his conversion to

Bundism in 1911. See his Simoni [Shimen Dobin], "Otto baur vegen di yuden," *Tsayt-fragen,* no. 1 (1909): 31–41. See *Leksikon fun der yidisher literatur, prese un filologye,* 4:750–56. Also see the note on Dobin in Jacobs, *On Socialists and the "Jewish Question" after Marx,* 231 n 26. Such major Bundist theoreticians as Medem, Kossovsky, and Ester Frumkin remained silent with regard to Bauer's position on the Jewish question, consciously avoiding an open confrontation with a leading west European Marxist. To my knowledge, Medem made no reference to Bauer's position on the Jewish question, instead praising his theories on the general national question. See, for example, Medem's "Di yidn-frage in rusland" (Apr. 1911), reprinted in *Vladimir medem tsum tsvantsigstn yortsayt* (New York: Bellemir Press, 1942), 316. Similarly, in his autobiography (*The Life and Soul of a Revolutionary Jewish Socialist,* 315–16), Medem remarks that he derived great satisfaction from Bauer's *The Question of Nationalities and Social Democracy,* which was "deeper, better, and clearer than mine. Indeed, his is an uncommonly brilliant mind (without question the finest mind in today's socialist movement), but on the essential matter we had found a common ground." The Bundist polemics on secular Yiddish schools in 1908–11 similarly ignored Bauer. It is interesting to note that on the occasion of the fiftieth anniversary of the appearance of Bauer's book, the Bundist periodical *Unzer tsayt* printed a positive appraisal without any mention of Bauer's position on the Jewish question. See Joseph Kisman, "50 yor zint otto bauers 'natsionalitetn-frage,'" *Unzer tsayt* 11–12 (Nov.–Dec. 1957): 67–69.

13. Lenin, "'Cultural-National' Autonomy," *Za Pravdu* 46 (28 Nov. 1913), reprinted in *Lenin on the Jewish Question,* ed. Hyman Lumer (New York: International Publishers, 1974), 91.

14. Otto Bauer, *Zagadnienie narodowości,* ed. Marjan Aleksandrowicz (Warsaw: Społeczeństwo, 1908). It should be noted that while the Polish edition was abridged, the section on the Jews was included in full. See pages 83–94.

15. Res [Feliks Perl], "W sprawie autonomii narodowej żydów," *Przedświt,* no. 11 (Nov. 1908): 441–42, 443, 446.

16. Citation from M. Śliwa, "The Jewish Problem in Polish Socialist Thought," *Polin* 9 (1996): 25.

17. Res [Feliks Perl], "W sprawie autonomii narodowej żydów," 446. Perl here argues against the position taken by Maks Horwitz, a leader of the PPS Left, in both his article in *Kuryer Codzienny,* the PPS's legal daily at the time, and in his booklet *W kwestyi żydowskiej* (Kraków, 1907).

18. Bronislav Groser, "From Pole to Jew," in Lucy Dawidowicz, ed., *The Golden Tradition* (New York: Schocken, 1967), 435; M. M. [Moshe Mishkinsky], "Grosser, Bronislaw," *Encyclopaedia Judaica,* 7:936; Sophia

Dubnow-Erlich, "Bronislav groser," *Doyres bundistn*, 1:319; B. Mikhalevich, *Zikhroynes fun a yidishn sotsialist*, 2:26–32.

19. Michalevich, *Zikhroynes fun a yidishn sotsialist*, 2:26–32.

20. Medem, *Life and Soul of a Legendary Jewish Socialist*, 306–7, 308.

21. Michalevich, *Zikhroynes fun a yidishn sotsialist*, 2:28.

22. Bronislav Groser, "Pro domo sua," *Wiedza* (1910): 240–48, 274–79.

23. For a response to Groser's article, see Tarski [Tadeusz Rechniewski], "Dyskusja w sprawie żydowskiej," *Wiedza* 16 (1910): 481–90.

24. Aldor Shtein [Bronislav Groser], "Shtrayt-fragen: diskusions-shtime iber dem artikel in 'glos' vegen asimilatsye bay yidn," *Der sotsial-demokrat* 47 (24 Nov. 1911): 1–2; continued in *Der sotsial-demokrat* 48 (1 Dec. 1911): 2–4; and in *Der sotsial-demokrat* 49 (8 Dec. 1911): 3–5.

25. Aldor Shtein [Bronislav Groser], "Shtrayt-fragen," *Der sotsial-demokrat* 48 (1 Dec. 1911): 2.

26. Ibid.

27. Aldor Shtein [Bronislav Groser], "Shtrayt-fragen," *Der sotsial-demokrat* 49 (8 Dec. 1911): 3.

28. Res [Feliks Perl], "Na bezdrożach żydowskiego 'renesansu'," *Głos* (6 Dec. 1911): 1; and *Głos* (7 Dec. 1911): 1.

29. *Głos* (7 Dec. 1911): 1.

30. "Uchwały Konferencyi PPS (opozycyi)" (Jan. 1913), folder 3, sygn. 305/III/41, AAN. Perl also discussed his views on the Jewish question in the organ of the PPS Opposition, *Walka*. See "W sprawie żydowskiej," *Walka*, no. 1 (Oct. 1913): 7. During the First World War, Perl never wavered from his assimilationist position. See Res [F. Perl], "O nacjonalizmie żydowskim," *Jedność Robotnicza* 11 (11 Mar. 1917): 1–3.

31. St. Os . . . arz. [Leon Wasilewski], "Pod hasłem 'ghetta,'" *Przedświt*, no. 6 (June 1911): 307, 311.

32. Leon Wasilewski, *Kwestya żydowska na ziemiach dawnej Rzeczypospolitej* (Lwów: Zjednoczenia, 1913), 29, 39–41.

33. Bolesław Limanowski, "Naród, państwo i międzynarodowość," *Krytyka* 1 (1908): 336.

34. W. Bieńkowski, "Gumplowicz, Władysław (1869–1942)," *PSB* (1960–61) 9:155.

35. *Sprawozdanie z X zjazdu Polskiej Partyi Socyalistycznej (I Zjazdu Frakcyi Rewolucyjnej)* (Kraków: Nakł. Józefa Wesołowskiego, 1907), 10. For a response to Gumplowicz, see 27–28.

36. *Przedświt*, no. 12 (Dec. 1908): 519.

37. Władysław Gumplowicz, *Kwestya polska a socyalizm* (Warsaw: Nakł. Wydawn. Dieł Społeczno-politycznych "życie," 1908), 55–56, 60, 60–61.

38. Ibid., 64.

39. Kmicic [M. Bielecki], *Przesądy antysemickie w świetle cyfr i faktów* (Warsaw: Wydawnictwo "Wiedzy," 1909), 73.

40. On the phenomenon of Polish "progressive" anti-Semitism, see Weeks, "Polish Progressive Antisemitism," 1905–1914," 49–68.

41. "Sprawa żydowska a socjalism," *Robotnik,* no. 222 (Aug. 1910): 4.

42. Ibid.

43. Tych, *PPS-Lewica, 1906–1918,* 1:624.

44. "Sprawozdanie z drugiej konferencji partynej" (Oct. 1910), reprinted in Tych, *PPS-Lewica, 1906–1918,* 2:661–62.

45. Seton-Watson, *Decline of Imperial Russia,* 292, 291.

46. *Istroricheskii arkhiv* (1962), 1:178–79, cited in J. N. Westwood, *Endurance and Endeavour: Russian History, 1812–1992,* 4th ed. (Oxford: Oxford University Press, 1993), 181.

47. Abramovitch, "Jewish Socialist Movement in Russia and Poland (1897–1919)," 2:391–92.

48. Corrsin, *Warsaw before the First World War,* 90.

49. See ibid., 89–106; and Blobaum, "Politics of Antisemitism in Fin-de-Siècle Warsaw," 275–306.

50. Hertz, Aronson, and Dubnow-Erlich, *Di geshikhte fun bund,* 2:593.

51. For the text of the PPS-Bund agreement, see "Zawiadomienie o naradzie Delegacji PPS i Bundu w sprawie wspólnej akcji wyborczej w Królestwie Polskim," folder 2, sygn. 305/III/41, AAN.

52. Hertz, Aronson, and Dubnow-Erlich, *Di geshikhte fun bund,* 2:594.

53. See "Do ogółu wyborców w Królestwie Polskim!" Central Committees of the PPS and Bund, Aug. 1912, folder 2, sygn. 305/III/41, AAN; and "Proletarier aller lender fareynigt eykh!," PPS-Bund, Nov. 1912, folder 20, MG7, Bund Archive.

54. Hertz, Aronson, and Dubnow-Erlich, *Di geshikhte fun bund,* 2:597.

55. See Corrsin, *Warsaw before the First World War,* 100–104, and Blobaum, "Politics of Antisemitism in Fin-de-Siècle Warsaw," 294–306.

56. For the PPS's condemnation of the Endecja and its economic boycott campaign, see "'Bojkot' żydów a klasa robotnicza," *Robotnik,* no. 234 (Dec. 1912): 9–10; and "Robotnicy wobec wyboru Jagiełły," *Robotnik,* no. 236 (Apr. 1913): 3–4.

57. Perl wrote two influential studies on French revolutionary thought under the PPS imprint. See Res [Feliks Perl], *Krótka historja Wielkiej Rewolucji Francuskiej* (London: PPS, 1898), which was published in Yiddish as *Di groyse frantsoyzishe revolutsie* (London: PPS, 1905). Also see Res [Feliks Perl], *Rewolucja 1848 we Francji* (Warsaw-Kraków, 1911).

## Conclusion

1. See "Pps vegn der yidisher arbayterbavegung," *Di arbeyter shtimme,* no. 30 (Oct. 1902): 6.

2. Feliks Sachs, Vilna, to the PPS Foreign Committee, London, 7 Aug. 1902, fols. 51–52, folder 1, sygn. 305/VII/34, AAN.

3. M. Luśnia [Kazimierz Kelles-Krauz], "Program narodowościowy socyalnej demokracyi austryackiej a program PPS II," *Przedświt,* no. 8 (Aug. 1903): 340–41.

4. Walicki, "Intellectual Elites and the Vicissitudes of 'Imagined Nation' in Poland," 249.

5. Hertz, "Bund's Nationality Program and Its Critics in the Russian, Polish and Austrian Socialist Movements," 66.

# Bibliography

## Archives

Archiwum Akt Nowych, Warsaw.
Archiwum Główne Akt Dawnych, Warsaw.
Archiwum Polskiej Akademii Nauk (PAN), Warsaw.
Archiwum Słownika Biograficznego Działaczy Polskiego Ruchu Robotniczego, Warsaw.
Biblioteka Narodowa, Warsaw.
The Bund Archives of the Jewish Labor Movement, New York.
Jewish Historical Institute, Warsaw (ŻIH).
Yivo Archives, New York.

## Newspapers

*Der arbeyter* (PPS, London-Vilna-Kraków-Warsaw), 1898–1906.
*Di arbeyter shtimme* (Bund, Vilna), 1897–1905.
*Der bund* (Bund, Minsk-Warsaw), 1904–5.
*Głos Bundu* (Bund, Geneva), 1904.
*Folkstsaytung* (Bund, Vilna), 1906–7.
*Fragen fun lebn* (Bund, Saint Petersburg), 1911–12.
*Fun partey-lebn* (Bund, 1908).
*Głos* (PPSD, Lwów [present-day L'viv]), 1911.
*Di hofnung* (Bund, Vilna), 1907.
*Der kampf* (PPS, Vilna), 1906.
*Kuryer Codzienny* (PPS, Warsaw), 1905.
*Lebens-fragen* (Bund, Warsaw), 1912.
*Łodzianin* (PPS, Łódź), 1900–1906.
*Myśl Socjalistyczna* (PPS Left, Kraków), 1907–8.
*Di naye tsayt* (Bund, Vilna), 1908–9.
*Nowe Życie* (PPS, Warsaw), 1905–6.
*Otkliki Bunda* (Bund, Geneva), 1909–11.
*Poslednia Izviestia*, (Bund, Geneva), 1901–6.
*Di proletarishe velt* (PPS, London), 1902–3.
*Di proletarishe velt* (PPS, Vilna-Warsaw), 1907.
*Przedświt* (PPS, Paris-London-Kraków), 1881–1914.
*Przegląd Socjaldemokratyczny* (SDKPiL, Kraków), 1902–4, 1908–10.
*Robotnik* (PPS, Warsaw), 1894–1914.
*Di shtime fun bund* (Bund, 1908–11).
*Sprawa Robotnicza* (SDKP, Paris), 1893–96.

*Światło* (PPS, London), 1898–1904.
*Tsayt-fragen* (Bund, Vilna), 1909–10.
*Der veker* (Bund, Vilna), 1905–6.
*Walka* (PPS Opposition, Warsaw), 1913–14.
*Wiedza* (PPS Left, Vilna), 1906–10.
*Der yidisher arbeyter* (Bund, Geneva), 1896–1904

## Works Cited

Abramovitch, Raphael. *In tsvey revolutsies: Di geshikhte fun a dor.* Vol. 1. New York: Arbeter ring, 1944.

———. "The Jewish Socialist Movement in Russia and Poland (1897–1919)." In *The Jewish People: Past and Present*, vol. 2, 369–98. New York: Central Yiddish Cultural Organization, 1948.

Agursky, S. *Di sotsyalistishe literatur oyf yidish in 1875–1897.* 2 vols. Minsk: Farlag fun der veysrusisher visnshaft-akademya, 1935.

Antkiewicz, Henry John. "Leon Wasilewski: Polish Patriot and Socialist." Ph.D. diss., Ohio State University, 1976.

Ascher, Abraham. *The Revolution of 1905.* 2 vols. Stanford, Calif.: Stanford University Press, 1988–92.

———. *P. A. Stolypin: The Search for Stability in Late Imperial Russia.* Stanford, Calif.: Stanford University Press, 2001.

Bartoszewski, W., and A. Polonsky, eds. *The Jews in Warsaw: A History.* Oxford: Basil Blackwell, 1991.

Bauer, H., A. Kappeler, and B. Roth, eds. *Die Nationalitäten des Russischen Reiches in der Volkszählung von 1897.* 2 vols. Stuttgart: F. Steiner, 1991.

Berman, L. *In loyf fun yorn: zikhroynes fun a yidishn arbeter.* New York: Unzer Tsayt, 1945.

Bernshtein, Leon. *Ershte shprotsungen (zikhroynes).* Buenos Aires: Farlag yid-bukh, 1956.

Blejwas, Stanislaus. *Realism in Polish Politics: Warsaw Positivism and National Survival in Nineteenth-Century Poland.* Columbus, Ohio: Slavica Publishers, 1984.

Blekhman, Leyb [Abram der Tate]. *Bleter fun mayn yugnt: zikhroynes fun a bundist.* New York: Unzer tsayt, 1959.

Blit, Lucjan. *The Origins of Polish Socialism: The History and Ideas of the First Polish Socialist Party, 1878–1886.* London: Cambridge University Press, 1971.

Blobaum, Robert. *Feliks Dzierżyński and the SDKPiL: A Study of the Origins of Polish Communism.* Boulder, Colo.: East European Monographs, 1984.

———. *Rewolucja: Russian Poland, 1904–1907.* Ithaca, N.Y.: Cornell University Press, 1995.

————. "The Politics of Antisemitism in Fin-de-Siècle Warsaw." *Journal of Modern History* 73 (June 2001): 275–306.

Bloch, Alfred. "Sprawa polska w Polskiej Partii Socjalistycznej w latch 1893–1904." Ph.D. Diss., Warsaw University, 1965.

Brauda, Ruth. "Hashpaat otto bauer al ha-bund." *M'asef* (1985): 77–104.

Bukhbinder, Naum Abramovich. *Di geshikhte fun der yidisher arbeter baveg-ung in rusland.* Vilna, Farlag "tomor," 1931.

Bund. "Di diskusye vegn der natsyonaler frage oyfn V tsuzamenfor fun bund yuni 1903 tsirikh (fun di protokaln fun tsuzamenfor)." *Unzer tsayt* 2 (15 Nov. 1927): 87–96; 3 (20 Dec. 1927): 82–91; 1 (15 Jan. 1928): 83–96.

*Der bund in der revolutsye fun 1905–6 loyt di materyaln fun bundishn arkhiv.* Warsaw: Farlag di velt, 1930.

Cała, Alina. "The Question of the Assimilation of Jews in the Polish Kingdom (1864–1897): An Interpretive Essay." *Polin* 1 (1986): 130–50.

————. *Asymilacja Żydów w Królestwie Polskim, 1864–1897.* Warsaw: Państwowy Instytut Wydawniczy, 1989.

————. "Jewish Socialists in the Kingdom of Poland." *Polin* 9 (1996): 3–13.

Charny, Daniel. *Vilne: memuarn.* Buenos Aires: Tsentral farlag fun poylishe yidn in argentina, 1951.

Cherikover, A. "Di onheybn fun der umlegaler literatur in yidish." *Historishe shriftn* (Vilna) 3 (1939): 577–603.

Chojnowski, Andrzej. "Problem narodowościowy na ziemiach polskich w początkach XX w. oraz w II Rzeczypospolitej." In *Z dziejów drugiej rzeczypospolitej,* edited by Olgierd Terlecki. Kraków: Krajowa Agencja Wydawnicza, 1986.

Cohn, N. "The Bund and Its Contribution to Cultural Life in Poland between the Two World Wars." In *Jewish Politics in Eastern Europe: The Bund at 100,* edited by Jack Jacobs, 112–30. New York: New York University Press, 2001.

Corrsin, Stephen D. "Polish-Jewish Relations before the First World War: The Case of the State Duma Elections in Warsaw." *Gal-Ed* 11 (1989): 31–53.

————. *Warsaw before the First World War: Poles and Jews in the Third City of the Russian Empire, 1880–1914.* Boulder, Colo.: East European Monographs, 1989.

————. "Aspects of Population Change and of Acculturation in Jewish Warsaw at the End of the Nineteenth Century: The Censuses of 1882 and 1897." *Polin* 5 (1990): 212–31.

————. "Literacy Rates and Questions of Language, Faith and Ethnic Identity in Population Censuses in the Partitioned Polish Lands and Interwar Poland (1880s–1930s)." *The Polish Review* 43, no. 2 (1998): 131–60.

Cottam, Kazimiera Janina. *Boleslaw Limanowski (1835–1935).* Boulder, Colo.: East Euroepan Monographs, 1978.

Czyński, Edward. *Etnograficzno-statystyczny zarys liczebności i rozsiedlenia ludności polskiej.* 2nd ed. Revised. Warsaw: Skład gł. w Księgarni E. Wende i Sp., 1909.

Daniszewski, T., ed. *SDKPiL w rewolucji 1905 roku: Zbiór publikacji.* Warsaw: Książka i Wiedza, 1955.

Davies, Norman. *God's Playground: A History of Poland.* Vol. 2. New York: Columbia University Press, 1982.

Davis, Horace B. *Nationalism and Socialism: Marxist and Labor Theories of Nationalism to 1917.* New York: Monthly Review Press, 1967.

Deutch, Lev. "Di ershte poylishe iden-sotsyalisten." *Tsukunft* 9 (Oct. 1916): 858–62.

Dimanshtein, Shimen, ed. *Revoliutsionnoe dvizhenie sredi evreev.* Moscow: Izd-vo Vsesoiuznogo Ob-va Polit. Katorzhan, 1930.

Dubnow, Simon. *History of the Jews of Poland and Russia.* Vol. 3. Philadelphia: Jewish Publication Society of America, 1920.

Dziewanowski, M. K. *The Communist Party of Poland: An Outline History.* Cambridge, Mass.: Harvard University Press, 1959.

Emmons, Terence. *The Formation of Political Parties and the First National Elections in Russia.* Cambridge, Mass.: Harvard University Press, 1983.

Falski, Leon. "Wspomnienia z dwóch lat (1892–1893)." *Z pola walki* (London, 1904): 28–34.

Feldman, Wilhelm. *Dzieje polskiej myśl politycznej, 1864–1914.* Warsaw: Instytut Badania Najnowszej Historji Polski, 1933.

Frankel, Jonathan. *Prophecy and Politics: Socialism, Nationalism, and the Russian Jews, 1862–1917.* Cambridge: Cambridge University Press, 1981.

Garlicki, Andrzej. *Józef Piłsudski, 1867–1935.* Warsaw: Czytelnik, 1988.

Gąsiorowska, Natalia, ed. *Źródła do dziejów rewolucji 1905–1907 w okręgu łódzkim.* 2 vols. Warsaw: Książka i Wiedza, 1957–64.

———. *Źródła do dziejów klasy robotniczej na ziemiach polskich.* 3 vols. Warsaw: Państwowe Wydawn. Naukowe, 1962–69.

Gassenschmidt, Christoph. *Jewish Liberal Politics in Tsarist Russia, 1900–1914: The Modernization of Russian Jewry.* New York: New York University Press, 1995.

Gelbard, Arie. "Ester frumkin: dmut mufla'ah be-toldot tnuat ha-poalim ha-yehudit." *M'asef* (1985): 61–76.

Goldhagen, Erich. "The Ethnic Consciousness of Early Russian Jewish Socialists." *Judaism* 23, no. 4 (fall 1974): 479–96.

Goldsmith, Emanuel S. *Modern Yiddish Culture: The Story of the Yiddish Language Movement.* London: Fairleigh Dickinson University Press, 1976; New York: Fordham University Press, 1997.

Golczewski, Frank. *Polnisch-jüdische Beziehungen 1881–1922: Eine Studie zur Geschichte des Antisemitismus in Osteuropa.* Wiesbaden: Steiner, 1981.

Górski, Piotr. *Socjalistyczno-niepodległościowa idea narodu polskiego, 1908–1914.* Kraków: Drukarnia "Apostrof," 1994.

Gozhanski, Shmuel. "Evreiskoe rabochee dvizhenie nachala 90-kh godov." In *Revoliutsionnoe dvizhenie sredi evreev,* edited by Shimen Dimanshtein, 81–93. Moscow: Izd-vo Vsesoivznogo Ob-va Polit. Katorzhan, 1930.

Greenbaum, Avraham. *The Periodical Publications of the Jewish Labour and Revolutionary Movements in Eastern and Southeastern Europe, 1877–1916.* Jerusalem: Dinur Center, 1998.

———. "The Historiography of the Russian Jewish Labor Movement." In *Proceedings of the Ninth World Congress of Jewish Studies.* Jerusalem: World Congress of Jewish Studies, 1986: 35–38.

Grossmann, Henryk. *Der bundizm in galitsien.* Kraków, 1908.

Grunberg, Karol. *Polskie koncepje federalistyczne, 1864–1918.* Warsaw: Książka i Wiedza, 1971.

Guttermann, Alexander. "Manhigei tnuat ha-poalim ha-polanit me-motsa yehudi: shorashehem, zehutam ve-yahasam le-klal yisrael (Mi-emantsi-patsia ve-hitbolelut le-radikalizm mahapkhani)." *M'asef* (1984): 141–56.

———. *Ha-miflagah ha-tsionit-sotsialistit be-rusya (ss) ba-shanim 1905–1906.* Tel Aviv: I. L. Peretz Publishing House, 1985.

———. "Manhigei tnuat ha-poalim ha-polanit mi-motsa yehudi: Shorashehem, zehutam ve-yahasam le-klal yisrael." *M'asef* (1985): 35–60.

———. "Assimilated Jews as Leaders of the Polish Labour Movement between the Two World Wars." *Gal-Ed* 14 (1995): 49–65.

Halevy, Zvi. *Jewish Schools under Czarism and Communism: The Struggle for Cultural Identity.* New York: Springer, 1976.

Harding, Niel, ed. *Marxism in Russia: Key Documents, 1879–1906.* Cambridge: Cambridge University Press, 1983.

Haustein, Ulrich. *Sozialismus und nationale Frage in Polen.* Cologne: Böhlau, 1969.

Hertz, Jacob. *Di geshikhte fun bund in lodz.* New York: Unzer Tsayt, 1959.

———. "The Bund's Nationality Program and Its Critics in the Russian, Polish and Austrian Socialist Movements." *Yivo Annual of Jewish Social Science* 14 (1969): 53–67.

———. "Di umlegale prese un literatur fun 'bund.'" *Pinkes far der forshung fun der yidisher literatur un prese,* 2:294–321. New York: Alveltlekhn yidishn Kultur-Kongres, 1972.

Hertz, Jacob, G. Aronson, and S. Dubnow-Erlich, eds. *Di geshikhte fun bund.* Vols. 1–2. New York: Unzer Tsayt, 1960–62.

Holzer, Jerzy. *PPS: Szkic dziejów.* Warsaw: Wiedza Powszechna, 1977.

———. "Relations between Polish and Jewish Left Wing Groups in Interwar Poland." In *The Jews in Poland,* edited by C. Abramsky, M. Jachimczyk, and A. Polonsky. New York: Basil Blackwell, 1986.

Hosking, Geoffrey. *The Russian Constitutional Experiment: Government and Duma, 1907–1914.* Cambridge: Cambridge University Press, 1973.

Jacobs, Jack. *On Socialists and the "Jewish Question" after Marx.* New York: New York University Press, 1992.

———."Friedrich Engels and the 'Jewish Question' Reconstructed." *Mega-Studien* 2 (1998): 3–23.

———. "Written Out of History: Bundists in Vienna and the Varieties of Jewish Experience in the Austrian First Republic." In *In Search of Jewish Community: Jewish Identities in Germany and Austria, 1918–1933,* edited by Michael Brenner and Derek J. Penslar, 115–33. Bloomington: Indiana University Press, 1998.

Jędrzejewicz, Wacław. *Piłsudski: A Life for Poland.* New York: Hippocrene Books, 1982.

Kaczyńska, Elżbieta, and Dariusz Drewniak. *Ochrana: Carska policja polityczna.* Warsaw: Gryf, 1993.

Kalabiński, Stanisław, and Feliks Tych. *Czwarte powstanie czy pierwsza rewolucja: Lata 1905–1907 na ziemiach polskich.* Warsaw: Wiedza Powszechna, 1969.

Kancewicz, Jan. "Zjazd Paryski socjalistów polskich (17–23 XI 1892): Jego geneza, przebieg i znaczenie." *Z pola walki* 4 (1962): 3–34.

———. "Działalność wydawnicza PPS w kraju w latach 1894–1896." In *Naród i państwo,* edited by Maria Zych. Warsaw: PWN, 1969.

———. "Związek zagraniczny socjalistów polskich 1893–1896: Działalność wydawnicza, transport i kolportaż." In *Studia z dziejów polskiego ruchu robotniczego,* edited by Ewa Szulc, vol. 2. Warsaw: Wydaw. Uniwersytetu Warszawskiego, 1983.

———. *Polska Partia Socjalistyczna w latach 1892–1896.* Warsaw: Państwowe Wydawn. Naukowe, 1984.

———. "Bund a rosyjski i polski ruch robotniczy (do 1914 r.)." In *Bund: 100 lat historii, 1897–1997.* Warsaw: Oficyna Wydawnicza, 2000.

Karwacki, Władysław Lech. *Łódzka orgnizacja Polskiej Partii Socjalistycznej-Lewicy 1906–1918.* Łódź: Wydawn. Łódzkie, 1964.

———. *Łódz w latach rewolucji 1905–1907.* Łódź: Wydawn. Łódzkie, 1975.

Kasprzakowa, Janina. *Ideologia i polityka PPS-Lewicy w latach 1907–1914.* Warsaw: Książka i Wiedza, 1965.

Katz-Blum, Hillel. *Zikhroynes fun a bundist.* New York: Arbeter ring, 1940.

Kaufman, Mojżesz. "Przyczynki do historji Żydowskiej Organizacji PPS." *Niepodległość* 12, no. 1 (1935): 22–52.

———. "Początki roboty żydowskiej PPS." *Niepodległość* 7, no. 3 (1933): 335–50.

Kazdan, S. *Di geshikhte fun yidishn shulvezn in umophengikn poyln.* Mexico City: Kultur un hilf, 1947.

———. *Fun kheder un "shkoles" biz tsisho*. Mexico City: Kultur un hilf, 1956.

Keep, John. *The Rise of Social Democracy in Russia*. Oxford: Clarendon, 1963.

Kelles-Krauz, Kazimierz. *Listy*. Edited by Feliks Tych. 2 vols. Wrocław: Zakład Narodowy im. Ossolińskich, 1984.

Kempinski, Hillel. "Yiddish Brochures of the Polish Socialist Party (PPS)." *Bulletin of the Bund Archives* 20 (Feb. 1965): 2–3.

Kiel, Mark. "The Jewish Narodnik." *Judaism* 19, no. 3 (summer 1970): 295–310.

Kieniewicz, Stefan. *The Emancipation of the Polish Peasantry*. Chicago: University of Chicago Press, 1969.

———. *Historia Polski, 1795–1918*. Warsaw: Państwowe Wydawn. Naukowe, 1983.

Kirzhnits, A. *Di yidishe prese in der gevezener ruslendisher imperie, 1823–1916*. Moscow-Kharkov-Minsk: Tsentraler felker-farlag fun fssr, 1930.

Kirzhnits, A., ed. *Der yidisher arbeter*. 2 vols. Moscow: Tsentraler farlag far di felker fun fssr, 1925.

Kopelzon, Tsemakh. "Di ershte shprotsungen: zikhroynes fun di yorn 1887–1890." *Arbeter-luekh* (Warsaw) 3 (1922): 49–70.

———. "Evreiskoe rabochee dvizhenie kontsa 80-kh i nachala 90-kh godov." In *Revoliutsionnoe dvizhenie sredi evreev*, edited by Shimen Dimanshtein: 65–80. Moscow: Izd-vo Vsesoivznogo Ob-va Polit. Katorzhan, 1930.

Kormanowa, Zanna. *Materiały do bibliografii druków socjalistycznych na ziemach polskich w latach 1866–1918*. 2nd ed. Warsaw: Książka i Wiedza, 1949.

Kremer, Arkadi. "Mit 35 yor tsurik." *Unzer tsayt* 2 (Feb. 1928): 83–87.

Kremer, Pati. "Zikhroynes vegen arkadi." In *Arkadi: zamlbukh tsum ondenk fun grinder fun "bund" arkadi kremer*, 22–72. New York: Unzer tsayt, 1942.

Król, Michał. "Żydowska Organizacja Polskiej Partii Socjalistycznej (1893–1903)." In *Żydzi-bojownicy o niepodległość Polski*, edited by N. Getter, J. Schall, and I. Schipper, 22–31. Lwów: Lwowski Instytut Wydawn, 1939.

———. "Żydowscy działacze w P.P.S. i 'Seckja Żydowska': ze wspomnień." In *Księga pamiątkowa ku czci Żydów bojowników sprawy polskiej, 1905–1918*, 22–31. Warsaw: Związek Żydów Uczestników Walk o Niepodległość Polski, 1936.

Krzesławski, Jan. "Dzieje PPS od 1904 roku do wybuchu wojny światowej w roku 1914." In *Księga jubileuszowa Polskiej Partji Socjalistycznej, 1892–1932*. Warsaw: Nakł. Spółki nakładowo-wydawniczej "Robotnik," 1933.

———. "Żydzi w polskim ruchu socjalistyczno-niepodległościowym." In *Żydzi bojownicy o niepodległość Polski*, edited by N. Getter, J. Schallond, and Z. Schipper, 32–34. Lwów: Lwowski Instytut Wydawn, 1939.

Kuhn, Rick. "The Jewish Social Democratic Party of Galicia and the Bund." In *Jewish Politics in Eastern Europe: The Bund at 100,* edited by Jack Jacobs, 133–54. New York: New York University Press, 2001.

Kula, Witold. *Historia gospodarcza Polski w dobie popowstaniowej, 1864–1918.* Warsaw: Spółdzielnia wydawnicza "Wiedza," 1947.

Kursky, Frants. *Gezamelte shriftn.* New York: Farlag der veker, 1952.

Ładyka, Teodor. *Polska Partia Socjalistyczna (Frakcja Rewolucyjna) w latach 1906–1914.* Warsaw: Książka i Wiedza, 1972.

Leslie, R. F., ed. *The History of Poland since 1863.* Cambridge: Cambridge University Press, 1980.

Lestschinsky, Jacob. *Dos yidishe folk in tsiferen.* Berlin: Klal farlag, 1922.

Levin, Sholem. *Untererdishe kemfer.* Edited by Moyshe Katz. New York: Sholem levin bukh komitet, 1946.

Lewis, Richard D. "The Labor Movement in Russian Poland in the Revolution of 1905–1907." Ph.D. diss., University of California, Berkeley, 1971.

Liesen, A. "Di ershte geheyme farzamlung in vilne." In *Vilne,* edited by Ephim H. Jeshurin, 127–34. New York: Workmen's Circle, 1935.

Limanowski, Bolesław. "Z moich wspomnień o narodzinach PPS." In *Księga pamiątkowa PPS w trzydziestą rocznicę.* Warsaw: Nakł. Spółki nakładowo-wydawniczej "Robotnik," 1923.

———. *Pamiętniki.* Vol. 2. Warsaw: Książka i Wiedza, 1958.

Litvak, A. *Vos geven: etiuden un zikhroynes.* Vilna: Vilner farlag fun b. kletskin, 1925.

Malinowski, Aleksander, ed. *Materiały do historyi PPS i ruchu rewolucyjnego w zaborze rosyjskim od r. 1893 do 1904.* 2 vols. Warsaw, 1907–11.

Marten-Finnis, Suzanne. "Bundist Journalism, 1897–1907." *East European Jewish Affairs* 30, no. 1 (2000): 39–59.

———. "The Bundist Press: A Study of Political Change and the Persistence of Anachronistic Language during the Russian Period." In *Jewish Politics in Eastern Europe: The Bund at 100,* edited by Jack Jacobs, 13–27. New York: New York University Press, 2001.

Martov, L. "Razvitie krupnoy promivlennosti i rabochi dvizhenie do 1892 g." In *Istoriia Rossii v XIX vieke.* Vol. 6. Saint Petersburg: A. I. Grant, 1909.

———. *Zapiski sotsial-demokrata.* Berlin: Izd-vo Z. I. Grzebina, 1922.

*Materialy k istorii evreiskago rabochego dvizheniia.* Saint Petersburg: Tribuna, 1906.

Mazowiecki, Mieczysław [Ludwik Kulczycki]. *Historya ruchu socyalistycznego w zaborze rosyjskim.* Kraków: Wydawnictwo "Proletaryatu," 1904.

Medem, Vladimir. *Zikhroynes un artiklen.* Warsaw: Farlag "yiddish,"' 1918.

———. *Vladimir Medem: Tsum tsvantsikn yortsayt.* New York: Amerikaner reprezentants fun algemaynem yidisher arbeyter bund in polyn, 1943.

————. *The Life and Soul of a Legendary Jewish Socialist.* Translated by S. Portnoy. New York: Ktav, 1978.

Mendel, Hersh. *Memoirs of a Jewish Revolutionary.* Winchester, Mass.: Unwin Hyman, 1989.

Mendelsohn, Ezra. "The Russian Jewish Labor Movement and Others." *Yivo Annual of Jewish Social Science* 16 (1969): 87–98.

————. *Class Struggle in the Pale: The Formative Years of the Jewish Workers' Movement in Tsarist Russia.* Cambridge: Cambridge University Press, 1970.

————. "A Note on Jewish Assimilation in the Polish Lands." In *Jewish Assimilation in Modern Times,* edited by Bela Vago. Boulder, Colo.: Westview Press, 1981.

Menes, A. "Di yidishe arbeter-bavegung in rusland fun onheyb 70-er bizn sof 90-er yorn." *Historishe shriftn* (Vilna) 3 (1939): 35–59.

————. "Di groyse tsayt." In *Arkadi: zamlbukh tsum ondenk fun grinder fun "bund" arkadi kremer,* 1–21. New York: Unzer tsayt, 1942.

Menes, Abraham, ed. *Der yidisher gedank in der nayer tsayt.* New York: Congress of Jewish Culture, 1957.

Miaso, Józef. *Uniwersytet dla Wszystkich.* Warsaw: Państwowe Zakłady Wydawnictw Szkolnych, 1960.

Michalski, Ryszard. *Socjalizm a Niepodległość w Polskiej Myśli Socjalistycznej (1878–1918).* Toruń: Uniwersytet Mikołaja Kopernika, 1988.

Mikhalevich, Beynish. *Zikhroynes fun a yidishn sotsialist.* 3 vols. Warsaw: Di velt, 1921–23.

Mill, John. "Di natsyonale frage un der 'bund.'" *Di tsukunft* 2 (Jan. 1918): 117–20.

————. "Der ershte tsuzamenfor fun 'bund.'" In *25 yor: zamlbukh.* Warsaw: Di velt, 1922.

————. "Di pionern epokhe fun der yidisher arbeter bavegung." *Historishe shriftn* (Vilna) 3 (1939): 369–93.

————. "Arkadi un der ershter tsuzamenfor." In *Arkadi: zamlbukh tsum ondenk fun grinder fun "bund" arkadi kremer.* New York: Unzer tsayt, 1942.

————. *Pionern un boyer: memuarn.* 2 vols. New York: Der veker, 1946–49.

Minczeles, Henri. *Histoire générale du Bund: Un mouvement révolutionnaire juif.* Paris: Éditions Austral, 1995.

Mishkinsky, Moshe. "Yesodot leumiyim be-hithavuta shel tnuat ha-poalim ha-yehudit be-rusya (me-reshita ve-ad 1901)." Ph.D. diss., Hebrew University of Jerusalem, 1965.

————. "Regional Factors in the Formation of the Jewish Labor Movement in Czarist Russia." *Yivo Annual of Jewish Social Science* 14 (1969): 27–52.

————. "Tnuat ha-poalim ha-yehudit be rusya ve-hatnuah ha-sotsyalistit ha-polanit." *Asupot* 1, no. 14 (1970): 81–131.

———. "The Jewish Labor Movement and European Socialism." In *Jewish Society through the Ages,* edited by H. H. Ben-Sasson and S. Ettinger. New York: Schocken Books, 1971.

———. "Al hug sotsialisti yehudi be-varsha be-shnat 1893–1894." *Gal-Ed* 11 (1975): 333–39.

———. *Reshit tnuat ha-poalim ha-yehudit be-rusya.* Tel Aviv: Ha-kibuts ha-me'uhad, 1981.

———. "A Turning Point in the History of Polish Socialism and Its Attitude towards the Jewish Question." *Polin* 1 (1986): 111–29.

———. "Polish Socialism and the Jewish Question on the Eve of the Establishment of the Polish Socialist Party and the Social Democracy of the Kingdom of Poland." *Polin* 5 (1990): 250–72.

Monasterska, Teresa. *Narodowy Związek Robotniczy, 1905–1920.* Warsaw: Państwowe Wydawn. Naukowe, 1973.

Naimark, Norman. *The History of the "Proletariat": The Emergence of Marxism in the Kingdom of Poland.* Boulder: East European Monographs, 1979.

———. *Terrorists and Social Democrats: The Russian Revolutionary Movement under Alexander III.* Cambridge, Mass.: Harvard University Press, 1983.

Nettl, J. P. *Rosa Luxemburg.* 2 vols. Oxford: Oxford University Press, 1966.

Pająk, Jerzy. *Organizacje bojowe partii politycznych w Królestwie Polskim 1904–1911.* Warsaw: Książka i Wiedza, 1985.

Pawlowski, Ignacy. *Geneza i działalność organizacji spiskowo-bojowej PPS, 1904–1905.* Wrocław: Zakład Narodowy im. Ossolińskich, 1976.

Peled, Yoav. *Class and Ethnicity in the Pale: The Political Economy of Jewish Workers' Nationalism in Late Imperial Russia.* New York: St. Martin's Press, 1989.

———. "The Concept of National Cultural Autonomy: The First One Hundred Years." In *Jewish Politics in Eastern Europe: The Bund at 100,* edited by Jack Jacobs, 255–70. New York: New York University Press, 2001.

Perl, Feliks. "Szkic dziejów PPS." In *Księga pamiątkowa PPS w trzydziestą rocznicę.* Warsaw: Nakł. Spółki nakładowo-wydawniczej "Robotnik," 1923.

———. [Res]. *Dzieje ruchu socjalistycznego w zaborze rosyjskim.* Warsaw: Życie, 1910.

———. [F. P.]. "Wspomnienia ze zjazdu paryskiego." *Jedność Robotnicza* (Warsaw) 26 (10 Dec 1916): 2–3.

Peskin, Jacob. "Di 'grupe yidishe sotsyial-demokratn in rusland' un arkadi kremer." *Historishe shriftn* (Vilna) 3 (1939): 544–56.

Piasecki, Henryk. "Feliks Perl—Historyk i działacz PPS." *BŻIH* 92 (1974): 59–70.

———. "Żydowska Organizacja PPS (1893–1907)." *BŻIH* 96 (1975): 37–66.

———. *Żydowska Organizacja PPS, 1893–1907*. Wrocław: Zakład Narodowy im. Ossolińskich, 1978.

Piłsudska, Aleksandra. *Memoirs*. London: Hust & Blackett, 1940.

Piłsudski, Józef. *Pisma-Mowy-Rozkazy: Wydanie zbiorowe prac dotychczas drukiem ogłoszonych*. Warsaw: Instytut Badania Najnowszej Historji Polski, 1930.

———. "Listy Józefa Piłsudskiego." Edited by L. Wasilewski and W. Pobóg-Malinowski. *Niepodległość* 12–20 (1935–39).

———. *Pisma zbiorowe*. 10 vols. Warsaw: Instytut Józefa Piłsudskiego, 1937–38.

———. *Joseph Piłsudski: The Memoires of a Polish Revolutionary and Soldier*. New York: AMS Press, 1977.

———. "Listy Józefa Piłsudskiego z okresu jego pracy w PPS." Edited by Wacław Jędrzejewski. *Niepodległość* 11–19 (1978–86).

———. *Pisma zbiorowe: Uzupełnienia*. Edited by Andrzej Garlicki and Ryszard Świętek. 2 vols. Warsaw: Krajowa Agencja Wydawnicza, 1992–93.

Poznanski, Ch. L. *Memuarn fun a bundist*. Warsaw: Druk "Grafia," 1938.

Piltz, Erasmus, ed. *Poland: Her People, History, Industries, Finance, Science, Literature, Art and Social Development*. London: H. Jenkins, 1909.

Pinson, Koppel S. "Arkadi Kremer, Vladimir Medem and the Ideology of the Jewish Bund." *Jewish Social Studies* 7 (1945): 233–64.

Pobóg-Malinowski. W. *Józef Piłsudski, 1864–1901: W podziemiach konspiracji*. Warsaw: Gebethner i Wolff, 1935.

———. *Józef Piłsudski, 1901–1908: W ogniu rewolucji*. Warsaw: Gebethner i Wolff, 1935.

———. *Najnowsza historia polityczna Polski, 1864–1945*. Vol. 1, *1864–1919*. Paris, 1953.

Próchnik, Adam. *Bunt łódzki w roku 1892*. Łódź: Nakł. Magistratu m. Łódzi, 1932.

———, ed. *Studia z dziejów polskiego ruchu robotniczego*. Warsaw: Książka i Wiedza, 1958.

"Proklamatsyes in yidish erev 'bund.'" *Historishe shriftn* (Vilna) 3 (1939): 750–56.

Rafes, Moyshe. *Ocherki po istorii Bunda*. Moscow: Moskovskii rabochii, 1923.

Rappaport, Herman, ed. *Narastanie rewolucji w Królestwie Polskim w latach 1900–1904*. Warsaw: Państwowe Wydawnictwo Naukowe, 1960.

*Recueil de matériaux sur la situation économique des Israélites de Russie, d'apres l'enquête de la Jewish Colonization Association*. 2 vols. Paris: Librairies Félix Alcan et Guillaumin Réunies, 1906–8.

Rieber, Alfred J. "Struggle over the Borderlands." In *The Legacy of History in Russia and the New States of Eurasia*, edited by S. Frederick Starr, 61–89. Armonk, N.Y.: M. S. Sharpe, 1994.

Römer, Michał. *Litwa: Studyum o odrodzieniu narodu litewskiego.* Lwów: Polskie Towarzystwo Nakładowe, 1908.

Sabaliunas, Leonas. "Social Democracy in Tsarist Lithuania, 1893–1904." *Slavic Review* 31, no. 2 (June 1972): 323–42.

———. *Lithuanian Social Democracy in Historical Perspective, 1893–1914.* Durham, N.C.: Duke University Press, 1990.

Samuś, Paweł. *Dzieje SDKPiL w Łódzi, 1893–1918.* Łódź: Wydawn. Łódzkie, 1984.

Samuś, Paweł, ed. *"Bunt łódzkie" 1892 roku: Studia z dziejów wielkiego konfliktu społecznego.* Łódź: Wydawnictwo Uniwersytetu Łódzkiego, 1993.

Schulman, E. *A History of Jewish Education in the Soviet Union.* New York: Ktav, 1971.

Seton-Watson, Hugh. *The Decline of Imperial Russia.* New York: Frederick A. Praeger, 1952.

———. *The Russian Empire, 1801–1917.* Oxford: Oxford University Press, 1967; Oxford: Clarendon, 1988.

Shatsky, Jacob. "Di yidn in poyln fun 1772 biz 1914." In *Di yidn in poyln fun di eltster tsayt biz der tsveyter velt milkhome,* 405–732. New York: Unzer tsayt, 1946.

———. *Geshikhte fun yidn in varshe.* Vol. 3. New York: Yivo Institute, 1953.

Shukman, H. "The Relations between the Jewish Bund and the RSDRP, 1897–1903." Ph.D. diss., Oxford University, 1961.

Shvarts, P. "Yuzef pilsudski, yiden un di yiden-frage." *Tsukunft* 6 (June 1935): 353–55.

———. "Pilsudski in milkhome mitn 'bund'." *Tsukunft* 11 (Nov. 1935): 663–66.

———. *Yuzef pilsudski: zayn batsyung tsu der yidn-frage un zayn kamf kegn Bund (1893–1905).* Warsaw, 1936.

———. "Di ershte yidishe oysgabes fun der pps." *Historishe shriftn* (Vilna) 3 (1939): 527–39.

Singer, Bernard. *Moje Nalewki.* Warsaw: Czytelnik, 1959.

Śliwa, Michał. *Feliks Perl.* Warsaw: Książka i Wiedza, 1988.

———. "Zagadnienie państwa w myśli politycznej Polskiej Partii Socjalistycznej." In *Państwo w polskiej myśli politycznej,* edited by W. Wrzesiński. Wrocław: Zakład Narodowy im. Ossslińskich, 1988.

———. "Kwestia żydowska w polskiej myśli socjalistycznej." In *Żydzi w Małopolsce.* Przemyśl: Południowo-Wschodni Instytut Naukowy w Prezemyślu, 1991.

Snyder, Timothy. *Nationalism, Marxism, and Modern Central Europe: A Biography of Kazimierz Kelles-Krauz.* Cambridge, Mass.: Distributed by Harvard University Press for the Ukrainian Research Institute, 1997.

Sobelman, Michael. "Polish Socialism and Jewish Nationality: The Views of Kazimierz Kelles-Krauz." *Soviet Jewish Affairs* 20, no. 1 (spring 1990): 47–55.

Stegner, Tadeusz. *Liberałowie Królestwa Polskiego 1904–1914.* Gdańsk, 1990.

———. "Na pograniczu dwóch obyczajów politycznych: Liberałowie Królestwa Polskiego wobec rewolucji 1905–1907." In *Społeczeństwo i polityka: Kultura polityczna w Królestwie Polskim na początku XX wieku,* edited by Anna Żarnowska and Tadeusz Wolsza. Warsaw: Wydawnictwo DiG, 1993.

Strożecki, Jan. "Wspomnienia Jana Strożeckiego (1887–1906)." *Archiwum ruchu robotniczego* (Warsaw) 4 (1977): 37–134.

Szmidt, B., ed. *Socjaldemokracja Królestwa Polskiego i Litwy: Materialy i dokumenty 1893–1904.* Moscow: Towarzystwo Wydawnicze Robotników Zagranicznych w ZSRR, 1934.

Szporluk, Roman. "Poland." In *Crises of Political Development in Europe and the United States,* edited by Raymond Grew. Princeton, N.J.: Princeton University Press, 1978.

———. *Communism and Nationalism: Karl Marx versus Friedrich List.* Oxford: Oxford University Press, 1988.

———. "Poland and the Rise of the Theory and Practice of Modern Nationality, 1770–1880." *Dialectics and Humanism* 17 (1990): 48–63.

———. "Polish-Ukrainian Relations in 1918: Notes for Discussion." In *The Reconstruction of Poland,* edited by Paul Latawski, 41–54. New York: St. Martin's Press, 1992.

———. "Ukraine: From an Imperial Periphery to a Sovereign State." *Daedalus* (summer 1997): 85–119.

Tobias, Henry. "The Bund and Lenin until 1903." *The Russian Review* 20, no. 4 (1961): 344–57.

———. *The Jewish Bund in Russia from Its Origins to 1905.* Stanford, Calif.: Stanford University Press, 1972.

Tomicki, Jan. *Polska Partia Socjalistyczna, 1892–1948.* Warsaw: Książka i Wiedza, 1983.

Trenam, Tracey L. "Polish Liberals and the Jewish Vote: The Duma Elections of 1906." Paper presented at the annual meeting of the America Association for the Advancement of Slavic Studies, Boston, November 1996.

Tych, Feliks. *Związek Robotników Polskich, 1889–1892: Anatomia wczesnej organizacji robotniczej.* Warsaw: Książka i Wiedza, 1974.

———. *Rok 1905.* Kraków: Krajowa Agencja Wydawnicza, 1990.

Tych, Feliks, ed. *PPS-Lewica, 1906–1918: Materiały i dokumenty.* 2 vols. Warsaw: Książka i Wiedza, 1961.

———. *SDKPiL: Materiały i dokumenty.* 3 vols. Warsaw: Książka i Wiedza, 1962.

————. *Polskie programy socjalistyczne, 1878–1918.* Warsaw: Książka i Wiedza, 1975.

Venturi, Franco. *Roots of Revolution: A History of the Populist and Socialist Movements in Nineteenth Century Russia,* translated by Francis Haskell. New York: Grosset & Dunlap, 1966.

Wajner, Monachim. "Do historji PPS na Litwie (wspomnienia o żydowskiej organizacji PPS w Grodnie)." *Niepodległość* 9 (Jan.–June 1934): 221–35.

Waldenberg, Mark. "Z problematyki narodu w polskiej myśli socjalistycznej okresu zaborów." In *Idee i koncepcje narodu w polskiej myśli politycznej czasów porozbiorowych,* edited by Janusz Goćkowski and Andrzej Walicki. Warsaw: Państwowe Wydawn. Naukowe, 1977.

Walecki, Henryk [M. Horwitz]. *Wybór pism.* 2 vols. Edited by Jan Kancewicz. Warsaw: Książka i Wiedza, 1967.

Walicki, Andrzej. *Philosophy and Romantic Nationalism: The Case of Poland.* Oxford: Clarendon Press, 1982.

————. *The Controversy over Capitalism: Studies in the Social Philosophy of the Russian Populists.* Oxford: Clarendon, 1969; Notre Dame, Ind.: University of Notre Dame, 1989.

————. *Poland Between East and West: The Controversies over Self-Definition and Modernization in Partitioned Poland.* Cambridge, Mass.: Distributed by Harvard University Press for the Ukrainian Research Institute, 1994.

————. "Intellectual Elites and the Vicissitudes of 'Imagined Nation' in Poland." *East European Politics and Society* 11, no. 2 (spring 1997): 227–53.

Wandycz, Piotr. *The Lands of Partitioned Poland, 1795–1918.* Seattle: University of Washington Press, 1974.

Wapiński, Roman. *Pokolenia Drugiej Rzeczypospolitej.* Wrocław: Zakład Narodowy im. Ossolińskich, 1991.

————. *Polska i małe ojczyzny Polaków: Z dziejów kształtowania się świadomości narodowej w XIX i XX wieku.* Wrocław: Zakład Narodowy im. Ossolińskich, 1994.

Wasilewski, Leon. "Z roboty zagranicznej PPS." *Księga pamiątkowa PPS w trzydziestą rocznicę* (Warsaw, 1923): 164–83.

————. "Polska emigracja londyńska na przełomie XIX i XX stulecia." *Niepodległość* 1 (1929–30): 236–61.

————. *Zarys dziejów Polskiej Partii Socjalistycznej.* Warsaw: Nowe Życie, 1925.

————. "Polska Partja Socjalistyczna w pierwszym okresie jej rozwoju (1892–1903)." In *Księga jubileuszowa Polskiej Partji Socjalistycznej, 1892–1932,* 28–61. Warsaw: Spółki nakładowo-wydawniczej "Robotnik," 1933.

————. "Walka o postulat niepodległości w polskim obozie socjalistycznym." *Niepodległość* 10 (1934): 1–20.

————. *Józef Piłsudski jakim go znałem.* Warsaw: Towarzystwo Wydawnicze "Rój," 1935.

————. "Kierownictwo PPS zaboru rosyjskiego (1893–1918)." *Niepodległość* 11 (1935): 351–63.

————. "Ze wspomnień." *Z pola walki* 2–3 (1973); 4 (1974).

Wasilewski, Leon, ed. "Dokumenty do historii zjazdu paryskiego 1892." *Niepodległość* 8, no. 1 (1933): 107–52.

Weeks, Theodore. "Polish 'Progressive Antisemitism,' 1905–1914." *East European Jewish Affairs* 25, no. 2 (1995): 49–68.

————. *Nation and State in Late Imperial Russia: Nationalism and Russification on the Western Frontier, 1863–1914.* DeKalb: Northern Illinois University Press, 1996.

Weinstock, Nathan. *Le pain de misère: Histoire du mouvement ouvrier juif en Europe.* Vol. 1. Paris: Éditions La Découverte, 1984.

Wereszycki, Henryk. *Historia polityczna Polski, 1864–1918.* 2nd ed. Wrocław: Ossolineum, 1990.

Wildman, K. Allan. *The Making of a Workers' Revolution: Russian Social Democracy, 1891–1903.* Chicago: University of Chicago Press, 1967.

————. "Russian and Jewish Social Democracy." In *Revolution and Politics in Russia: Essays in Memory of B. I. Nicolaevsky,* edited by Alexander and Janet Rabinowitch. Bloomington: Indiana University Press, 1972.

Wistrich, Robert. *Socialism and the Jews: The Dilemmas of Assimilation in Germany and Austria-Hungary.* Rutherford, N.J.: Fairleigh Dickinson University Press; London and Toronto: Associated University Presses, 1982.

————. "Rosa Luxemburg, Leo Jogiches and the Jewish Labour Movement, 1893–1903." In Ada Rapoport-Albert and Steven J. Zipperstein, eds., 529–45. *Jewish History: Essays in Honour of Chimen Abramsky.* London: P. Halban, 1988.

Wojciechowski, Stanisław. *Moje wspomnienia.* Vol. 1. Lwów-Warsaw: Książnica-Atlas, 1938.

Wojtasik, J. *Idea walki zbrojnej o niepodległość Polski 1864–1907: Koncepcje i próby ich realizacji.* Warsaw: Wydawn. Ministerstwa Obrony Narodowej, 1987.

Woodhouse, C. E. and Henry J. Tobias. "Primordial Ties and Political Process in Pre-Revolutionary Russia: The Case of the Jewish Bund." *Comparative Studies in Society and History* 8 (Apr. 1966): 331–60.

————. "Political Reaction and Revolutionary Careers: The Jewish Bundists in Defeat 1907–10." *Comparative Studies in Society and History* 19 (1977): 367–96.

Wróbel, Piotr. "Jewish Warsaw before the First World War." In *The Jews in Warsaw: A History,* edited by A. Polonsky and W. Bartoszewski, 246–77. Oxford: Basil Blackwell, 1991.

———. "Przed odzyskaniem niepodległości." In *Najnowsze dzieje Żydów w Polsce*, edited by Jerzy Tomaszewski, 13–142. Warsaw: Wydawnictwo Naukowe PWN, 1993.

Żarnowska, Anna. *Geneza rozłamu w Polskiej Partii Socjalistycznyej 1904–1906.* Warsaw: Państwowe Wydawnictwo Naukowe, 1965.

———. *Klasa robotnicza Królestwa Polskiego, 1870–1914.* Warsaw: Państwowe Wydawnictwo Naukowe, 1974.

———. *Robotnicy Warszawy na przełomie XIX i XX wieku.* Warsaw: Państwowy Instytut Wydawniczy, 1985.

———. "Religion and Politics: Polish Workers c. 1900." *Social History* 16, no. 3 (Oct. 1991): 299–316.

———. "Rewolucja 1905–1907 a kultura polityczna robotników." In *Społeczeństwo i polityka: Kultura polityczna w Królestwie Polskim na początku XX wieku.* Warsaw: Wydawnictwo DiG, 1993.

———. "Rewolucja 1905–1907 a kultura polityczna społeczeństwa Królestwa Polskiego." In *Społeczeństwo i polityka: Kultura polityczna w Królestwie Polskim na początku XX wieku.* Warsaw: Wydawnictwo DiG, 1993.

Zeira, Asher. "Ben ha-pps ve-habund." *M'asef* 1 (May 1971): 165–84.

Zimmerman, Joshua D. "Józef Piłsudski and the 'Jewish Question,' 1892–1905." *East European Jewish Affairs* 28, no. 1 (summer 1998): 87–107.

———. "The Influence of the 'Polish Question' on the Bund's National Program, 1897–1905." In *Jewish Politics in Eastern Europe: The Bund at 100*, edited by Jack Jacobs, 28–45. New York: New York University Press, 2001.

Żychowski, Marian. *Polska myśl socjalistyczna XIX i XX wieku.* Warsaw: Państwowe Wydawnictwo Naukowe, 1976.

# Index

Abramov, Yudel, 85, 296n7

Abramovitch, Raphael, 233, 235, 236–37, 241

Abramowski, Edward, 21–22, 25, 150

Adler, Victor, 258

Aid Alliance of the Jewish Workers' Movement in the Russian Empire, 130–31. *See also* Aid Alliance of the Polish Socialist Party

Aid Alliance of the Polish Socialist Party (Związek Pomocy PPS), 132, 140–41, 145, 305n31

Aizenshtat, Isai, 39, 54, 235, 236

All-Austrian Social Democratic Party (Brünn Congress, Sept. 1899), 113–15, 121, 258

All-Russian Union of Railroad Employees and Workers in Moscow strike (Oct. 1905), 202–3

Alter, Isaac (Grodno), 235

anti-Semitism: the Bund on, 182, 271; Endecja (National Democrats) and, 216–17, 268, 270–72; Jewish separateness and, 148; in the Polish press, 262; PPS and, 89, 97–98, 146–48, 169, 172, 182, 217, 219, 268–69, 271; *Vi kumt a yid tsu sotsyialismus* (brochure), 146–47

*Der arbeyter* (periodical), 134t6.1, 136; Aid Alliance of the Polish Socialist Party and, 140–41; the Bund and, 107, 109, 139, 140, 141; Christians as ethnic group in, 143; factory articles in, 141, 142; fourth conference, Jewish Section of PPS (Feb. 1906) proceedings in, 211–12; Leon Gottlieb and, 133, 137, 141–42; Maks Horwitz and, 131, 132–33, 135, 210; Jewish as ethnic group in, 143; Jewish-Christian worker alliances discussed in, 138, 141; the Jewish question in, 126, 133–35, 137–38, 144,

170–71, 210; Jewish workers in, 138, 139; Lithuanian nationality in, 170–71; Polish independence in, 142–43, 153, 170–71; Teresa Reznikowska-Perlowa and, 135–37, 142; Russian Poland printing of, 170; Feliks Sachs and, 141–42; Yiddish use in, 135, 137, 140, 141–42, 210; Zionism discussed in, 138

*Di arbeyter shtimme*, 134t6.1; as central Bund periodical, 86, 296n15; on Jewish national idea, 175–77; on Lithuanian nationalism, 182; "Our Aims" (central committee) in, 91–92, 93, 95, 106, 298n50; police raid on, 92–93, 106, 296n15; on Polish independence, 177; PPS allegations of Russification, response to, 92–93; response to Feliks Sachs in, 173–74; on schisms in Polish socialist movement, 174–76; on sixth congress of, PPS (1902), 173

assimilation: *asymilacja państwowa* (state assimilation), 166; Otto Bauer and, 258; Jewish separateness and, 266–67, 269; national cultural autonomy, Jewish, 258; Polish positivism, 10, 282n4; PPS Left and, 255, 268–70; PPS Right and, 255, 264–67; PPS Yiddish press and, 154; secular education, 10; the Vilna Group and, 44–45. *See also* education; the Jewish question; Russification; Yiddish

Association of Christian Workers (SRCh), 214

Austria-Hungary, 109, 113–14, 258, 267–68

Bauer, Otto, 258–60, 262–63, 328n12

Becker, Joseph, 245

Berman, Pavel, 39, 54, 85, 118

Białystok: arrests of socialists in, 131; Bund fourth congress in (April 1901)

**349**

Jewish Social Democratic Party of Galicia. *See* ŻPS
Jewish Social-Democratic Workers' Party-Poale Zion, 230
Jewish Socialist Post from America to Poland, 128–29, 130
Jewish workers: adult evening schools for, 242–44, 324n93; as artisans, 17t1.8; the Bund and, 178–79; Christian workers, alliances with, 71–72, 129–30, 138, 141, 144, 149–50; in factories, 17t1.8; *A Letter to Agitators* (Gozhanski), 47, 48–49; national rights of, 116–17; Polish independence and, 109, 151, 153, 167–68; Polish language and, 70, 71–72, 144; propaganda *kruzhki* (circles), 45–46; Sabbath observance by, 228, 251, 253, 265; tsarist system and, 133–35; Yiddish and, 47–48, 51, 97, 176
Jodko-Narkiewicz, Witold, 159; *Di yidn in poyln* (brochure), 147–48; Jewish workers' alliances with Christian workers, 149–50; on Jewish working class representation by the Bund, 178; Old Guard representative to PPS council (1905), 200; on Polish independence, 32–33
Jogiches, Lev, 33, 39, 55
Joselewicz, Berek, 149

Kaplansky, Israel, 85
Katz, Dovid, 85, 107, 116, 118, 120
Katz-Blum, Hillel, 85, 116–17, 296n7
Kaufman, Mojżesz, 54, 71, 143, 226, 292n63
Kautsky, Karl, 109, 110–11, 114, 121, 259
Kelles-Krauz, Kazimierz, 163, 166, 167, 184–85, 187–88, 310n4
Kempner, Stanisław, 216
Kielce, 16t1.6, 196, 212
Kingdom of Poland. *See* Congress Poland
Klimowicz, Paulin, 30
Kopelzon, Tsemakh, 27, 39, 41–44, 54, 286n51
Kossovsky, Vladimir, 62; on Bauer's position on the Jewish question, 328n12; on the Bund and Yiddish culture, 253–54; on foreign committee

(Bund), 117; on an independent Jewish socialist party, 54, 85, 86; on Jewish nationalism, 117; on PPS allegations of Russification, 91, 92; on PPS-Jewish working class relations, 313n1; the Vilna Group and, 39; *The War of the Polish Socialist Party against the Jewish Worker's Bund,* 93, 95–98, 299n50; at Zurich congress (1905), 208
Kowalski, Henoch, 139
Kremer, Arkadi ("father of the Bund"), 57; *On Agitation* (brochure), 47, 48; on foreign committee (Bund), 117; Group of Free Labor, 83; on Jewish nationalism, 41, 117; on a Jewish Social Democratic party, 79, 84, 85–86, 296n7; Tsemakh Kopelzon and, 27, 39, 41–44, 54, 286n51; Maskilic background of, 40–41; John Mill and, 41, 84; Jacob Notkin and, 40; Józef Piłsudski and, 27, 30, 167, 286n51; on PPS allegations of Russification, 91, 92; radicalization of, 40–41. *See also* Róg, Kazimierz; the Vilna Group
Kristan, Etbin, 113
Kulczycki, Ludwik, 297n28
*Kurjer Codzienny* (Daily Courier), 209–10, 212
Kwiatek, Józef, 170, 223; on the Jewish question, 187, 188; "Our Political Declaration," 195, 196; on PPS-Bund relations, 177, 183, 184; Saint Petersburg massacre demonstrations, 195, 196

Latvia, 265; LSDP's support for federation with, 88; Piłsudski's recognition as oppressed nationality, 31
LDSP (Lithuanian Social Democratic Party), 87–88, 96, 112–13
League for the Attainment of Full Rights for the Jewish People of Russia, 216, 229
Lederhendler, Eli, 288n8
Lednicki, Aleksander, 216
Lemberg/Lvov: Bund eighth conference (1910), 251–53, 265; PPS eighth congress (1906), 212–13; ŻPS fourth conference (1910), 252
Lenin, Vladimir, 3, 184, 187, 235, 259

Lestschinsky, Jacob, 240
Levin, Gershon, 240
Levin, Nora, 313n1
Levin, Sholom, 233
Levinson, Boris, 246, 247–48
Levinson, Liuba, 39, 65
Levit, Roza (Frieda), 241–42
Lewis, Richard, 204
Liber, Marc, 3, 64, 121, 208, 235, 236
Limanowski, Bolesław, 20, 265–66
Lithuania: added to Bund's name
    (General Jewish Workers' Bund in
    Lithuania, Poland and Russia), 123,
    273; Bund and Lithuanian national-
    ism, 182, 186–87; Jews in, 36–37, 38,
    169; LDSP, 87–88, 96, 112–13;
    Lithuania-Belarus, 16t1.7, 36–38;
    national question in, 88, 169–73;
    Polish language and, 88, 297n28; PPS
    on, 171–72; Russian Social Democrats
    territorial claims of, 167; Russification
    of, 27, 89. *See also* the Bund; Vilna; the
    Vilna Group
Lithuanian Social Democratic Party. *See*
    LDSP
Litvak, A. (Haim Helfand), 228, 233, 236,
    242, 249–50
Łódź: Bund activity in, 235, 239; demo-
    graphics of, 12, 16t1.6; Harfe, 241;
    NZR in, 202; PPS in, 9, 137, 144; rebel-
    lion in (May 6, 1892), 18, 47; Society
    for the Spread of Education
    (Towarzystwo Krzwienia Oświaty,
    TKO), 241
London: PPS Jewish émigrés in, 131–32;
    PPS propaganda brochures in
    Yiddish, 145t6.3; zhargonists in,
    140–42. *See also Der arbeyter*; ZZSP
Luxemburg, Rosa, 33–34, 53–55, 113

Malinowski, Aleksander, 198, 200
Marchlewski, Julian, 73–74
Martov, Iulii, 9, 52–53, 54, 94, 111, 291n58
Maskilim, 10, 39, 40, 149
Medem, Vladimir, 63; on assimilation,
    248–49; on Bauer's position on the
    Jewish question, 328n12; on Bund's
    decline, 233; and Bund sixth congress,
    208; and conference, Bund (Grodno:
    March 1908), 235; on the national

question, 205; neutralism of, 248–51,
    263–64
Mendelsohn, Ezra, 6, 36, 288n2
Mendelson, Stanisław, 22, 156; on a fed-
    eral republic of equal nations, 287n69;
    Jewish Social Democrats and, 24;
    Jewish Social Democrats and
    Russification, 286n52; Józef Piłsudski
    and, 25, 26, 27; Polish socialists and,
    19; polonized background of, 70; ZRP,
    Second Proletariat and, 25; Workers'
    Unification and, 25
Miklaszewski, Bolesław, 127–29
Mill, John, 58; American Yiddish publica-
    tions, 81; background of, 41–43;
    General Jewish Workers' Bund in
    Russia and Poland, 84–85, 296n7; on
    Jewish national rights, 116–17; on the
    Jewish question, 51–52, 109; on
    Jewish workers, 47, 74, 78–79, 293n25;
    Tsemakh Kopelzon, and, 42–44; on
    Arkadi Kremer, 41, 84; Rosa
    Luxemburg and, 53–55; Julian
    Marchlewski and, 73–74; on the
    national question in *Der yidisher
    arbeyter*, 107–11; on Feliks Perl, 54,
    292n63; on the Polish cause, 41,
    43–44; Polish cultural knowledge of,
    73–74; on Polish independence, 54,
    55, 108–10; review of *Der arbeyter*
    (PPS), 107–9; Kazimierz Róg alliance
    with, 79–81, 294n41; on "Zionism or
    Socialism?" (Zhitlovsky), 112; ZRP,
    47, 74, 78, 293n25; at Zurich congress
    (1905), 208. *See also* the Vilna Group
Minczeles, Henri, 313n1
Minsk, 16t1.7, 73, 270
Mishinsky, Moshe: on Bundist historiog-
    raphy, 6, 281n8; General Jewish
    Workers' Bund in Russia and Poland,
    86; on Jewish identity of the Vilna
    Group, 46–47; Jewish nationality in *A
    Letter to Agitators*, 48; on Jewish
    Section (ŻO) of the PPS, 82; Lithuania
    and the Jewish labor movement,
    36–37; on the PPS, 313n1; on propa-
    ganda *kruzhki* (circles) education,
    46–47; Russian Jewish socialists,
    Jewish identity of, 38; Russia's impor-
    tance in the Bund, 123

*Światło*, 139
Świętochowski, Aleksander, 216
Szporluk, Roman, 10
Szumow, Piotr, 170, 316n35

Terman, Moshe (Mohilev), 235
Tobias, Henry, 48, 253
Tomicki, Jan, 88, 296n16
Trunk, Isaiah, 241, 295n48

Ukraine: Jewish support for independence of, 122; as location of 1881 pogroms; LSDP's proposal for federation with, 88; Piłsudski's support for autonomy of, 190; Polish support for federation with, 4, 23; Ukrainian nationality, Polish recognition of, 4; Bund's fourth congress, 123
Union of Polish Socialists Abroad. *See* ZZSP
Union of Polish Workers. *See* ZRP
University for All (Uniwersytet dla Wszystkich), 239–41

Vandervelde, Emile, 34
Veiter, A., 239
*Der veker*, 134t6.1, 231
Vilna: adult evening school, Yiddish instruction in, 243; Bund central committee in, 238; Bundist cultural Yiddish movement in, 239; Bundist periodicals in, 231, 233; demonstrations of Jewish workers in, 270; founding congress of Bund in, 85–86; Galician Jewish publications in, 30–31; Jewish autonomous culture and identity in, 38; Jewish population of, 16t1.7; Jewish Social Democrats in, 23, 27–28, 30, 286nn51, 52, 296n16; PPS in, 6, 9; PPS Jews identification with Polish national struggle, 184; Feliks Sachs, 170; Yiddish socialist periodicals in, 23, 30
the Vilna Group: in Congress Poland, 72–73; founders of the Bund, role in, 85, 296n7; founding of, 44–45; on an independent Jewish socialist movement, 51–52, 54; international view of, 45–47; Jewish identity of, 46–47; on the Jewish question, 51–52; Jewish workers and, 45, 47–48; non-territori-

ality of, 39; propaganda *kruzhki* (circles) in, 45–46; Russian Social Democratic party and, 83–84; Russian spoken in, 45; secular education of, 40; in Warsaw, 72–75; Yiddish propaganda literature in, 74, 75t3.1; Yiddish used by, 47–48, 50, 74; ZRP and, 47, 74, 78–79, 293n25. *See also* Gozhanski, Shmuel; Kopelzon, Tsemakh; Kremer, Arkadi; Mill, John
Vital, David, 313n1
*Voskhod* (periodical), 229, 231

Wajner, Monachim, 184
Walecki, Henryk. *See* Horwitz, Maks
Walicki, Andrzej, 274
Warsaw: arrests of socialists in, 131; Bundist cultural Yiddish movement in, 239–40; Central Circle (Centrale Koło), 29; demand for constituent assembly in, 199; demonstrations of Jewish workers, 270; *Haynt* (newspaper), 231; Jewish population of, 16t1.6; Jewish Social Democrats in, 74, 80, 295n48, 296n16; Yitzhok Pesakhson group in, 77–78, 80, 295n48; PPS in, 9, 70, 74, 144; PPS May Day proclamation (1902), 153; Regional Workers' Committee of PPS, 198–99; Kazimierz Róg group in, 77; socialist-led strike in (1905), 196; Society to Combat Illiteracy (Di gezelshaft tsu bakempfen dem analfabetizm), 244; Union of Jewish Workers (Mill), 47, 74, 78–79, 293n25; the Vilna Group in, 73–75; Workers' Committee (Komitet Robotniczy), 30; Yiddish-language literature in, 74, 75t3.1, 152, 206–7, 231
Warszawski, Adolf, 33
Wasilewski, Leon, 162; *Der arbeyter* (periodical), 135; on Jewish national-cultural autonomy, 135, 265; *The Jewish Question on the Lands of Old Poland*, 265; on Józef Piłsudski, 29; on PPS Jews in London, 132; on revolution, 256
Weinreich, Max, 68
Weinstein, A. (Rakhmiel), 115, 116, 233, 235, 236